NONVIOLENCE: AN ALTERNATIVE FOR DEFEATING GLOBAL TERROR(ISM)

NONVIOLENCE: AN ALTERNATIVE FOR DEFEATING GLOBAL TERROR(ISM)

SENTHIL RAM

AND

RALPH SUMMY

EDITORS

Nova Science Publishers, Inc.
New York

For permission to use material from this book please contact us:
Telephone 631-231-7269; Fax 631-231-8175
Web Site: http://www.novapublishers.com

NOTICE TO THE READER
The Publisher has taken reasonable care in the preparation of this book, but makes no expressed or implied warranty of any kind and assumes no responsibility for any errors or omissions. No liability is assumed for incidental or consequential damages in connection with or arising out of information contained in this book. The Publisher shall not be liable for any special, consequential, or exemplary damages resulting, in whole or in part, from the readers' use of, or reliance upon, this material.

Independent verification should be sought for any data, advice or recommendations contained in this book. In addition, no responsibility is assumed by the publisher for any injury and/or damage to persons or property arising from any methods, products, instructions, ideas or otherwise contained in this publication.

This publication is designed to provide accurate and authoritative information with regard to the subject matter covered herein. It is sold with the clear understanding that the Publisher is not engaged in rendering legal or any other professional services. If legal or any other expert assistance is required, the services of a competent person should be sought. FROM A DECLARATION OF PARTICIPANTS JOINTLY ADOPTED BY A COMMITTEE OF THE AMERICAN BAR ASSOCIATION AND A COMMITTEE OF PUBLISHERS.

LIBRARY OF CONGRESS CATALOGING-IN-PUBLICATION DATA
Nonviolence : an alternative for defeating global terror(ism) / Senthil Ram and Ralph Summy (editors).
   p. cm.
 Includes index.
 ISBN-13: 978-1-60021-812-5 (hardcover)
 ISBN-10: 1-60021-812-1 (hardcover)
 1. Terrorism--Prevention--International cooperation. 2. Nonviolence. 3. Passive resistance. I. Ram, Senthil. II. Summy, Ralph.
 HV6431.N666 2007
 363.325'17--dc22
                2007022581

Published by Nova Science Publishers, Inc. ✦ New York

CONTENTS

PREFACE

AN IMPORTANT BOOK FROM IPRA

It is a pleasure to introduce this book from the Nonviolence Commission of the International Peace Research Association (IPRA) that provides a way out of the folly of the war against terrorism. Today's interactions of governmental and non-governmental terrorism repeat themselves in ever greater tragedies. Gilbert Achcar calls them 'macabre serials.' Ralph Summy and Senthil Ram — and some of the best peace researchers — see the probable shape of things to come as grave if no efforts are undertaken to replace the accelerating incompetence of the counter-terrorism policies by nonviolent and more effective responses to terrorism.

The nonviolent alternative, they propose, implies courage and intellectual solidarity with the victims of violence. It pleads for a new strategic culture that is open enough to perceive that both terrorism and antiterrorism are harming rather than serving self-interests, is self-confident enough to acknowledge it, and wise enough to reverse it in time. It urges us to read the writing on the wall. Terrorism cannot be condoned but it can be understood. It pleads for a more pro-active backfire analysis of governmental and non-governmental terrorism. It recommends support to specific groups that are waging nonviolent struggles for rights, freedom, and justice, and the development of a new discourse about the effectiveness of strategic nonviolent action compared to terrorism and antiterrorism and other forms of insurrectionary and anti-insurrectionary violence.

Nonviolence: An Alternative for Defeating Global Terror(ism) is a remarkable contribution to today's discourse on terrorism, not only because it highlights the stupidity of today's twin terrorisms, but above all, because it invites the reader to ponder a more realistic and effective alternative.

Luc Reychler
Secretary General, IPRA
Leuven, Belgium

THE DALAI LAMA

FOREWORD

This is an important book. We live in an era in which attention is dominated by terrorism and violence. Despite offering important ways of understanding and dealing with terrorist threats, nonviolent alternatives are rarely explored. Now this book does so creatively and in depth.

We all want to live in peace and happiness, but we seem at a loss about how to bring it about. Under the threat of violence that currently prevails, the gift of fearlessness is an important act of generosity. I have often spoken about the need for individuals to accomplish a sense of inner disarmament, to cultivate a sense of inner peace, to contribute to the wider goal of world peace. But this does not mean that we should allow ourselves to be pushed around and intimidated.

The terrorist attacks that have lately taken place in many parts of the world are the negative result of destructive emotions. Therefore, when we respond to such acts of violence we need to think very carefully and use our intelligence according to non-violent principles. This is very important. Terrorist attacks are always shocking, but avenging them by going to war is unrealistic and inappropriate. Nonviolence can contain terrorism in the long run. Terrorism is a human problem and should be solved in a humanitarian way, and nonviolence provides the proper approach for this.

I am quite sure that if the circumstances that give rise to terrorism can be discussed calmly according to nonviolent principles, as several of the contributors to this book have done, with the long-term safety of the world as the prime concern, then various solutions can be found.

Retaliatory military action may bring some immediate satisfaction, but it will not ultimately root out the underlying problem of terrorism. Far-sighted measures need to be taken. Force is not the long-term answer to this complicated problem. In fact, the use of force rarely solves any problems, for it so often only leaves destruction and suffering in its wake. Human conflicts should be resolved with compassion and understanding, and the key should be the use of nonviolence. As terrorism is something that affects all of us, and nowhere seems to be entirely free of this threat, it is important that we work together to examine the factors that breed and give rise to terrorism and develop lasting solutions. Responding to violence with more violence does not serve the purpose, nor does mere talk about nonviolence when things are going smoothly. It is precisely when things become really difficult, urgent and critical that we need to think and act with nonviolence. Moreover, peace and calm can only be achieved if the basis for understanding and nonviolence are well established right from the beginning.

Human conflicts occur as a result of causes and conditions, many of which are within the protagonists' control. In the case of violent conflict it is important to restrain the situation before it gets out of hand. Once the causes and conditions for violent clashes have ripened, it is very difficult to calm them down again, because without an effort to break the cycle of violence with restraint and understanding, more violence ensues. If we instinctively retaliate against violence done to us, how can we expect our opponent not to feel justified to retaliate in turn? Preventive measures and restraint have to be adopted at an earlier stage. Clearly leaders need to be alert, far-sighted and decisive. Mahatma Gandhi, who was such a leader, pointed out that, if we are seriously interested in peace, it must be achieved through peaceful and nonviolent means.

The contributors to this book give a lead in taking a more holistic view of the problems we face. They have thought rationally about how we can work to avert future disasters in a nonviolent way. As one of them remarks, terrorism can never be condoned, but it can be understood. I am impressed by the suggestion that the use of violence and war have made a relatively recent appearance in our history and that human behavior has involved nonviolent strategies for much longer. Under present circumstances many of our fellow citizens are filled with fear and feel powerless to defend themselves or influence events. To transform this situation into a more positive democratic solution requires instead our compassionate and considered participation.

I commend the editors for their dedication in gathering together these essays that explore the use of nonviolence as a long-term measure to eliminate all kinds of terrorism. This book should be read not only by policy makers, but also by everyone who is interested in achieving genuine peace in the world. It is my prayer that, just as nonviolent strategy has proved victorious in countering suppressive governments in the past, nonviolent elements in the international strategy against global terrorism shall be equally successful today.

March 16, 2007

March 16, 20

PART I: INTRODUCTION

In: Nonviolence: An Alternative for Defeating...   ISBN: 978-1-60021-812-5
Editors: S. Ram and R. Summy, pp. 3-9

NONVIOLENT COUNTER TO GLOBAL TERROR(ISM) AND PARADIGMS OF COUNTER-TERRORISM

Senthil Ram and Ralph Summy

Counter-terrorism is a controversial subject. The field is marred by tensions: Is terrorism a war or crime? Are terrorists freedom fighters or psychopaths? Should counter-terrorism focus on terrorists' actions or on their intentions and purposes? Should liberal democracies deal with root causes that produce terrorists or just eliminate terrorists? Should countries affected by terrorist violence focus on fear management or terror eradication?

While the chapters in this book deal with most of these issues, the main purpose is directed towards a broader theme. The focus is on extending the debate to what at first blush might appear an absurd proposition: that the best way to counter global terrorism is through the cogent application of nonviolence theory and practice. If the book can make some inroads into placing this dissenting view on the public agenda, its goal will have been achieved. A paradigm shift will have been initiated to challenge the orthodoxy depicted in Table I under the heading of 'Military/Security/War.'

Criticism of this prevailing view is usually confined to a legal response. While legal options form part of the nonviolence response, the arguments advanced in the following chapters are far more provocative, and it is hoped will open up new avenues of possibilities. Violence as a counter to terrorism has a dismal record in the long run — often in the short run, too. The existing legal methods are more apt to succeed than violence in the short term, but they offer little prospects of a permanent solution. What is required is radically new thinking, which means bringing to the forefront a paradigm that has existed since the beginning of human time but, following the introduction about 10,000 years ago of agricultural and pastoral settlements, has been out of vogue. The age of nonviolence, however, appears to have re-arrived in the 21st century. Its appearance stems from an imperative to survive. One of the first tests of survival comes in the way the world deals with the many forms of non-state and state terrorism.

The following chapters aim to awaken, to evoke dialectical tension, and to help usher in alternatives and unconventional ideas that will one day replace the dominant cycle of enduring violence. Readers are invited to contact the authors, their friends and associates — whatever their views might be — so that more and more people begin to enter into a dialectic of peaceful language and peaceful action about a peaceful world that counters the various forms of terror and violence. A good place to begin that dialectic is by discussing the foundation chapter, written by Piero Giorgi.

His chapter confronts critics who claim that nonviolence defies humankind's innate nature. He argues that nonviolent behavior is the result of the biocultural evolution of humans and thus a functional potentiality of our species. Consequently, a reintegration of nonviolence into everyday life and world affairs should constitute a natural condition of human beings; it should become a way of overcoming, among other things, all forms of violence including terrorism.

The role of fear, which can cover up real and underlying issues and encourage violence, is analyzed concisely by Anna Alomes. In particular, she looks at the issue of terrorism from the Gandhian and Kingian perspectives and argues that nonviolence transformation is the essence of reducing violence and effecting peaceful change. Similarly, Michael Nagler draws inspiration from the Gandhian example. He analyzes the underlying theory and some of the practical measures which Gandhi developed over his lifetime and which have relevance today in meeting the challenge of terrorism with nonviolent alternatives. Nagler emphasizes the importance of understanding the sources of terrorism, along with the mass mediated culture of violence, when developing a principled nonviolent approach that fosters real security.

Brian Martin, in his chapter 'Terrorism as a Backfire Process,' explains the 'backfire' nature of terrorism — how it works to the disadvantage of the terrorists — and outlines its implications for nonviolent resistance in defeating terrorism. But terrorist actions can also trigger 'backfire' to the advantage of the terrorists. Senthil Ram describes the construct of a psychological process that induces the victim of an attack to make a 'counter-productive response.' Terrorists aim to generate so much fear, hatred and vengeance in their enemy that there is apt to be an overreaction of military firepower that will strike at the innocent (causing so-called 'collateral damage') and gain the terrorists' additional support. The response will be equally counter-productive in the homeland if the state responds by enacting security laws and regulations that infringe on civil rights and liberties. Ram outlines the basic weaknesses of the terrorist's strategy when the victim/state acts intelligently and refuses to overreact. He argues for a nonviolent strategy that recognizes the terrorists' ploy. Terror is the bait that lures the attacked society into a trap of mindless fear in which the impulse to strike out blindly and counter-productively becomes an overwhelming compulsion.

In similar fashion, Hardy Merriman and Jack DuVall highlight the need to address the root causes of terrorism and propose that support should be given to specific groups that are waging nonviolent struggles for rights, freedom, and justice. A new discourse needs to be developed about the effectiveness of strategic nonviolent action compared to terrorism or other forms of insurrectionary violence. At the same time, Tom Hastings stresses the importance of acting locally in countering terrorism nonviolently. He describes how one group of local actionists in Portland, Oregon have woven a nonviolent response to terrorism into their struggle against the terrorism of war and occupation conducted by their own country. Kevin Clements in his chapter on 'Terrorism: Violent and Nonviolent Responses' moves the argument to another dimension. He calls for a general de-legitimating of all violence since war and violence have no place in contemporary geo-politics, and no state has the right to pursue a war of its choosing. If this revolutionary concept truly permeated the world's cultures and was practiced on the world stage of international politics, those who strayed from the field would shortly be brought into line. Empowered citizens would marginalize the offenders. Terrorist organizations would be unable to generate counter-productive responses. Eventually their ranks would fade away.

Timothy McElwee writes about 'The Role of UN Police in Nonviolently Countering Terrorism.' He analyzes the various missions undertaken by UN peacekeeping forces to minimize armed conflicts around the world, and explains the potential role of UN police in countering the global terrorist threat. The ultimate goal is the establishment of a UN permanent body of trained peacekeepers that can move quickly into trouble spots. For Donna McInnis, nonviolent education could be the affective remedy to the problems of violence, a way to arrest and then reverse the spiral of self-imposed violence. From her perspective, a critical and humanely-based education program will form the long term solution to overcoming the paralysis of fear and to containing terrorism at a tolerable societal level. She sets out such a program. Similarly, Roland Bleiker looks at the aesthetic reactions of people to terrorist acts, focusing on literature, the visual arts and architecture. He argues persuasively that emotional insights could be a valuable resource in the development of nonviolent alternatives to the problems of terrorism.

In her chapter, 'Understanding Islamic Terrorism: Humiliation Awareness and the Role for Nonviolence,' Victoria Fontan carefully peruses the speeches of Usama bin Laden to understand the root causes of international terrorism. She concludes that the pragmatic nonviolent ways to counter non-state terrorism range from engaging in standard nonviolent practices to promoting initiatives in grassroots socio-economic empowerment. Christine Mason, on the other hand, seeks to demystify some of the perceived linkages between terrorism and Islam. She does this in 'Terrorism, Gender and Nonviolent Islam' by, among other things, comparing the nonviolent responses of Eritrea's Muslim women in the war against Ethiopia with those of their sisters who fought alongside the male guerillas of the Eritrean People's Liberation Front. Her study discloses 'that those women who fought nonviolently garnered more respect and acceptance from the Eritrean community than those women who fought in combat.' The subject of violence/nonviolence in Islam is also taken up by Chaiwat Satha-Anand. He argues that Muslims, due to the *jahiliyya* factor (ignorance), are reluctant to employ the language of nonviolence in characterizing their actions. Their reluctance stems mainly from an inadequate understanding of both the concepts of power and the dynamics of nonviolent action. However, he contends, such conceptual misunderstandings can be overcome by gaining an adequate language that will characterize the Muslims' present day struggles. The historical absence of Muslim's legacy of nonviolence will be replaced by another legacy that features nonviolence. Thus the original meanings of the *jahiliyya* conducive to nonviolence in Islam can be rediscovered.

In the final offering, Ralph Summy projects the broad outline of a nonviolent strategy against terrorism. He emphasizes six main elements to be implemented immediately, including a staged withdrawal of the occupiers from Iraq. Longer term developments include the redeployment of funds away from military expenditures into education, health and food programs. Educational curriculums at all levels should promote peace values through special peace courses and indirectly through attachment to other courses and classroom pedagogy. The pervasive dominator/subservient model can be radically transformed by an informed public whose powers of critical thinking have been honed in schools and across a band of responsible media.

PARADIGMS OF COUNTER-TERRORISM

The debates on counter-terrorism should be preceded by a mapping out of various past and present responses to terrorism, irrespective of whether they were violent or nonviolent. Therefore, as pointed out previously, this introductory chapter offers an analytical framework for studying the principal paradigms of counter-terrorism. The framework enables this book to be contextualized within the body of existing literature on terrorism, and it also will hopefully assist readers in positioning the broad approach and specific features of this book's contributions.

Counter-terrorism typically falls into two categories, the *criminal justice* model and the *military:security/war* model. Here we include a third category called, *the peace and development* model. However, this model is not new. It has been discussed and debated on various occasions by parties across the divide: hawks and doves; establishment and anti-establishment; and national parliaments, regional and international bodies, including the United Nations. Having these three main approaches to counter-terrorism, a particular country can either confine its response to its national boundaries or pursue the terrorists at the international level. Thus, there are six options for dealing with terrorists. However, these approaches are not mutually exclusive. They are elaborated in the following paragraphs.

Table I. Paradigms of counter-terrorism

		PEACE and DEVELOPMENT	CRIMINAL JUSTICE	MILITARY: SECURITY/WAR
		NONVIOLENCE	LEGAL MEANS	VIOLENCE
		Positive Orientation	Neutral	Negative Orientation
International	End/Goal	Preventive & Constructive	Punitive & Preventive	Destructive of Enemy
	Target	Structures that Produce Terrorists	Terrorists and Their Supporters	Terrorists, Bases and Networks
	Means	Development/Reconciliation	International Law	War
	Methods	Foreign Development Aid, Education & Alternative Media	Courts, Mediation, Negotiation, Arbitration & UN Policing	Military Strategy, Arms Transfers & Alliances
	Costs	Monetary	Monetary	Human Life & Injury, Monetary & Material
National	End/Goal	Avoidance	Punishment/Constraint	Wiping out by any means the possibility of terrorist actions locally
	Target	Terrorists, their Supporters & Potential Supporters	Terrorists and Their Supporters	Terrorists and Their Networks
	Means	Nonviolent Political Action & Realistic Empathy with 'Other'	Rule of Law & Human Rights	Violent Crackdowns, Security Alerts, Anti-Liberal Constitutional Changes, and Repressive New Laws and Policies
	Methods	Nonviolent Protest & Persuasion, Non-Cooperation, Intervention, Education, and Alternative media	Community Intelligence, Court Trials & Democratic Policing	Intelligence, Undercover Operations & Policing
	Costs	Monetary & Lots of Time	Monetary & Reform of Legal and Police Systems	Monetary, Denial/Restriction of Civil Liberties and Freedom & Growth of Public Administration

MILITARY MODEL

In the military model terrorism is considered 'as an act of revolutionary warfare with the onus of response placed on the military and entailing the use of retaliatory strikes, campaigns of retribution and troop development' [Chalk 1998, 376]. This model is essentially a war model rooted in direct, retaliatory, unilateral and often excessive violence. From a peace research point of view this approach has a negative orientation.

1. National Military Model

The goal of national governments who engage with terrorists in a military model is to defeat or prevent terrorist actions globally or locally. Countries restructure their security framework, amend constitutions and existing laws, enact new laws and fashion new policies out of old laws. All these will give virtually unrestricted and protective power to civilian police, intelligence and military authorities to target terrorists. This model demands a great deal of human, material and monetary resources. In most cases the money is diverted from other developmental expenditures to sustain new security initiatives and infrastructures. It has also been observed that such an approach in general erodes civil liberties and fundamental democratic values in Western societies. However, military means may in the short term be of some help in reducing the frequency and destructiveness of terrorist actions, though it may also have the opposite effect. Nor is it apt to eradicate terrorism in the long term [Mueller 2005: 223]. In some cases, like Israel and Palestine, it may even lead to a prolonged internal war.

2. International Military Model

In an international military model, national governments fully mobilize their resources in pursuit of the terrorists throughout the world. The main objective is to destroy the terrorists, their bases and networks completely. The national governments declare an open, unlimited war with the terrorists and with countries that are believed to harbor the terrorists. Countries develop global military strategies, mobilize and arm their forces and form alliances. The approach involves the tremendous output of human, monetary and material resources. The prospect of a complete victory is unlikely. At the same time, the withdrawal of coalition forces could be considered a defeat by the opponent and bystanders.

CRIMINAL MODEL

This model is the most commonly used one. Terrorism is treated as a crime where the responsibility to control it lies within the national and international criminal legal systems. Particularly, liberal democratic states treat terrorism as a crime and seek to deter it with punishment meted out within the criminal legal system [Chalk 1998, 376]. Understandably terrorism, like other types of crime, cannot be completely eradicated. Nonetheless, its frequency and destructiveness can be reduced [Mueller 2005, 223]. Government officials and media play a key role. 'Risk assessment and Communication' will be included in the policy discussions [Mueller 2005: 228]. From a peace research perspective this model is somewhere in between a positive and negative orientation.

3. National Criminal Model

National governments that utilize the criminal model strive to deter terrorists and their supporters with the threat of punishment. The main objective of governments is to constrain the terrorists and prevent their terror actions. The rule of law and human rights become the foundations upon which the governments build their legal and criminal counter-responses to terrorism. Governments hope to contain — or at worse absorb — any terrorists' damage with carefully executed judicial, intelligence and policing measures. However, 'overreaction' is the most important problem in dealing with terrorism within the legal means. The standard judicial and law enforcement procedures can be gradually violated as the 'state is progressively drawn into a parallel grey zone of illegality which mirrors the one in which the terrorist operates' [Chalk 1998: 377]. As a result, the notion of criminal justice gets politicized and becomes 'political justice'; where the principles of due process are severely undermined [Chalk 1998, 377].

4. International Criminal Model

In this model national governments extend their legal web to the international scene. With the legal cooperation of other countries and international institutions, it is hoped terrorist operations will be contained or eliminated within the individual country. Terrorists can be effectively captured, deterred and punished with the use of existing or new international laws. In addition to the punitive international court systems, mediation, negotiation and arbitration are some of the other means of dealing with terrorists within the legal framework. Countries jointly resolve to contribute funds to the development and operation of international judicial systems. And the United Nations is at times called upon to play a key role in monitoring and evaluating, as well as initiating, an aspect of the criminal justice approach.

PEACE AND DEVELOPMENT MODEL

In the peace and development model, terrorism is attributed to a history of deep-rooted humiliations and conflicts. Its prevention is possible only through economic and social development in the repressed and repressing societies that breed terrorists. The full range of nonviolent methods (protest and persuasion, non-cooperation and intervention) is available in contending with terrorism. In true Gandhian style the target to be opposed is the *act* of terrorism, not the terrorist. This nonviolent model projects a highly positive orientation.

5. National Peace and Development Model

In this model governments try not to fall into the terrorist's trap of being provoked into overreacting. 'Since the creation of insecurity, fear, anxiety and hysteria is central for terrorists, they can be defeated simply by not becoming terrified and by resisting the temptation to overreact' [Mueller 2005, 497]. Governments try to avoid falling into the trap by understanding why terrorists exist and what motivates them to attack certain targets. The fear and terror unleashed by terror attacks are countered through education and realistic empathy with terrorists. More importantly, the politicians, bureaucrats, officials and the media need to inform the public reasonably and realistically about the terrorist threats and risks, instead of terrifying them and falling prey to the terrorist's strategy [Mueller 2005, 497]. Thus, by not overreacting to terrorist violence Governments prevent a new cycle of violence. Nevertheless, the strategy is not all carrot but may contain some stick in the form of nonviolent sanctions.

6. International Peace and Development Model

At the international level, governments offer assistance to the society that produces the terrorists. This constructive action targets the structures that have thwarted the terrorists' basic needs like security and identity. Education and economic development that overcome lack of opportunity and previous humiliation represent the corner stones in the building of a new, less violent society. This approach requires large scale financial commitment from a coalition of developed countries. International institutions like the United Nations Development Program can be vital to the success of the strategy. Some terrorists — for example the leadership and cadre — may be so ideologically driven that they will not, under any circumstances, respond to positive gestures. In that case, the nonviolent strategist resorts to the repertoire of nonviolent tools he or she thinks are appropriate to the situation. Another consideration is to overlap with the legal model, as the two models usually work well in tandem.

REFERENCES

Chalk, P. (1998). 'The Response to Terrorism as a Threat to Liberal Democracy.' *Australian Journal of Politics and History*, 44(3), 373-388.

Mueller, J. (2005). 'Simplicity and Spook: Terrorism and the Dynamics of Threat Exaggeration.' *International Studies Perspectives*, 6(2), 208-234.

Mueller, J. (2005). 'Six Rather Unusual Propositions about Terrorism.' *Terrorism and Political Violence*, 17, 487-505.

Wilkinson, Paul. (2006). *Terrorism versus Democracy: The Liberal State Response*. London, New York: Routledge.

In: Nonviolence: An Alternative for Defeating...   ISBN: 978-1-60021-812-5
Editors: S. Ram and R. Summy, pp. 11-27   © 2008 Nova Science Publishers, Inc.

Chapter 1

THE ORIGINS OF VIOLENCE: NEW IDEAS AND NEW EXPLANATIONS AFFECTING TERRORISM

Piero P. Giorgi

ABSTRACT

The use of nonviolence in countering terrorism is readily dismissed by critics who claim, among other things, that it defies humankind's innate nature. However, in the present chapter it is suggested that nonviolent behavior is the result of the biocultural evolution of humans, thus a functional potentiality of our species. Modern neuroscience, anthropology and archaeology point to such an idea, while the classic authors who are still followed by mainstream political theorists (Hobbes, Freud, Lorenz, Wilson) hold that humans are congenitally violent. A serious discussion on these theoretical premises is essential for peace studies and the design of future programs of positive and negative peace. Nonviolent strategies may have been adopted by humans for about 90,000 years, while structural violence and war may be the unavoidable result of domesticating nature about 10,000 years ago, which resulted in the emergence of agricultural settlements and pastoral cultures. The position of Sigmund Freud, the role of religion, the training of soldiers and terrorists, and the case of global terrorism are then discussed in the context of the origins of nonviolence and violence. In the conclusion, a reintegration of nonviolence in everyday life and world affairs is suggested as the natural condition of human beings and as a way of overcoming, among other things, all forms of terrorism.

1. INTRODUCTION

What defines human behavior is still a controversial issue in biomedical science and a weak aspect of peace theory. In fact, one cannot discuss the rejection of violent behavior and the promotion of nonviolence in defeating terrorism without some understanding of the origins of these behavioral strategies. In order to clarify terminology, the definitions of key terms are listed in an Appendix[1].

In this chapter I discuss the origins of nonviolence with an initial criticism of the Freudian idea of aggressive instincts in the light of modern findings in neuroscience, anthropology and archaeology. As an alternative to Freud's outdated position, I will argue that nonviolence is an adaptive biocultural trait of our species, and violence is a consequence of the relatively recent invention of food (agriculture and stock raising). In the light of this hypothesis, I will then discuss the recent phenomenon of global terrorism on the basis of new evidence concerning human nature.

2. FREUD AND THE HUMAN MALAISE

Sigmund Freud addressed the question of human aggressiveness in his *Civilisation and Its Discontent*. He should be recognized for having proposed for the first time that the social evolution undertaken by human beings in the last few thousand years — the period of so-called 'civilization' — took a direction that was not conducive to their neurological imperatives. Freud then suggested that this would explain our diffuse sense of malaise and the emergence of neuroses. This novel approach to the causality of psychiatric conditions should have stimulated a critical investigation of human nature in the academic world, but it did not, because the vast majority of social thinkers accepted Freud's unsubstantiated explanation of this human malaise. He suggested that neuroses were caused by our basic needs to express aggression against each other and to satisfy unrestrained sexuality. These needs were seen as clashing with society's repression of the behavioral traits associated with these very needs. However, his basic intuition of a mismatch between neurological imperatives and social evolution can support quite a different causal explanation, as discussed below. A critical re-assessment of Freud's contention is warranted by advances in neuroscience and anthropology that occurred since he wrote *Civilisation and Its Discontent*.

In his essay, Freud [1952, 767-806] follows an interesting line of reasoning. He starts by considering the question 'What is the purpose of human life?' [771]. This question is normally considered within the domain of religion, but Freud contends it must be addressed with scientific arguments. While the aim of life is to be happy, this human aspiration is not included in the scheme of Creation [772].[2] Then Freud offers his materialistic definition of happiness: the gratification of basic instincts [773]. Problems of terminology and scientific anachronism undermine his thesis.

---

[1] More information about the concepts briefly defined in the Appendix can be found in Giorgi (2001). This book can be ordered by e-sale at <http://www.365bookmark.it > by sending an email for instructions to <p.giorgi@uq.edu.au> (cost: A$ 25. A third edition is in preparation. A warning about terminology: some authors believe that terms should be univocally bound to concepts only in science, while the humanities need flexibility in order to allow creativity and new interpretations. I disagree, as academic communication requires knowing what the other is talking about in order to compare ideas, whatever discipline is involved. In my experience, an agreed and precise terminology for basic concepts does not prevent creativity around complex concepts.

[2] It is important to note that Freud talks about human beings in general, but he then refers only to the Judeo-Christian world of Creation. Let's not condemn him of cultural narrow-mindedness too quickly, however. Contemporary social psychologists draw conclusions about human psychology from analyses carried out in England or USA, not necessarily models for humans in Nepal or even Sicily.

The term 'instinct' refers to specific congenital behavior, such as the running of newborn turtles towards the sea, which is not dependent on postnatal experience. Modern textbooks of developmental psychology tell us that *Homo sapiens* can be placed at the end of the evolutionary strategy of reducing instincts to a minimum in order to adapt more successfully to specific environments through a postnatal definition of behavior. Of course this requires long periods of parental care and high levels of learning capacity, which are typical of primates. As a consequence, the repertoire of human instincts is limited to the specific behavior of newborn babies in finding the nipple and knowing how to suckle, and one-year old children swimming without any teaching. No other social behavior is based on congenital factors, i.e. is instinctive [See Halliday and Slater; Gallagher and Craig].[3]

The list of gratifying behaviors considered by Freud — those seeking libido, eroticism, intoxication, enjoyment of beauty, etc [773-776] — are not instincts, as they all require complex postnatal experience in order to be defined and are exquisitely different in different cultures — hardly good material to investigate the congenital character of human happiness. But it is necessary to be kind to Freud, as he formulated these ideas about one hundred years ago, when cultures, different from Judeo-Christian, had hardly been studied. Developmental neurobiology was not even born as a discipline, and Cesare Lombroso at that time was busy photographing prisoners to work out the phrenology of criminal behavior.

The central argument of Freud is that

> The gratification of instincts is happiness, but when the outer world lets us starve, refuses us satisfaction of our needs, they become the cause of very great suffering [773] … our so-called civilization itself is to blame for a great part of our misery, and we should be much happier if we were to give it up and go back to primitive conditions [776].

Rightly so, Freud never refers to Jean Jacques Rousseau in presenting his explanation of human unhappiness or discontent, because the Austrian psychiatrist does not deal with morality, such as the good, noble savage vs. the bad, immoral civilized man, as Rousseau did. Freud deals only with instinctive social behavior — as if humans had such a thing — and considers it to be a basic characteristic of *Homo sapiens*, just like having one nose and two feet.

The other alleged instinctive social behavior considered by Freud — namely our instinct for killing other people — is more relevant to peace theory and the origins of nonviolence, and our focus on countering terrorism. A person's neighbor allegedly represents

> a temptation … to gratify … aggressiveness on him … to humiliate him, to cause him pain, to torture and kill him. *Homo homini lupus*; who has the courage to dispute it in the face of all evidence in his own life and in history? This aggressive cruelty … also manifests itself spontaneously and reveals men as savage beasts to whom the thought of sparing their own kind is alien. Anyone who calls to mind the atrocities of early migrations, of the invasion by the Huns … even indeed the horrors of the last World War, will have to bow his head humbly before the truth of this view of man [787].

---

[3] In spite of a good scientific consensus in developmental human neurobiology, the public is not informed about such a simple but important aspect of human behavior.

In the case of aggression and terrorism — the aspect we are interested in — Freud uses the same line of reasoning used for sexuality: 'Men clearly do not find it easy to do without satisfaction of their tendency to aggression that is in them; when deprived of satisfaction of it they are ill at ease.' And then he concludes:

> If civilization requires such sacrifices, not only of sexuality but also of the aggressive tendencies in mankind, we can better understand why it should be so hard for men to feel happy in it. In actual fact, primitive man was better off in this respect, for he knew nothing of any restrictions on his instincts [787].

We are facing here a severe case of scientific anachronism and historical short-sightedness. Serious studies of anthropology only started about two decades after the publication of *Civilisation and Its Discontent*. Therefore Freud could not know that *Homo sapiens* had inhabited the earth between 50,000 and 100,000 years before his 'Huns and World War.' Moreover, modern scientists have no reason to believe that prehistoric people, our true ancestors,[4] used violence against each other, either individually or in an organized manner similar to war. The best evidence in support of our nonviolent prehistory is the general lack of man-to-man direct violence in prehistoric rock art [See Giorgi and Anati 2004, 263-269] and the nonviolent social organization of hunter-gatherers who were studied in the 20th century before being physically eliminated or acculturated [Lee 1979].

Freud's intuition of a mismatch between human nature and modern society is interesting and worth pursuing. His line of reasoning is, however, not in agreement with recent advances in neuroscience and anthropology. Freud's ideas of human nature were derived from Thomas Hobbes' *homo homini lupus* (man as a wolf to other men, *Leviathan*, 1651), a 350-year old view which lacks the support of modern human biology. It is amazing that the same idea should remain an acceptable explanation for the origins of the State in political science [Bobbio 1993].[5] The persistence of communication barriers between disciplines, particularly between the sciences and social sciences, is a serious limitation for the advancement of knowledge in this field.

Freud is right about one thing: human 'discontent' is definitively there. It currently takes the form of a dramatic increase in cases of depression throughout the world. But Freud's explanation for this discontent can be turned on its head. It may well be that the high level of structural and direct violence in modern society is not conducive to happiness for human beings, whose neurological make-up was selected to live in small, nonviolent, relaxed communities.[6] My explanation is just the opposite of Freud's, as he believed that 'primitive

---

[4] Popular reports often refer to other species of Hominids (*Australopitecus, Homo habilis, H. erectus*, etc.) as 'our ancestors,' while our ancestors are only *Homo sapiens*, a species that underwent a very unique path of natural selection. We have only common evolutionary origins with other Hominids, just as we have common origins, much earlier on, with rats. Simply attributing to us behavioral traits of other Hominids, or rats as it is often done, is not good evolutionary biology.

[5] Interestingly, anthropologists are still struggling with an explanation of the origins of the State. For example, [Bodley 1997, 182]: 'The rise of centralized state political power is perhaps the greatest anthropological mystery of all.' Most authors take a descriptive, historical approach, while the few who attempt a causal explanation [Spenser, Sahlins, Carnerio, Service] are basing their findings on very local, specific cases that lack the necessary generality.

[6] Note that modern population biologists and anthropologists agree that *Homo sapiens* has maintained its basic neurological make-up and behavioral potentialities since its emergence 50,000-100,000 years ago. In fact a

man' — a meaningless term in modern science — was free to kill and fornicate as his nature required, and now he suffers from prohibitions imposed by 'civilization.'

3. FREUD'S IDEAS LIVE ON IN OTHER DISCIPLINES

Freud's outmoded view of human beings leads to wrong conclusions about the causation of violence and represents a serious impediment to advances in peace studies and the promotion of nonviolent political action. Without a serious discussion about the origins of violence we cannot choose between the project of negative peace (if men are congenitally violent) and that of positive peace (if that is not correct).

Unfortunately Freud's idea of congenital violence in humans has permeated into several important fields of study that are relevant to peace studies. Cesare Lombroso, the founder of *criminology*, considered antisocial behavior as congenital atavism; Konrad Lorenz, the founder of animal and human *behavioral studies*, accepted the idea of congenital human violence, and so did Edward Wilson, the father of *socio-biology*. Modern *psychiatry* is still wondering whether aggression should be considered a disease [See Marzuk 1996].[7] In view of the positions of so many relevant disciplines, it is not surprising that most sociologists and political scientists are convinced that human beings are violent by nature. In the best of cases, psychiatrists and psychologists subscribe to what might be called the fifty/fifty theory — antisocial behavior is in part due to genetic 'factors' and in part due to postnatal learning.

Elsewhere I have explained that this position is contrary to what we know about genetic information and the development of the human brain [Giorgi 2001, chapter 2]. Briefly, genetic information can only determine personal predisposition, which is not behavior (see Appendix). Moreover, as sources of information, genetic information and postnatal experience are different in nature and therefore cannot be added together to explain behavior.

4. THE SEVILLE STATEMENT IS NOT ENOUGH

In 1986 twenty qualified experts issued the Seville Statement, which defined as unscientific the belief in congenital human violence. They did so because the modern scholarship of political science, psychiatry, human ethology and sociobiology is strongly influenced by the biologically deterministic stand taken by the disciplines' founders, Thomas Hobbes (1651), Sigmund Freud (1929), Konrad Lorenz (1966), and Edward Wilson (1975), respectively. In these disciplines the discussion is politically polarized, affected by the sterile polemic of nature/nurture, and at best settled on the basis of the unscientific fifty/fifty theory mentioned above. But how useful is the Seville Statement?

The idea of the Seville Statement is acceptable, but it also requires an explanation of the origins of violence, i.e. 7,000-10,000 years of social injustice, exploitation, torture, maiming, and killing of other human beings. Elsewhere in my writings a hypothesis is offered of how structural violence was an unavoidable consequence of the domestication of plants and

---

species with large populations and continuous mixing and genetic flow would be prevented from undergoing significant evolutionary changes.

[7] The peculiar position of psychiatry within the medical sciences has been discussed by Eric Kandel (1998).

animals, and how wars of defense and of conquest followed as a consequence of structural violence [Giorgi 2001, 144-158]. A summarized version of this hypothesis is reported in two sections down.

By way of an introduction to follow the above critique of Freud's *Civilisation and its Discontent*, it is proposed to analyze those authors who have already expressed strong doubts about congenital violence in human beings. The first author who systematically investigated human cooperation was the Russian sociologist Peter Kropotkin who in 1914 published *Mutual Aid* (probably not read by Freud). He found that in both social animals and humans, instances of solidarity and cooperation were far more common than competition and direct violence. The English anthropologist Ashley Montagu [1957, 1968] also came to the conclusion that structural violence and war were social constructs and nonviolence was a more obvious characteristic of human beings. The psychologist Erich Fromm [1973] effectively contested Freud's idea of congenital human violence. The anthropologist Richard Lee [1979, 1988], among others, lived for several years with the Kalahari Bushmen, who were essentially hunter-gatherers (i.e. not food producers), and described the nonviolent strategies they used (but now have lost) to solve conflicts of interest. Unlike hard sociobiologists, the ethologist, Robert Hinde [1974], made a clear distinction between the origins of animal and human behavior, and between aggression toward members of other species for nutrition and aggression toward members of one's own species, as only humans do. In fact (see Section 6) human aggression to its own species is a recent (7,000-8,000 years) invention of food-producing cultures, which are still passing it faithfully from one generation to the next together with DNA and its consequent traits. The poor understanding of these different mechanisms of inheritance has caused much confusion in the so-called nature/nurture debate (See Sections 5 and 6).

5. THE ORIGINS OF NONVIOLENCE

An objective approach and multidisciplinary reading of modern research leads to the inescapable conclusion that nonviolence originated with the human species itself. The cultural trait of nonviolence, cooperation and mutual aid go back to the very emergence of *Homo sapiens*. The development of the new cerebral connections required for sophisticated social interactions occurred at the same time. As a species humans are not equipped with physical qualities such as speed, sharp vision, powerful claws, sharp teeth, strong bodies. Long before the invention of special clothing, weapons and tools, *Homo sapiens* survived natural selection by group cohesion and solidarity. Our species is the end result of the evolutionary strategy of sophisticated communication for collective problem solving. If brutal force and aggression had been the evolutionary strategy leading to our species, what would have been the purpose of developing a large frontal lobe and its rich associative connections for internalizing complex social relations? What use would it have been to develop very sophisticated cortical connections for speech and language if the evolutionary strategy was not to advance communication for group cohesion and to find nonviolent solutions to conflicts of interests? It does not take much brain power or communication to settle a conflict of interest with a punch-up, or a war.[8]

Interestingly, anthropologists found that special skills for nonviolent solutions of conflicts of interest had survived with the few hunter-gathering cultures they studied before colonization and its physical and cultural genocide — African Bushmen, Polar Eskimos, Australian Desert Aborigines and others [Bonta 1993]. Therefore one should not refer to 'primitive' or 'tribal,' or 'nomadic' people when discussing the origins of nonviolence. The important distinction is between *food-gathering cultures* and *food-producing cultures*, i.e. between hunting and gathering, on the one hand, and agricultural and pastoral economy, on the other. The latter types of cultures invented violence (direct, structural and cultural violence) and war independently in three distant regions of the earth soon after the domestication of nature (i.e. in the Middle East about 10,000 years ago, Southeast Asia 9,000 years ago and Central America 5,000 years ago). How such a cultural transition occurred is briefly discussed in the next section.

One should not confuse the hypothesis of nonviolence as an intrinsic characteristic that results from the biocultural evolution of *Homo sapiens* with Rousseau's 'noble savage' vs the 'bad civilized man.'[9] Just like Hobbes and Freud, Rousseau did not have the benefit of the knowledge brought about by modern science and was the victim of his own imagination and prejudices of the time. Nonviolence is not a moral choice, as Rousseau put it, but an evolutionary adaptive strategy that became particularly developed in *Homo sapiens*,[10] but was lost by food-producing cultures in the last few thousand years. The reason why modern anthropologists are not investigating such a transition from nonviolence to violence will hopefully be elucidated by future historians of science.

---

[8] In the past, war, as a strategy to solve conflicts of interests, was simply unethical; in recent times it is also rapidly becoming stupid. During the last 60 years or so, military solutions have provided no solution at all. Previously large armies confronted each other to settle simple questions of supremacy. Since the defeat of the French army in Indochina in the 1950s, we have witnessed the failure of powerful military countries to impose their will by force when confronting a determined resistance from small countries or groups. The complex issues behind these wars have generally not been solved; if anything they have been made even worse and more complicated by the military intervention.

[9] The popular association of Jean Jacques Rousseau (1712-1778) with the concept of the 'noble savage' is highly inappropriate. A few words have been quoted out of context by generations of writers who obviously never read Rousseau's original works [Rousseau 1952]. When referring to 'man in nature' or 'negroes and savages' or 'Caribbeans,' he actually describes them as 'Solitary, indolent ...' [Rousseau 1952, 337], '... destitute of every species of intelligence ...' [338] and having no morality [393]. The nonviolent nature of pre-historical humans is then described by him in a rather negative way: '... [H]e would have spent his days insensibly in peace and innocence ...' [338], '... fortunate enough to be ignorant of those excellences, which whet the appetite ...[and] consequently fall into fewer and less violent disputes.' [346], '... without speech and without home, an equal stranger to war and to all ties ...' [346]. It is difficult to detect any degree of nobility in this idiot of the woods who helped Rousseau to show '... that man is naturally good.' [362]. This is a far cry from modern anthropological thinking. The position of the present work is therefore not neo-Rousseauian. Evidence from modern neuroscience, anthropology and peace research warrants a very different optimistic view of human nature [see Giorgi 2001, Parts 2 & 3].

[10] Nonviolence as an evolutionary adaptation is particularly evident in the species of chimpanzee living in the tropical forests of Zaire, the bonobo *(Pan paniscus)*, whose social behavior is quite different from the ordinary chimpanzee *(Pan troglodytes)*, as it includes several nonviolent strategies [Kano 1993].

6. THE TRANSITION FROM NONVIOLENCE TO VIOLENCE

As indicated above, the 1986 Seville Statement refuted the idea of violence as a congenital characteristic of human beings. However, the obvious question generated by this statement, but not addressed, is why have human beings then oppressed, wounded and killed each other during the last 8,000 years or so?

The hypothesis of the origins of structural violence and war, summarized below,[11] does not require humans to be 'bad' or 'good', as Thomas Hobbes and J. J. Rousseau suggested, nor does it refer to biological determinism as contemporary hard sociobiologists do to support congenital violence. It is, instead, based on an inescapable chain of causes and effects in our cultural evolution that followed the domestication of plants and animals, i.e. the production of food instead of the collection of food, which was the original adaptation of *Homo sapiens*.

- Food production caused the breakdown in the biocultural evolution of humans, as rapid cultural changes could not be paralleled by suitable (slow) biological modifications, i.e. changes in behavioral predisposition. As a result, the brain of hunter-gatherers (the same as yours and mine) found itself dealing with a new alien social environment for which it was not conceived by its biocultural evolution.
- Optimal food supply and the consequent settlement in large communities led to the breakdown in communication necessary to find nonviolent solutions for conflicts of interest.
- Surplus of food led to division of labour, as some people stopped tilling the fields in order to build dwellings, agricultural tools, pottery, the means to store food, fences for domestic animals, etc.
- Goods and services offered by some professions obviously became more desirable than others, which unavoidably led to social stratification, and a minority – astronomers perhaps – exercising authority over the majority (a situation our brain is not designed for).
- The dominant minority (the embryo of the State) soon had to use reward/punishment systems (the embryo of police) to impose their authority over a disempowered majority. This is structural and direct violence. Other types of violence and war unavoidably followed.
- *War of defense* appeared when professional hunters were commandeered to staff a defense army against local hunter-gatherers who threatened the live stock of settled communities, as they arguably did not know the difference between wild game and domesticated animals.
- *War of conquest* appeared when smaller agricultural communities refused to be 'protected' by the defense army of larger communities and stopped paying previously agreed tributes.

This hypothesis just attempts a causal explanation, which can be challenged by further studies. One way of challenging it would entail investigating accurately the emergence of violence through rock art, and to study possible cases of violence that may be identified in art

---

[11] For an extended version of this hypothesis, see Giorgi [2001, 144-158].

dating back to prehistoric times, i.e. before the domestication of plants and animals. Such a research will require multidisciplinary work and a critical discussion about assumptions so far accepted concerning human nature and the origins of social behavior. A preliminary analysis [Giorgi and Anati 2004, 263-269] has indicated that instances of direct violence (man to man combat) are very rare indeed in prehistoric rock art, in the order of ten cases among the hundreds of thousands of art items discovered and described thus far. These rare cases could be explained by special social circumstances that may have disturbed existing cultures. Further studies are planned in order to understand the specific causality of violence.

7. THE ROLE OF RELIGION

The current debate about radical Islamic terrorism forces us to include religion in the discussion offered in this chapter. Indeed, spirituality and religion are, by themselves, important aspects when discussing the origins and evolution of nonviolence. Spirituality (see Appendix) engages in the metaphysical questions of origins (the mythologies of creation, origins of people and natural features), of welfare (the psychic dimensions of health, as practiced by shamans), and the afterlife (the mythologies of immortality). Interestingly, these ancient spiritual postures are fundamentally similar in all cultures. One could therefore argue that spirituality is an integral trait of human nature. Religion, on the other hand, is an institutionalized practice of spirituality with dogmas, behavioral instructions, and a hierarchical administration that usually works in close collaboration with secular authorities.[12]

In discussing the origin of nonviolence, the most important aspects are the first appearance of religion in large agricultural settlements and the novel introduction of religious behavioral instructions. Almost without exception, all religious behavioral instructions (e.g. the Ten Commandments) urge the faithful to be nonviolent.[13] As discussed above, hunter-gatherers did not need the recommendation of being nonviolent from their spiritual practitioners (shamans), because nonviolence was the essence of their culture. Nonviolence was lived and practiced in their every day life, transmitted to younger generations through initiation, and reinforced when needed with decisions taken by the elders to prevent violence.

The appearance of religion (institutionalized spirituality) at the same time when food production was generating violence is, in my view, of great significance. The nonviolent instructions of religion probably became necessary in order to counterbalance the new trends of competition and violence, a kind of remedial education for men who were testing the limits of their neurological imperatives: *frustrated assassins* for Freud, *unfulfilled cooperators* in my analysis. Unfortunately, behavioral instructions of religion are affected by a great degree of hypocrisy. Unlike the spirituality and nonviolence of food-gathering cultures, the religiosity of food-producing cultures is not put into practice in everyday life. Among major world religions, Christianity would arguably win first prize for not following the teachings of its founder as enshrined in the New Testament, especially the Sermon on the Mount. Even the

---

[12] These characteristics did not exist in the original 'religions,' which I therefore prefer to call 'forms of spirituality,' in order to distinguish two different expressions of human metaphysical concern.

[13] I am referring to the golden rule: 'Do onto others as you would have them do onto you' [Luke 6, 31], which can be found in very similar terms in Judaism [Talmud, Shabbat, 31a], Islam [Surah 6, 151-164], Buddhism [Udana-Varga 5, 18], Hinduism [Mahabharata], Confucianism [Analects XV, 23] and the Baha'i Faith [Gleanings of Baha'u'llah, 315].

Ten Commandments (which belong to Judaism) are largely ignored. Could this explain the higher level of violence as well as depression in the so-called Christian world? If Freud were right, this part of humanity should be the happiest one.

8. ANTITHETIC CULTURAL MESSAGES

For about 2,500 years, religion has been the main source of inspiration for nonviolence. Important social and religious thinkers – such as Prince Siddhartha, Joshua of Nazareth, Guru Nanak, Baha'u'llah, to name only a few – preached nonviolence in structurally violent cultures in order to return some degree of humanity to human beings. In other words, these leaders saw the need to recapture the social skills that food gatherers had mastered to avoid violence. At the same time, however, the secular side of food-producing cultures — especially their men — resisted these teachings in practice engaging in behavior such as competition and accumulation of wealth.

This contradiction in behavioral instructions does not seem to worry too many people, as exemplified in their institutions, for two reasons. First of all, individuals can select one particular role in society, and become monks or soldiers or businessmen, and thus avoid contradiction. Next, aggression is discouraged within a given polity, by making it illegal and punishable, although it will be encouraged when directed toward another political entity called 'the enemy.' Thus in the Ten Commandments one needs to understand that 'your neighbor' is someone living quite literally next to you, not the person living in a town nearby that may be allied with your enemy. In-group cooperation and out-group aggression has been the norm for thousands of years in food-producing, violent cultures.

9. SECULAR NONVIOLENCE

One can therefore argue that the rise of peace studies in the mid-20th century introduced a secular dimension to the pursuit of nonviolence and, more importantly, challenged the hypocrisy of promoting both violence and nonviolence in the same culture. The new secular promotion of nonviolence — still in its infancy and poorly understood in most cultures — is removing political contradictions in society and reconstructing humanity in both its material and spiritual dimensions. The establishment of the first center for peace studies and the first journal of peace studies in the 1960s by Johan Galtung, followed by the publication in 1973 of Gene Sharp's seminal work, *The Politics of Nonviolent Action*, were turning points in understanding the role of nonviolence, so that today it is the object of academic studies and practical applications, not just the intuition of men and women of good will.

10. THE METAPHOR OF MEDICINE

This chapter on the origins of nonviolence cannot avoid recalling the important metaphor of medicine. The same mechanisms that maintain a strategy of violent solutions to conflicts of interest also operate in the focusing on curative medicine at the expense of preventive medicine, the type of medicine comparable to the nonviolent approach.

As noted above, psychiatry is of central importance. If aggressiveness were an intrinsic characteristic of human beings or an evolutionary adaptive trait — as Hobbes, Freud, Lorenz, and Wilson argued — an increase in structural violence and aggression in a given culture would result in an improvement in health. We observe, on the contrary, that in a social environment characterized by intense competition and aggressive behavior (large cities, cut-throat work places, highly competitive business, military units in combat, etc) people experience high levels of psychological and psychosomatic diseases, as well as so-called 'organic' diseases. In fact chronic stress, a rapidly increasing malady, is known to inhibit the immune system and increase the susceptibility to diseases.

11. ABOUT SOLDIERS

The way soldiers are trained seems to support the idea that nonviolence is part of the human biocultural make-up (see Appendix). If human beings — men in particular — were intrinsically violent, military training would only concern technical aspects, such as the functioning of weapons. On the contrary, recruits are initially subjected to a barrage of interventions destined to humiliate, depersonalise and then subordinate them. When they have become obedient pawns, the 'enemy' is slowly but efficiently outlined in their mind and the logic of arrogance and aggression is then gradually nurtured in the soldier's whole way of life. The training schedule is meant to remove the very qualities of a nonviolent (normal) human being: dignity, personality, independent thinking, solidarity and empathy with everyone (not just one's friends), and trust in one's fellow human (however alien 'the other' may be).[14]

Of course, the rhetoric of the gallant soldier requires some embellishment for the strange creature that emerges from the training camp. For this we have elegant uniforms, snappy military parades, and a discourse promoting the idea of the good soldier's qualities: courage, devotion to country, loyalty to comrades, obedience to his superiors.

12. ABOUT TERRORISTS

Wars have not always been fought between armies confronting each other in the field. Sometimes one's opponent has no proper army, less men and limited armaments, as in the case of the resistance against occupation by a defeated country. The resistance against an occupying army can also be nonviolent [see Sharp 1990; Ackerman and Kruegler, 1994]. Whether violent or nonviolent, resistance fighters have the advantage of operating on familiar home ground and the potential benefit of local support. Instances of people and guerrilla

---

[14] Explorers and colonialists reported many times about 'first encounters.' Generally speaking, coming from structurally violent cultures (food producers), they were very suspicious of the strange creatures they encountered in the 'new lands.' Their response was to act prudently or to try and conceal their fear, while the behavior of nonviolent cultures (food gatherers) was characterized by curiosity.

struggles have been known since ancient times, but events of the last decades have highlighted violent asymmetric confrontations in the form of terrorism.

The apparent brutality and single-mindedness of terrorists force us to re-consider the question of the causality of violent behavior. Would such a high level of indiscriminate violence undermine the idea of human being's nonviolent nature? Are those we label terrorists any different from 'normal' uniform soldiers? (Posing this last question should not be interpreted as an attempt to justify terrorism.)

Let us consider terminology first. Confusion with regard to fighters without uniforms transpires from the terminology used by the international media covering the recent invasion of Iraq. The perpetrators of violence against the occupying forces and their collaborators have been called 'terrorists', 'insurgents' and 'rebels'; these terms have their own distinctive meanings. However, the media has a strong tendency to refer to terrorists as those who kill kidnapped civilians and bomb others indiscriminately, but to label insurgents or rebels as those who blow up military vehicles. In my view this infers an ethical tolerance not only for killers in uniform, but also for killers of killers in uniform. The uniform seems to represent an external symbol of the institutionalized function of killing or being killed, a kind of priestly cloak that relieves those who wear it from having to obey the commandment 'Thou shalt not kill.'[15]

What is the difference between shooting indiscriminately into a crowd from a military helicopter, and cutting off the head of a kidnapped civilian? They are both acts of cruelty and forms of terrorism. The only difference lies in the remoteness of the killer from his victim. The soldier in uniform can more easily fire the hail of bullets than draw the knife across a human throat, because he has been trained and allayed of responsibility for the former act. But the effect for the victim is the same.

The technical and ethical analogy between killers without uniform and in uniform is closer than most people would imagine. Both killers have to overcome their natural disinclination to kill. Just as regular soldiers must be de-humanised during their basic training period, guerrilla fighters, rebels and terrorists must be prepared ideologically and emotionally for the same purpose of killing. A culture of intense hatred nurtures volunteers for terrorist training camps, where specific ideological motivations are provided, along with fighting skills and technical know-how. Lacking any killing instinct, these future terrorists would have continued to attend their sheep, cultivate their fields, and trade their goods, if someone had not brain-washed and effectively trained them to hate. This is because modern advances in neuroscience, human evolution, social anthropology and paleoethnology support the idea that killing other human beings is not a neurological imperative of *Homo sapiens*. It requires intensive post-natal channelling of behavior, whether one wears a uniform or not.

---

[15] One should note that some translations of the Old Testament read 'Do not kill,' while others read instead 'Do not commit murder,' which includes the possibility of just war and capital punishment. In my view, a discussion

13. CONCLUSION

I would argue that nonviolence is part and parcel of humanity. It probably represents the most significant evolutionary strategy among Hominids that led to the emergence of *Homo sapiens*. Adopting it again after a few thousand years of neglect will be essential for the survival of our species. Academics and intellectuals should urgently discuss the modalities of doing so, but they do not do so because of the widespread idea that we are congenitally violent. This outlook limits us to considering only negative peace as a social/political strategy. Such a scientifically anachronistic situation has been greatly facilitated, in my view, by an exaggerated academic specialisation that prevents a multidiscipinary understanding of human behavior and related world events, and by the current political interference with academic freedom.[16]

Old-fashioned views about human nature and the origins of behavior are limiting our options for nonviolent solutions to counter global terrorism — in particular the advancing of long-term solutions. If we continue to ignore the historical and psychological causes of terrorism and follow a Freudian concept of terrorists as evil or atavistic criminals, we will promote greater violence rather than reduce and eliminate it. But if we analyze the origins of violence and terrorism and their root causes, 'the course of action [will flow] from the discourse,' as Johan Galtung has said [2001, 158].

APPENDIX

Short definitions of terms used in this chapter. An asterisk after an entry means that the usage by this author differs from the use normally adopted in the general literature.

*Aggressiveness** – A functional potentiality, not a behavior. Persons born with a high level of aggressiveness acquire very quickly aggressive behavior, but they need to be shown what to do (behavior) by a given culture. In the general literature one uses 'aggression', 'aggressiveness', and 'violence' as synonyms.

*Aggression** – Aggressive behavior, which is part of the behavioral traits acquired by children within a given culture in order to hunt and defend themselves from predators, not to kill other people. See 'Aggressiveness' and 'Violence'.

*Behavior** – Motor activity directed toward a conscious or subconscious goal. Note that 'emotion' and 'aggressiveness' are not behavior.

Biocultural evolution – Parallel evolution of behavioral predisposition (congenital characteristics of the brain) and specific behavior acquired by youngsters after birth from the cultural context. In general, evolution (modification of species) is the result of the natural selection of traits in the course of adaption for survival. In the current climate of exaggerated biological determinism, biocultural evolution is little known, but it occurs in all social animals and specifies their social behaviour [Lopreato 1984].

---

on the interpretation of this commandment remains within the realm of Jewish theology, while those individuals calling themselves Christians should simply follow Jesus' exhortation of turning the other cheek.

[16] The selective support of certain lines of research recently adopted by national governments has reduced universities to the role of governmental institutions for applied research. Innovative ideas and creative research, the engines of human progress, have been sacrificed to the advantage of conservative technical progress.

Congenital characteristics – It literally means 'born with.' It refers to both genetic characteristics (specific DNA sequences) and specific physiological conditions experienced by the foetus in utero. The popular literature often uses the term 'genetic' to mean congenital. For example, mental deficiency due to malnutrition of the mother is congenital but not genetic. See also 'Genetic characteristics.'

Conflict – Situation of antagonism existing after the parties have selected violence to resolve their conflict of interest. The terms 'conflict of interest' and 'conflict' should not be confused, but one normally does so

Cultural violence – See Violence (cultural).

Direct violence – See Violence (direct).

*Functional potentiality** – A function which is characteristic of a species, but it does not develop without postnatal information from the physical and social environment of the baby or child or person. Examples: erect posture, hand dexterity, speech and specific social behavior. These functions are important because they are used to distinguish *Homo sapiens* from our most similar Primates, *Pan troglodytes* (chimpanzee) and *Pan paniscus* (bonobo).

Genetic characteristics – Physical and behavioral traits that are directly defined by the specific sequences of nucleotides of DNA.

*Genetic predisposition** – A genetic characteristic (DNA sequences) that just speeds up or slows down the acquisition of a functional potentiality. Note that a genetic predisposition does not contribute to the specific definition of that function. Practically all body functions, and diseases, are indirectly affected (not defined) by genetic predisposition. For example, with a high genetic predisposition to lung cancer, one might get cancer with minimal cigarette smoking, which is the true cause of the disease (genes are not the cause). Or, with a genetic predisposition to dancing, one learns classic ballet quicker (genes do not define dance movements, just the time needed to learn them). Aggressiveness is a personal predisposition, not behavior.

Human beings – Members of the species *Homo sapiens* who have existed on this Earth for only about 100,000 years. The study of human nature should not be limited to historical men. Other species of the genus *Homo* or of Hominids or Primates are not 'our ancestors', we only share common ancestry with them.

*Neurological imperative** – A functional limitation of the human nervous system, which is not infinitely plastic. Every stage of development probably has its own neurological imperative, the lack of which hinders the progress of normal development.

Negative peace – Temporary absence of violence or war.

Nonviolence – Mental attitude and behavioral posture that favours consultation and negotiation in order to set in place win-win solutions of conflicts of interest. Nonviolent solutions are not passive or appeasing.

*Pacifism** - Rhetorical opposition to war, which is normally professed by religious groups. Seventeenth century Quakers were among the early denominations to oppose war. Jews, Christians and Muslims are not pacifists, because of their concept of 'just war'. Buddhism, the Baha'i Faith and some other religions profess pacifism: by this they mean that international disputes should not be settled by armed conflicts. Some modern Constitutions state the same (e.g. art. 11 of the Italian Constitution), hence the recent rise of secular pacifist movements. Unfortunately, pacifism does not deal with the causes and prevention of war (positive peace). I am not just a pacifist.

Peace studies – Multidisciplinary studies that aim at understanding the causes of violence and war and possible nonviolent solutions. The theoretical bases of peace studies are weak, because academics and intellectuals avoid dealing with the issue of human nature and the origins of human behavior.

Positive peace – Absence of violence or war because their causes have been eliminated. Those who think that violence is a human congenital characteristic, only pursue negative peace.

Postnatal acquisition* – The completion of functional potentialities in parallel with the definition of neural circuitries and muscular-skeletal structures. Erect posture, hand dexterity, speech, and social behavior, for example, are acquired, not learned. The general literature uses 'acquiring' and 'learning' as synonyms.

Postnatal learning* – Information added to the memory bank of the brain after all functional potentiality have been acquired. In fact, the function of transforming short-term memory into long-term memory (learning) is one of these functional potentialities.

Religion* – Spirituality is an intrinsic characteristic of human beings (see below). A violent superstructure appeared mainly with the emergence of settled agricultural and pastoral cultures (see Section 6). Religion is spirituality organised by a hierarchical authority, which mediates between human spirituality and a divinity (or divinities) that can be benign, if rituals and/or appropriate behavior are adopted, or unfavourable if displeased. Behavioral instructions and collaboration with civil authority in structural violence are the main features that distinguish religion from spirituality.

Spirituality* – The human cerebral cortex has an area in the frontal lobe that becomes particularly active during meditation and mental concentration on metaphysical issues [see Goleman 2003]. Prehistoric cultures and contemporary hunter-gatherers demonstrated sophisticated forms of metaphysical association with elements of nature and other human beings. They did not consider themselves masters of nature (rather guardians of it) nor masters of other people (but as equals in society). These features in ecology and democracy were part of their culture, not separate instructions added by clergy and political movements.

Structural violence – The mother of all forms of violence. It is the sum of those ideas and institutions that limit the development of the functional potentialities of a person. Falling ill of a preventable disease, lacking education, or love or cultural identity, are only a few examples of structural violence.

Violence (direct) – Aggressive behavior displayed by a person against another person; it can be verbal or physical (wounding, torturing and killing). Intentional killing is the extreme form of man-to-man aggression and is typical of (historical) human beings. As this is not practiced by animals, one needs a term (violence) different from aggression. In this sense, animals are aggressive not violent, and human hunting is aggression against another species, not violence.

Violence (cultural) – A special case of structural violence that affects the way a person thinks. Indoctrination and political propaganda is a form of cultural violence.

War - A state of conflict involving a sophisticated social organization and a dominant minority that has a vested interest in staging war.

ACKNOWLEDGEMENTS

Piero P. Giorgi, BSc PhD FAIBiol, is a member of the European Research Centre, 25084 Gargnano, Brescia, Italy, and a Research Associate of the Australian Centre for Peace and Conflict Studies, University of Queensland, Brisbane, Qld. 4072 Australia. Dr Giorgi is the author of *The Origins of Violence by Cultural Evolution* [Giorgi, 2001], see note 1.

REFERENCES

Ackerman, P. and Kruegler, C. (1994). *Strategic Nonviolent Conflict: The Dynamics of People Power in the 20th Century.* Westport, CT: Praeger.

Bobbio, N. (1993). *Thomas Hobbes and the Natural Law Tradition.* Chicago: University of Chicago Press.

Bodley, J. H. (1997). *Cultural Anthropology: Tribes, States and the Global System.* London: Mayfield Publishing Co.

Bonta, B. (1993). *Peaceful People: An Annotated Bibliography.* Metuchen, NJ: The Scarecrow Press.

Freud, S. (1952). *'Civilisation and Its Discontent.'* In The Major Works of Sigmund Freud (pp.767-806). Chicago: William Benton (Encyclopaedia Britannica, The Great Books of the Western World, vol. 54).

Fromm, E. (1973). *The Anatomy of Human Destructiveness.* Greenwich: Fawcett Crest.

Gallagher, J.J. and Craig T.R. (1987). *The Malleability of Children.* Baltimore: Paul H. Brooks.

Galtung, J. (2001). *'September 11, 2001 – Diagnosis, Prognosis and Therapy.'* Convivio, vol. 7/2, 152-167.

Giorgi, P.P. (2001). *The Origins of Violence by Cultural Evolution.* (2nd edition). Brisbane, Qld: Minerva E and S.

Giorgi, P. P. and Anati, E. (2004). 'Violence and Its Evidence in Prehistoric Rock Art – A Comparison of Ideas.' In E. Anati, P.A. Fradkin and P.P. Giorgi (Eds), *New Discoveries, New Interpretations, New Research Methods – 21st Valcamonica Symposium on Prehistoric and Tribal Art.* (263-269). Capo di Brescia, Italy: Centro Camuno di Studi Preistorici.

Goleman, D. (Ed.). (2003). *Destructive Emotions.* (342-346). London: Bloomsbury.

Halliday, T.R. and Slater, P.J.B. (1983). *Genes, Development and Learning.* Oxford: Blackwell.

Hinde, R. (1974). *Biological Basis of Human Social Behavior.* New York: McGraw-Hill.

Kandel, E. (1998). 'A New Intellectual Framework for Psychiatry.' *American Journal of Psychiatry,* vol. 155, 457-469.

Kano, T. (1993). *The Last Ape: Pygmy Chimpanzee Behavior and Ecology.* Stanford, CA: Stanford University Press.

Koprotkin, P. (1914). *Mutual Aid: A Factor of Evolution.* (Reprinted edition). Boston: Porter Sargent Publishers.

Lee, R.B. (1979). *The !Kung San – Men, Women and Work in a Foraging Society.* Cambridge, MA: Cambridge University Press.

Lee, R.B. (1988). 'Reflections on Primitive Communism.' In T. Ingold, D. Riches and J. Woodburn (Eds.), *Hunters and Gatherers.* (vol 1, 252-268). New York: Berg.

Lopreato, J. (1984). Human Nature and Biocultural Evolution. London: Allen and Urwin.

Marzuk, P.M. (1996). 'Violence, Crime, and Mental Illness.' *Archives of General Psychiatry,* vol. 53, 481-486.

Montagu, A. (1957). *Anthropology and Human Nature.* New York: McGraw-Hill.

Montagu, A. (1968). (Ed.). *Man and Aggression.* New York: Oxford University Press.

Rousseau, J.J. (1952). *On the Origin of Equality and The Social Contract.* (trans G.D.H. Cole). Chicago: William Benton (Encyclopaedia Britannica, The Great Books of the Western World).

Sharp, G. (1990). *Civilian-Based Defense: A Post-Military Weapons System.* Princeton, NJ: Princeton University Press.

PART II: NONVIOLENCE AND TERRORISM

In: Nonviolence: An Alternative for Defeating...
Editors: S. Ram and R. Summy, pp. 31-46

ISBN: 978-1-60021-812-5
© 2008 Nova Science Publishers, Inc.

Chapter 2

SEARCHING FOR AN EXIT IN THE CORRIDOR OF FEAR: REVISITING GANDHI AND KING IN TIMES OF TERROR[ISM]

Anna Alomes

ABSTRACT

This chapter considers how Mohandas K. Gandhi and the Rev. Dr Martin Luther King Jr. might reflect on the contemporary threat of terrorism (considering both state and non-state actors). They would consider the 'corridor of fear' that has been created and demonstrate how to uncover and address the real issues, concluding that a nonviolent response to terror is possible given at least five presuppositions for change: 1) people have the capacity to change and are not stuck in a predetermined social grid of hatred, violence and suffering from which there is no escape; 2) violence is about the action of the agent, not a set of circumstances; 3) every individual is accountable for their actions, including intentions; 4) there is a false moral distinction between 'self' and 'other' to be bridged; and 5) by disengaging from the false distinction and adhering to nonviolence, value is attributed to the other as a person, while still allowing opposition to injustice. Humans are relational beings, and developing a cooperative approach to conflict resolution — even toward those who intend to harm us — will provide an exit from the corridor of fear. Gandhi and King argued that nonviolence offers the moral person a sustainable basis for decision-making and a viable course of action to confront and reduce violence in ourselves and others. This transformation is the building block for peaceful change in society.

INTRODUCTION

Twenty-first century notions of fear, terror, hatred, discrimination and uncertainty are no different in kind to those faced in the preceding century by Mohandas Karamchand Gandhi and the Rev. Dr Martin Luther King Jr. The leadership, practical approach through nonviolence, and the hope they provided a few decades ago can be usefully called upon to make sense of these troubled times. How would their ideas, actions and guidance be applied today? Briefly, they would shift the focus from the current 'future-based, risk-oriented' view of life (to be outlined shortly) to the present. The relational nature of human beings and the particular development of those relationships become crucial to transform fear and anxiety into peace and stability. Counter-terrorist action on Gandhi's and King's terms would only make sense inside the nonviolence spectrum. They would ask us to use our 'moral imagination' (to borrow John Paul Lederach's term) to reinterpret actions in the present and to sow the seeds of a different future for humanity.

To begin with, Gandhi and King would consider the signs of today's concerns: fear of the 'others' religious extremism; calls for the state to increase borderline protection; the amplification of national security aligned with international security; and a disposition to identify allies and express hatred toward those who threaten a sense of daily stability, security and happiness. They would acknowledge pain and suffering while emphasizing the need to dig underneath this surface action and examine the real issues — for example, they would say: 'It's not about religion, it's about violence. It's not about borderline protection, it's about demonizing "the other." It's not about inclusion for those on our team, but about the exclusion of all other teams.'

Using the framework of nonviolence to understand the real causes of these problems may begin to illuminate the exit sign in this 'corridor of fear.' Moving towards it and through it is a longer-term task, requiring immediate action. To begin the discussion from a commonsense perspective, it is proposed to examine the broader issues that contribute to violence and then move to a moral consideration of violent action before calling on practical nonviolent solutions from Gandhi and King.

THE PROBLEM WITH VIOLENT ANTI-TERRORIST ACTIONS OF HEROES

Albert Einstein says that we cannot use the same approach to solve a difficult problem with the same thinking that created it. Therefore, it does not make sense to try to solve an outbreak of violence using violence as the solution. But despite the obvious historical evidence — 'We have already tried and tested every form of violence, and not once in the entire course of human history has anything good or lasting come from it' [Lech Walesa, Polish Nobel Peace Laureate, 1983] — attempts are made, shoulder-first, to charge at the door of violence. It is time to step back and give serious consideration to an alternative approach.

The Rev. Dr Martin Luther King Jr. builds on a commonsense approach and moves toward a moral evaluation:

> The ultimate weakness of violence is that it is a descending spiral, begetting the very thing it seeks to destroy. Instead of diminishing evil, it multiplies it .... [T]hrough violence you may murder the hater, but you do not murder hate. In fact, violence merely increases hate [King 1967, 179].

On this view, violent acts of counter-terrorism cannot possibly defeat the violence of terrorism, no matter how worthy the intention.

THE CAUSAL CHAIN

It is not difficult to understand how the core issue of 'truth' has been made opaque: the morning newspaper headline reads, 'anti-Islamic hate crimes' and below it is recounted an almost clinical description of the violent deaths of individuals and groups that appear as a shopping list of facts. The presentation of these facts — such as the number of casualties, the types of explosive devices, and the statistics on remote detonators and geographic areas — diverts attention from the main issue. The 'truth' is presented as simple matters of fact about the world; truth as a sanitized shopping list.

As an alternative, thinkers such as Michael Nagler encourage people to step back and see the larger picture. Everything has a cause and the links in the causal chain need to be examined in order to understand where this violence is coming from. Nagler talks about the process required to reach this understanding as 'letting ourselves down a chain into murky waters, hand over hand' [2001, 23], and explains that we must backtrack in our thinking from anti-Islamic hate crimes

- To hate crimes
- To hate [2001, 23].

Hate is the real problem. To take Nagler's example further, the more hate there is, the more it will express itself in whatever form. Some of those forms will be illegal — crimes in other words — and some of those will be directed against Islamic practitioners. But in Nagler's view, the underlying reason that anti-Islamic hate crimes are on the rise would have little to do with Islam or even racism. Today, the focus could be Islamists; tomorrow it could be Jews; next week it could be homeless people or gays and lesbians; yesterday it was communists. But since these groups are only the targets of some people's hate, trying to cope with each victimized group individually is like trying to fix one leak at a time in a rusted plumbing system. Would it not be more effective to shut off the water? [Nagler 2001, 21-22]. Even better to install a new plumbing system....

From this perspective, anti-Islamic and anti-Western hate crimes would not exist without hate. Rather than getting sidetracked by an interpretation of 'truth' as an endless lists of facts, consider French philosopher Michel Foucault's more complex notion of archaeologically digging down through the facts to discover the real cause of the problem. For both Gandhi and King, this is the 'truth' of *how things ought to be*: where reference is made directly to the ethical domain, and not merely to matters of fact about the world; and where the focus is on understanding and reducing hate itself and not just the shopping list of hate-crimes. At this ethical level it is straightforward to argue for common ground — agents are not heroes or enemies, but members of the human race who share common rights and depend upon one another in social relations. This point will become more significant later when it is discussed how nonviolent action is required to dissolve the (false) moral distinction between self and other.

Such a dissolution provides a convincing rejoinder to those who would attempt to justify violence, but whose argument can only gain coherence by separating agents into heroes and enemies. Subsequently, it becomes logical for the perpetrators of violence to remove the barriers to freedom by obliterating the enemies. It may sound plausible to some, but herein lies the problem: because the enemies are terrible people who commit unacceptable acts of cruelty and harm by inflicting violence on their own citizens and members of outside nations, they become morally repugnant, prompting aggressive action from the heroes. But when heroic violent action is undertaken, the justification is that the hero is using violence *legally* and the enemy is using violence *illegally*, achieving a different ruling from exactly the same action of violence and cruelty (known as 'double-morality').

Both Gandhi and King would argue that it is not rational to attain freedom as an end by destroying the very freedom of others in order to achieve it. They would point out that using violence to further a moral cause copies 'the enemy' and sanctions as 'right' those aspects that only moments before were considered morally 'wrong.' This violent action, which causes fear, suffering, harm and death, is followed closely by an attempted justification by modern anti-terrorist heroes to describe their actions as the 'legitimate use of force.' By this careful sleight of hand (switching to the sanitized terms of 'legitimacy' and 'force'), the ideas of 'violence', 'harm' and 'accountability,' do not even enter the discourse.

Recalling William James, the military party denies neither the bestiality, nor the horror, nor the expense [1950, 96]. It only says that war is *worth* them; that wars are human nature's best protection against its weaker and more cowardly self, and that humankind cannot afford to adopt a peace economy. In contrast to this view, Gandhi and King demonstrate that violence is neither legitimate nor the legitimator of power. Today, an alternative is needed as a matter of urgency.

WHAT DOES GANDHI HAVE TO OFFER?

Gandhi rejects the idea of 'justified violence:' according to him, all violence is opposite to the natural 'law of love,' which he refers to as the law of the universe and the 'law of our being,' expressed through the term *ahimsa* and relevant to all regardless of religious or cultural differences. (On this basis, the 'war on terror' makes no sense and would not be supported, nor would an increase in state-based structures of violence: for example, US\$441 billion on US military spending in 2006). An understanding of Gandhi's idea of truth, and how violence represents falsity or error, provides a convincing rejoinder to the present climate of terror and fear. Gandhi insists 'the truth is far more powerful than any weapon of mass destruction' [Bose 1948, 181].

Aware of the exclusion entailed by a theistic doctrine, Gandhi places 'truth' at the top of the pedestal of importance. For Christians, this truth is God. For Muslims, Allah; for others, truth can be represented by something outside of this framework. Early in his public comments, Gandhi identified God with truth. Later, Gandhi claimed that for him 'God and Truth are convertible terms' [1948, 67]. The following year, in an address at Wardha, he declared: '...to me Truth is God and there is no way to find Truth except the way of nonviolence' [1948, 172].

Truth is conceived as relative. It is not permanent and fixed, nor does it belong only to one religion or spiritual tradition (spawning heroes and enemies who undertake the last great cataclysmic battle for good over evil). Gandhi's life can be described as an 'experiment with truth.' He offers an inclusive secular account of truth (inclusive of all religious views, and dependent upon none).

He admitted that he had drunk deeply from many springs, including Indian traditions, Christianity and Islam. It can perhaps be said that his perceptions reflect the harmony or similarity that he saw in their views on nonviolence as well as in what he describes as the unbroken testimony that humanity has from seers and saints of different times and continents. Yet, he did not quote the authority of Gods or revelations or religious texts for his views on nonviolence. He did certainly say that they supported his perceptions. But the arguments that he advanced in support of nonviolence or *ahimsa* were philosophical, sociological and spiritual, and not religious. They were related to the spiritual life of the individual as well as the dynamics of action oriented to social goals, human behavior in situations of conflict or opinions and interests and struggles for social justice [Varma and Alomes, in press].

At this juncture, consider humankind's perennial struggle for social justice, the urgent desire for protection and security, and the contemporary climate of fear that is escalating on a daily basis. Understanding what is going on in the present is the necessary first step before seeking guidance from the two nonviolent titans, Gandhi and King.

THE CORRIDOR OF FEAR

In September 2006, UN Secretary General Kofi Annan lamented: 'Internationally, the world is seeing an increasing misuse of what I call the "T-word" — terrorism — to demonize opponents, to throttle freedom of speech and the press, and to delegitimize legitimate political grievances.' He continued, pointing out that the 'collateral damage' of this misuse includes damage to the presumption of innocence, to precious human rights, to the rule of law, and to the very fabric of democratic governance [Humphrey 2004, 1]. If this is true (and it appears to be), there exists the misplaced notion of 'burning down the village in order to save it' — or using violent tactics that regrettably destroy the very values and freedoms that governments are trying to preserve.

As Humphrey points out, the discourse on terrorism and security is about the justification of counter-terrorism measures. In the name of national security, counter-terrorism seeks to ensure protection of citizens through defensive policing at home and offensive military intervention abroad. The world has moved from protection of the individual against state-terrorism, that is, protecting the rights of individuals against unjust state law and oppression — and King and Gandhi have much to say about this aspect — to a point where Humphrey says state-terrorism is now imagined as 'globalized terrorism' (terrorism that is extremist, networked, highly symbolic and clandestine). The danger is that all separate and random acts of terrorist violence are now unified and assimilated into politically related events. His examples include the World Trade Centre attacks, a bombing of a Jerusalem bus, and a Baghdad UN truck bombing. He astutely points out that, irrespective of whether or not the perpetrators of terrorist violence are part of international networks with common aims, 'globalized terrorism' effectively assimilates diverse forms of political violence with the consequence of unifying and amplifying the threat. Differences are further de-politicized by essentializing the terrorist act, ignoring the political projects behind it and thereby reducing terrorism to a problem of security and counter-terrorism policy for the state. This results in the need for individuals to be protected from apocalyptic violence and world-ending events [Humphrey 2004, 2-3].

National and international security agendas become inextricably entwined and the individual is in a different type of environment — not one of stability, comfort and predictability, but one where future possibilities of cataclysmic risk increasingly determine daily decision-making. A 'risk society' is created where 'the concept of risk becomes a peculiar intermediate state between security and destruction, where the perception of threatening risks determines thought and action' [Adam, Beck and van Loon 2000, 213]. The 'risk society' is 'an epoch in which the dark sides of progress increasingly come to dominate social debate' [Beck 1995, 2].

No wonder individuals feel vulnerable, fearful and confused. They have been suddenly dropped into a situation where their neighborhood-based life in general (and daily events within their reach and control, in particular) has been replaced by the risk of a cataclysmic uncontrollable tidal wave of violence ready to impact and destroy all of their lives, hopes and dreams at some unknown future moment. They begin to build mental and physical fortresses; they have no time to speak to strangers; they develop suspicion toward those who look and sound different to them; and they are constantly murmuring about a feeling of insecurity. As Humphrey points out:

> Terrorism only heightens the individual sense of insecurity by revealing governments' inability to guarantee individual security. The stream of non-specific terrorism warnings we receive from governments in the form of travel alerts or vigilance advice [such as the Australian government's 'Be Alert, Not Alarmed' fridge magnet campaign] heighten risk consciousness (and fear) and make individual security the primary measure of national security. This global terrorism becomes something experienced as potentially world-ending violence beyond our control [2004, 3-4].

Is it any wonder that a large number of people have completely lost hope of ever having a happy and meaningful life?

Both Gandhi and King would call for a refocus on the present. This future-based scenario of risk, fear and misery is something that is an artificial construction. It does not reflect the fact that the majority of people on the planet have never killed anybody and would not intentionally harm anything; or that most people are united in wanting happy and meaningful lives devoid of suffering. What would happen if society rejected the legitimacy of this pre-determined, risk-based future; rejected the labels frequently appearing about 'these cataclysmic times;' and borrowed John Paul Lederach's approach that this can be the 'era that finishes fear and violence' and the one that 'opens pathways to meaningful, cooperative dialogue and peace' [2002, 4].

TRANSFORMING THE PRESENT TO CREATE A NEW FUTURE — INSIGHTS FROM GANDHI AND KING

With a quick sketch of current circumstances, the remainder of this discussion will focus on how Gandhi and King would approach the task of transforming the future-based 'globalized terrorism' view into a present-based tool kit that moves societies toward a more peaceful existence. At the core of their different views would be the idea of constructing a web of relationships — in a particular kind of way. According to Lederach,

... [T]he moral imagination requires the capacity to imagine ourselves in a web of relationships that includes our enemies; the ability to sustain paradoxical curiosity that embraces complexity without reliance on dualistic polarity; the fundamental belief in and pursuit of the creative act; and the acceptance of the inherent risk of stepping into the mystery of the unknown that lies beyond the far too familiar landscape of violence [2005, 5].

Rather than absorbing statements like 'smoke them out of their fox-holes' or 'obliterate the enemy,' which have been used by government officials, individuals could ask themselves questions like: 'What would it be like to listen to the issues of those who would attack us?;' or 'Even if we disagree with their views, as fellow human beings how do we treat them with dignity and respect?' Individuals could imagine how it would be to co-exist cooperatively with those who are labelled terrorists.

Gandhi wants people to understand that all of these people are fellow 'seekers after truth,' persons who espouse various or no religions, and those who hold vastly differing views as to the proper social structures or constructive programing in a society [Varma and Alomes, in press]. He admits of error and indecision at many stages of his applied experiment, but the one principle that he adheres to is the theme of *ahimsa* — the supreme and only means to the discovery of social truths. 'Those who join the Ashram have literally to accept that meaning,' he insists. That meaning of *ahimsa* takes him into a realm that is much higher than simply non-killing. In his words,

Ahimsa really means that you may not offend anybody, you may not harbor an uncharitable thought even in connection with one who may consider himself to be your enemy ... that does not mean that we practice the doctrine in its entirety. Far from it. It is an ideal which we have to reach, and it is an ideal to be reached even at this very moment, if we are capable of doing so. [Gandhi 1927, 324].

Statements like this make it easy to see why some critics argue that this type of lifestyle is relevant to only a few exceptional individuals. But perhaps there is another way to think about *ahimsa*. Think about the North Star. Using the North Star as an accurate guide to travel in that direction does not entail a belief by the travellers that they will literally reach the star. Likewise, the pursuit of *ahimsa* can provide a useful guideline for action based on an understanding of incremental improvement in the direction of tolerance, compassion and nonviolence. According to Gandhi, any small step we take today in denying violence and moving toward human dignity, respect and valuing difference is a step in the right direction.

The view of Shri Ravindra Varma [2006], a leading Gandhian commentator, that there are diametrically opposed views from both state and non-state actors, is obvious in these difficult times. The conflict that results cannot be advanced through coercion and force, it can only be resolved by approaching conflict in a cooperative way (peace is not the absence of conflict, but a different way of approaching and resolving it). For example, rather than setting down a pathway of hatred towards all practitioners of Islam for the acts of a handful, it would be more helpful to ask the question: 'Why would someone hate us so much that they would fly planes into buildings?' [Hanh 2001, 100].

According to Lederach:

Anger of this sort (what we could call generational identity-based anger) is constructed over time through a combination of historical events, a deep sense of threat to identity, and direct experiences of sustained exclusion. This is very important to understand because our response to the immediate events will have everything to do with whether we reinforce and provide the oil, seeds and nutrients for future cycles of revenge and violence or whether it changes... the myth they carefully seek to sustain: That they are under threat, fighting an irrational and mad system that has never taken them seriously and wishes to destroy them and their people. What we need to do is to destroy the myth, not their people [2001, 2].

The task is to replace the myth with truth. Gandhi proposes that a perception of truth cannot be transferred to another or made acceptable to another through violence. Varma says that violence can suppress expression of differences, but cannot eliminate different perceptions [2006]. If one depends on violence to ensure the acceptance of one's perception, or one's perception of truth, one will always have to depend on violence. The acceptance will depend on violence and will endure as long as violence prevails. It will therefore result in a vicious cycle of violence, not a change of views or perceptions.

Since differences arise because of the nature of the human mind — and this is unique to our species — the need to be consistent with the paradigms of co-existence is also unique to humans. Since differences arise due to mental processes and the flaws in these methods, a countervailing or correcting force has to be employed by the mind and in the mind, whether it is one's mind or the mind of another. Gandhi called this countervailing force of nonviolence 'the law of our being,' or the law of our species. In practical terms, to allow a space for change to occur, people must learn to listen in order to reduce the feelings of frustration, anger and hatred as they arise in the mind, and to apply these ideas consistently over time.

Gandhi insists that 'Truth is God' and the quest for Truth or God is the highest quest that a human being can embark on. It is the quest for self-realization. Since the way to Truth lies through love, the way to this realization also lies through nonviolence. For Gandhi, this is the spiritual basis of nonviolence [Varma, 2006].

The law of cause and effect is an inexorable law that governs the universe. Since 'means' are the causes that are used to create the effects, which are seen as the goals or 'ends,' the causes that are employed will determine the effects that are created. In other words, the means will determine the ends. Gandhi [1948] proposed that means and ends are two sides of the same coin. They are convertible terms. Violence cannot generate nonviolence. Hatred cannot generate love. The object of a peaceful or nonviolent society can be created only through nonviolent means, not violent means. The emotions, attitudes, responses and states of mind that are desirable in a nonviolent society cannot be created through violent methods.

As Varma points out, 'we can see that none of these arguments bases itself on the revelations of prophets or texts of religions. All of them arise from the nature of the human mind and the paradigms that govern the existence of the human species (and the demands of co-existence in society) [Varma and Alomes in press].

Gandhi would want people to give up the notion of deadly conflict as an inevitability, and to recognize that it is not a two-fold choice — cooperation or conflict — but that cooperation can be used as the most successful method for dealing with conflict. The whole notion of security (individual, state and international) rests on cooperation, and cooperation rests on two-way relationships based on trust and respect. If what constitutes human nature is about 'being in relation,' then the basis of those relationships must be established. As Kevin

Clements correctly points out [2006], it is also necessary to determine how to undertake relationships with those who are feared or who have been outspoken about intending to do harm.

The popular way of approaching this type of difficult relationship is indeed lacking wisdom: namely, the only recourse is to annihilate 'the other' in an attempt to annihilate their views. At least one problem with this approach is that as soon as this 'other' has gone, another will inevitably pop up to take their place. And if the opposing camp also holds this misguided view, the only logical way to proceed is toward complete extinction of both sides. As King says, 'we must learn to live together as brothers or perish together as fools.' He eloquently continues: 'We are caught in an inescapable network of mutuality, tied in a single garment of destiny. Whatever affects one directly affects all indirectly' [1967, 45].

If we are going to declare eternal hostility toward anything, it will need to be toward narrow nationalism, religious and cultural conflict, racial disharmony, economic disparity and environmental degradation — the five causes of violence identified by His Holiness the Dalai Lama in conversation with the author. However, when people are overtaken by a new fear, they are disinclined to worry about the gaping chasm between rich and poor, the hundreds of thousands of displaced persons, the overflowing refugee camps and the destruction of natural resources on the planet (the key global problems left to fester in the wake of the war on terror). As Varma [2006] suggests:

> The fear that sophisticated versions of the weapons of mass destruction may percolate into the hands of groups of terrorists has further aggravated the sense of universal vulnerability. Humanity seems to find itself wedged in between these two threats to its survival — one from weapons of mass destruction, and the other, the tactics and operations of terrorism, which too depend on creating the sense of universal vulnerability.

A little reflection should illuminate whether these two threats are separate and distinct or two sides of the same coin. Both seem to have a common origin: faith in the use of physical force or violence — that the only or ultimate test to determine justice or truth is violence, and that it is therefore legitimate to mobilize and use the weaponry necessary to effectively realize that goal.

Once one accepts violence as the sole or ultimate instrument, two corollaries follow: first, anyone who wants to engage in combat and deploy violent force has to acquire greater determinant force; and second, they have to choose weapons and tactics that give them greater strike power. The first leads to an inevitable arms race, including the manufacture and inclusion of weapons of mass destruction, and the second to the adoption of forms and tactics of warmaking like guerrilla warfare and terrorism. Those people who want to save the world from the threat of weapons of mass destruction and terrorism must oppose the source that has created both of these threats — the mindset that sees violence as the answer to differences of opinion [Varma, 2006].

Gandhi gave us an insightful metaphor to understand how to deal with conflict cooperatively. If we have seven people present, we will most likely get seven completely different versions of the 'truth', so how can we move forward? He tells the much-repeated story of 'the seven blind men and the elephant.' Imagine them standing around the elephant in a circle. The one at the trunk reports that the elephant is a long snake-like creature, the one at the tail reports that the elephant is a thin wispy creature, the one at the side says it is a vast mountainous creature and so on. Each captures some aspect of the elephant, but that version alone is not what an elephant is. Through a network of relations with others, guided by the operation of reason, each of us comes to an understanding or a 'measure of reality,' which may be true at that time but is open to modification and refinement. Gandhi holds that truth is not something at which we arrive in isolation, waiting for a moment of revelation. Truth is discovered by persons in relations with others. The individual can only use objective truth as a guiding principle. What is achievable is truth in relative terms; and in this respect the individual searches for truth in terms of the community of which they are a part. For Gandhi, truth and *ahimsa* are inseparable ... *ahimsa* is the means and truth is the end.

Ahimsa is not a negative state of harmlessness but a positive state of compassion, love and understanding, of doing good even to the evil-doer. But what it does not mean is helping the evil-doer to continue the wrong or tolerating it by passive acquiescence. Gandhi's philosophy and practice, as evidenced through his life, demonstrates the basic commitment to reduce violence in ourselves and meet the violence of others with the power of nonviolence. It also demonstrates an unswerving dedication to interdependence. Gandhi argues that all phenomena and all sentient and non-sentient beings are interdependent. The universe arises, exists and survives or disintegrates on the basis of interdependence. In the paradigm of interdependence, all are equal.

On this view it makes no sense to maintain the distinction between 'self' and 'other,' where the other can readily become 'the enemy.' This flawed logic continues that if 'the other' is destroyed, the problems of 'the self' are over. Lederach paints a graphic picture to represent the futility of this notion:

> In all my experiences of deep-rooted conflict what stands out most are the ways in which political leaders wishing to end the violence believed they could achieve it by overpowering and getting rid of the perpetrator of the violence ... [Using] military action to destroy terror ... will be like hitting a fully mature dandelion with a golf club ... ensuring yet another generation of recruits [2001, 4].

Bishop Desmond Tutu reminds us that the false distinction between 'self' and 'other,' between 'friend' and 'enemy,' is the cause of much of the world's violence. An 'enemy' is a situation-dependent convention, a label, and the very same person can be a stranger, an enemy and a friend over a lifetime. In a discussion with the author in 1998, he said that to transform our thinking, we should consider: 'an enemy as a friend one has not yet made.'

If breaking down the barriers between individuals and groups is the first step towards peaceful co-existence, then rejecting the need for deadly conflict and denying the legitimacy of the violent action of state and non-state actors would be the next item on Gandhi's and King's agenda. Two things happen in the exercise of power through violence — a claim to *authority* and a claim to *legitimacy*. Following Gandhi's lead, King utilized non-cooperation or civil disobedience campaigns — based on the withdrawal of recognition of the authority to rule or enforce its values — and the denial of the legitimacy of violence. Gandhi demonstrated the success of these ideas and techniques in his practice of *satyagraha* or 'truth insistence,' evidenced in historically famous campaigns like the Salt March and the Vykom Temple Road *satyagraha*. Later, King transmitted this technique of nonviolent activism and self-suffering into the Montgomery Bus Boycott. It turns out that fearlessness in the face of oppression is the key, and the only test of truth is action based on the refusal to do harm.

Believing in the soundness and success of this philosophy does require faith, however, and on King's terms: 'faith is taking the first step even when you don't see the whole staircase.'

For King, demonstrating power through nonviolence requires recognition of the equality and inherent rights of all humankind; and an insistence on the truth of equality, justice and compassion. The means/ends dichotomy must undergo a conceptual turn; the agent must realize that means and ends are one and the same. 'There is no way to peace, peace is the way; there is no way to truth, truth is the way' [Hanh 1993, 5]. This understanding requires a necessary commitment to nonviolence in thought and application every minute of every day. Rather than a useful technique to be used once or twice a year for the purpose of protest, it becomes the desirable way of life for a moral agent.

With foundational beliefs in the dignity and worth of all humankind, and an insistence on the truth of this, Gandhi and King showed how the moral agent can use nonviolent action, not only as a defense against violence, but as a positive and constructive force to bring about social change. By not only believing this, but by demonstrating this belief through action, the agent can influence others seeking truth, and influence the oppressor to correct wrong views in a way that may move both players to a new position of understanding amid power relations. Power exercised in this way can be enormously successful and it does not involve injury or harm. Neither does it involve cowardice or compromise. The moral agent acts from a position of strength, while always aware and empathetic to the needs of the 'interlocutor.' In Gandhi's view, it is the power of the activists' will, together with their reason, that effects change in society.

All of Gandhi's campaigns reflect the following themes: (1) pursuit of the Truth or God, which for Gandhi was the search for realizing the truth of human unity; (2) *satyagraha* as the means for achieving this realization; (3) power existing in the hands of the individual, with any individual able to learn how to access it; (4) the holding of a moral truth that fosters nonviolent action, is supported by self-suffering, and supplies a force that any individual can learn to wield against an opponent of any proportion with an expectation of success; (5) while apparent differences remain (each individual will have a different visual appearance, different hopes fears and desires), when the individual accepts nonviolence s/he ceases to be different to others. Nonviolence calls on the feature common to all persons — humanity — and insists on the removal of the (false) distinction between self and other. This goes beyond mere theorizing and becomes a call for individuals to act.

Varma [2006] advises that in honing the ability to identify truth, the *satyagrahi* (one who insists on truth) must remove the imperfections of the instrument of observation — that is, the mind's facile distractions — and adopt the scientific temper and the scientific method of rigorous enquiry. Gandhi saw no distinction between the methods that are used to establish truth in the field of the 'sciences' and in the field of *satyagraha* when formulating truth as one saw it in the social situation. He would have also considered it applicable to today's war on terror. In addition to the discipline familiar in the field of empirical enquiry (such as observation, the collection and objective examination of data and their verification), Gandhi also included experience as an element of understanding or comprehension. What would make people so full of hate that they are prepared to blow themselves up? What are their concerns? Are they legitimate? What additional facts are influencing beliefs and behavior? Are there other ways to respond than to employ violence? What is needed to create the opportunity for listening and dialogue? What would it take to transform the situation?

In order to move forward toward peace, Gandhi wants the *Satyagrahi* to free him/herself of all prejudices and obsessions; to be meticulous in the collection and assessment of facts to ensure that when a solution is proposed it can be supported and is fair to the genuine interests (as distinct from imagined interest or the interests of aggrandisement) of the one whose position s/he wants to alter; to be ready therefore to subject the facts or evidence behind the conclusions to constant scrutiny by the other side, by impartial intermediaries or by the public at large, and to revise our own views, without considerations of prestige, if it was found on the scrutiny of evidence or other considerations that we had fallen short [Varma 2006, 49-50].

In this way, Gandhi combines the scientific method with relentless efforts to improve the efficiency of his instruments, i.e. his head and heart, by shedding all untruth, violence, lack of love, in other words by purifying himself, by ridding himself of what he was fighting in others [Varma 2006, 27].

Gandhi demonstrates that nonviolence is inclusive; it can break down political and religious barriers and provides a position of strength and optimism. Perhaps the most persistent element in Gandhi's work is the recurring theme that nonviolence is truth-creating.

Inevitably, conflict and the threat of uncontrolled violence are conditions of the human circumstance. It is not enough that the agent should take unreasoned 'flight from violence.' As expressed by Bondurant, "The Gandhian experiments suggest that if man is to free himself from fear and threat alike, he pause in his flight from violence to set himself the task of its conquest' [1965, 233].

In an attempt to conquer violence, King's famous *Letter from Birmingham Jail* [1963] shows how, with tireless persistence, he confronted the myths used to justify violence, and how, one by one, he aimed to demolish them. This elegant piece of work (outlined below) provides additional tools to confront state and non-state terror today.

Like Gandhi, reason for King, is the measure of humanity. He argued that affirmative action is a reasonable policy in compensating against ongoing historical discrimination; further, that American habits are stubbornly racist, even after the victories of the civil rights campaigns. He argued that racism is one mechanism of systematic oppression, bolstered by class conflict and violence. King sought to purge violence from social relations in order to alleviate oppressive mechanisms and conditions. He drew distinctions between justice and injustice by providing a philosophical justification for his militant involvement in the affairs of Birmingham: 'I am in Birmingham because injustice is here' [1964, 77]. Similarly, he would have had no hesitation in confronting the war in (the term 'in' is now used more than 'on') Iraq because injustice is here (where 'here' is increasingly becoming global).

In Birmingham, King found three reasons to judge segregation laws as unjust: (1) they degrade personality; (2) they are inflicted upon a minority while the majority is unaffected; and (3) they are enacted by a majority while the minority is prevented from participating in deliberations. Thus, King argued that he is obliged to present his body in protest. When Ralph Waldo Emerson asked Henry Thoreau why he was in jail, Thoreau replied by asking Emerson why he was not. King routinely defended his philosophy of nonviolence for its unique ability to meet the demands of universal liberation. It becomes quite feasible that King would have responded to state and non-state perpetrators of violence today with similar logic.

King challenged America to a higher destiny (then and now). Key clauses of the American creed affirm self-evident truths such as equal rights, freedom and justice for all; yet these pronouncements in practice are applied with systematic double standards. He asserted that human affairs should be guided by universal moral principles. Moreover, the difference between right and wrong cannot be evaded because each has different consequences:

His classic *Letter from Birmingham Jail* was written while he was imprisoned for leading a civil rights demonstration without a permit. In the letter, he responded to eight Alabama clergymen who found his tactics too extreme. 'In a reply abounding in references to the Jewish and Christian Scriptures and to philosophers ancient and modern, Dr King met his critics head on, and left a written legacy of his nonviolent approach to oppression' [Fahey and Armstrong 1992, 113].

Reviewing the long record of police brutality and unsolved bombings of churches in Birmingham, King instructed his critics in the 'four steps of any nonviolent campaign:' (1) collection of the facts; (2) negotiation; (3) self-purification; and (4) direct action. Focusing on these points, he denied that he had acted irresponsibly. In the crisis created by direct action, King saw hope for 'creative tension' — through the tolerance of beatings and other suffering — which as we have seen in Gandhi's project, can change an enemy into an ally (in this, King echoes Gandhi's appeal to self-suffering).

King turned to the issue of equality: 'if white Americans would not accept equality for black Americans, then what might be their excuse?' King's answer to his own question was direct: white America had calculated the cost of equality and decided it would not pay. Even though the country was founded upon the principle that 'all men are created equal', white America still reserved the right to interpret the principle in its own interest. As King explained elsewhere, 'Jefferson's majestic words "all men are created equal" meant for him, as for many others, that all *white* men are created equal' [1967, 23.].

This concept of equality outlined by King is fundamental to his later writings on nonviolence. Here again, King echoed Gandhi: 'when compared to other philosophies of power — white or black — nonviolence alone insisted upon a single meaning for equality. Under the terms of the logic of nonviolence, opponents also were considered equal' [Moses 1997, 29].

This outlook can be instructive for the present circumstances where one is either part of the 'Coalition of the Willing' or an enemy. No exceptions. No equality. On the other hand, evident in King's writing is the call to dissolve barriers and realize a common structure. He referred to a type of occlusion where a privileged white version of reality obstructs the value of marginalized black persons, 'as if there were no ethical considerations...to respect' [Moses 1997, 57]. By resisting this view, individuals assert their value and point to a common structure, in order to 'reassert the regulatory value of ethical imperatives that favor the development of each and every personality' [57]. King stated:

> Soon the doctrine of white supremacy was embedded in every textbook and preached in practically every pulpit. It became a structural part of the culture. And men then embraced this philosophy not as the rationalization of a lie, but as the expression of a final truth [1967, 75].

When the evils of racism, poverty and militarism are defeated, a new set of values emerges. The economy must become more person-centered than property-and-profit-centered; and the government must depend more on its moral power than its military power. King persistently recasts oppressive power in terms of a common corruption that diminishes *everyone's* humanity. Injustice concerns every person imaginable.

CONCLUSION

We have seen that for both Gandhi and King nonviolence involves moral courage, discipline, strength and wisdom. But most of all, it requires a recognition of violence, not an acceptance of it, and a determination to resist it, to deny its authority and its legitimacy. French philosopher Jacques Ellul made the shrewd observation that our era 'is not at all the age of violence; it's the age of the awareness of violence ... what really characterizes our time is not so much that there is so much violence ... but that we are challenged, possibly as never before, to deal with it' [cited in Nagler 2001, 18].

Dealing with violence in a practical way would characterize Gandhi and King's constructive program. They would require a shift from a future-oriented focus to the present. Instead of people dealing with cataclysmic events beyond their control, the task would be to bring relationships back within their control. Effective and morally legitimate management means denying the legitimacy of violence and creating a space for dialogue, even with those who intend harm. Gandhi and King would insist on mobilizing grass-roots community-based resources. (The task of non-government organizations becomes important to provide accurate information for the general public and to liaise with government decision-makers.) A plan would need to be created for dealing with difference in a cooperative way. Attitudes of domination would need to be transformed to dialogue, requiring a massive shift at a community level to withdraw support for war and violence as the only problem-solving strategy.

Gandhi and King would argue that there is no such thing as a 'just war' and cite the alarming trend in the ratio of civilian deaths. At the beginning of the twentieth century, the ratio of military to civilian casualties in wars was eight to one. Today, this has been almost exactly reversed. For our two nonviolence leaders this statistic would be totally unacceptable. Gandhi and King would point to contemporary examples for social change through nonviolence. In 2003, the 'Rose Revolution', a mass nonviolence campaign in the country of Georgia, displaced President Eduard Shevardnadze; and in 2004/5 in the Ukraine, orange-clad supporters of Victor Yushchenko gathered in Independence Square in Kiev to protest nonviolently against the violence, corruption, voter intimidation and electoral fraud that resulted in an election re-run and successful conclusion for Yushchenko.

Finally, Gandhi and King would highlight the five significant factors required to challenge violent action:

1. that people have the *capacity to change* (that life in general, power relations in particular, and agents as conductors of those power relations are not confined to a predetermined and rigidly fixed social grid of hatred, violence and suffering from which there is no escape);

2. that violence is about the *action* of the agent, not a set of circumstances;

3. that every individual is *accountable* for their actions (including intentions);

4. that the *false moral distinction* between self and other (which so frequently leads to notions of the other as 'enemy' or the enemy as 'inhuman,' and on that basis acts of violence are said to be justified) must be recognized;

5. that by disengaging from the false distinction of 'self' and 'other' and adhering to nonviolence, value is attributed to the other as a person, while still allowing opposition to injustice.

The nonviolent votary claims power from an ethically sound position and having this power is not committed to domination or coercion (violence in, violence out) but the way one leads one's everyday life, insisting on the truth and skillfully dealing with the complexities of social interaction through compassion — compassion in, compassion out.

Humans need to deal with violence by picturing themselves as part of a whole, as Albert Einstein observed in a letter reprinted in *The New York Times* on March 29, 1972:

A human being is a part of the whole, called by us the 'universe,' a part limited in time and space. He experiences his thoughts and feelings as sometimes separate from the rest — a kind of optical delusion of his consciousness. This delusion is a kind of prison for us, restricting us to our personal decisions and to affection for a few persons nearest us. Our task must be to free ourselves from this prison by widening our circle of compassion to embrace all living creatures and the whole of nature in its beauty [cited in Nagler 2001, 172].

To paraphrase Gandhi: Our greatness as human beings lies not so much in being able to remake the world — that is the myth of the atomic age — as in being able to remake ourselves. The urgent questions become: How can people remake themselves? How do they reduce the causes of violence in their minds, like anger, frustration, fear and hatred? How can they increase their connection to others and promote unity, compassion and harmony? How do they deal with difference in a cooperative rather than violent way? As Ury [1999] points out, far from eliminating differences, the challenge is to make the world safe for differences.

King would close this discussion by urging individuals to move beyond their selfish narrow view and realize the possibility of a cooperative future. There is a choice: to look at 'life as a mirror in which we see only ourselves or as a window through which to see other selves' [1963, 14]. It is becoming increasingly difficult for people to evade the window King encourages them to look into and through, to see themselves as agents in the moral community. They can choose to exit the corridor of fear, and have the capacity to do so by utilizing the window of nonviolence.

The logic of nonviolence seeks power within a disciplined framework that views violence as harmful and inevitably short-sighted. 'True nonviolence is more than the absence of violence. It is the persistent and determined application of peaceable power to offences against the community — in this case the world community' [King 1967, 184].

ACKNOWLEDGEMENTS

Dr Anna Alomes is a philosopher, primarily interested in nonviolence, reconciliation, conflict resolution and comparative philosophy issues. She is Director of the Centre for Applied Philosophy and Ethics [CAPE] at the University of Tasmania, and works part of each year in India. She is the co-author of a book, *Towards a Nonviolent Mind,* due out shortly.

REFERENCES

Adam, B., Beck, U., and van Loon, J. (2000). (Eds.). *The Risk Society and Beyond: Critical Issues in Social Theory*. London: Sage Publications.

Beck, U. (1995). *Ecological Politics in the Age of Risk*. Cambridge: Polity.

Bondurant, J. V. (1965). *Conquest of Violence: The Gandhian Philosophy of Conflict*. Los Angeles: University of California Press.

Bose, N. K. (1935). 'An Interview with Mahatma Gandhi.' *The Modern Review*, LVIII, October 1935, 45-46.

Clements, K. (2006). Nonviolent Response to Terror and Terrorism. Public lecture delivered at the University of Tasmania. 31 July.

Fahey, J., and Armstrong, R. (1992). (Eds.). *A Peace Reader: Essential Readings on War, Justice, Non-violence and World Order*. New York: Paulist Press.

Foucault, M. (1980). In C. Gordon (Ed.). *Power/Knowledge: Selected Interviews and Other Writings 1972–77*. Brighton, Sussex: Harvester Press.

Gandhi, M. K. (1927). *An Autobiography or The Story of My Experiments with Truth*. Ahmedabad: Navajivan Publishing House.

Gandhi, M. K. (1948). *Satyagraha in South Africa*. V.G. Desai (trans.) Madras: Ganesan.

Hanh, T. N. (2001). *Anger*. London: Rider.

Humphrey, M. (2004). *Human Rights Counter-Terrorism and Security*. Sydney: Australian Human Rights Centre, University of New South Wales.

James, W. (1950). *The Principles of Psychology*. New York: Dover.

King, M. L. Jr. (1958). *Stride Toward Freedom: The Montgomery Story*. San Francisco: Harper and Row.

King, M. L. Jr. (1963). *Letter from Birmingham Jail*. San Francisco: Harper.

King, M. L. Jr. (1964). *Why We Can't Wait*. New York: Mentor.

King, M. L. Jr. (1967). *Where Do We Go from Here: Chaos or Community?* Boston: Beacon Press.

Lederach, J. P. (2005). *The Moral Imagination: The Art and Soul of Building Peace*. New York: Oxford University Press.

Lederach, J. P. (2001). *The Challenge of Terror: A Travelling Essay*. Retrieved August 14, 2006, from http://www.mediate.com/articles/terror911.cfm

Lederach, J. P. (2002). *A Holiday Wish*. Retrieved August 14, 2006, from http://www.wagingpeace.org/articles/2002/12/31_lederach_holiday-wish.htm

Moses, G. (1997). *Revolution of Conscience: Martin Luther King Jr. and the Philosophy of Nonviolence*. New York: Guilford.

Nagler, M. N. (2001). *Is There No Other Way? The Search for a Non-violent Future*. Maui, Hawaii: Inner Ocean.

Ury, W. (1999). *Getting to Peace: Transforming Conflict at Home, at Work and in the World*. New York: Viking.

Varma, R. (2006). *Spiritual Perceptions of Mahatma Gandhi* New Delhi: Rupa and Co.

Varma, R., and Alomes, A. (in press). *Towards a Nonviolent Mind*.

In: Nonviolence: An Alternative for Defeating... ISBN: 978-1-60021-812-5
Editors: S. Ram and R. Summy, pp. 47-55 © 2008 Nova Science Publishers, Inc.

Chapter 3

THE MAHATMA AND THE MUJIHADEEN: GANDHI'S ANSWER TO TERRORISM

Michael N. Nagler

ABSTRACT

While it is intuitively obvious that nonviolence and terrorism are opposites, and almost as obvious that the one must annihilate the other, i.e. that if properly understood nonviolence would be the solution to this form of violence (as it would to any other) yet it is far from clear how to implement nonviolence for this purpose. In this study I explore both the underlying theory and some of the practical measures by which we could set about responding to that challenge. I begin with Gandhi's challenge to the British after Bhagat Singh threw a bomb into the state legislative assembly at Lahore at the end of 1929: 'I urge you then to read that writing on the wall. Nobody throws away his life without some motive behind.' In other words, as a friend of mine said shortly after 9/11, 'Terrorism cannot be condoned, but it can be understood.' Understanding is possible only when one separates the person from the deed; and here we see the first of many 'nonviolence dividends,' or lessons to be learned from Gandhi, i.e. principled nonviolence that is immediately applicable to the situation of all of us who are caught in one position or another by the 'Global War on Terror.' Other characteristics of principled nonviolence to be treated in this chapter will include: (1) Terrorism and deception are weapons not of the strong but of the weak. Restraint, forgiveness, compassion and humility are signs of strength. It is these responses that lead to real security; (2) Nonviolence has in actual fact been used to overcome terrorism; (3) Nations can - and in two cases actually did - adopt nonviolence; (4) It is far more effective to correct the conditions giving rise to terrorism than to attempt to thwart terrorists who are responding, however wrongly, to those conditions. Finally (5) I will address a problem that has taken on far greater proportions since Gandhi's day: namely, the culture of violence promoted by the mass media that has become the dominant culture of most people today.

INTRODUCTION

On April 8, 1929, a young man named Bhagat Singh entered the visitors' gallery of the Lahore assembly, threw a bomb and began firing an automatic pistol at the British and Indian officials who were conferring there. Singh, who had assassinated the British Assistant Superintendent of Police the previous December, was captured on this occasion and hanged in March of 1931.

Gandhi utterly condemned Singh's 'dastardly' acts of violence, but wrote,

> Bhagat Singh and his companions have been executed and have become martyrs. . . I join in the tributes paid to the memory of these young men. And yet I must warn the Youth of the country against following their example. We should not utilize our energy, our spirit of sacrifice, our labors and our indomitable courage in the way they have utilized theirs. This country must not be liberated through bloodshed [CWMG vol. 51, 1931, 341].

No one loathed terrorism more than Gandhi. He stood to lose everything he had worked for with a single bomb, for he knew full well how rulers seize on the chance to condemn nonviolent movements for the slightest lapse, just as today's media will ignore a highly disciplined nonviolent demonstration to seize on the odd outbreak of sabotage. (I have ventured to call this, somewhat facetiously, 'Nagler's Law: V+NV = V.') But Gandhi's aversion to terrorism went much deeper. Terrorism is in many ways the worst form of violence. Indeed, it is often tinged with a kind of cowardice, which is even worse than violence, if anything can be. As one who gave his whole life to eradicate violence in every compartment of life, he could not possibly condone one of its worst forms.

Yet, as a friend of mine said in connection with our nation's response to 9/11, 'terrorism cannot be condoned, but it can be *understood*.' And therein lies both the subtlety and the contemporaneity of Gandhi's position.

SEPARATING PERSON FROM DEED

The first difference to observe between Gandhi's views and the prevailing reaction to terrorism that we are seeing today is that no matter how much terrorism sickened him (I am not being hyperbolic; there are eye-witness accounts of Gandhi being physically revolted by open violence), he did not hate *terrorists*. For him, precisely because he was nonviolent, the doer was never identical with his deed. Thus we find him pleading in vain with the Viceroy to commute the death sentence for Singh and his accomplices, and not just because it might make the misguided terrorist a martyr. In the Mahatma's eyes, violence is violence whether handed down by a legally constituted court or hurled by a lone assassin. It was by the same reasoning that while he hated 'from the bottom of my heart the system of government that the British have set up in India' and the force required to sustain it, he 'refuse[d] to hate the domineering Englishman,' just as he refused to hate the domineering Hindu.

Thus Gandhi warned the Government repeatedly not to overreact as other youth, particularly in Bengal, ignored his advice and followed Bhagat Singh down the road of despair; and in these warnings he pleaded with them to do something Governments so rarely do — listen to the voice, however hoarse and inarticulate, that was issuing from the deeds of their attackers: 'Will you not see the writing that these terrorists are writing with their blood? Will you not see that we do not want bread made of wheat, but we want bread of liberty; and without that liberty there are thousands today who are sworn not to give themselves peace or to give the country peace.' In other words he did not ask that the terrorism be condoned but pleaded, largely in vain, that it be understood — and the first step in such understanding was to separate the person from the deed. This could not be more pertinent for us, who are caught up one way or another in the 'Global War on Terror' now being conducted with such misguided vigor by the United States.

ACKNOWLEDGING THE COUNTER-PRODUCTIVITY OF ALL TERRORISM

It goes without saying that the second principle in Gandhi's approach, one that is more recognized by many critics of government policy today, is that if you are going to condemn terrorism, as of course we must, we must condemn it even-handedly. Terror is terror whether it comes strapped to the body of a suicide bomber or launched from hundreds of miles away onto targets that may just turn out to include innocent civilians.

As we know now to our cost — those of us who are free to admit it, at least — the use of violence against terrorism is counter-productive, then as now. We can almost hear our own sad case in Gandhi's further observation from the same letter just quoted:

> About the Government I cannot help feeling that it has missed a golden opportunity, to win over the rebels to its side. . . The reliance on violence . . . suggests that in spite of high-sounding and pious proclamations, it does not want to part with power.

As many military personnel are now saying about the quagmire in Iraq: 'We are making terrorists faster than we can kill them.' It could not be otherwise. From a nonviolent perspective, violence is violence; more of the same poison does not cancel the previous dose. It is only because the vast majority of people lack the habit of asking themselves, is this violence or not, that they are caught up in relatively superficial distinctions like whether the violence comes from a state or a less organized actor.

If we are not to use violence to protect ourselves against such attacks, though, what on earth are we to use?

ANTIDOTE TO TERRORISM

On one level the answer is so simple that it appears on a bumper sticker I have outside my office at Berkeley: NONVIOLENCE: ANTI-TERRORISM THAT WORKS. I believe this is a case where intuition works: nonviolence is the only possible antidote to terrorism, and the only reason we do not use it for that purpose is that we are still so unfamiliar with nonviolence, even though it has been used in an ever-widening array of situations since Gandhi's time. And a kind of terrorism was one of them.

Vinoba Bhave, considered by many to be the Mahatma's closest disciple in terms of spiritual orientation, was passing through the Chambal Valley in Madhya Pradesh on one of his *padayatra's* or 'walking pilgrimages' in 1960. The area was 'infested' with *dacoits*, or hereditary bandits, but Bhave, wisely eschewing the dehumanizing imagery, said no, it was not 'infested with dacoits' but 'inhabited by virtuous people.' Using his nonviolent authority, he sent word to the offenders that if they would come forward and surrender to him they would be dealt with fairly by the law, but no further punishment would be visited on themselves or their families. Many of them came and laid their arms at his feet, forestalling a bloody confrontation with the police [See for example Nargolkar 1995, 127-129, with illustration at the end]. Peace researchers will think of Kenneth Boulding's First Law: 'If something has happened, it is possible.'

But is this relevant to us, who no longer have a Bhave, not to mention a Gandhi, in our midst? It is relevant, though possibly more difficult. Gandhi was adamant that given proper training and proper generalship, nonviolence could be practiced by masses of humankind. Indeed, he said, 'That non-violence which only an individual can use is not of much use in terms of society. Man is a social being. His accomplishments to be of use must be such as any person with sufficient diligence can attain' [CWMG vol. 98, 6 December, 1947 - 30 January, 1948, item 9]. If the last thirty or so years have shown anything, they have shown that masses of people, in many cases without a single, 'charismatic' leader, can carry out campaigns that are largely free from violence at least in action and that not only persuade (or if that is not possible, coerce) their governments to change course but simply sweep them aside [Zunes et al 1999; Schell 2003; Schock 2005].[1]

To take this one step further, governments themselves have been known to adopt nonviolent modes of behavior even — or perhaps especially — under threatening conditions. I am thinking here of the historical examples of Ashoka's India and William Penn's Pennsylvania; of even more relevance would be the nonviolence that, amazingly enough, drew in nearly 100,000 devoutly Muslim Pathans (Pakhtuns) from what was then the North-West Frontier Province of India to follow Khan Abdul Ghaffar Khan; the famed Khudai Khidmatgars or 'Servants of God' who played a conspicuous role in the larger freedom struggle. And yet, perhaps we should not be so amazed. Nonviolence is for the brave, and there was no one braver than the Pathan even though he expressed that bravery in revenge and violence before — and now, unfortunately, after — Gandhi's transformative power swept over the country. Perhaps the fact that we find it unlikely that such violent men can be won over by nonviolence only betrays how little we still understand it.

Nonviolence, then, can be used not only as an attitude of humanity for which Gandhi pleaded, largely in vain — an attitude that would allow us to listen to the grievances of those who feel compelled to use terror against us regardless of how strongly we condemn that method — but also as a method for direct confrontation.

Terrorism and deception are weapons not of the strong but of the weak. Restraint, forgiveness, compassion and humility are signs of strength. It is these responses that lead to real security. I hope I have established that nonviolence, properly understood, can be an effective recourse against the threat of terrorism — the only effective recourse, I actually believe — and that it can be carried out by individuals, by groups or by entire states, if necessary even without the kind of leadership it has occasionally enjoyed. Gandhi was partly

---

[1] Schell, it should be noted, does not distinguish carefully between movements free of or marred by violence.

thinking of the Khudai Khidmatgars when he said it was nothing short of 'blasphemy to say that non-violence can be practiced by individuals and never by nations which are composed of individuals' [CWMG vol. 74, 194].

As if in illustration of his words, during the virulent racial attacks of 2003 in Bihar, a 'Hindu' mob descended on a rural village at a time when most of the Hindu men, being farmers, were out in the fields. The women reacted quickly however, and took in their Muslim neighbors to protect them. We are talking about mostly one-room cottages, so this often meant 'hiding' their Muslim neighbors in the *puja* corner, underneath their household altar (a pregnant symbolism) and taking their stand at the door, armed with nothing but courage. The mob stormed up to home after home accusing these women, 'You are hiding Muslims in there! 'Yes,' the women calmly replied, not moving aside. 'We want them out of there,' the mob would order, and one after the other the women replied, 'First kill me, then only you may enter.' And the mob turned back. This scene was repeated in ten villages throughout Bihar.[2]

These mobs were a pure form of state terrorism (assuming that, as seems true, it was elements of the ruling BJP that supported them). The women refused to 'buy' their dementia, and the fear they had to master in themselves defused the anger that was boiling in the mob. This is the essential dynamic of all nonviolent response to violent threat. As Gandhi had explained nearly a century earlier in response to the Jallianwalla Bagh massacre in the Punjab,

[General Dyer] wanted us to run away from his fire, to crawl on our bellies and draw lines with our noses. That was part of the game of 'frightfulness.' When we face it with eyes front, it vanishes like an apparition. The might of the tyrant recoils on itself when it meets with no response, even as an arm violently waved in the air suffers dislocation' [Gandhi 1921].

These words of his are once again borne out by history. When the Montgomery bus boycott had passed the point sometimes called the 'nonviolent moment,' when (violent) force meets (nonviolent) force and the latter prevails, some desperate segregationists tried to regain control of the situation by throwing a bomb. This time, however, no one reacted. The experiment was not repeated. Of course, many will say, this is dangerous. It is not one hundred percent reliable. We would answer, is violence one hundred percent reliable?

FAILURE TO UNDERSTAND VIOLENCE

The London-based International Institute for Strategic Studies recently stated that 'al-Qa'ida's recruitment and fundraising was greatly boosted by the US invasion of Iraq.'[3] Militants expanded their influence across the region, be it the Muslim Brotherhood in Egypt, the growing militant threat on Pakistan's border with Afghanistan, increased al-Qa'ida influence in Afghanistan, the distressing electoral coup of Hamas in Palestine, and the growing influence of hard-liners in Iran. Iraq is now a breeding ground for terrorism, or as

---

[2] Collected from eye-witness accounts by Nirmala Deshpande, MP, and orally reported to the author.

one military spokesman said, 'We are breeding terrorists faster than we can kill them.' In fact, government analysts seem to have suggested that the State Department stopped counting terrorist incidents not, as they averred, because these had become too difficult to track accurately, but because such 'incidents worldwide had jumped threefold' after 2003 [Cole 2006, 15].

This is the logic of violence. 'Ironically,' writes Benjamin Schwartz in the *Atlantic Monthly,* 'America's nuclear dominance may dramatically diminish its security' [Schwartz 2006, 33]. Ironic perhaps, but not the least paradoxical or — if one understands the logic of nonviolence — too surprising.

There are a number of negatives in the dilemma facing us. Our national policy has been a disaster — and remains that at the time of this writing. 'Everybody hates America now because of the policies of President [George W] Bush,' said a prominent cleric in Fallujah, 'and his own people condemn him, so what can we do? They slaughtered the Geneva Accords that we were insisting upon every Friday in our mosques, and they killed human rights' [quoted in al-Ubeidi 2004]. We Americans are not in a strong position. But that may actually give us a kind of entry into a new relationship with those who hate or distrust us. In July, 1988 the American cruiser Vincennes on duty in the Persian Gulf shot down an Iranian Airbus by mistake, killing 290 civilians (among them 66 children). Senior President Bush announced, 'I don't care what the facts are. I will never apologize for the American people.' The President, speaking for all of us, added peace, the possibility of living in peace, to the casualty list. We, the American people, must find a way to bypass his legacy and do for ourselves precisely what he lacked the manhood to do for us. To admit that one's assailant has a kind of point is not comforting — at first. It requires a kind of courage. As Gandhi said about the Bhagat Singh, 'have we the courage to ask what is [his] motive?' There is no way to respond to terrorism without courage — except, of course, by mimicking its violence.

We have other disadvantages to cope with: there are no Vinoba Bhaves around. The 'peace army' concept that could provide a nonviolent equivalent to armed intervention is still in an early stage of development,[4] and perhaps most importantly, we are facing an enormous wall of ignorance on the part of millions upon millions — the received opinion of the world, that violence alone is 'realistic,' indeed all that exists. What could be our options in such an uphill battle?

I still believe that Gandhi's first recommendation must be followed: condemn terrorism, but not (except as the law provides) terrorists. Do not confound the doer and his deed; not only because it costs us something humanly when we do that, but because it closes the door to any possibility of removing his hatred. What the mass media and political leaders have done in the wake of September 11 could not be more wrong, you can never convert terrorists if you dehumanize them, e.g. by calling them 'jackals,' 'varmints,' 'cave-dwellers' and similar metaphors. Even the word 'terrorist' is a dangerous mistake. You can communicate with a person who has been driven by desperation to commit a heinous act against you (provided he is still alive); it is much harder to communicate with a 'terrorist' who is cast beyond the pale of reason by that very designation. Gandhi even recommended dropping the word 'criminal' from our vocabulary — or applying it to everyone!

---

[3] Full report available from Daniel Jordan, PhD (drdanj@adelphia.net) or Neil Wollman; PhD. (njwollman@manchester.edu).

[4] Cf. www.nonviolentpeaceforce.org.

In this connection, it is a mistake to take the defiant rhetoric of Islamist terrorists at face-value, when they claim, for example that they 'seek death the way we (in the West) want to live.' It is folly to take anyone's bluster at face value when they are greatly agitated, and we would do well to recall the by-and-large quiet departure of Jewish families from Gaza, some of whom had proclaimed they would never leave their biblically covenanted settlements alive, and how the leader of the Kurdish resistance in Turkey immediately announced a ceasefire when Prime Minister Recep Tayyip Erdoğan did no more than admit that the Kurds had in fact been mistreated. Such is the power of 'compassionate listening,' acknowledging the other's pain. When the first President Bush refused to do that in 1988 he not only condemned us to the present cycle of violence, he deprived us of a major opportunity for personal and political growth.

The Global War on Terror is unwinable from its very conception, for 'war against terrorism' is only a metaphor; terrorism is not a country, but a technique. We would do far better to consider a terrorist attack not an act of war but a crime, which is after all the truth, and having realized that to adopt the kind of response to it that is likely to succeed. In other words, we need to shift from retributive justice, the failures of which on the domestic level are now evident, to restorative justice. In this frame we would regard perpetrators the way Gandhi regarded Bhagat Singh: as a seriously misguided human being, but a human being.

No one who is truly nonviolent, it therefore seems to me, will either condone such attacks nor simply be passive in the face of them (which is never the response of nonviolence to anything). We are talking about responding, but in a manner that will not perpetuate the very offenses we are trying to control by unconsciously adopting their logic. Just as the death penalty *increases* the rate of homicide, retaliation increases terrorism. The world's remaining superpower has recently tried to stand above the law; but even it cannot evade the natural law that violence begets violence.

However, this would still be only the response to make *after* an attack. It is the height of folly to wait until any form of violence has happened: as in medicine, prevention (or what John Burton calls *provention,* wisely distinguishing it from merely trying to thwart an attack by those who are already enraged) is the infinitely saner and more effective remedy. As President Jimmy Carter recently observed, the biggest problem in the world today is the huge and growing gap between the rich and poor, and if we could solve that problem 'there would be fewer people willing to kill themselves to hurt an American.' Robert Fisk's magisterial history of the Middle East, *The Great War for Civilisation: The Conquest of the Middle East* puts beyond doubt that behind what we may like to consider ranting by an Osama bin Laden is a misuse of grievances that are very real. As Gandhi said, 'Will you not see the writing that these terrorists are writing with their blood?'

Nonviolence advocates are wearily familiar with the logic, 'how can you reason with terrorists, who are no more rational than Hitler?' But was WWII caused by a lone madman or by the millions who were so readily provoked into listen to him? This is the answer. We can change the conditions that give extremists their compelling force and the support system they need to do their work. There is no reason not to listen to the grievances of the people who attack us. Indeed this way alone leads to security.

Realistically, the American people as a whole, and the world as a whole, will not be able to take this way until they abandon the culture that has turned consumerism into a religion, and by so doing made violence into a way of life. This is not the place to launch into a full analysis of materialism and the mass media [Nagler 2004]. Suffice it to say that this culture

creates both the material reason for America's aggressive behaviour around the world —
particularly to secure oil — and the mindset that makes us act so violently.

CONCLUSION

There have been four 'wars' launched in the United States within recent times: the 'war
on poverty,' the 'war on drugs,' a subset of the 'war on crime,' and now the '(global) war on
terrorism.' The first three, especially the one on drugs, have been huge, expensive failures.
That is because they were wrongly conceived. The war on poverty should really have been a
war on greed (if we must stick with the metaphor); the struggle against the shockingly
widespread culture of substance abuse should have addressed the emptiness of life in a
consumerist culture and the way it alienates us from others, our environment, and our own
deeper selves.

And so it is with the 'war on terrorism,' but with far more dangerous consequences. This
'war' also is proving to be a much more expensive and more drastic failure. The devil is in
the nomenclature. There is no way to wage a 'war' on terrorism, which, to repeat, is not a
state but a technique, and a technique of desperation for those who see no other recourse.
Rather, we must reconceptualize our whole approach, and here is where Gandhi's legacy is
invaluable. He shows that we can, and must imagine and work towards a world where no
warlord or pathological hater or religious fanatic will be able to play upon the legitimate
grievances of others and seduce them into following his mad remedy.

The ruins of the World Trade Towers have ceased hissing and burning under the streets
of Manhattan, but the embers of hatred that hurled such devastating fury into them have been
fanned even higher by an insanely dangerous policy of returning violence for violence. It is
time to heed Mahatma Gandhi's plea to acknowledge and repair the causes of that rage.

ACKNOWLEDGEMENTS

Michael Nagler is Professor emeritus of Classics and Comparative Literature at
University of California, Berkeley, where he founded the Peace and Conflict Studies Program
in which he still teaches nonviolence and related subjects. He is the author of *The Search for
a Nonviolent Future* (American Book Award, 2002) and many other books and articles, most
recently *Hope or Terror: Gandhi and the Other 9/11* (published by the Metta Center and the
Nonviolent Peaceforce). He is the director of Metta (www.mettacenter.org) and a frequent
speaker on peace and spiritually-based nonviolence issues around the world.

REFERENCES

al-Ubeidi, S.D. (2004). *Online Asia Times*, 21 July.
Cole, D. (2006). 'Are We Safer?' *The New York Review of Books*. 9 March.
Gandhi, M.K. (1921). *Young India*. 20 October.

Gandhi, M.K. (1931). *Collected Works of Mahatma Gandhi (CWMG)* vol. 51. Statement on execution of Bhagat Singh and comrades (reprinted from paper *Gujarati*). New Delhi, 23 March, 1931. 341.

Gandhi, M.K. (1939) *CWMG* vol. 74.

Gandhi, M.K. (1947). *CWMG* vol. 98, 6 December, 1947 - 30 January, 1948, item 9.

Nagler, M. (2004). *Search for a Nonviolent Future.* Maui, HI: Inner Ocean.

Nargolkar, V. (1995). *The Creed of Saint Vinoba.* Bombay: Bharatiya Vidya Bhavan.

Schell, J. (2003). *The Unconquerable World: Power, Nonviolence, and the Will of the People.* New York: Holt.

Schock, K. (2005). *Unarmed Insurrections: People Power Movements in Nondemocracies.* Minneapolis: University of Minnesota Press.

Schwartz, B. (2006). 'Perils of Primacy.' *Atlantic Monthly,* Jan/Feb.

Zunes, S., Kurtz, L.R. and Asher, S.B. (1999). (Eds.). *Nonviolent Social Movements: A Geographical Perspective.* Oxford: Blackwell Publishing.

In: Nonviolence: An Alternative for Defeating...
Editors: S. Ram and R. Summy, pp. 57-69

ISBN: 978-1-60021-812-5
© 2008 Nova Science Publishers, Inc.

Chapter 4

TERRORISM AS A BACKFIRE PROCESS

Brian Martin[1]

ABSTRACT

Terrorism is widely seen as an injustice, naturally enough because it is a blatant violation of human rights. The reaction against actions that are perceived as unjust can be called 'backfire.' The concept of backfire is an extension of Gene Sharp's political jiu-jitsu concept. The strange thing about terrorism is that it seems designed to backfire. Look in turn at each of the five methods of inhibiting backfire. First is cover-up. Terrorists commonly carry out their actions publicly and announce responsibility for them. They expose their actions rather than covering them up. Second is devaluing the target. Usually terrorists have lower status than their targets, especially when prominent citizens are targeted. The potential for devaluing the targets of terrorism is not great. Third is reinterpreting the action. Terrorists seldom say that there was not really a bombing or that the number of dead is exaggerated or that the attack was a mistake. Fourth is using official processes to give the appearance of justice. Terrorists usually have no access to courts, commissions of inquiry or other official processes for justifying their actions. Fifth is intimidation and bribery. Terrorists can threaten those who criticize them, especially those in their own milieu. But their ability to bribe targets and witnesses is limited. In summary, terrorists have limited capacity to inhibit outrage about their actions. Indeed, they often go out of their way to magnify the sense of outrage, for example by seeking media coverage. Therefore it is predictable that most terrorist actions backfire against the terrorists. This analysis applies only to non-state terrorists, the ones that receive the bulk of attention by governments and the media. The question remains why non-state terrorists often behave in a way that is almost guaranteed to backfire. This chapter will analyze both state and non-state terrorism using backfire analysis and spelling out implications for nonviolent resistance to and prevention of terrorism.

---

[1] I thank Greg Scott and Steve Wright for helpful comments on a draft. This work is supported by the Australian Research Council.

INTRODUCTION

On the face of it, terrorism seems to be an incredibly counter-productive method of action.[2] When violent attacks are made against innocent civilians, the usual response is outrage and increased popular support for government action against the terrorists and those associated with them. In short, terrorism is almost guaranteed to backfire. This suggests that the motivation for terrorism may often be something other than effectiveness.

The attacks on 11 September 2001 were a challenge to US corporate and military power, but rather than weakening the US, they instead had the effect of generating enormous sympathy around the world for the US people and mobilizing US public opinion in favor of attacks on anyone held responsible. The 9/11 attack legitimized the unleashing of US military power in ways previously only contemplated.

The same pattern can be observed time and again in other terrorist incidents. Every Palestinian suicide bombing gives greater legitimacy to the Israeli government for taking a harsh line. The spectacular attacks by Chechen rebels against the Russian people have led to greater support for brutal methods used by the Russian government in Chechnya.

This pattern has prevailed for a long time. Uruguay used to be a model liberal democracy, known as the Switzerland of South America. In the 1960s, the Tupamaros, left-wing revolutionaries, challenged the government, eventually engaging in urban terrorism. Rather than leading to revolution, the result in 1973 was destruction of democracy and descent into repressive military rule.[3]

In the next section, I explore the dynamics of outrage from injustice in order to explain why terrorism is so predictably counterproductive, following this with some possible reasons for the persistence of non-state terrorism despite its poor record of instrumental success. Then I use the same framework to examine state terrorism, which is far less likely to cause outrage. Finally, I look at the implications for nonviolent responses to terrorism.

TERRORISM AND OUTRAGE

Terrorism is widely seen as an injustice, naturally enough because it is a blatant violation of human rights. What is striking is that terrorism flouts all the techniques usually used to dampen outrage over injustice.

Premier nonviolence researcher Gene Sharp coined the expression 'political jiu-jitsu' to refer to how a violent attack on nonviolent protesters can recoil against the attackers [Sharp 1973, 657-703].[4] Examples include beatings of protesters during the 1930 salt raids in India [Weber 1997], the 1960 massacre of black South African protesters by white police at Sharpeville [Frankel 2001], and the 1991 massacre of mourners at a cemetery in Dili, East Timor by Indonesian troops. Each one of these attacks generated enormous outrage, especially in other countries, and thus was seriously counterproductive for the attackers. On

---

[2] Carr (2002) argues that all forms of violence against civilians have been counterproductive throughout history.

[3] After the restoration of representative government in 1985, the Tupamaros became a political party. I owe this example to Andrew Mack.

[4] Sharp built on the concept of 'moral jiu-jitsu' developed by Gregg (1966).

closer inspection, though, it is apparent that most violent attacks on protesters do *not* generate much outrage. For example, there were numerous massacres in East Timor before 1991, none of which drew much attention. The Dili massacre was different in that western journalists witnessed the attack and captured it on camera.

Sharp's model of the dynamics of nonviolent action can be considered to be a form of grounded theory. Sharp looked at a large number of nonviolent campaigns and noticed a recurring set of processes; political jiu-jitsu was frequently, but not always, one of these processes. Using the same grounded theory approach, I have examined a wide variety of injustices, from censorship to torture, looking at the conditions that create or reduce outrage [Jansen and Martin 2003; Jansen and Martin 2004; Martin and Wright 2003; Martin 2004; Martin and Rifkin 2004].

Two fundamental conditions are necessary to maximize outrage about an event: first, the event is perceived as unjust; second, information about the event is communicated to relevant audiences. Perpetrators can act in ways that reduce outrage; their methods can be classified into five standard categories:

- cover up the event;
- devalue the victims;
- reinterpret the event as something else;
- set up formal inquiries or refer the matter to official bodies that give the appearance of justice;
- use intimidation and bribery against victims, witnesses and anyone else involved.

Cover-up serves to block communication to relevant audiences. Devaluation, reinterpretation and official channels serve to change the perception of injustice. Intimidation and bribery serve to deter action by those who are outraged.

Each of these five methods can be observed in the salt raids, the Sharpeville massacre and the Dili massacre. Consider for instance the Dili massacre, in which Indonesian troops opened fire, without warning, on a large peaceful gathering of East Timorese people entering Santa Cruz cemetery during a funeral procession on 12 November 1991 [Kohen 1999, 154-158; McMillan 1992]. Immediately after the shooting there were attempts at cover-up, with the Indonesian military cutting off telephone connections out of East Timor and alerting Australian customs officials in an attempt to confiscate the videotapes taken of the events.

Indonesian officials devalued the victims by making derogatory comments about the protesters, for example calling them 'scum.' This continued a longstanding pattern of cultural contempt, by the Javanese rulers, for the East Timorese people. Indonesian officials reinterpreted the shooting by simply lying about what had happened. They blamed the events on East Timorese agitators and initially gave a figure of 19 dead, later raising this to 50. A separate assessment found that at least 271 people had died. The Indonesian government, under pressure, set up an inquiry into the events. It applied mild penalties to a few individuals. The Indonesian military set up its own inquiry, with a similar result. These inquiries gave a superficial appearance of justice. Immediately after the massacre, Indonesian troops arrested, beat and killed many East Timorese independence supporters, in an attempt to intimidate those opposing Indonesian rule. Thus all five methods of inhibiting outrage can be found associated with the Dili massacre.

The same methods had been used in other massacres in East Timor, with the difference that in these earlier cases cover-up was more effective, so there was less need for the other methods. For example, there had been no Indonesian formal inquiries into East Timor killings prior to the Dili massacre.

Protesters can amplify the sense of outrage by countering each of these five methods, for example by exposing the attack, humanizing the victims, interpreting the events as an injustice, avoiding or discrediting official processes, and resisting and exposing intimidation and bribery. In a sense, protesters and attackers are engaged in a struggle over how people perceive and react to events. The main reason that the Dili massacre backfired is that quite a few western journalists were present and filmmaker Max Stahl caught the events on videotape. These eyewitnesses and the photographic and video evidence escaped the usual process of cover-up. Indonesian slurs on the East Timorese had little salience for western audiences, and likewise the lies by the Indonesian government and the official inquiries had insufficient credibility to dampen international outrage. Repressive tactics in East Timor may have intimidated some East Timorese, but these tactics only increased international concern. The result was a tremendous increase in international support for the East Timorese independence support movement, which laid the basis for independence in 1999.

This same analysis can be applied to injustices well beyond the scenario of violent attacks on nonviolent protesters. For example, there was a massive public reaction against the beating of motorist Rodney King by Los Angeles police in March 1991, even though Rodney King was neither a protester nor nonviolent [Martin, in press]. I refer to this reaction against actions that are perceived as unjust as 'backfire.' The struggle between attackers and targets thus becomes a backfire process. The concept of backfire is an extension of the concept of political jiu-jitsu.

The strange thing about terrorism is that it seems designed to backfire. The two fundamental conditions for backfire are a perception of injustice and communication to relevant audiences. Terrorism is widely perceived as unjust and it is often intended to generate attention. Indeed, terrorism has been called 'communication activated and amplified by violence' [Schmid and Graaf 1982, 54; see also Nacos 2002 and Tuman 2003].

Look in turn at each of the five methods of inhibiting outrage. First is covering up the event. Terrorists commonly carry out their actions publicly or announce responsibility for them or both. They expose their actions rather than covering them up. Second is devaluing the target. Usually terrorists have lower status than their targets, especially when prominent citizens are kidnapped or assassinated. The potential for devaluing the targets of terrorism is not great. If al-Qa'ida has used derogatory labels for the victims of 9/11, these labels have little public currency. Third is reinterpreting the event. Terrorists seldom say that there was not really a bombing or that the number of dead was exaggerated or that the attack was a mistake. Indeed, they are more likely to celebrate and exaggerate their attacks. Fourth is using official processes to give the appearance of justice. Terrorists usually have no access to courts, commissions of inquiry, panels of prestigious experts or other official processes for justifying their actions.[5] Quite the contrary: these processes are regularly used against them, for example when alleged terrorists are brought to trial. Fifth is intimidation and bribery. The

---

[5] Al-Qa'ida leaders have sought opinions from Islamic scholars to justify their killing of civilians, but the purpose of this seems mainly for ideological support within the network. (Note that the search for theological justification for killing is peculiar neither to terrorists nor to Islam.)

power of terrorists to intimidate opponents and critics — politicians, military forces, intelligence agencies, journalists, ordinary citizens — is seldom very great, as evidenced by the number of people willing to publicly denunciate terrorists and their attacks. After the March 2004 Madrid train bombings, large numbers of Spaniards joined public protests against the bombings. On the other hand, terrorists are usually more able to intimidate those who criticize them from within their own milieu. Finally, their ability to bribe targets and witnesses is limited.

In summary, terrorists have limited capacity to inhibit outrage about their actions. Indeed, they often go out of their way to magnify the sense of outrage, for example by seeking media coverage. Therefore it is predictable that most terrorist actions backfire against the terrorists.

WHY TERRORISM BY THE WEAK?

The question thus arises of why terrorists behave in a way that is almost guaranteed to be counterproductive. It is possible to identify several explanations. First, terrorism can be an expressive act, rather than an instrumental one. It can be an expression of resistance against humiliation or degradation experienced, consciously or unconsciously, or an expression of revenge against previous acts by the opponent. Expressive acts can serve emotional purposes even when they are not effective in practical terms.[6]

Second, terrorism is a characteristically masculine act [Morgan 1989]. Nearly all terrorists are male. The very few female terrorists are so unusual that they generate excessive attention. Males are far more likely than females to be involved in all types of violence, not just terrorism. Violence is seen by some — such as Frantz Fanon, theorist of decolonization — as a psychologically liberating act.[7] This psychology is largely masculine.

Third, some terrorists believe that violence is an effective way of achieving their goals. The belief in the potency of violence is pervasive in many cultures, for example in underlying news reports that concentrate on violence and ignore low-profile nonviolent action, in Hollywood movies where good guys use violence more effectively than bad guys, and in history books that concentrate on wars and governments. So, despite the dismal record of terrorists in promoting their causes, many of them assume that what they are doing must be effective.

Fourth, terrorism can be used instrumentally to provoke counter-violence from the state. If this counter-violence is seen as excessive — as it sometimes is — then this can create more support for the cause espoused by the terrorists. In other words, although terrorism backfires, it can lead to state terrorism that itself backfires by generating greater support for the terrorists' cause. This sort of process can be seen in many encounters, for example in British military actions against IRA terrorists and in Israeli military actions against Palestinian terrorists. The military actions are sometimes so excessive that many civilians are humiliated, injured or killed, leading to greater support for the anti- government cause.[8] After all, state

---

[6] Scheff (1994) highlights the role of unacknowledged shame in protracted conflict, especially war.

[7] According to Fanon [1963, 94]: 'At the level of individuals, violence is a cleansing force. It frees the native from his inferiority complex and from his despair and inaction; it makes him fearless and restores his self-respect.'

[8] According to Cullison (2004), internal communications of al-Qa'ida reveal that 'its aim was to tempt the powers to strike back in a way that would create sympathy for the terrorists' (p. 58).

terror is sometimes motivated by revenge rather than a calculated assessment of benefits and costs. Thus, sometimes, non-state terrorism does 'work' by provoking an even greater state terror that causes more people to oppose the government. But a full assessment of terrorism in this scenario should look at its costs — lives, property damage, loss of civil liberties — as well as its benefits, and should also look at alternative routes to the same ends, as discussed later.

Fifth, terrorism can be part of a cycle of violence that cements the role of leaders at the expense of the success of the struggle. A viable struggle using conventional, legal and/or nonviolent means can be derailed by a terrorist campaign that gives greater power to the terrorist leaders, most commonly when violence provokes counter-violence. For example, in Kosovo, there was a decade-long nonviolent struggle for independence. But after the Kosovo Liberation Army adopted terrorist tactics, leading to counter-violence by the Serbian rulers and then NATO intervention, the KLA gained leadership of the independence struggle [Clark 2000].

The other side of this dynamic is the value to some government leaders when opponents resort to violence. Every Palestinian suicide bombing cements the position and policies of Israeli leaders who take a punitive stance towards Palestinian aspirations. In this context, nonviolent struggle is a threat, which many people believe is the reason why Palestinian nonviolence advocate Mubarak Awad was deported by the Israeli government. Some governments — operating either in a calculating or an instinctive fashion — may provoke or fail to prevent terrorism by their opponents to both discredit the opponents and cement the government's own position. This is a version of the process of using *agents provocateurs* to instigate or provoke violence in protest movements in order to discredit them and justify the use of state force against them. More generally, conventional government anti-terrorism policies, by killing, subjugating and humiliating members of oppressed groups, seem ideally designed to foster the terrorism they ostensibly seek to oppose.

There are thus many possible reasons for adopting terrorism, most of which have nothing to do with being effective in bringing about social change.

STATE TERRORISM

This analysis so far applies only to non-state terrorists, the ones that receive the bulk of attention by governments and the media. States that exercise terror, in contrast, are able to use all the five methods of inhibiting outrage: they routinely cover up their actions, for example by hiding the use of torture and by using death squads and proxy armies [Campbell and Brenner 2000]; they smear their targets as criminals or terrorists; they say that they are protecting borders, dealing with crime or countering subversion and that abuses are aberrations; they often establish legal processes for their actions to give the appearance of justice; and they can intimidate or bribe those who might challenge or expose their actions. So it is not surprising that state terror, though it leads to vastly more deaths and suffering than non-state terror, seldom generates much public outrage.

Consider for example the killings carried out by the military in Indonesia in 1965-1966 [Cribb 1990]. The trigger for the launching of terror was an alleged Communist Party coup attempt against the left-wing Sukarno government, though this explanation has been disputed.

In any case, the military action was justified as necessary to defend the nation against a communist takeover. Western governments largely supported this interpretation, and raised little protest against the scale of killing. Those targeted were labeled communists — some, certainly, were members of the very large Communist Party, but many were not — and maligned as such. The killings thus constituted what Chomsky and Herman call 'constructive terror,' namely for a good cause and against a suitably stigmatized enemy [Chomsky and Herman 1979, 205-217]. Although the slaughter was not secret, there was no systematic documentation of what happened. Considering the vast scale of killing — many hundreds of thousands of people died — the events received relatively little international attention. This was a sort of *de facto* cover-up. Legal processes were not deployed against perpetrators of the slaughter, but instead used to impose lengthy prison sentences on thousands of targets who were fortunate to have their lives spared. It is hard to obtain evidence of intimidation and bribery used to prevent opposition, but it is reasonable to presume that Indonesians who protested against the killing would have themselves become targets, whereas those who cooperated might be rewarded.

Another example of state terror is Stalinism, in which many millions died in purges and prison camps and as a result of forced relocation and starvation. The scale of the terror was hidden by pervasive censorship and by disinformation, for example guiding visitors through carefully staged tours that gave the impression of a successful socialist state [Hollander 1981]. The victims of Stalinism were vilified as reactionaries, members of the bourgeoisie, traitors, criminals, mentally ill and enemies of the revolution. The whole process was portrayed as one of building a socialist society. Legal processes were established to give the appearance of justice, with show trials the visible face of false justice.[9] Internal opponents of the terror could themselves become targets, whereas supporters stood to gain. Fellow travelers from other countries, who whitewashed the terror, could expect to be received favorably by the Stalinist regime. Thus, the Stalinist state was able to use, with good effect, every one of the five methods for reducing outrage from injustice. On the other hand, these methods had little effect on the most vocal opponents of Stalinism, anti-communists in the West, who were unconvinced or unaffected by vilification of victims, by Stalinist justifications, by show trials and by the potential for intimidation or bribery.

The success of states in minimizing outrage from their terrorist activities is revealed in the great discrepancy between the massive media coverage of non-state terrorism and the scant attention to state terrorism. Usually governments only condemn state terrorism when perpetrated by certain enemy states, as when the US government applies the label 'rogue state.' The research literature on terrorism follows the agenda set by governments and the mass media, concentrating on non-state terrorism, with relatively few treatments of state terrorism.[10]

Even the conventional definition of terrorism, as violence exercised by non-government groups against civilians for political ends, reflects the interests of states.[11] A less one-sided

---

[9] Show trials were public and thus went against the tendency to cover up terror. A possible interpretation is that, for the state, the benefit of formal legitimacy outweighed the benefits of secrecy.

[10] This observation is documented in Reid (1997). I thank Steve Wright for informing me of this reference. Treatments of state terrorism include Chomsky and Herman (1979), George (1991), Ross (1995), Ross (2000), Stohl and Lopez (1984), and Stohl and Lopez (1980).

[11] This point is made emphatically by Herman (1982).

definition of terrorism, as violence used for political ends, would immediately identify states as the world's leading terrorists, through torture, warfare and the usual range of repressive tactics.[12] The very words 'terror,' 'terrorism' and 'terrorist' thus are political labels, typically directed at opponents rather than used in a precise and consistent fashion.[13]

NONVIOLENT ACTION AS AN ALTERNATIVE TO TERRORISM

Nonviolent action is usually far more effective than violence in generating support and bringing about desirable change. Consider for example a peaceful protest against government policies. If police beat or kill protesters, this can backfire against the government — indeed, this is the canonical scenario for Sharp's political jiu-jitsu. Consider each of the five methods for inhibiting backfire.

- Many nonviolent actions are carried out in public, so that covering up attacks is not easy.
- When protesters dress conventionally and behave moderately and respectfully — rather than dressing outrageously and behaving aggressively — then it is difficult for the government to devalue them.
- When protesters explicitly commit themselves to nonviolence and are open about their goals and methods, it is more difficult for governments to be convincing with alternative interpretations.
- If, when activists come under attack, they appeal directly to the public — including allies, opponents and third parties — they are more likely to obtain support than by relying on official channels such as making complaints about police misconduct.
- Nonviolent action is itself a stand in the face of potential intimidation.

Contrasting each of these with the corresponding method when violence is used, it is apparent that nonviolent action is far more likely to build support.

One of the keys to backfire is that people perceive violent attacks on peaceful protesters as unjust. This is the reason that nonviolence proponents continually stress the importance of maintaining nonviolent discipline.[14] A breakdown in discipline — even a brief scuffle or some verbal abuse — changes the nature of the interaction and alters the perception of injustice when police use violence. In contrast, bombings and assassinations completely undercut this dynamic.

Nonviolent action has a good track record in liberation struggles. The Palestinian Liberation Organization used terrorism for years but with limited success. The spontaneous development of the first intifada in 1987 — an unarmed struggle, not a perfectly nonviolent struggle — was far more effective in mobilizing support among Palestinians, winning

---

[12] Markusen and Kopf (1995) point to similarities between genocide and strategic bombing. Similar parallels exist between terrorism and warfare.

[13] Geerty (1997) gives a cogent critique of the content of the term 'terrorism' as evolving from its origins as state terror to an incoherent expression of condemnation.

[14] Sharp (1973, 573-655) includes 'solidarity and discipline to fight repression' as one of the stages in his 'dynamics of nonviolent action,' just before political jiu-jitsu.

international sympathy and splitting Israeli public opinion. Arguably, a completely nonviolent struggle would have been even more effective [Dajani 1994; Rigby 1991]. Instead, in the second intifada from 2000, suicide bombings have weakened support for the Palestinian cause.

In apartheid South Africa, armed struggle was fairly easily crushed by the state. Liberation occurred only after nonviolent action became the main mode of struggle [Zunes 1999]. Similarly, the East Timorese struggle for independence achieved success after the armed struggle was subordinated to nonviolent action [Fukuda 2000].

The failures of armed struggle are legion. Not only do many armed struggles completely fail, but in many of those that lead to independence — such as in Vietnam and Algeria — the death toll is horrific.[15] Furthermore, successful armed struggle is more likely to lead to a centralization of power in the subsequent government. Armed struggle is especially ineffective against systems of representative government: there is not a single successful case of a revolutionary overthrow. This can be understood in terms of backfire. Armed struggle has far greater legitimacy when used against repressive and corrupt regimes. Against a system based on the rule of law and majority rule, violent opposition has far less legitimacy. Indeed, it can be argued that a potent way to reduce non-state terrorism is to ensure that realistic opportunities exist to work through the system for progressive social change (including by using nonviolent action).[16]

Despite nonviolent action's success record, terrorism is still attractive to many for the reasons outlined earlier.

NONVIOLENCE AGAINST TERRORISM

I have argued that nonviolent methods are usually far more effective than violent methods in promoting beneficial social change, because violence commonly leads to reduced support and lower legitimacy. Therefore one of the ways to reduce terrorism is to convince those who are considering violence as an option that nonviolent alternatives are superior. This line of argument is most relevant to reducing non-state terrorism, in other words terrorism of the weak.

Opposing state terrorism is another matter, because states have a vastly greater capacity to reduce outrage from their own injustices. The challenge is to make state terrorism backfire by countering each of the five standard methods of inhibiting outrage. Countering cover-up involves exposing state violence and cruelty, for example through whistleblowing, investigative reporting, courage of editors and alternative media. Countering devaluation can be done through humanizing of targets, for example through personal contact, speaking tours and human interest stories. Countering government interpretations — sometimes sincere, sometimes spin and lies — requires ongoing efforts to communicate understandings from the point of view of victims and critics. Countering the pacifying effect of official channels — such as investigations that whitewash what is happening — requires trusting official

---

[15] Two or three million Vietnamese died in the wars for independence and up to a million Algerians.

[16] Rubenstein (1987) makes a well-informed assessment of the driving forces behind terrorism, especially terrorism associated with social revolution and national liberation. He supports an anti-terrorism policy that permits 'young intellectuals to be reunited through collective action with their people' (p. 236).

procedures less and exposing and discrediting processes that give a false appearance of justice. Countering intimidation and bribery involves refusing to be cowed or co-opted and exposing attempts to intimidate and bribe.

In the 1980s, the US government supported state terrorism in Central America by assisting governments and paramilitary groups that imprisoned, assaulted, tortured and killed opponents. The US government disguised its role by use of proxy armies — notably the Contras in Nicaragua — and client governments. It stigmatized opponents as communists and terrorists and claimed that all its actions were in the interests of democracy. Opponents in the US came under surveillance and were subject to disruptive interventions by government agencies.

The Central America peace movement blossomed in opposition to this US state terrorism [Smith 1996]. One of the most potent challenges was support for refugees from Central America, often undertaken through church networks. The stories told by these refugees to groups of church people avoided government censorship and media spin. When church people met refugees face to face, the refugees became flesh-and-blood humans rather than anonymous victims, thereby countering attempts at devaluation. The refugees' stories were a direct challenge to the government's interpretations of its policy. Seeing the way that the law was used against refugees helped to discredit formal channels for justice in the eyes of movement participants. Finally, the church and associated personal networks provided support for resisting government intimidation. The Central American solidarity movement thus was effective in countering each of the five methods for inhibiting outrage from injustice.

CONCLUSION

Terrorism, as a tool for bringing about a better world, has remarkably poor prospects, even when the cause being supported is a worthy one. Examining the dynamics of outrage from injustice leads to the conclusion that nonviolent action is usually far more effective than violence in challenging repression and oppression. In spite of this, violence has a continuing appeal to some challengers, partly due to cultural assumptions and partly due to the way that violence serves to cement the role of group leaders and the way that violence by non-state groups serves to justify state violence.

State terrorism also has a continuing appeal, because it often achieves its immediate ends, though these seldom are supportive of values such as peace and freedom. Because terrorism so often serves the interests of powerholders in states and in non-state groups — almost always male dominated, hierarchical and secretive — it is unlikely that violence will be renounced any time soon. Nonviolent action is a continuing challenge to violent options, both as an exemplary alternative to non-state violence and as a method of opposing state violence. Examining the five main methods for inhibiting outrage over injustice offers a checklist for nonviolent campaigns, as shown by the example of the Central America peace movement. It is also possible to use this same checklist to suggest ways to highlight the ways that nonviolence is superior to violence.

- Reveal the value of nonviolence by further studies of historical and contemporary use of nonviolent action.

- Counter devaluation of nonviolence practitioners by emphasizing their courage and suffering and unwillingness to harm others.

- Counter interpretations of nonviolence as passive and ineffective by documenting its successes and documenting the failures of violence.

- Avoid relying on government support for promotion of nonviolent alternatives, and avoid assuming that government initiatives — peace plans, disarmament negotiations, treaties, laws — are going to solve problems or, indeed, are intrinsically nonviolent.

- Refuse to be intimidated by critics of nonviolence and refuse to be bought off by opportunities within the mainstream.

The backfire framework offers a way of analyzing tactics against injustice. In doing so, it reveals the shortcomings of terrorism and the strengths of nonviolent action. Nonviolent action is both an alternative to non-state terrorism — a method of challenging the social conditions that can breed non-state terrorism — and a method of challenging state terrorism. It is thus a potent but neglected anti-terrorist tool.[17]

ACKNOWLEDGEMENTS

Brian Martin is a Professor in Science, Technology and Society, University of Wollongong, Australia. He is researching on the dynamics of power, with special attention to strategies for challenging repression and exploitation. Martin has written twelve books and over 200 major papers and chapters. His most recent books are (1) with Wendy Varney, *Nonviolence Speaks: Communicating against Repression* (Cresskill, NJ: Hampton Press, 2003) and (2) *Justice Ignited: The Dynamics of Backfire* (Lanham, MD: Rowman & Littlefield Publishers, 2007). Phone: +61-2-4228 7860 (h), +61-2-4221 3763 (w), Fax: +61-2-4221-5341, Email: bmartin@uow.edu.au Website: http://www.uow.edu.au/arts/sts/bmartin/

REFERENCES

Campbell, B.B. and Brenner, A.D. (2000). (Eds.). *Death Squads in Global Perspective: Murder with Deniability.* New York: St. Martin's Press.

Carr, Caleb. (2002). *The Lessons of Terror.* New York: Random House.

Chomsky, N. and Herman, E.S. (1979). *The Political Economy of Human Rights, Vol.1: The Washington Connection and Third World Fascism.* Montréal: Black Rose Books.

---

[17] There are at least two other ways that nonviolent approaches can be mobilized against terrorism. The first is to replace large, potentially dangerous technological systems, such as large power plants, dams and refineries, with small-scale decentralized systems, such as energy efficiency and renewable energy systems, thereby reducing the vulnerability of societies to terrorists [Martin 2001]. The second is to replace the present 'intelligence' (spying) services, based on secrecy and centralized control, with agencies that openly publish their findings, thereby becoming more accountable as well as more reliable [Martin 2002].

Clark, H.. (2000). *Civil Resistance in Kosovo.* London: Pluto.

Cribb, R.. (1990). (Ed.). *The Indonesian Killings 1965-1966.* Melbourne: Centre for Southeast Asian Studies, Monash University.

Cullison, A. (2004). 'Inside Al-Qaeda's Hard Drive.' *Atlantic Monthly,* 294 (September), 55-70.

Dajani, S.R. (1994). *Eyes Without Country: Searching for a Palestinian Strategy of Liberation.* Philadelphia: Temple University Press.

Fanon, F. (1963). *The Wretched of the Earth,* trans. C. Farrington. New York: Grove Press.

Frankel, P. (2001). *An Ordinary Atrocity: Sharpeville and its Massacre.* New Haven, CT: Yale University Press.

Fukuda, C. M. (2000). 'Peace through Nonviolent Action: The East Timorese Resistance Movement's Strategy for Engagement.' *Pacifica Review,* 12(1), February, 17-31.

Geerty, C. (1997). *The Future of Terrorism.* London: Phoenix.

George, A. (1991). (Ed.). *Western State Terrorism.* Cambridge: Polity Press.

Gregg, R. (1966). *The Power of Nonviolence.* New York: Schocken Books.

Herman, E.S. (1982). *The Real Terror Network: Terrorism in Fact and Propaganda.* Boston: South End Press.

Hollander, P. (1981). *Political Pilgrims: Travels of Western Intellectuals to the Soviet Union, China, and Cuba 1928-1978.* New York: Oxford University Press.

Jansen, S.C. and Martin, B. (2003). 'Making Censorship Backfire.' *Counterpoise,* 7(3), July, 5-15.

Jansen, S.C. and Martin, B. (2004). 'Exposing and Opposing Censorship: Backfire Dynamics in Freedom-of-Speech Struggles.' *Pacific Journalism Review,* 10(1), April, 29-45.

Kohen, A.S. (1999). *From the Place of the Dead: The Epic Struggles of Bishop Belo of East Timor.* New York: St. Martin's Press.

Markusen, E. and Kopf, D. (1995). *The Holocaust and Strategic Bombing: Genocide and Total War in the Twentieth Century.* Boulder, CO: Westview.

Martin, B. and Rifkin, W. (2004). 'The Dynamics of Employee Dissent: Whistleblowers and Organizational Jiu-Jitsu.' *Public Organization Review,* Vol. 4, 221-238.

Martin, B. and Wright, S. (2003). 'Countershock: Mobilizing Resistance to Electroshock Weapons.' *Medicine, Conflict and Survival,* 19(3), July-September, 205-222.

Martin, B. (2004). 'Iraq Attack Backfire.' *Economic and Political Weekly,* 39(16), 17-23 April, 1577-1583.

Martin, B. (in press). 'The Beating of Rodney King: The Dynamics of Backfire'.

Martin, B. (2002). 'Nonviolence Versus Terrorism.' *Social Alternatives,* 21(2), Autumn, 6-9.

Martin, B. (2001). *Technology for Nonviolent Struggle.* London: War Resisters' International.

McMillan, A. (1992). *Death in Dili.* Sydney: Hodder and Stoughton.

Morgan, R. (1989). *The Demon Lover: On the Sexuality of Terrorism.* New York: Norton.

Nacos, B.L. (2002). *Mass-Mediated Terrorism: The Central Role of the Media in Terrorism and Counterterrorism.* Lanham, MD: Rowman and Littlefield.

Reid, E.O.F. (1997). 'Evolution of a Body of Knowledge: An Analysis of Terrorism Research.' *Information Processing and Management,* 33(1). 91-106.

Rigby, A. (1991). *Living the Intifada.* London: Zed Books.

Ross, J.I. (1995). (Ed.). *Controlling State Crime: An Introduction.* New York: Garland.

Ross, J.I. (2000). (Ed.). *Varieties of State Crime and Its Control.* Monsey, NY: Criminal Justice Press.

Rubenstein, R. E. (1987). *Alchemists of Revolution: Terrorism in the Modern World*. New York: Basic Books.

Scheff, T.J. (1994). *Bloody Revenge: Emotions, Nationalism, and War*. Boulder, CO: Westview.

Schmid, A.P. and de Graaf, J. (1982). *Violence as Communication: Insurgent Terrorism and the Western News Media*. London: Sage.

Sharp, G. (1973). *The Politics of Nonviolent Action*. Boston: Porter Sargent.

Smith, C. (1996). R*esisting Reagan: The U.S. Central America Peace Movement*. Chicago: University of Chicago Press.

Stohl, M. and Lopez, G.A. (1984). (Eds.). *The State as Terrorist: The Dynamics of Governmental Violence and Repression*. Westport, CT: Greenwood.

Stohl, M. and Lopez, G.A. (1988). (Eds.). *Terrible Beyond Endurance? The Foreign Policy of State Terrorism*. Westport, CT: Greenwood.

Tuman, J.S. (2003). *Communicating Terror: The Rhetorical Dimensions of Terrorism*. Thousand Oaks, CA: Sage.

Weber, T. (1997). *On the Salt March: The Historiography of Gandhi's March to Dandi*. New Delhi: Harper Collins.

Zunes, S. (1999). 'The Role of Non-violent Action in the Downfall of Apartheid.' *Journal of Modern African Studies*, 37(1), 137-169.

In: Nonviolence: An Alternative for Defeating...

Editors: S. Ram and R. Summy, pp. 71-89

ISBN: 978-1-60021-812-5

Chapter 5

UNDERSTANDING THE INDIRECT STRATEGY OF TERRORISM: INSIGHTS FROM NONVIOLENT ACTION RESEARCH

Senthil Ram

'... [I]n its approach to confronting terrorism, whether prosecuting wars abroad or pursuing security at home, America has conjured the very fear that is terrorism's principal weapon.'

Benjamin Barber in *Fear's Empire* [2003]

ABSTRACT

The conceptual framework of this chapter is built on strategic and psychological perspectives of terrorism. The central argument is that the strategy of terrorism is to carry out violent acts on a target state's population and initiate a psychological process of terror called 'terror jiu-jitsu' that will have damaging behavioral consequences on the target state and provoke a reaction beneficial to the terrorists. Insights are drawn from nonviolent action research to understand the process of 'terror jiu-jitsu' initiated by violent action — as an opposite parallel to the processes of 'political jiu-jitsu' initiated by nonviolent action. While the first section of the chapter deals with various perspectives on the strategy of terrorism and sketches a general theoretical background, the second section argues that terrorism is an indirect strategy which actively stages a violent act to spread terror in a targeted society. The terrorists then hopefully await the target's overreaction and consequent implosion. The third section on the dynamics of terrorism includes three dimensions. The first features the construction of the strategy of 'terror jiu-jitsu' which aims to initiate violence on the part of the terrorists that will evoke irrational fears among the target's public, create an exaggerated sense of threat, and enable the media, politicians and officials to engage in fear mongering to their manipulative advantage. The second dimension explains how the behavioral consequences of 'terror jiu-jitsu' weaken the target state at both individual levels and institutional levels. Thirdly, the two kinds of engagement commonly anticipated by terrorists are analyzed: accommodation and aggression. In conclusion the weaknesses of the strategy of terrorism are outlined, in addition to suggestions for future research.

INTRODUCTION

The strategy of terrorism is a relatively unresearched subject. As a specific form of political violence, terrorism serves a strategic purpose and comprises distinct strategic elements. It appears that underlying the strategy, there is a psychological process of inducing terror, fear, anger and hatred on a targeted society and in turn the policies of that society. However, until recently psychological aspects of terrorism have received very little scholarly attention and notably most of the older works have focused on the personality of terrorists as psychopaths (particularly the positivist psychological theories) and the negative psychological effects of terrorism on targeted populations.[1] The present growth in literature largely focuses on terrorists as rational individuals and on the psychological effects of the terrorist actions on opposing societies. For instance, the four volumes on *The Psychology of Terrorism* edited by Stout [2002] are a good example of this; among others are Crenshaw [1983 & 2000], Wardlaw [1989], Reich [1990], Pearlstein [1991] and Juergensmeyer [2000].

Arguments that depict terrorists as crazy, suicidal psychopaths and terrorism as individual pathology not only undermine the strategic perspectives of terrorism but also trivialize as well as complicate the issue. On the other hand, works that deal with terrorists as rational individuals applying terror for strategic purposes do not explore the entire spectrum of the strategy of terrorism including how the dynamics of the psychological processes induce behavioral consequences favorable to the terrorists [e.g., McCauley 2003). Noticeably, works that especially deal with the strategy of terrorism rightly highlight that terrorism is an indirect [Fromkin 1974] and coercive [Pape 2003] strategy which builds on the fear and pain it unleashes on the target society. However, even these works do not elaborate the underlying psychological processes that produce behaviors and reactions sought by the terrorists. In this context, this chapter attempts to explore, what is termed by Crenshaw [2000, 415] as the 21st century's research agenda on the psychology of terrorism: 'terrorist perceptions of goals and of the effectiveness of terrorism as a strategy.'

This chapter is based on two inter-related perspectives, the strategic and psychological, and brings them together to develop a broader understanding of the psychological dynamics of terror. More specifically, the chapter argues that the strategy of terrorism is to carry out violent acts on a targeted state's population and initiate a psychological process of terror called *terror jiu-jitsu*. This in turn will affect self-damaging behavioral consequences by the targeted state — a reaction that rebounds to the benefit of the terrorists. Insights are drawn from nonviolent action research's opposite description of *political jiu-jitsu* where the violence of the nonviolent activists' opponent rebounds on him, and not the intended target of the violence.

Although many scholars [Fromkin 1974; McCauley 2002; Barber 2003] have recognized the *jiu-jitsu*[2]-like damaging and self-defeating psychological process initiated by terror and

---

[1] Psychologists have observed that after the September 11 attacks on the US, some Americans have suffered from a range of fears including fear of flying, work place fears and more general fears associated with future terror attacks [McCauley 2003, 21]. At the same time patriotism — both good and blind — and the development of a sense of common identity among different racial and ethnic groups have increased. Paradoxically, terrorism on the one hand threatens those who identify with the target group and, on the other, increases identification within the target group.

[2] *Jiu-jitsu* is a Japanese martial art which defeats the opponent by using his own power. The authors quoted here have used the analogy of *jiu-jitsu* to understand the mechanism of terrorism which aims to turn the state's

facilitated by fear, a framework for understanding this process has been largely absent. The main effect of academics taking the psychological element of 'terror' out of terrorism makes the phenomenon of terrorism a methodologically non-demanding exercise [Weinberg, Pedahzur et al. 2004].In other words, methodology is the culprit, since politically motivated actions are more easily observed and studied than processes dealing with internal mental states. Not surprisingly, only a handful of researchers [Walter 1964; McCauley 2002] have dared to include distinctive psychological elements — such as the emotional reaction and social effects caused by violent acts — in their analysis of the terrorism process (along with the act, threat and target of violence). For my part, having acknowledged the methodological caveats in studying the psychological process of terrorism — and noted the dearth of such research in contemporary literature on terrorism — I make no claims for this study other than to have attempted an exploratory broadening of our understanding of terrorism.

Although *terror jiu-jitsu* influences three groups — the target group, the terrorists' in-group and third parties, I shall be focusing only on the target group. As the chapter is not event driven, it does not address who are the terrorists, why they exist and when and where they attack. Nor is there any attempt to prescribe solutions to terrorism. Rather, the analysis deals with theoretical concerns about the technique of terrorism, particularly the strategy of terrorism, and why terrorists chose to use this strategy. In considering these questions the focus is on the dynamics of terrorism.

Throughout the chapter whenever the word 'terrorism' is used, it refers to anti-state acts by non-state actors. The word 'terrorist,' therefore, takes on the limited meaning of non-state actors.[3] Examples for analysis are drawn largely from the September 11 terrorist attacks and the reaction to them of the US government and its population.

PERSPECTIVES ON TERRORISM AS A STRATEGY

Although terrorism from 'above' emerged dramatically during the French Revolution's 'reign of terror', terrorism from 'below' did not come to the general public's attention until the Irish treaty of 1921 [Fromkin 1974]. Since then it has been used as a technique of political violence by nationalists, guerrillas, revolutionaries, anarchists, rightists and religious fundamentalists in both east and west. Of these, the most prominent and moderately successful were waged during the colonial period, and subsequently mainly against governments of the developing nations.

In his *Strategy of Terrorism*, Fromkin [1974]] demonstrates how terrorism served as a fitting strategy for nationalists and revolutionaries in the fight against foreign powers in

---

power against itself. Since my understanding of *jiu-jitsu* originally came from the concept of 'political *jiu-jitsu*' coined by Gene Sharp [1973] in reference to nonviolent action research, I prefer to use his spelling of *jiu-jitsu* instead of *jujitsu*.

[3] The term terrorism was originally used to refer to state terror. State terror is the basis of terror; not only in terms of its origin but also in its destructiveness. In the twentieth century alone a total of 170 million people were killed by governments (excluding war casualties) whereas terrorists, guerrillas and other non-state groups killed around 50,000 people — a ratio of 260 to 1. Along with that, the same century witnessed a massive increase in the state's power to influence individuals' lives and also to threaten the interests of minority groups. States not only unleashed terror to control their own population but elsewhere where their economic and political interests were involved. It is in this context that anti-state terrorism, now widely regarded as *the* terrorism, appeared on the scene. For further discussion, see McCauley [2002].

colonial situations in the 1950s and 60s. For instance, Britain's reaction to terror actions of the Irish revolutionaries, particularly the Black and Tan methods, were so repressive that it turned against the empire and eventually led to the independence of Southern Ireland in 1921. Similarly the Irgun Zvai Leumi, a tiny group of Jewish militants, used terror tactics in the 1940s to successfully expel the then global power Great Britain from Palestine. In the 1950s, the nationalist rebel group in Algeria, the National Liberation Front, used random violence to polarize the Europeans and native population in the struggle for independence from France. Failure of the governments to fully understand the strategy of terrorism was the main reason for its political success.

On the other hand, irrespective of understanding the strategy, suicide terrorism paralyzed many governments in the 1980s and 90s. In his recent work on the *Strategic Logic of Suicide Terrorism*, Pape [2003] argues that armed rebels and terrorist gangs have been using suicide terrorism particularly against democratic governments to withdraw their military forces from territories that are viewed by terrorists as their homeland. Among the eleven suicide campaigns examined by Pape during 1980-2001, six cases stand apart. In one case terrorists achieved complete success: Hezbollah forced American and French troops to withdraw from Lebanon in 1983. In three cases terrorists partially realized their territorial aims: Hezbollah against Israel in withdrawing from Lebanon in 1983-85, and HAMAS against Israel in withdrawing from Palestine in April 1994 and again during October 1994-August 1995. In the case of the Liberation Tigers of Tamil Eeelam (LTTE) — a militant group in the island state of Sri Lanka which is fighting for a separate homeland and staged 75 of the 186 suicide attacks from 1980 to 2001— the government entered into negotiations during 1993-94. Another suicide campaign of HAMAS in 1997 resulted in the release of its top leader from an Israeli prison.

Fromkin and Pape have sketched a lucid outline of the strategy of terrorism respectively in its colonial period and in contemporary times. Fromkin rightly observed that terrorism is an indirect strategy and fear is its weapon. It is used in a special way to make governments react. During the colonial era the common reaction of governments was repression. Highly brutal in many cases, it boomeranged against the colonial powers and led to their downfall. Terror in itself was unable to realize any political goals; rather it was the responses that it generated which provided the success for the terrorists. The essence of the strategy of terrorism, as outlined by Fromkin [1974, 688], entails

> using an opponent's own strength against him. It was a sort of *jujitsu*. First the adversary was made to be afraid, and then, predictably, he would react to his fear by increasing the bulk of his strength, and then the sheer weight of that bulk would drag him down (emphasis added).

In short, terrorists seek to achieve their goal, not directly through their terrorist acts but indirectly through the responses to these acts.

Pape [2003, 346] argues that suicide terrorism is a strategy of coercion. It aims to compel the targeted government to change policy. The strategic logic is to 'inflict pain on the opposing society, to overwhelm their interests in resisting the terrorist demands, and so to cause either the government to concede or the population to revolt against the government.' By shrewd timing, along with targeting democratic governments and pinpointing their nationalistic symbols, terrorists execute their strategic logic and successfully coerce targeted governments.

Similarly, political scientist Benjamin Barber [2003] in his *Fear's Empire* argues that fear is terrorism's only weapon. Therefore, 'the terrorist's primary job (as with any infectious agent) is merely to initiate the contagion. The contaminated body's immune system does the rest as the body struggles to neutralize the infection by making war on its own infected systems' [Barber 2003, 42]. He continues [Barber 2003, 43]: 'terrorism's strategic *jujitsu* cannot win other than by leveraging others into losing, overcoming them by dint of their own forceful momentum' (emphasis added). For Barber, both the terrorist's strategy of fear as well as the preventive counter-terrorist's military strategy of using fear to defeat fear have serious limitations. Nonetheless, what makes the terrorists' strategy weak and how terror, accompanied by other emotions like anger and hatred, impacts on larger populations with negative behavioral consequences are not elaborated by him.

Like Barber [2003], Fromkin [1974, 686], too, demonstrates that '*fear* can paralyze the will, befuddle mind, and exhaust the strength of an adversary…and *persuade* an opponent' to accommodate to the point of view of terrorists (emphasis added). However, the psychological processes of fear that could persuade and cause behavioral changes like accommodation remain ambiguous. In similar fashion, Pape points out that *inflicting pain* is central to the strategic logic of suicide terrorism, but he does not go any further to explain how this psychological process created in the minds of people pressures a government to give concessions to terrorists. Insufficient theoretical perspectives on underlying psychological processes pose a problem of causality not only to his central argument where concessions to terrorists by democratic governments are the result of this pain, but also to his other claim that pain (inflicted on the targeted society) might drive the 'population to revolt against the government' [Pape 2003, 346].

Recent studies by psychologists approach terrorism as strategic and normal psychology and terrorists as normal and rational people. The focus of the literature has largely been on the social-psychological influences that produce terrorism — like causes, comrades, and reactions to crises. For instance, McCauley [2003] argues that anger evoked by insults and frustrations leveled at the group drives normal middle class people to commit acts of terrorism against Western societies in the hope that favorable policies will ensue toward Muslim states. It is a strategy that uses violent intimidation as an instrument or means to achieve ends far beyond the terrorism. Among the two kinds of aggression noted by psychologists, emotional and instrumental, terrorism falls within the latter. The goals of terrorists are twofold: (1) to cause material and political damage to the enemy (make him suffer), and (2) to use the enemy's counter-terror responses as a means of mobilizing support within their own group. Because the state's superior strength is gradually turned against itself, McCauley calls this strategy '*jujitsu* politics' [emphasis added, quoted in Friedberg 2004]. Though McCauley accurately points out that the 'response to terrorism can be more dangerous than the terrorists,' the process that weakens the attacked government by turning its own power against itself remains unclear [McCauley 2006, 9].

Contrary to the above perspectives on strategic terrorism, Merari [1993] contends that terrorists do not have a logical strategy. The terrorists' 'operational inventory is rather limited,' he says, and hence they are 'rarely clear enough as to lay down a complete, coherent strategic plan' [Merari 1993, 18]. However, he identifies the following strategic ideas that have been operationalized within the range of terrorism: propaganda by the deed, intimidation to spread fear, provocation leading to repression, strategy of chaos, strategy of attrition, and expressive terrorism. More specifically he agrees with the established notion that the 'psychological impact is the most essential element in terrorism as a strategy' [Merari 1993, 19].

Two consensus points stand out from the above discussion: the psychological impact of terrorism and the strategic elements of terrorism. This is the point of departure for this chapter. In the analysis so far there are no clear explanations about the working of the psychological process on the one hand, and the development of a comprehensive framework connecting the strategic elements on the other. Arguably, both of these factors, when joined, form the dynamics of terrorism. Without a clear theoretical understanding of the dynamics, any analysis of the strategy of terrorism remains incomplete.

THE INDIRECT STRATEGY OF TERRORISM

The strategy of terrorism is to carry out violent acts on a targeted state's population and initiate a psychological process of terror with damaging behavioral consequences that serve the interests of the terrorists. It is an indirect strategy; it is passive.

Terrorists are in control of this strategy while they perform the violent act. Following that, they lose control of the process, both in a psychological and behavioral sense. Although there are media opportunities for them to claim responsibility for the event, enabling them to publicize their cause, the underlying framework in which the message is received and interpreted features the terror of the violent act. Terrorists gamble their hopes, dreams and lives specifically on the violence of their act.

Terrorists are constantly inventing, discovering and improving the array of weapons and operational and organizational techniques that will maximize their strategy under a range of different political conditions. Their weapons have been — at least to date — conventional and low-tech. Nonetheless, their delivery or execution, their credibility and deterrence are significantly improved by using humans who are willing to die or be killed in the process of using such weapons. Widely known as 'suicide bombers,' this latest addition to the terrorist arsenal has become the ultimate weapon of the 'strategy of the weak' in terrorizing and coercing the strong. As observed, most researchers treat suicide terrorism as just another tactic [e.g. Hoffman 1998; Jenkins 1985; Laqueur 1987] or suicide terrorists as deranged psychopaths hiding behind apocalyptic reasons [e.g. Kramer 1990; Merari 1990; Post 1990]. However, Pape [2003] argues that suicide terrorism is the most powerful and reliable technique of violence that can be strategically applied by a minority of rational individuals to express communal grievances against a dominant and powerful state.

Choosing when, where, on whom, and by whom; and planning; training and finally performing a violent act capable of initiating a psychological process does not appear any less strategic than what we commonly regard as 'strategic' in the military context. However, crucial issues like whether terrorists are content with a 'credible-kill capacity' or will aspire for 'overkill' by acquiring weapons of mass destruction (WMD) — or whether effective coercion depends on one heavy attack or a series of moderate attacks — raise questions that require lengthy analysis beyond this chapter's scope. Suffice it to say that as long as terrorists are able to perform acts that kill people, the strategic purpose is served.

The second aspect of this strategy concerns the capacity of violent acts to initiate a psychological process that attains what the terrorists want. As opposed to the guerilla or military soldier, a terrorist does not aim to produce a 'physical result'; rather his main objective is a 'psychological result' [Fromkin 1974].[4] The randomness of a terrorist act in itself is strategic enough to cause a tremendous psychological effect. The notion that the terrorists can strike anytime, anywhere, with any weapons and without any warning spreads a pall of deep anxiety over the potentially targeted society. On the other hand, from Pape's [2003] observation of various suicidal terrorist attacks from 1980 to 2001, terrorists seem to have carefully selected democratic countries that are perceived to be soft targets and have committed alleged offenses against the terrorists' values and interests.[5]

The last element that determines the strategic aspect of terrorist acts is the goal or motive. Most of the definitions of terrorism do not clarify the motives of terrorism — or they simply state that they are political — and focus on the target and the relationship to conventional warfare.[6] However, research on the targets of terrorists, at least in the last two decades, suggests a strategic pattern. Among the 188 suicide terrorist attacks identified by Pape [2003] between the 1980s and 1990s, the majority targeted democratic countries that were perceived by terrorists as soft. Given the historical examples [Fromkin 1974] and contemporary cases [Chalk 1998] of many states' self-defeating counter-terror measures, it can be highly expected that terrorists will notice the temptation of affluent democratic countries to resort to repression with complex and often illegal and unconstitutional counter-terror activities that eventually undermine the government's legitimacy, creating a situation that tends to serve the interests of the terrorists. Therefore, terrorists are strategically compelled to commit their violent acts against highly democratic and developed Western states rather than the less democratic and poorer countries [Hamilton and Hamilton 1983]. By ear-marking the democracies as their target, the terrorists aim to achieve the following: the communication of their grievances to an international audience, the coercion of the targeted state to change its policies, and the mobilization of support within the terrorist group/society.

DYNAMICS OF TERRORISM

How do violent acts achieve the above mentioned objectives for terrorists? Or in other words, what are the passive processes that terrorists hope to initiate through their violent acts so as to effect favorable results? Or more specifically, what are the underlying processes or components of terrorism? One of the best places to look for answers is in the various definitions of terrorism.

---

[4] However, since 9-11, terrorists also aim to produce great physical damage on the targeted country through their terror actions.

[5] The meaningless, random, and violent acts on democratic countries that are capable of producing tremendous psychological results can be distinguished from other forms of political violence like guerrilla or military. As argued by Merari [1993, 4], the challenge is to limit the definition of terrorism 'to more specific types of phenomena, distinguishable from other forms of political violence.'

[6] However, Stevens [2002] noted a consensus among scholars that terrorism emerges when people confront economic, political and religious oppression. Given the limited scope of this article, no attempt is made to pursue questions of the terrorists' motives. Similarly, who are the terrorists and why they take up terrorism are also not dealt with here.

Merari [1993] observed three central elements constituting the US, UK and German governments' definitions of terrorism: violent acts, intention to sow fear on the targeted population, and the political objectives. The broader academic definitions also have these three elements at their core. For instance, among the 109 definitions on terrorism collected by Schmid and Jongman [1988], 83.5 percent emphasized violence, 65 percent political goals and 51 percent the motivation to inflict fear and terror. However, given the initiation of fear on the targeted population by guerrillas and also by the military in a conventional war situation for political objectives, these elements are not unique to terrorism alone; rather they are a common feature in all forms of political violence [Merari 1993]. At the same time, the most often cited definition of the US State Department, Department of Defense, and Central Intelligence Agency (CIA) does not mention the fear factor explicitly: 'terrorism' means premeditated, politically motivated violence perpetrated against noncombatant targets by sub-national groups or clandestine agents, usually intended to influence an audience.

Taking a cue from this, let's look at what might be missing in these definitions and relevant to our analysis of terrorism's dynamics. Weinberg, Pedahzur et al [2004] have developed a consensus definition through an empirical analysis of various definitions. They compared the 22 'definitional elements' of terrorism gathered by Alex Schmid [1983] with that of the definitions of authors whose articles appeared in three major journals; *Terrorism, Studies in Conflict and Terrorism,* and *Terrorism and Political Violence,* and developed the following definition: '(T)errorism is a politically motivated tactic involving the threat or use of force or violence in which the pursuit of publicity plays a significant role' [782]. They observed that this academic definition points to a 'virtual absence of reference to the psychological element...widely thought to be at the heart of the concept' [Weinberg, Pedahzur et al. 2004, 777].

Building on the strategy of terrorism outlined at the beginning of this section, I intend to highlight three distinct processes encompassing the psychological element: (1) the attitudinal influence; (2) the immediate behavioral consequences; and (3) the reaction as well as the overreaction against terrorists. The psychological process of terror *jiu-jitsu* initiated by the terrorists' violent acts on a targeted society influences the latter's attitudes, and produces damaging behavioral consequences to the targeted state. The spectrum of a targeted state's reaction falls between accommodation to the terrorists' demands, which might improve the terrorists' position, and aggression against the terrorists which might help terrorists to mobilize within the in-group. The above three psychological stages (attitude, behavior and reaction) in the dynamics of terrorism are passive from the point of view of the terrorists. They have no or very little control over this process once it has been initiated. Clearly the three elements are unique to the strategy of terrorism when compared with other forms of political violence. In the subsequent sections each of these processes is elaborated.

1) Attitudinal Influence: Terror *Jiu-Jitsu* in Action

Most scholars consider that fear is the weapon of terrorists without distinguishing it from terror [for e.g., Fromkin 1974; Barber 2003; Pape 2003]. Instead I argue that it is terror that serves terrorists' purpose and fear is a by product. Though the word 'terror' is used ambiguously on many occasions, it is commonly understood as the psychic state of extreme fear and the terrifying violent event that produces this psychic state [Walter 1964]. On the other hand, fear is produced in response to objective threats [Sparks 2003]. The experience of terror is very different from other forms of fear and anxiety.[7] Creation of terror which is central to the politics of terrorism, argues Sparks [2003, 204], 'requires acts that are deliberately destructive to the people being terrorized'. Thus, a violent act becomes central to terrorism.

While terrorism is violence used in order to create terror, terror *jiu-jitsu* is the process that triggers the dynamics of terrorism. Terror *jiu-jitsu* is understood as the psychological process initiated especially in the minds of a targeted society by terrorists' staging random violent acts on a few of the target's members[8]. Terror *jiu-jitsu* is not the end of terrorism. It is just a first step. It aims to influence the targeted population to perform various actions that fulfill the terrorists' objectives. It is very similar to the function of fear outlined by Fromkin [1974, 693]. Fear created by a terrorist act, 'will lead somebody else — not the terrorist — to embark on some quite different program of action that will accomplish whatever it is that the terrorist really desires.' More fittingly, the mechanism of terror *jiu-jitsu* can be coherently understood by drawing a parallel to the process of political *jiu-jitsu* produced in a nonviolent resistance situation.

Political *jiu-jitsu* is one of the important theoretical concepts underlying nonviolence theory and in turn nonviolent action research. Gregg [1966], in his significant work on nonviolence theory in 1935, constructed the concept of moral *jiu-jitsu* to refer to the underlying psychological process of nonviolent action. According to him, when a nonviolent activist confronts the violence of the opponent, the asymmetry in the choice of means to settle the conflict — particularly the activists' refusal to use violence — throws the opponent morally off balance. It works like the Japanese martial art *jiu-jitsu,* which defeats the opponent by strategically using his own power. In a nonviolent conflict situation, the witnessing role of bystanders strengthens the moral *jiu-jitsu* and gradually weakens the opponent. According to Gregg, 'Violence which is not opposed by violence, but by courageous nonviolence, if it is in the open, is sure sooner or later to react against the attacker' [quoted in Martin, Varney et al. 2001, 145].

Gene Sharp, the prominent nonviolence researcher, expanded the concept of moral *jiu-jitsu* by incorporating strategic elements like timing, organization, preparation, etc., and called it political *jiu-jitsu*. In his words:

> Political *jiu-jitsu* is one of the special processes by which nonviolent action deals with violent repression. By combining nonviolent discipline with solidarity and persistence in struggle, the nonviolent actionists cause the violence of the opponent's repression to be exposed in the worst possible light. This, in turn, may lead to shifts in opinion and then to shifts in power relationships favorable to the nonviolent group. These shifts result from withdrawal of support from the opponent and the grant of support to the nonviolent actionists [Sharp 1973, 657].

According to Sharp, political *jiu-jitsu* is a psychological process initiated when the opponent's violence is unleashed against the unarmed nonviolent activists. It is rooted in the

---

[7] While 'anxiety may be caused by a number of other factors, including intra-psychic tensions, interpersonal conflicts, and unsettled social conditions, the "terror" analyzed here is restricted to the emotional state caused by specific violent acts or threats' [Walter 1964, 248].

suffering of activists and thrives on the sympathy of three groups of people: functionaries of the opponent, the grievance group and third parties. Mere persistence of nonviolent action and more suffering at the hand of the opponent gradually mobilizes support for the activists from these three groups. The oppressor, who is dependent on a multitude of power bases to retain his position, is alienated and weakened when these groups withdraw their consent. In some cases he loses his power completely whereas in others he accommodates to the demands of the nonviolent activists. Sharp [2005, 45-46] identified four mechanisms by which political *jiu-jitsu* could produce results: conversion, accommodation, coercion and disintegration.

Similarly in a terror situation, terrorists initiate terror in the minds of a few in a targeted society through performing violent acts. This terror kick starts a psychological process encompassing a range of emotions like fear, anger and hatred and spreads to the larger population which I call terror *jiu-jitsu*. Just like political *jiu-jitsu,* terror *jiu-jitsu* influences the attitudes and eventually the behavior of the aforementioned three groups: the target group, the terrorists' in-group and third parties, and alters the power relations. That is, the reaction of these groups is designed to gradually strengthen the terrorists' power position and weaken his opponents within these three groups. The two prominent processes that realize the terrorists' objectives are coercion and aggression; coercion is what the terrorists' action does, while aggression is the reaction of the targeted state.

Terror *jiu-jitsu* is a combination of various feelings and emotions like anger, fear, hatred, anxiety and insecurity that are produced by actual or perceived credible and random threats to people's lives. Terror *jiu-jitsu* might improve the terrorists' image within their in-group and bring in more recruits. It influences third parties to take positions supporting the targeted state's reaction or condemning the targeted state's overreaction. It works to influence the attitudes within the targeted state's society. It may damage people's sense of wellbeing and bring about a change in their thinking that causes political instability. The targeted society's reaction can prove destructive across a range of social, political and economic spheres. Thus the reasoning goes: if a government can be provoked to overreact, it may be weakened, civil society may be greatly affected, people may turn against their own government, greater understanding may develop for the terrorists' grievances, and additional support may swell the ranks of the terrorists.

1a. Initiation of Terror Jiu-Jitsu

Terrorist acts are aimed at killing some people and initiating terror in the entire targeted population. This act of especially killing civilians, who are considered innocent, initiates the process of terror *jiu-jitsu*. It expands from a few to a larger society through the spread of a combination of emotions like anger, fear and hatred.

What produces anger among the targeted population is the seemingly pointless and paradoxical nature of the act itself [Fromkin 1974]. It is pointless because a terrorist does not necessarily believe that persons killed by him deserve it; and it is paradoxical because he goes ahead and kills them despite their particular death being a matter of indifference to him. By comparison, a murderer, or a soldier kills somebody because they want that particular person out of the way — to be dead. Thus, from an objective point of view, a terrorist act is utterly

---

[8] Although mostly non-combatants, even the killing of soldiers in remotes battlefields might set in train a psychological process — though different from terror *jiu-jitsu*.

meaningless. The act is so apparently meaningless that 'it is a natural reaction to turn on those who perpetrated it in anger and hatred' [Fromkin 1974, 695].

Although anger and hatred seem related — or at least the latter appears to represent a more severe form of the former — there does exist a fundamental difference. For instance, a parent may become angry with a misbehaving child and even go to the extent of beating him/her, but would rarely hate the child. While anger is hot, hatred seems cold. 'Anger is a response to a particular incident or offense; hatred expresses a longer-term relation of antipathy' [McCauley 2002, 7]. More relevantly, Aristotle says: 'The angry man wants the object of his anger to suffer in return; hatred wishes its object not to exist' [quoted in [McCauley 2002, 7].

Therefore, violent acts of terrorism are capable of arousing anger — at least, among the targeted population. But are they sufficient to make them hate the terrorists? Or, what makes people hate terrorists in a manner to support actions to eradicate them? Plausible answers can be drawn from research on offences and offenders [McCauley 2002, 7]: 'offences that include long-term threats are more likely to elicit the desire to eliminate the offender.' An immediate emotional reaction to a life-threatening situation is fear. This fear, accompanied by anger, becomes hatred. That is, threat and the ensuing fear seem to be the key elements that convert anger into hatred, and the willingness to support actions that will eliminate the source of the threat.

The violent acts of terrorists are capable of posing a threat to entire populations. According to Pape [2003] the 'threat to inflict low to medium levels of punishment on civilians' is central to terrorism. Two crucial elements make a terrorist act threatening: randomness and credibility. While randomness is the terrorists' capacity to launch an attack at anytime and anywhere with any weapons, credibility is the assurance that such an attack will most likely cause extensive damage, including loss of life. The use of suicide bombers as a means to carry out terrorists' acts guarantees both randomness and credibility.

The credibility of suicide attacks is simply raised by the fact that the would-be attackers cannot be deterred from carrying out future attacks [Pape 2003; Mueller 2005]. Suicide bombers present a 'threat of continuing limited civilian punishment that the target government cannot completely eliminate' [Pape 2003, 356]. Secondly, suicide attacks are more destructive than other forms of terrorist attacks. According to Pape [2003, 346], the 188 suicide terrorist attacks that occurred between 1980-2001 killed an average of 13 people each (without including 9-11 casualties), whereas during the same time the 4,155 other forms of terrorist attacks killed only 3,207 people, an average of less than one person per attack. Thirdly, death due to a suicide attack seems credible. For instance, suicide attacks which account for just 3 percent of all terrorist attacks from 1980-2001 caused 48 percent of total deaths excluding the 9-11 counts [Pape 2003]. Lastly, it is not a one-time event but often occurs in a series of suicide attacks. A suicide bomber sacrificing his life shall logically make the attack worth it. Therefore, it plausibly raises the risk to civilians [Pape 2003, 346].

The credibility of the threat of terrorist attacks is reinforced due to the randomness of the event. Suicide bombing has improved considerably the randomness of an attack. The bomber is able to penetrate very ordinary, as well as unimaginable places, due to the range of options available to him in concealing weapons or becoming a weapon himself. He is presented with more options of access to a site than a murderer because his mission is 'one-way' and he has no intention to escape or return. All these factors make the randomness of dying in a terror attack similar to the chances of winning a lottery. As Mueller points out [2005, 228], 'one's chances are as good or bad as those of others.'

With the threat of overwhelming terror, the targeted population develops a mixture of feelings like anger, fear and hatred. Though in actual fact the violence of terrorism is only experienced by a few people, the fear is felt by many and stays in their minds for a long time.[9] This expansion of terror into fear and feelings like hatred, anxiety and insecurity (which ultimately terrorizes people) characterizes the nature of terror *jiu-jitsu*. It can be strengthened by further terror attacks or the issuance of threats of more terrorist actions. On the other hand, as explained below, it can also be intensified by other factors — like irrational public responses and the fear mongering and threat exaggerations of the media, politicians and so-called terrorism industry — that are beyond the terrorists' control.

1b. Intensification of Terror Jiu-Jitsu

Following Mueller's [2005, 221] remark, 'anything that enhances fear gives in to terrorists,' I argue that anything that also enhances, anger, hatred and insecurity advances terror *jiu-jitsu*. The commonly observed tendency of threat exaggeration and fear mongering in democratic countries — typically after a terror attack, undoubtedly intensifies terror *jiu-jitsu*. For instance, in the US, after the 9-11 attacks, commentators felt that the country had become 'vulnerable' and 'fragile.' Moreover, some observers, especially politicians, have perceived that 'terrorists armed with weapons of mass destruction present an existential threat to the United States' and for some 'it is a threat to civilization itself.' In similarly alarming language, a CIA official's book states that the USA's 'survival' is at stake and is engaged in a 'war to death' [Mueller 2005, 225].

After the September 11 attacks, McCauley [2002] observed at least three kinds of fear reactions among the American public. First, fear was related to the work place among those persons who survived the terrorist attack on the Word Trade Center (WTC). Second, fear of flying was generated by those who did not have any personal link to the destruction of WTC. And third, general fears were expressed of dying due to 'uncontrollable and unpredictable terrorist attacks.' The last two categories of fears pose special problems because the perceived risks — in threats like shark attacks, flying and even terrorism — are highly unrealistic [Mueller 2005; Mueller 2005a]. For instance, the chances of an American dying in a terrorist instigated air crash is one in 13 million whereas to take the same level of risk one has only to travel 11.2 miles on an inter-state highway. Similarly, the number of Americans killed by international terrorism since 1960, including 9-11, parallels the number killed by lightening or an allergic reaction to peanuts. The 'false sense of insecurity' over terrorism can be compared with the rise of fear about crime in the 1990s despite the actual decline in crime rates. These 'irrational fears' acquired by the American public on 'remote dangers,' contends Mueller [2005, 228], are very difficult to deal with or control. While it is impossible for the public to escape the genuine threat of terrorism, politicians and the media exaggerate the danger and fan their fears.

The downplaying of risks and threats is arguably more precarious than to exaggerate them [Mueller 2005]. Therefore, assuming the politicians and the media are sincerely

---

[9] For instance, the IRA bombed to 'terrorize those relatively few people who were in the blast range when they went off, but the warnings which attended the bombs instilled fear into far more people — often to the level of panic — and this fear, felt by many, lasts longer than the terror felt by the few' [Sparks 2003, 204].

concerned about the dangers of terrorism, they are inclined to exaggerate its potential threats. For politicians to understate the threat of terrorism or be insensitive to public concerns can prove fatal to a political career. As for the media, despite claiming fair and balanced coverage on terrorism, there is a temptation to amplify the risks and threats and eventually generate fear because it attracts readers and viewers. Both the media and the politicians, for whatever their reasons, stress 'extreme possibilities so much and so exclusively' [Mueller 2005, 227]. They rarely reveal mitigating considerations such as international terrorism does not kill more than a few hundred people every year (barring 2001). Instead they focus on domestic terrorism and on predictions about some yet-to-happen gigantic terrorist strike.

According to Mueller [2005a, 492-497], the so called terrorism industry — which includes 'risk entrepreneurs, bureaucrats, most of the media, and nearly all politicians'— induces terrorism by stoking fears and encouraging overreactions. The terrorism industry concentrates on raising alarms instead of assessing 'realistic risks and probabilities.' For instance, the Department of Homeland Security, which was created by US President George W. Bush in response to 9-11, warns in its manifesto that 'today's terrorists can strike at any place, at any time, and with virtually any weapon'[Document 2002]. If 'terrorism were to be back-burnered,' the terrorism experts would be out of business. But on account of incentives, as Rosen argues, they 'exaggerate risks and pander to public fears' [quoted in Mueller 2005a, 494]. Thus it seems the terrorists would be hard pressed to 'spread fear more effectively than the American Government inadvertently has done as it dutifully passes on random threats against unspecified targets and warns that further attacks are a virtual certainty' [Barber 2003, 43].

2) Behavioral Consequences: Weakening of a Targeted State

As observed by Sparks [2003, 201],

> Fear drives the desire to hunt out and destroy agents of danger without and within. Where there is cultural heterogeneity, this fear-driven quest for safety can become twisted into a drive for the security of sameness. The potential cost of such activity is the loss of civil society itself.

In other words, the terror *jiu-jitsu* evoked by the terrorists' violent acts and intensified by the public's irrational fears — which have been fanned by the threat exaggeration and fear mongering of the media, politicians, administrators and the terrorism industry generally — tends to generate behavioral consequences, at both the individual and institutional levels, that are damaging to the targeted state. While these behavioral consequences are detailed below, due to space considerations, a theoretical mapping of the factors determining the attitudes behind the behaviors is excluded.[10]

2a. Individual Level
Following the 9-11 attacks two kinds of damaging behavioral reactions can be noted in the US: reactions leading to the loss of more lives, and reactions affecting the business and

economic sector. Firstly, the fears caused by the attacks have made people choose the more dangerous automobile transportation rather than the airplane. As a result, from 11 September to 31 December 2001 alone, there was an increase of more than one thousand deaths in automobile accidents. Looking at another statistic presented by Mueller three and a half years later,

> if a small percentage of the one-hundred-thousand-plus road deaths since 2001 occurred to people who were driving because they feared to fly, the number of Americans who have perished in overreaction to 9-11 in road accidents alone could well surpass the number who were killed by the terrorists on that terrible day' [Mueller 2005a, 492].

Secondly, peoples' reaction to 9-11 greatly affected the tourism and airline industries. Even three years after 9-11, the US domestic airliners were less than 7 percent below pre- 9-11 profits [Mueller 2005a, 492]. Reportedly, there was a loss of nearly 1.6 million jobs — mainly in the tourism industry [Mueller 2005a]. According to Osama bin Laden, the 9-11 attacks cost al-Qa'ida $500,000, whereas for the US, the attacks and their consequences cost more than $500 billion [Mueller 2005a, 497].

2b. Institutional Level

Whether a reaction to terror will lead to repression, which in turn will lead people to revolt against their government, remains a contentious subject. Many analysts argue that repressive counter-terror institutional measures can erode the democratic foundations of a state and threaten its democratic way of life, finally producing an outcome desirable to the terrorists. Notably, the classic objective of terrorism is to 'try and trap authorities into overreaction by provoking the use of illegal or unconstitutional counter-measures' [Chalk 1998, 386].[11] Thus, the terror situation tempts a state to resort to illegal and unconstitutional counter-terror measures, which on the one hand undermine its own legitimacy and on the other create a situation more dangerous than the one it seeks to eliminate. [Chalk 1998, 374].[12]

Since one of the most important duties of a liberal democratic state is to provide security for its citizens, the threat of random terrorist acts compels a state to respond firmly to prevent any future attacks. However, the reaction often undermines the 'defining principles that

---

[10] According to McCauley, social norms play a greater role in determining the behavioral expressions of attitudes. For further discussion, see McCauley [2002].

[11] On philosophical grounds, repressive counter-terrorist methods seem to undermine the 'liberal notion that all human beings have the right to be protected against the arbitrary and coercive actions of institutions which have legal and political power.' On strategic grounds, it erodes the 'perceived legitimacy of the fight against terrorism.' See Chalk [1998, 386].

[12] However, the revolutionary terrorists, who violently attempted to overthrow the liberal-pluralistic regimes in 1960s, suffered setbacks. They believed that 'terrorist attacks would force hitherto liberal regimes to become repressive, a change which in turn would alienate the masses, thus setting the stage for revolution' [Fromkin 1974, 690]. But it did not work out as they expected. However, some revolutionary groups have argued that since 'liberal democracies are already police states, the object of revolutionary terrorist action should be to reveal this hidden reality to the population at large. An unthinking reaction by the authorities to terrorist provocation would accomplish the desired result. Thus, the aim of terrorism would be to trick the government into taking off its mask.' Fromkin [1974, 690] argues that, 'Similarly in the USA, terrorist bomb attacks have not led to any change at all in the form of government, much less to a transformation of America into a police state.' This argument is disputable in the present context. Indeed, the liberal democracies are being challenged to prove that they are 'face' and not 'mask' [Fromkin 1974, 690].

underpin liberal democratic forms of government' [Chalk 1998, 374]. As exemplified by Chalk, the 'strategy of tension' in Italy between1969 and 1974; the 'dirty war' against ETA in Spain between 1983 and 1987; and the 'brutal insurgency' in Peru from 1992 to 1996 brought the liberal democracies of these countries to launch (with only minor restraints) institutionalized and bureaucratized terror from 'above' [Chalk 1998: 373]. Such an overreaction to terrorist acts and threats initially affects the criminal justice system. And due to the politicization of the criminal justice system, justice becomes 'political justice.' The principles of due process are seriously undermined, and gradually the state is 'drawn into a parallel grey zone of illegality which mirrors the one in which the terrorist operates' [Chalk 1998, 377].

After 9-11, an enormous amount of money has been redirected from essential and important parts of the budget to cover expenses incurred in managing the terrorist threat. Irrespective of how remote the threat of terrorism might be, enormous resources of labor and money are invested in countering the presumed threat [Mueller 2005, 223]. The newly instituted US Department of Homeland Security (DHS) — with approximately 184,000 employees — is the third largest cabinet department in the federal government after the Departments of Defense and Veterans Affairs (also institutions directly related to national security). The current budget for DHS is $35.6 billion while state and local governments spend additional billions. The priorities of the US, according to Clark Chapman and Alan Harris, 'remain radically torqued toward homeland defense and fighting terrorism at the expense of objectively greater societal needs' [quoted in Mueller 2005a, 492].[13] In particular, the money is spent on: (1) the further reduction of threats that have already been minimized, and (2) engaging in reassuring actions rather than reducing risks [Mueller 2005, 224]. The fear factor, and not the danger, is claimed by Barber [2003] to be the main reason for the closing down of the US stock markets after the 9/11 attacks. Finally, the additional half-hour security check at the US airports after the attacks seems to have cost the economy $15 billion a year, whereas the total profit of the airline industries in the 1990s never exceeded $5.5 billion [Mueller 2005a, 492]. This 'speculative immune reaction to attacks', argues Barber [2003, 43], did more damage to the US than al-Qa'ida could ever have done.

3) Engagement with Terrorists

The most favorable reaction for the terrorists is either that the targeted government is pressured by its citizens to listen to the terrorist's demands or the targeted government is overthrown by its own people [Pape 2003, 346]. This section will examine two common ways a targeted government deals with the terrorists: 1) it accommodates to the terrorists' demands; or 2) it mobilizes its aggressive forces against the terrorists' in-group. Outlining the entire range of counter-terror options is not attempted in this section, since the basic purpose is to demonstrate how the strategy of terror *jiu-jitsu* produces reactions that can work — and have worked thus far — in favor of the terrorists.

---

[13] According to Banks, 'if terrorists force us to redirect resources away from sensible programs and future growth, in order to pursue unachievable but politically popular levels of domestic security, then they have won an important victory that mortgages our future' [quoted in Mueller 2005a, 492].

3a. Accommodation through Coercion

Coercion is an important outcome that terrorists hope to achieve through their violent acts. As observed by Fromkin [1974, 686], terrorism 'can persuade an opponent that a particular point of view is taken with such deadly seriousness by its few adherents that it should be accommodated, rather than suffering casualties year after year in a campaign to suppress it.' Although fighting abroad 'suffers the disadvantage of fighting the battle away from its own base,' well established foreign powers like the US are under no compulsion to fight a loosing war to the bitter end [Fromkin 1974, 691]. Therefore, when US President Ronald Regan decided to withdraw from Lebanon, he said, 'The price we had to pay in Beirut was so great, the tragedy at the barracks was so enormous....We had to pull out....We couldn't stay there and run the risk of another suicide attack on the Marines' [quoted in Pape 2003, 352].

The capacity to coerce, according to Pape [2003], is central to the strategy of terrorism. However, thus far terrorists have only managed to successfully coerce states to yield minor or insignificant concessions, 'such as withdrawal from territory of low strategic importance or, as in Israel's case in 1994 and 1995, a temporary and partial withdrawal from a more important area' [Pape 2003, 355]. At the same time, suicide terrorists are unable to coerce governments to give up goals they consider crucial to their security and economic survival. For instance, the US was prepared to withdraw from Lebanon only because none of its vital security, economic or ideological interests was at stake. In Pape's view [2003], terrorist have learned that moderate punishment on targeted states reaps moderate benefits whereas more destructive attacks might lead to greater coercive results.

3b. Aggression and Terrorists' in-Group Mobilization

The counter-violent aggression of a targeted state seems to gain it short term benefits — in terms of jailing, isolating or killing terrorists or monitoring their communities — but it has generally proved ineffective in curbing the long term violence of the terrorists. The experience of Israel and a few other states including the US proves that counter-aggression has 'met with meager success' [Pape 2003, 356]. Even after the US had 'successfully toppled the Taliban in Afghanistan in December 2001, al Qa'ida launched seven successful suicide attacks from April to December 2002, killing some 250 Western citizens, more than in the three years before September 11, 2001' [Pape 2003, 356].

Aggression against terrorism in most cases has either helped the terrorists or harmed people not responsible for the terrorism. The US bombing of Osama bin-Laden's terrorist training camps in Afghanistan has 'made him into an international celebrity, essentially created his al-Qa'ida organization and made it possible to attract funds and recruits, and converted the Taliban from reluctant hosts to allies and partners' [Mueller 2005a, 491]. In response to the terrorism of the Chechen rebels, Russia waged a war against the breakaway republic in 1999 that added to the cost of Russian lives and property. When terrorists connected to Libya bombed a discotheque in Germany killing two people, Ronald Regan authorized a bombing on Libya in 1986 killing 270 people and destroying an airline company [Mueller 2005, 222]. Similarly, when al-Qa'ida bombed two American embassies in Kenya and Tanzania killing over 200 people (including a few Americans) in 1998, President Bill Clinton sanctioned a bombing on a suspected pharmaceutical company that exposed countless Sudanese to the dangerous effects of chemical poisons that will impact on their lives for many years to come. [Mueller 2005a, 491].

As well, counter-aggression can directly benefit the terrorists' in-group by mobilizing additional supporters. As observed by McCauley, a terrorist group represents the top of a pyramid whose base is 'composed of everyone who agrees with the terrorist's goals, even those who disagree with the violent means' [cited in Friedberg 2004]. In between the terrorists and sympathizers are a group of active supporters with a high level of commitment to the terrorist cause but have not yet crossed over to the ranks of the terrorists. Since terrorists mostly advance nationalistic goals like 'expelling a foreign military force from their territory,' there is always a reasonable number of supporters who represent a pool of potential recruits [Pape 2003, 348]. Contrary to popular perception, Pape [2003] contends that the primary aims of suicide terrorists are of a political nature, and that they will always find some support for their goals against the targeted state, as long as those goals correspond to what other nationalists want. By way of an extreme example, 95 percent of Saudi society shares the al- Qa'ida objective that US troops should withdraw from the Saudi Peninsula [Pape 2003]. Terrorists — despite resorting to an ambitious strategy of violence — still identify with societies and pursue goals that are supported by many of their fellow nationals. In short, the terrorist group is dependent on the pyramid for its 'cover, support and recruits,' and often finds that backing. By committing violent acts against a state, 'terrorists hope to provoke a response from the state...thereby expanding the terrorists' support base, increasing the number of recruits and building sympathy for their cause' [Friedberg 2004, 2].

CONCLUSION

The strategy of terrorism is to carry out violent acts on a targeted state's population that will initiate a psychological process of terror called terror *jiu-jitsu*. While the immediate effect of the violent act is confined to a few persons, it soon produces anger and fear among an entire society. The anger is due to the meaningless savagery of the violent act, and the fear of future violence. The combination of fear and anger results in hatred, from which swells an overwhelming urge to eliminate the terror threat. Fear-mongering and threat-exaggeration become rampant and grip the entire population. The resultant behavior of individuals and institutions damages the political, economic and social fabric of the targeted state. Lastly, as anticipated by the terrorists, terror *jiu-jitsu* either coerces the state to accommodate to the terrorists' interests or to instigate aggression against the terrorists, thereby facilitating the growth of the terrorists' pyramid of supporters. This is a brief summary of terrorism's dynamics driven by the psychological process of terror *jiu-jitsu*.

However, there is a vital weakness in the strategy of terrorism, namely that it is an indirect and passive strategy. Terrorism achieves its goals not directly through its acts, but through reactions to its acts. A strategy that provides its target with the opportunity to deny its purpose — depending almost exclusively on how its opponent acts — is naturally a weak strategy. Terrorists play an active role only with the staging of the violent act and initiating terror *jiu-jitsu*. Afterwards, the dynamics of terror *jiu-jitsu* is passive, because what happens is beyond the terrorist's direct control.

Terror techniques tend not to be very effective against less democratic and more authoritarian governments. In the first place, it is difficult for suicide terrorists to gain access to a totalitarian state. Even if they do, and the state overreacts to the extent that it collapses, the terrorists are in no position to form a new government.

It should be self-evident that to defeat the strategy of terror *jiu-jitsu*, the starting point of a counter-strategy needs to minimize the psychological effect of any terrorist act and to conduct a controlled and effective response. While a concerted effort to eschew the goal of terror *jiu-jitsu* is central to the defeat of terrorism, it is only the beginning — a short term antidote against terrorism. Its long term prevention requires going to the deep-rooted sources of the conflict. It means assisting in the putting together of a broadly-based program of economic and social development inside the breeding grounds of terrorists. These kinds of viable alternative models that focus on rationality, peace and the fulfillment of ontological needs are explored in some of the remaining chapters.

ACKNOWLEDGEMENTS

Senthil Ram is presently a researcher at the School of Social Science, Media and Communication, Wollongong University, Australia and also a South Asia Fellow 2007 at the East West Center, Washington D.C. He has received a PhD on the nonviolent aspects of Tibetan exile politics. His current projects include nonviolent responses to global terrorism and peaceful resolution of Maoist revolutionary violence in India/South Asia. He is also coordinating a collaboration project with Gothenburg University, Sweden that is based at the University of Madras, India to introduce peace studies in Indian/South Asian universities. His forthcoming monograph, *Nonviolent Conflict Transformation of Tibetan Conflict*, is being published by the University of Tromso, Norway. He has been a co-convener of the Nonviolence Commission of the International Peace Research Association (IPRA) from 2002 to the present.

REFERENCES

Barber, B. R. (2003). *Fear's Empire: War, Terrorism and Democracy*. New York, London: W. W. Norton.

Chalk, P. (1998). 'The Response to Terrorism as a Threat to Liberal Democracy.' *Australian Journal of Politics and History*. 44(3): 373-388.

Crenshaw, M. (1983). 'Introduction: Reflections on the Effects of Terrorism.' *Terrorism Legitimacy and Power: The Consequences of Political Violence*. Middletown, CT: Wesleyan UP.

Crenshaw, M. (2000). 'The Psychology of Terrorism: An Agenda for the 21st century.' *Political Psychology*. 21(2): 405-420.

Document. (2002). 'The National Strategy for Homeland Security, July.' Retrieved 14 June, 2006, from http://www.whitehouse.gov/homeland/book/sect2.pdf.

Friedberg, M. (2004) 'Understanding the Psychology of Terrorism.' *Science and Technology*, Bryn Mawr College, DOI:

Fromkin, D. (1974). 'The Strategy of Terrorism.' *Foreign Affairs*. 53: 683-698.

Gregg, R. B. (1966). *The Power of Nonviolence*. New York: Schocken.

Hamilton, L. C. and Hamilton, J. D. (1983). 'Dynamics of Terrorism.' *International Studies Quarterly.* 27(1): 39-54.

Juergensmeyer, M. (2000). *Terror in the Mind of God: The Global Rise of Religious Violence.* Berkeley, CA: University of California Press.

Martin, B., Varney, W. et al. (2001). 'Political *Jiu-jitsu* against Indonesian Repression: Studying Lower-Profile Nonviolent Resistance.' *Pacifica Review.*13(2): 143-156.

McCauley, C. (2002). 'Psychological Issues in Understanding Terrorism and the Response to Terrorism.' in C. E. Stout (Ed.). *The Psychology of Terrorism: Theoretical Understandings and Perspectives, Volume III.* Westport, Ct: Praeger. III: 3-29.

McCauley, C. (2006). 'The Psychology of Terrorism.' Retrieved 30 May, 2006, from http://www.ssrc.org/sep11/essays/mccauley_text_only.htm.

Merari, A. (1993). 'Terrorism as a Strategy of Insurgency.' *Terrorism and Political Violence.* 5(4): 213-251.

Mueller, J. (2005). 'Simplicity and Spook: Terrorism and the Dynamics of Threat Exaggeration.' *International Studies Perspectives.* 6(2): 208-234.

Mueller, J. (2005a). 'Six Rather Unusual Propositions about Terrorism.' *Terrorism and Political Violence.* 17: 487-505.

Pape, R. A. (2003). 'The Strategic Logic of Suicide Terrorism.' *American Political Science Review.* 97(3): 343-361.

Pearlstein, R. M. (1991). *The Mind of the Political Terrorist.* Wilmington, DE: Scholarly Resources, Inc.

Reich, W. (Ed.) (1990). *Origins of Terrorism: Psychologies, Ideologies, Theologies, States of Mind.* Cambridge: Cambridge University Press.

Schmid, A. P. (1983). *Political Terrorism: A Research Guide to Concepts, Theories, Data Bases and Literature.* Amsterdam: North-Holland Publishing Company.

Schmid, A. P. and A. Jongman (1988). *Political Terrorism.* New Brunswick, NJ: Transaction Books.

Sharp, G. (1973). *The Politics of Nonviolent Action.* Boston: Porter Sargent.

Sharp, G. (2005). *Waging Nonviolent Struggle: 20th Century Practice and 21st Century Potential.* Boston: Porter Sargent.

Sparks, C. (2003). 'Liberalism, Terrorism and the Politics of Fear.' *Politics.* 23(3): 200-206.

Stout, C. E. (Ed.) (2002). *The Psychology of Terrorism- IV volumes.* Westport, CT: Praeger.

Walter, E. V. (1964). 'VIolence and the Process of Terror.' *American Sociological Review.* 29(2): 248-257.

Wardlaw, G. (1989). *Political Terrorism: Theory, Tactics and Counter-Measures.* Cambridge: Cambridge University Press.

Weinberg, L., Pedahzur, A. et al. (2004). 'The Challenges of Conceptualizing Terrorism.' *Terrorism and Political Violence.* 16(4): 777-794.

PART III: NONVIOLENT ISLAM AND ISLAMIC TERRORISM

In: Nonviolence: An Alternative for Defeating...
Editors: S. Ram and R. Summy, pp. 93-106

ISBN: 978-1-60021-812-5
© 2008 Nova Science Publishers, Inc.

Chapter 6

UNDERSTANDING ISLAMIC TERRORISM: HUMILIATION AWARENESS AND THE ROLE FOR NONVIOLENCE

Victoria Fontan

ABSTRACT

While counter-terrorism research currently revolves around heavy militarism and offensives that seldom win the hearts and minds of the people involved, nonviolence and counter-terrorism are not necessarily exclusive of one another. By way of an analysis of Usama bin Laden's speeches, this chapter seeks to understand the root causes of international terrorism in order to conceptualize its nature as well as to find pragmatic nonviolent ways to counter it at the grassroots level. In the chapter it is argued that an understanding of the difference between terrorism and insurgency can lead to new ways of addressing the al-Qa'ida problem. These ways range from nonviolent counterinsurgency practices to grassroots socio-economic empowerment initiatives already instigated by various US development agencies abroad.

INTRODUCTION

In the immediate aftermath of the September 11th attacks on the World Trade Centre and the Pentagon, the world was led to believe that the course of history had been changed forever. On September 16th 2001, US President George W. Bush declared in a press conference: '[t]his crusade, this war on terrorism is going to take a while. And the American people must be patient. I'm going to be patient' [2001]. While this statement was immediately judged to be too hostile against the Muslim world, its blatant anachronism nevertheless captured some of the zero-sum intentions of the Bush Administration: i.e. wage a long-term war against terrorism on Middle Eastern soil [AP 2001].

On October 7th 2001, immediately after the US launch of a massive bombing assault on Afghanistan, with British and French air support, Qatar-based Al-Jazeera satellite channel issued the following pre-recorded statement by Usama bin Laden, 'Neither America nor anyone who lives there will enjoy safety until safety becomes a reality for us living in Palestine and before all the infidel armies leave the land of Muhammad' [bin Laden 2001, 105]. Usama bin Laden's defiant response to George W. Bush was remarkably clear; we will not stop until we consider ourselves free from your occupation. Far from being new, the exact same message was sent by bin Laden to bin Baz, Chief Mufti of Saudi Arabia, more than seven years before. At the time, bin Laden denounced the occupation of Saudi Arabia as well as the collusion of some other Middle East regimes with the West. This letter had for a return address a London-based think tank, the Advice and Reform Committee. From think-tank affiliate to world terror giant, what had gone wrong for Usama bin Laden to elevate his struggle from words to actions?

This chapter will seek to understand the root causes of Usama bin Laden's anger towards the West, in order to extract from his writings concrete nonviolent (tactics, methods, approaches) in which to potentially diffuse the appeal that his message generates among his disciples. Instead of dating the beginning of the war on terror to September 11th 2001, the author will argue that the 'War on Terror' has for its origin Usama bin Laden's polarization against what he perceives as Western terror against the Muslim world. In the reality of the currently declared 'war on terror' — harboring extreme polarization on either side of the Bush/bin Laden divide — can one still consider nonviolence as a means of waging counter-terrorism?

This chapter will seek to answer the question by first coming to grips with Usama bin Laden's message to the *Umma* or Muslim world. His message will then be placed in the context of an intended global insurgency, using humiliation as a vector for its conceptualization as well as an understanding of how to initiate a counter-insurgency. In the light of this analysis, the effectiveness of the US response becomes easier to evaluate.

1. USAMA BIN LADEN'S MESSAGE TO THE MUSLIM WORLD AND THE WEST

Five years after the inception of the War on Terror, the world may not be considered a safer place. Iraq is on the verge of a civil war triggered partly by al-Qa'ida, and Taliban fighters have regained control of parts of Afghanistan, so that the threat of terrorism against the West and its allies remains high [Krueger & Laitin 2004; CNN 2006)]. Overall, security threats are elevated, air travel is becoming increasingly difficult, and the price of crude oil has more than doubled since September 11th 2001. While the causes of this state of affairs are debatable and open to interpretation, a careful analysis of the 'works' of Usama bin Laden leads to an understanding of his overall aim. What does Usama bin Laden really want of the West? Will an understanding of his thoughts lead to alternative ways to counter terrorism?

1a. Censorship and the Malaise of Counter-Terrorism Research

Not only is it acceptable for a doctor to research an illness, no-one would deny that it is highly recommended. Mainstream counter-terrorism, however, does not seem to apply comprehensively this cardinal rule of scientific research: that is, to know your enemy in order to combat him better. Indeed, when a Senior CIA official writes on this very subject, dutiful caution compels him to publish his ground-breaking work under the name of 'Anonymous.'[1] True, a plethora of researchers now populate think tanks and academic institutions across the US, producing an endless series of books and essays on *jihad* and terrorism. These efforts, however, tend to be those of the converted writing for an elite, whose passport to gentrification in US terms seems to be a softened one-sided outlook on Middle Eastern politics and US foreign policy, seldom asking the crucial question behind the War on Terror: why do they hate you/us so much? In a Manichean *us* versus *them* framework, such an approach might be deemed unnecessary, let alone seditious. Who needs to understand a terrorist since their overall aim is only to spread terror within a population? The perceived irrationality of terror seems to be ample grounds for not seeking to understand it. Indeed, the policy of the Bush administration towards terrorism is remarkably one-eyed in its solution: no negotiation, only complete eradication of the enemy.

While it is only reasonable to expect that any US administration will want to rally massive public support behind a war to which it is committed, it is in the interest of everyone, including that administration, to understand the background and origins of the conflict. This role ought to be assumed by an intellectual elite, but its attempts to analyze the decision-making on both sides and rally the public towards an informed assessment of government actions, is both subtly and openly discouraged by the reigning US political leadership. Academics find themselves scrutinized for what they assert in class, for what they decide to write and research. It is in this difficult context that Professor Bruce Lawrence chose to analyze the messages of Usama bin Laden towards the Muslim world, as well as to the West, in order to better understand the motivations behind Muslim terrorism. He compiled every statement ever made by Usama bin Laden between December 1994 and 2004. He decided to undertake this task after discovering that 'official pressures have ensured that, for the most part, his (bin Laden's) voice has been tacitly censored, as if to hear it clearly and without cuts or interruption would be too dangerous' [Lawrence 2005, xi]. What, then, emerges from a reading of Usama bin Laden's messages? These can be sorted according to (1) the issues they expose, (2) the villains and their regional acolytes deemed responsible for all the problems, (3) the suggestions for restoring justice in the Muslim world, and (4) the symptoms they denounce.

1b. The Issues, Villains and Methods

Since December 1994, two issues are recurrent in all his messages: the Arab/Israeli crisis, referred to as the Jewish usurpation of Palestinian land; and the Western occupation of Saudi Arabia, referred to as the 'invasion of Arabia' by the 'Judeo-Christian,' the 'Crusader' alliance or simply the 'locusts' [bin Laden 1995, 15 & 17; bin Laden 1996, 25; bin Laden 1998a, 59]. The villains are mostly but not exclusively the infidel regimes of the US, Israel and the UK, and their regional allies, most importantly Saudi Arabia.

---

[1] Michael Scheuer, former head of the CIA Unit in charge of hunting Usama bin Laden, wrote *Imperial Hubris* under the pen name 'Anonymous' [Potomac Editions 2004]. Scheuer resigned from the CIA in 2004.

The methods to restore justice within the Middle East focus on a call for *jihad* and a boycott of the US and all its allies. Of interest with regard to Usama bin Laden's declaration of *jihad* is his mention of *jihad* as uniquely defensive. According to Scheuer [quoted in Lawrence 2005, 46, n.3], *jihad* can also be offensive, for the spread of Islam as a religion and the conquest of new territories. Such *jihad* must be ordered by a supreme religious authority. With regard to defensive *jihad*, however, no leadership endorsement is needed and its necessity stems from an attack by non-Muslims on Islam, on Muslims, on Muslim territory or some combination of the three. Usama bin Laden uses this defensive theme on many occasions throughout his statements.

1c. The Symptoms

The defensive theme can be understood as an underlying dynamic behind many of the denounced symptoms, primarily relating to a perception of US double standards in its policies. These double standards are perceived to relate to the US denunciation of Usama bin Laden's actions as terrorist acts, while the US has allegedly a track record of being directly responsible for the death of thousands of individuals worldwide and for 'perpetrat[ing] deeds which [one] would not find the most ravenous of animals debasing themselves to do' [bin Laden 1996b, 40]. On a more sweeping note, Usama bin Laden denounces the US as the 'leader of terrorism and crime in the world' [bin Laden 1997, 51]. The Truman Administration's dropping of atomic bombs over Hiroshima and Nagasaki on August 6th 1945 constitutes a recurrent theme in his speeches, as do the sanctions against Iraq [bin Laden 1996b, 40].

Another case of claimed double standards pertains to the allies that the US supports in the Middle East and the Gulf Region. America's friends are said to be guilty of social injustices, political corruption and severe repression. Therein lies the core of the appeal that Usama bin Laden utilizes to gain support from the socially and politically disenfranchised within the Middle Eastern and Gulf regions. A stern indignation against the abject poverty and lack of development suffered as a result of the corruption of a few is illustrated by the every day 'struggling even with the basics of everyday life [such as] economic recession, price inflation, mounting debts, and prison overcrowding,' the former denounced as usury on the part of the government, sanctioned as being *haram* in Islam [bin Laden 1996a, 27-28].

The condemnation of these actions has for a special target the fifteen to twenty-five age bracket, thought to best fit the criteria of the unattached and jobless youth that would be most malleable to become a *jihad* fighter. Indeed, as a twenty-five year old and above man 'will have a wife and children, ... his mind becomes more mature, but the ability to give becomes weaker' [bin Laden 1998b, 91] — hence the recourse towards utilizing younger men for waging *jihad*.[2] This candid admission of the necessity for no terrestrial attachment in order for prospective fighters to freely give their lives to the *jihad* leads to an understanding of the necessity to comprehend the socio-economic issues that matter the most for Muslim males. According to Bucaille's (1998) analysis of the widespread appeal for *jihad* within Palestinian

---

[2] Indeed, a prospective suicide bomber, whom I interviewed in Iraq, deplored being still alive because of the fact that all men younger than he managed to be sent to their 'holy' mission before he could go. This was because he already had a wife and children to be looked after as a result of his death.

society, young Muslim men — and women — are not necessarily driven only by religion but also by the social status that becoming a *shaheed* provides.[3] In the case of young men, at an age when one is not necessarily a functional member of society according to Middle Eastern standards of masculinity, such as being employed and being rich enough to be able to marry, being a *jihad* fighter or a *shaheed* places these young men on the highway to becoming men [Ghoussoub & Sinclair-Webb 2000]. True, the 9-11 *shaheeds* did not directly match those criteria [9-11 Commission Report 2004]. However, what is important here is the fact that Usama bin Laden's corresponding message is specifically directed towards the *umma* and not only a selected few.

1d. Jihad and Justice

What does a soul waging *jihad* gain upon accession to heaven? The emergence of suicide bombing in Palestine over the past decade has led the international media to exploit this question in its most essentialist expression. Part of the answer is nowadays known to many and even pertains to popular culture. The pornography of violence attached to this topic by the media has reached a peak since 9-11, whereby Islam is intrinsically connected to sexualized violence [Karim 2002]. While many believe that a suicide bomber (not necessarily a *jihad* fighter) reaches sexual nirvana through the granting of virgins, not many are aware of the exact number involved, let alone the cultural and religious signification of this specific pledge. Moreover, the rest of the promises made to *jihad* fighters are seldom introduced, for *jihad* warriors not only marry virgins when they access to paradise, they also regain their human dignity, among other things.[4]

This loss of human dignity is of crucial importance to the discourse of Usama bin Laden, for the theme of humiliation is recurrent throughout the years preceding the 9-11 attacks. Humiliation was first characterized as the loss of self-respect of the *Umma* or Muslim world for 'abandoning' the *jihad* against the Western 'invasion of Arabia' [bin Laden 1995, 18]. It was then mentioned in the context of political repression and abject poverty suffered by the *menu peuple* of the Gulf and Palestine, then in a perspective of double standards and lack of sanctity of Muslim life. In the current context of the war in Iraq and other issues related to Israel/Palestine, the promise of restoration of human dignity to the *Umma* gives particular strength to Usama bin Laden's populist message. The means prescribed to achieve this self-restitution is a global Muslim insurgency against the humiliating forces of the US, the UK, Israel and their allies.

---

[3] *Shaheed*: a person engaged in self-sacrificing operations, refereed to as suicide bombers in simplistic popular culture.

[4] 'The martyr has a guarantee from God: He forgives him at the first drop of his blood and shows him his seat in Heaven. He decorates him with the jewels of faith, protects him from the torment of the grave, keeps him safe on the day of judgment, places a crown of dignity on his head with the finest rubies in the world, marries him to seventy-two of the pure virgins of paradise and intercedes on behalf of seventy of his relatives' [Lawrence 2005, 29].

2. INSURGENCY OR TERRORISM?

Usama bin Laden refers to his action throughout the world as the provocation of an insurgency of the global Muslim community, while the Bush administration refers to it as pure acts of terrorism. Is the latter an accurate labeling? This part will transcend the common cliché that one person's terrorist is another person's freedom fighter, and will problematize the relationship between terrorism and insurgency?

2a. An 'Auxiliary Weapon'

The labeling of the hunt for Usama bin Laden as a 'war on terror' by the Bush administration was not an exceedingly smart initiative. Not only did it set the time narrative of the conflict opposing the US to al-Qa'ida from the 9-11 attacks onwards — thus suppressing years of warnings and opposition on the part of Usama bin Laden — it also contained the potential for self-scrutiny about the reasons that led nineteen men to commit suicide on the day of the attacks. However, any initial attempts by the media, academics or other members of the community to carefully raise the question were repressed as unpatriotic or treasonable [Bird 2002]. Is the 'civilized world' rightfully involved in a 'war on terror'?

While the crime against humanity that constitutes 9-11 cannot be justified, a careful analysis of its surrounding narrative can lead a counter-terrorism expert to find potential remedies for its populist drive. Before engaging in this exercise, let us understand what terrorism represents in relation to insurgency. Terrorism has been qualified by Paul Wilkinson [2001, 2] as an 'auxiliary weapon' to insurgency. Defining insurrency as a rebellion or rise against any governmental power or authority, excludes any superpower or coalition member within the definition. An insurgency can be identified as anything ranging from guerilla warfare to terrorism and sabotage. Of importance in relation to guerilla warfare is the involvement of potentially very few people advancing the political struggle with quite specific tactics. For example, the element of surprise is fundamental to its operation. Due to its small numbers, the insurgency's repeated guerilla attacks can exhaust the State politically and psychologically over time. It retains the advantage of being able to choose the time and place of the next attack, the latter element being a strong expression of psychological warfare [Taber 2002]. According to Wilkinson, the use of terrorism in guerilla warfare is geared towards enhancing popular support for the guerilla, since almost invariably the State's recourse to violent retaliation will act as a self-fulfilling prophecy, validating the political assertions of the insurgency. Thus, a state that engages in *quid pro* quo Taliban-like terror will ultimately not only escalate the conflict, but also strengthen the insurgency, in the same manner that oil will always add to a fire. As Wilkinson [2001, 13] observes, not only is there a distinction to be made between state and non-state terror, the former 'has been vastly more lethal and has often been an antecedent to, and a contributory cause of, the (non-state) terrorism.' What if the 'war on terror' was just a counter-productive approach to the Usama bin Laden problem?

2b. Don Quixote and the Insurgency of the Umma

Usama bin Laden has always been straightforward in defining his mission as the 'duty ... to motivate [the] *umma* to *jihad* for the sake of God against America and Israel and their allies' [bin Laden 1998b, 69]. By placing this quote in the context of the use of terror as an auxiliary weapon of insurgency, the overall aspiration of Usama bin Laden becomes clearer. The aim of his use of terror throughout the years, initially within the Muslim world and later on Western territory, was twofold. First, it was to elicit a regional state response that would motivate a few young men to pledge their lives to his cause. After preparation and careful selection, the best of these young men would be trained to target strategic interests on Western soil in order to accede to the second phase of the plan, a massive Western retaliation towards the Muslim world that would motivate the *umma*, namely the 'Global Islamic Front for *Jihad* against Jews and Crusaders,' to finally engage in collective *jihad* to liberate Muslim holy territories from the perceived 'infidel enemy' [bin Laden 1998b, 69].

The 9-11 attacks on the World Trace Center and the Pentagon were therefore carefully planned to initiate the second phase of Usama bin Laden's objective: provoking a response from the US and its allies that would be strong enough to arouse a massive hostile reaction of the *umma* against the West. Far from seeking to exclusively lead and plan all future al-Qa'ida attacks, Usama bin Laden is more interested in his ideology and message translating into further acts of terrorism that will lead to increased state retaliation, hence place him and his organization closer to their aim of having motivated a global insurgency. Once again, the clarity of the written messages of Usama bin Laden leads to an obvious clue of dire consequences to be feared should the West act as an involuntary accomplice to his aim. Al-Qa'ida does not seek to direct or plan the global insurgency, but simply to *motivate* it. Therefore, not only will a retaliatory counter-terrorist attack against al-Qa'ida be a counter-productive fight against windmills, it will have the reverse impact of strengthening the ranks of the insurgency that provoked the state, since the organization seeks to develop more as a 'franchise' or an ideology than a structure. As economic globalization has facilitated the exponential spread of franchises such as MacDonald fast-food restaurants, al-Qa'ida seeks to develop in a similar way.

While insurgency is not exact science, the fact that several terrorist attacks have already been successfully carried out by 'in-country' bred cells in Europe, such as the London bombings of July 2005 — and planned in the US and Canada — does not lead one to optimism in relation to the success of the US-led 'War on Terror.'[5] If anything, the world is growing increasingly unsafe. The use of violence as a counter-terrorism method can therefore be questioned as a viable option against what amounts more to an emerging *ad hoc* insurgency than a terrorist monolith.

On a more positive note, the motivational strategy of Usama bin Laden did backfire in Iraq with the creation of the al-Qa'ida Mesopotamia movement of Abu Musab al-Zarqawi, a local organization that gave a bad name to its global cousin, especially due to the beheading of Western hostages, a practice that fostered shame, disgust and resentment against al-Qa'ida

---

[5] Recently, terror plots have been dismantled in Canada (June 2006) and England (July 2006) to respectively attack the Canadian Parliament and to introduce and activate liquid explosives on transatlantic flights. Both had been masterminded by individuals of ethnic origin born and raised in Canada and England, hence never having directly suffered the humiliations denounced by Usama bin Laden.

throughout the Muslim world [Brisard 2005]. For once, the insurgency superseded the state in the scale of its horrific methods — an absolute 'no-no' in insurgency practices, thus triggering a backlash in local participation and ideological support.[6] To be added to this is the realization on the part of many Iraqis of all confessions that al-Qa'ida had for its ultimate aim in Iraq the triggering of a civil war.[7] Even though Usama bin Laden ultimately condemned the beheadings, the credibility of his message of every Muslim being a victim of Western oppression was tarnished. While this short-term decrease in popular support for al-Qa'ida is a uniquely tangible positive development in a five-year 'war on terror,' the fact that this was not the direct result of a US-led initiative leads to pessimism in an evaluation of the long-term viability of current violent counter-terrorist initiatives.

3. NONVIOLENCE AND COUNTER-INSURGENCY: AN IMPOSSIBLE MATCH?

If the narrative that opposes Usama bin laden is no longer one of terrorism, can one that is labeled counter-insurgency prove effective in the long-run? Moreover, can counter-insurgency ever become nonviolent? This part will seek to answer these questions in light of the necessity for the West to become aware of how to transform grassroot grievances into a partnership for sustainable peace.

3a Counter-Insurgency as a Viable Alternative to Counter-Terrorism?

What is it with counter-terrorism that brings out the worst in people? The 2003 National Strategy for Combating Terrorism sheds light on this question. In an apparent realization that social ills condone terrorism, it underlines possible causes other than the madness of a few individuals. It even provides a chapter on 'diminish[ing] the underlying conditions that terrorists seek to exploit,' a proposal that appears to be nonviolent at least in its rationale. The conditions listed are 'poverty, deprivation, social disenfranchisement, and unresolved political and regional disputes,' and the solutions advocated are to resolve 'regional disputes, [and] foster economic, social, and political development, market-based economies, good governance, and the rule of law' [NSCT 2003, 22-23].

While these conditions are the same conditions exposed and denounced by Usama bin Laden in his writings, the proposed solutions appear to be different in their nature. Usama bin Laden advocates a global insurgency, and the US seeks to foster democratization, good governance and economic growth. After careful examination of these solutions, one tends to be more dubious in relation to the nonviolent nature of US-based solutions, for they are based on close work with regional allies through the strengthening of weak states and prevention of the re-emergence of terrorism. When translated on the ground, for instance, in the case of Saudi Arabia, an unconditional support for this allied regime leads one to realize that the

---

[6] Unattributable interview with former al-Qa'ida operative in Baghdad, July 2006. The interviewee attributed his departure from the organization to its un-Islamic nature and inhumane acts of cruelty perpetrated against Iraqis as well as foreigners.

[7] Interview with Patrick Cockburn, correspondent for the London Independent, al-Jadriyah, Baghdad, July 2006.

support of a strong rule of law will undeniably lead to additional mass arrests, torture, political repression and corruption.[8] Those are the very same underlying conditions 'that terrorists seek to exploit' and that the US seeks to diminish. Sadly, while the Bush Administration has accurately identified the conditions that foster terrorism in the 2003 National Strategy for Combating Terrorism, its 2006 version does not even mention these and can be identified as a hawkish version of its 2003 counterpart, systematically relying on denouncing old issues such as Weapons of Mass Destruction and ignoring the importance of soft power.[9] Once again, violence for violence is a dead-end solution. If counter-terrorism fails, will counter-insurgency succeed?

Until very recently, counter-insurgency in the US military doctrine has been heavily influenced by counter-terrorism dogma and measures. Post-Saddam Iraq provides an ideal illustration of this. Brigadier Nigel Aylwin-Foster, from the British armed forces, was as an exchange officer serving with US forces in Iraq throughout 2004, and on that occasion observed their counter-insurgency (COIN) tactics. Highly critical of these tactics, he wrote a document in which he pointed out the major shortcomings he had witnessed. Throughout the very critical year of 2004, in the struggle against a growing Iraqi insurgency against the presence of the US-led coalition, the fighting culminated in two sieges of the Sunni city of Fallujah in April and November, and one of Najaf in July-August. The year 2004 can be seen as the most active — insurgency-wise — in post-Saddam Iraq. A decline in the insurgency's focus was observed in 2005 due to the actions of al-Qa'ida Mesopotamia to initiate a civil war between Sunnis and Shi'ites, as well as the development of rifts within different insurgency groups over mostly financial and corruption matters [Hashim 2006].[10]

Aylwin-Foster's worst constructive criticism of COIN practices stems from the idea that, while it excels in conventional combat activities, the US military is not prepared adequately for what it calls Operations Other Than War, that is to say, peacekeeping and effective counter-insurgency missions. Indeed, Aylwin-Foster takes the example of the United States Military Academic at West Point, which only grants COIN the status of an elective in its academic program. More importantly, he asserts that while the firepower of conventional warfare is important, the sheer insensitivity to cultural differences between Iraqis and US personnel 'arguably amounted to institutional racism,' and provoked an escalation in the many grassroot conflicts that pitted coalition soldiers against Iraqis [Aylwin-Foster 2005, 3]. In the case of Fallujah, these cultural insensitivities led to the destruction of more than eighty percent of the city in November 2004 [Fontan 2006]. The fact that US army personnel were told they were facing a terrorist enemy did not place them in an adequate frame of mind to attempt to win the hearts and minds of the Iraqis. Moreover, upon realization that this was becoming a problem, the 'can do attitude' of the army — arguably commendable in itself — made it slow to change the tactical course of its COIN approach away from counter-terrorism.

While an increasing number of US military personnel slowly came to realize the flaws of past COIN tactics, it took the Bush Administration more than three years to re-shape, self-evaluate and reconsider its policy on the subject. This came about after a disastrous electoral

---

[8] A perusal of human rights advocacy organizations' websites such as Human Rights Watch and Amnesty International will inform the reader on the appalling human rights records that this country has acquired.

[9] The 2006 National Strategy for Combating Terrorism is available online: http://www.state.gov/s/ct/rls/wh/71803.htm

[10] Interview with Omar, former insurgent fighter of the Abu Ghraib section of the 'Army of 1920' group, Baghdad, July 2006.

defeat in November 2006 and from calls within the US armed forces for a change of COIN tactics. One can speculate that this reluctance in admitting that another course of action was necessary in relation to COIN in Iraq probably stemmed from the 'war on terror' narrative that had been applied by the Bush Administration since the tragic events of 9-11. After all, if blunt force will defeat terror, why then would one change course in the middle of a war? The answer lies in the crucial differentiation that exists between terror and insurgency.

3b. Better Late than Never: A Re-Evaluation of US Army COIN Tactics

Far form being an ideological monolith, the US army is an organization that at times benefits from an anachronistic sense of democracy, good governance and self-reflection. The sheer number of its personnel makes it possible to observe a microcosm of society, from rich to poor, educated to less educated and politically left to right-wing. While not necessarily widely developed, the characteristics mentioned above make the US army stand out in comparison to other more traditionalist and autocratic armed forces throughout the world. While it is at times reluctant to react to erroneous policy courses of action, in the case of Iraq — partly due to a political realization that admitting to shortcomings would not be politically attractive — two of its brightest and most experienced generals, Dr. David Petraeus of the Army and Jim Mattis of the Marines, wrote a new COIN manual that was released in June 2006. The 241page-document places an emphasis on many nonviolent aspects of COIN, that range from a heavier reliance on human intelligence to a strong emphasis on cultural, political and social sensitivities towards the populations caught in counter-insurgency operations. Human rights violations are condemned throughout the manual as counter-productive and leading to an upsurge of insurgent fighters. The commonly understood equation according to which one dead insurgent leads to ten more insurgents is very accurately explained [Petraeus & Mattis 2006].

More importantly in the context of the 'war on terror,' the manual's innovative strength features an analysis of the driving forces behind an insurgency, such as the importance of popular support and the place that terrorism has in relation to an insurgency. Significantly, all the arguments that are utilized by Usama bin Laden to justify his struggle, such as the humiliation of a people through occupation, political repression, poverty and lack of economic opportunities, are mentioned in this manual.

Should these reflections be utilized in the fight against Usama bin Laden and his ideas, the US might have a chance to defeat him. Despite the appointment in January 2007 of Lieutenant-General Petraeus as the new US ground commander in Iraq, a question remains whether the introduction of a radical change in counter-insurgency strategy comes too late. Moreover, adopting his approach leads to a major political shift that amounts to an admission of complete failure on the part of the current US Administration, a point that will not be lost by the Democratic candidate against his/her Republican counterpart when contesting the forthcoming presidential elections in November 2008.

3c. The Role of Nonviolence in Countering Terrorism

If it is established that counter-insurgency (COIN) needs to be reassessed in light of current developments in Iraq; as well as the 'war on terror' following an analysis of the writings of Usama bin Laden, one might ask how to address these crucial issues in a manner that will not foster their resurgence in the long-term. If counter-terrorism applied to an insurgency does not work, then what does?

During the night of Saturday November 18th 2006, dozens of Palestinians formed a human shield in order to foil an air strike that was planned by the Israeli Defense Forces on the house of an HAMAS official localized in the Northern Gaza strip. It was reported the next day that this initiative did prevent the planned air strike. Two days later, the same type of meeting was organized in and around the house of another HAMAS official.

Organized and promoted by HAMAS supporters, this type of action against the Israeli government was a clear departure of tactics previously and regularly used by the same party, such as suicide operations or violent defiance of Israeli troops. This nonviolent tactic was active in its essence; it mobilized the gathering of individuals; it publicized the defiance of Israeli authority; it impacted both politically and socially on the restructuring of community ties through the sharing of a common political goal; and most importantly, it did not advocate nor represent an act of violence.

The action has the potential to foster the use of more nonviolent tactics among the population of Gaza. In the savagery of the Palestinian-Israeli conflict this tactical action showed that nonviolence can be successful in countering an act of violence that may amount to state-terrorism for some. Nonviolence — a moral philosophy that discards the use of violence in efforts to bring about social or political change — may have different motivations that can stem from ethical to pragmatic concerns [Abu Nimer 2003]. Whether one decides to resort to nonviolence based on moral grounds or on the realization of its practical effectiveness, or for both reasons, the end result is the same. Nonviolence is being used to bring about change.

In relation to COIN in Iraq, or to the war on terror generally, resorting to nonviolence on the part of the US Army and the Bush Administration may derive solely from pragmatic considerations. A careful analysis of the Petraeus and Mattis COIN document illustrates that point. In its 'successful and unsuccessful counter-insurgency operational practices' table, the document asserts that violent practices — such as 'placing priority on killing and capturing the enemy' and 'not engaging the population' — constitute a grave mistake in the US previous tactical approach. Instead, the manual advocates a 'focus on the population, their needs, and security.' Another illustration denounces the ignoring of 'peacetime government processes, including legal procedures,' calling instead for an 'amnesty and rehabilitation for insurgents' and 'expand(ing) and diversify(ing) the police force' [Petraeus & Mattis 2006, 1-24].

While the document was cast in the light of the Iraqi war, it is deemed to 'fill a doctrinal gap' in COIN practices in general [Petraeus & Mattis 2006, foreword]. If the 'war on terror' were shifted to a counter-insurgency mode, then not only could these nonviolent practices be applied to the Usama bin Laden problem, but others such as democratization, good governance and grassroots economic growth could also be introduced in a sustainable manner. Moreover, an awareness of the political, ideological, economic and cultural humiliation — perceived by millions of Muslim around the world — could form the starting point of a comprehensive nonviolent foreign policy within those regions where Usama bin Laden's message resonates the most effectively.

CONCLUSION

On October 12th 2006, Britain's Home Secretary John Reid warned that al-Qa'ida might be winning the war of ideas. The timeliness of this realization can be imputed to the fact that no-one making the political decisions had realized the importance of these ideas until now, let alone the importance of understanding al-Qa'ida as a force striving towards the motivation of a global insurgency against the West. While realizing that counter-terrorism only fuels an insurgency, one must also appreciate that nonviolence and counter-terrorism are not an impossible match, and that nonviolence does not belong to the sole prerogative of the peace movement. Although one starts from the proposition that counter-terrorism is not the answer to the Usama bin Laden problem, it is imperative that a joint initiative to resolve the problem is implemented by all camps. At this stage of the 'war on terror,' the peace movement must make a special effort to reach out to its hitherto declared nemesis, the hawks, to solve a global problem that needs everyone's involvement. Not only do the 'hawks' have the resources to combat a common plague, they have the decisional power that a dissenting group, like the peace studies camp, can only aspire to.

Nonviolent exponents should avoid being indirectly violent in their opposition to the so-called perpetrators of violence. They should include them in their thinking and mandate. Viable nonviolence is already present within the US Administration, in relation to counter-insurgency doctrine, international development and democratization initiatives. The US military and organizations such as the United States Agency for International Development must work jointly in counter-insurgency efforts that respect human dignity and human rights. The capability is possible and the will appears present. Nonviolence starts when the segregation of discourse ends.

It is only upon fully comprehending the futility of counter-terrorism that the message of Usama bin Laden will be defused once and for all. The *Umma* must be made aware that the Western world has understood their malaise and is striving towards equality and the promotion of human dignity for all. On a positive note, it is possible to surmise there are signs that the insurrection of the *Umma* wished by Usama bin Laden will not occur in its projected form. Recent developments in Lebanon, for instance, have elevated Sayeed Hassan Nasrallah, Secretary General of the Lebanese Hezbollah, to the position of champion of the Muslim rights against Western oppression. He represents a potentially strong competitor for winning the hearts and minds of the *Umma* and undermining the influence of al-Qa'ida. Once again, this positive development was not initiated by conventional violent counter-terrorist measures.

ACKNOWLEDGEMENTS

Victoria Fontan is the Director of Academic Development and Assistant Professor of Peace and Conflict Studies at the University for Peace, Costa Rica. She is researching on the development of terrorism and political violence in post-conflict areas, more specifically on humiliation and social polarizations. She worked as a journalist in Iraq and carried out field research in Lebanon, the Spanish Basque country, and more recently post-Saddam Iraq where she was an Assistant Professor of Conflict Resolution, Salahaddin University, Erbil, Iraq. Send any correspondence to <vfontan@upeace.org>

REFERENCES

Abu-Nimer, M. (2003). *Nonviolence and Peace Building in Islam: Theory and Practice.* Tampa: Florida University Press.

Agence France Presse. (2006a). 'Evolution of Crude Oil Prices Since 1970,' wire report, Paris, April 23rd; available online on September 21st 2006, *http://www.lebanonwire.com/0604MLN/06042303MAF.asp.*

Agence France Presse. (2006b). 'British Minister Warns Al-Qa'ida Is Winning War of Ideas,' wire report, London, October 21st, available online on November 20th 2006, *http://news.yahoo.com/s/afp/20061022/wl_afp/britainattackspolitics.*

Associated Press. (2001). *'White House Apologizes for Using "Crusade" to Describe War on Terrorism,'* available online, September 21st 2006, *http://www.freerepublic.com/focus/f-news/526718/posts.*

Aylwin-Foster, N. (2005). 'Changing the Army for Counterinsurgency Operations.' *Military Review*, Fort Leavenworth, (November-December).

Bird, S. E. (2002). 'Taking It Personally: Supermarket Tabloids after September 11th.' In B. Zelizer & S. Allan (Eds.), *Journalism After September 11*. London: Routledge.

British Broadcasting Corporation. (2006). 'Gazans Gather to Foil Airstrike,' available online, November 20th 2006, http://news.bbc.co.uk/2/hi/middle_east/6164666.stm.

Brisard, J.-C. (2005). Zarkaoui : *Le Nouveau Visage d'al-Qa'ida.* Paris: Fayard.

Bucaille, L. (1998). *Gaza: La Violence de la Paix.* Paris: Presses de la Fondation Narionale de Sciences Politiques.

Bush, G. W. (2001). 'Remarks by the President Upon Arrival,' available online, September 21st 2006. *http://www.whitehouse.gov/news/releases/2001/09/20010916-2.html.*

Cable News Network. (2000). 'Poll: 1 in 4 Americans Believe U.S. Was Safer Before 9/11,' available online, September 21st 2006, *http://www.cnn.com/2006/US/08/23/terror.poll/index.html.*

Fontan, V. 2006. 'Polarization Between Occupier and Occupied in Post-Saddam Iraq: Humiliation and the Formation of Political Violence.' *Terrorism and Political Violence*, 18 (Spring 2006), 217-238.

Ghoussoub, M. & Sinclair-Webb, E. (Eds.). (2006). *Imagined Masculinities: Male Identity and Culture in the Modern Middle East.* London: Saqi Essentials.

Hashim, A. S. (2006). *Insurgency and Counter-Insurgency in Iraq.* Ithaca: Cornell University Press.

Karim, H. H. (2002). 'Making Sense of the "Islamic Peril": Journalism as Cultural Practice.' In B. Zelizer & S. Allan (Eds.), *Journalism After September 11*. London: Routledge.

Krueger, A. B. & Laitin, D. D. (2004). '"Misunderestimating" Terrorism.' *Foreign Affairs*, 83 (45), September-October.

Laden (bin), U. (1995). 'The Invasion of Arabia.' In B. Lawrence (Ed.). *Messages to the World: The Statements of Osama bin Laden.* London: Verso (2005).

Laden (bin), U. (1996a). 'Declaration of Jihad.' In B. Lawrence (Ed.). *Messages to the World: The Statements of Osama bin Laden.* London: Verso (2005).

Laden (bin), U. (1996b). 'The Saudi Regime.' In Bruce Lawrence (Ed.). *Messages to the World: The Statements of Osama bin Laden.* London: Verso (2005).

Laden (bin), U. (1997). 'From Somalia to Afghanistan.' In B. Lawrence (Ed.). *Messages to the World: The Statements of Osama bin Laden.* London: Verso (2005).

Laden (bin), U. (1998a). 'The World Islamic Front.' In B. Lawrence (Ed.). *Messages to the World: The Statements of Osama bin Laden.* London: Verso (2005).

Laden (bin), U. (1998b). 'A Muslim Bomb.' In B. Lawrence (Ed.). *Messages to the World: The Statements of Osama bin Laden.* London: Verso (2005).

Laden (bin), U. (2001). 'The Winds of Faith.' In B. Lawrence (Ed.). *Messages to the World: The Statements of Osama bin Laden.* London: Verso (2005).

Lawrence, B. (2005). 'Introduction.' In B. Lawrence (Ed.). *Messages to the World: The Statements of Osama bin Laden* (pp. i-xi). London: Verso.

National Commission on Terrorist Attacks upon the United States. (2004). *The 9/11 Commission Report.* New York: W.W. Norton & Company.

National Strategy for Combating Terrorism. (February 2003), available online on September 21st 2006, *http://www.iwar.org.uk/homesec/resources/counter-terror/national-strategy.htm.*

Petraeus, D. & Mattis, J. (2006). 'Counterinsurgency (Final Draft –Not for Implementation).' Headquarters, Department of the Army, United States of America, available online on September 21st 2006, *http://www.fas.org/irp/doddir/army/fm3-24fd.pdf#search=%22* Counterinsurgency%20Petraeus%20final%20draft%22.

Taber, R. (2002). *The War of the Flea: The Classic Study of Guerilla Warfare.* Washington, DC: Potomac Books.

Wilkinson, P. (2001). *Terrorism Versus Democracy: The Liberal State Response* (chapters 1 and 2, pp. 1-40). London: Frank Cass.

In: Nonviolence: An Alternative for Defeating...
Editors: S. Ram and R. Summy, pp. 107-129

ISBN: 978-1-60021-812-5

Chapter 7

TERRORISM, GENDER AND NONVIOLENT ISLAM: THE CASE OF ERITREA

Christine Mason

ABSTRACT

Terrorism and Islam have a long history of association. Even before September 11th, terrorism was frequently linked by the press, foreign governments and academics alike, to Islamic practices and Muslims in general. Post September 11th, the linkage has become something of a global obsession, as the fear of communism is swiftly replaced with the fear of Islamic terrorism. This chapter seeks to demystify some of this linkage by examining nonviolent Islamic responses to terrorism by Muslim women. In order to do so, the case of Eritrea will be used.

The Eritrean case study examines the nonviolent movement led by female members of the Eritrean Liberation Front (ELF). The ELF fought from 1961-1991 against the acts of Ethiopian terrorism that swept Eritrea in the former's bid to crush the Eritrean anti-colonial rebellion. In response, many Muslim ELF women drew upon Islamic principles and practices to create a movement of Islamic nonviolence. Reinterpreting concepts such as *jihad* (holy struggle) and *jitihad* (reinterpretation of Islamic scripts), ELF women resisted Ethiopian terrorist actions through nonviolent acts. These acts varied from protests to refusals to comply and consent to Ethiopian demands. In the face of terrorist acts such as bombings, mass rape, destruction of houses and fields, women stood firm in their nonviolent responses and in doing so challenged their male compatriots in the ELF who desired violent responses.

The war eventually ceased with Eritrean victory and independence, though largely due to the other, violently orientated movement, the Eritrean People's Liberation Front (EPLF). In this Front, however, women were frontline fighters and made up 30% of the armed forces. Yet, the impact of pre-independence violence in post-conflict Eritrea is palpable for women. It is argued in this chapter that those women who fought nonviolently garnered more respect and acceptance from the Eritrean community than those women who fought in combat. This lends support to the idea that nonviolence has a strong feminist component that can benefit women in long term peacebuilding in post-terrorist situations.

INTRODUCTION

The world watched in horror at the September 11 destruction of the World Trade Center, two bombings in Bali, and a series of attacks in London and Spain. These attacks were carried out by Islamic extremists, yet it leads people to believe that all Muslims are terrorists and that Islam itself is inherently violent. However, terror comes in many forms and so does the interpretation and use of Islam in conflict. This chapter is focusing on a different kind of terror: thirty years (1961-1991) of ghastly war wreaked upon Eritrea by Ethiopia as the former struggled for independence. More specifically, it analyzes the role and approach of women to this state terror within the two major liberation fronts that fought Ethiopia: the Eritrean Liberation Front (ELF) and its successor, the Eritrean People's Liberation Front (EPLF). One of the significant differences between these two Fronts is that in the ELF, women were largely of the Muslim faith, very rarely entered armed combat, and practiced various strategies of nonviolence against Ethiopian oppression. By contrast, the EPLF encouraged women to fight and participate in all forms of the armed conflict with up to 35% in the frontlines alone. Although many were Christians, there were also some Muslim female fighters who later joined the ranks as part of the ELPF's policy of 'uniting' all Eritreans in combat. This chapter compares the violent and nonviolent roles that existed in each Front, acknowledging that the dichotomy of violence/nonviolence is frequently blurred for various reasons. It examines the impact this had upon women socially and spiritually and especially in the post-war period. It asks the question: does it make a difference socially if women bear arms compared to opting for nonviolent resistance?

The chapter is divided into four sections. The first will examine two issues: the discourse of women and nonviolence, and then the discourse of Islam and nonviolence and how this ties into thoughts about women. The second section will examine the ELF and explore the nonviolent tactics of various women and why they undertook such an approach. This is followed by the third section which moves onto an exploration of the EPLF where women participated as active combatants against Ethiopian terror. Finally, the last section examines what happened to women from the ELF and EPLF once the war was over and assesses whether or not violent or nonviolent resistance had any ramifications upon them socially.

A. GENDER, NONVIOLENCE AND ISLAM

I. Gender Troubles

Sadly, nonviolence theorists have tended to be men [Holmes 1990, 80]. However, a small number of women authors, such as Boulding [1995], Deming [1982], Cook and Kirk [1984], The Feminism and Nonviolence Study Group [1983] and McAllister [1982], have added vital theoretical contributions to the nonviolence debate. They point out that women activists have frequently left the nonviolence movement since it directly conflicted with their own commitments to feminism. As Meyerding [1982, 6-7] explains,

> feminists have found it necessary to *un*become members of nonviolent groups, movements and/or communities…[O]n the whole, nonviolent men have not been eager to

study or accept feminist analysis nor to make the changes in their lives and work which a commitment to feminism would demand.

Nonviolent activists have described how they were frequently relegated to traditionally perceived 'female tasks' within nonviolent movements such as typing, taking minutes, washing and cooking for the collective and so forth [McAllister 1982].

Writers and activists in the tradition of feminist nonviolence have pointed out that most of the key male historical nonviolent theorists and activists, such as de la Boètie, Thoreau, and Tolstoy, excluded women not only from their theoretical writings but also from nonviolent protest outside the domestic sphere. The de la Boètian tradition 'further strengthened a model of dissent based on the image of a male revolutionary riding towards freedom while ignoring and even entrenching the patriarchal social order that made this heroic fight possible' [Bleiker 2000, 147]. Tolstoy argued that women's rights were 'nonsense' and that women were naturally inferior to men, serving only as necessary breeders for humanity [Bleiker 2000, 152]. To these ends, he treated his own wife, Sofia, as a domestic slave, as documented in her diaries [Tolstaia 1985].

These male pioneers of nonviolence display clear misogyny towards women. More complex are the cases of Gandhi and Sharp. Gandhi did a great deal to improve the rights of women in India and included them in his nonviolent resistance to British rule. Gandhi's principles of *satyagraha* (adherence to truth) and *ahimsa* (nonviolence) were for all peoples, as were his calls for suffering and self-sacrifice. He was clear in his directives, '[o]f all the evils of men…none is as degrading as the abuse of…the female sex' [Gandhi cited in Fisher 1962, 246]. However his own personal life and many of his writings are plagued with inconsistencies towards women and nonviolence. For example, Gandhi supported the notion of suicide for women who had been sexually assaulted since, he argued, that 'if women find their chastity is in danger of being violated, they must develop courage enough to die rather than yield to the brute in man' [*Harijan*, 31 December 1938]. He regularly structured his nonviolent protests to enforce gender segregation and divisions, relegating women to more 'domestic' activities [Shivers 1982, 182-194]. Women were intended to shut shops, continue weaving and avoid marches, lest it hindered the demonstration by their 'feminine' presence.

More complexly, his own personal life was riddled with contradictions. He had been married at 13 to Kasturbai and in his autobiography, explained detailed accounts of extreme jealousy, anger and violence towards her, to the point where he insisted for a long period that she stay confined to their house. He noted he was 'forever on the look-out regarding her movements, and therefore she could not go anywhere without my permission' [Gandhi 1993, 12]. This led to frequent struggles and fights [Gandhi 1993, 12-13] and he confessed that he frequently beat his wife. One pertinent example is an issue that arose between them about cleaning chamber pots, which she detested and frequently opposed in tears. During one such event Gandhi explains:

> I was far from being satisfied by her merely carrying the pot. I would have her do it cheerfully. So I said, raising my voice: 'I will not stand this nonsense in my house.' The words pierced her like an arrow. She shouted back: 'Keep your house to yourself and let me go.' I forgot myself, and the spring of compassion dried up in me. I caught her by the hand, dragged the helpless woman to the gate…and proceeded to open it with the intention of pushing her out. The tears were running down her face in torrents, and she cried: 'Have you no sense of shame? Must you so far forget yourself? Where am I to go?

I have no parents or relatives here to harbor me. Being your wife, you think I must put up with your cuffs and kicks?'...I put on a brave face but was really ashamed and shut the gate. If my wife could not leave me neither could I leave her [Gandhi 1993, 277-278].

Gandhi fought his own inner demons in an attempt to reach the truth and meditated for days on his actions and thoughts. Eventually, he saw lust and commitment to his family as hindering this higher goal and took a life long vow of celibacy under *brahmacharya*. He explained this concept of celibacy in the following way: 'A true *brahmachari* will not even dream of satisfying the fleshy appetite, and until he is in that condition, he has a great deal of ground to cover [Gandhi 1993, 317]. Certain events took place that led many, especially female writers in the field, to question his personal behavior and desires. Of particular note was his practice, utilized to 'reinforce' and 'test' his chastity, by sleeping in a room with naked female followers to challenge his own willpower and commitment to *brahmacharya*. Gandhi [cited in Wolpert 2002, 17] explained the practice in the following way:

One who never has lustful intention, who by constant attendance upon God, has become capable of lying naked with naked women, however beautiful they may be, without being in any manner whatsoever sexually excited. Such a person should be incapable of lying, incapable of intending doing harm to a single man or woman, free from anger and malice and detached.

The comments above in no way undervalue the valuable life and literature of Gandhi; it simply explains a more complex vision of Gandhi as a person and a writer in his struggle to achieve nonviolence, viewed through a nonviolent feminist lens.

Sharp's work, while remaining instructive for nonviolent activists, and free from the questions about his own personal behavior, is also questionable from a nonviolent feminist perspective. Sharp [1973, 65] divides society into rulers and subjects with power deriving purely from the consent of the subject. It therefore follows that withdrawal of consent is the central mechanism for addressing oppression in an active, nonviolent way. However, the social practices that facilitate male domination over women do not exist in terms of a ruler/subject dynamic. Thus, 'without any analysis of patriarchy as a structured set of social relations which can hardly be "turned off" by the simple withdrawal of consent, Sharp does not provide the basis for studying this power dynamic' [Martin 1989, 216]. Generally absent in Sharp's work is the complicated notion of consent [Pateman, 1980, 1988; McGuiness, 1993; Mason, 2001]. 'Women are not fully constituted individuals in civil society and thus they do not necessarily have consent at their disposal' [Pateman cited in McGuiness 1993, 104].

II. Islam, Nonviolence and Gender

Ever since the end of the Cold War Islam has become the specter of evil in many people's eyes [Esposito, 1992; Said, 1981]. It is associated with '*erhab* (terror/terrorism), *jihad* (struggle), *kafir* (heretics/nonbelievers), *shaheed* (martyrdom) and the repression of women (through such means as *purdah* (seclusion), honor killings, female circumcision and so forth.[1] However, many people know very little about Islam, the variegations of interpretation of Islam globally, its discursive variants and key religious issues deriving from *al-Qu'ran, al-Hadith* and the *Sunnat*. Many therefore conclude that Islam and nonviolence are mutually exclusive, without allowing for a more complex view of Muslims and Islam beyond simplistic interpretations of notions such as *jihad* (frequently translated incorrectly into English as 'Holy War'), terrorism and violence for example [Partner, 1997]. Yet, Islam is far more complex than this and prominent Islamic scholars argue that to solve the demonization of Islam and conflict that is arising between faiths, all peoples need extensive knowledge of Islam and the strength to have open minds [Said 2000 and 2001]. As Abdalla [2001/2002, 152] argues, 'historical misuses, abuses and misinterpretations of Islamic sources have diluted the very strong emphasis on justice, equality and freedom in Islam as a value system.' To delve back in history, all Muslims know that the Prophet Muhammad himself practiced nonviolence, tolerance and kindness when others maltreated him [USIP 2002, 2].

Within the broad edicts and traditions of Islam are concepts of nonviolence. There is no Arabic equivalent to the English term 'nonviolence', some scholars associate it with the word *salam* (peace), yet still find it 'foreign' [Salleh, 2001, 109]. There are perhaps clearer edicts on violence: 'From the definition of violence and the standards set by Islam, immediately it can be said that violence is sinful and forbidden. It is possible for a Muslim to restrain acts of violence if his [sic] behavior follows the principles of Islam.' [Salleh 2001, 110].

In interviews with Eritrean women they made it clear they were talking about the same concept by describing their adherence to practicing *la 'unf* (literally being 'not violent') and *la mushta* (not killing). Many quoted central tenets of *al-Qur'an* and *al-hadith* such as the following:

- And if any one saved a life,
- It would be as if he saved
- The life of the whole people [*Al-Qur'an, Surah* 5, *Ayat* 32].

This is how many Eritrean Muslim women resisted the terror of the Ethiopians, by being 'not violent' and 'not killing.' It would not be part of their culture and duty as Muslims to do otherwise. This will become apparent when we examine the two liberation fronts in Eritrea and the role of women against Ethiopian terrorism.

B. The Case of Eritrea: The Eritrean Liberation Front

Eritrea is a small poor state in the Horn of Africa. It is a state defined by roughly nine ethnic groups and two religions, Islam and Coptic Christianity. It also has two distinct geographical zones: the highland regions, where the capital Asmara is, and the Lowland regions. Having being colonized by Italy in 1890 it was later federated to Ethiopia by the United Nations after the end of World War Two. This Federation was a bitter one. As a result, Eritrea fought a bloody war for independence from Ethiopia from 1961-1991, finally emerging victoriously. The path to this victory is enshrined in the activities of two liberation

---

[1] For clear translations and explanations of Arabic and Islamic terms, see Nicholas Awde [2000].

movements[2]: first, the Eritrean Liberation Front (ELF) and second the Eritrean Peoples Liberation Front, which was the last Front standing during the 1991 victory and went on to become the Government, the People's Front for Democracy and Justice (PFDJ).

I. The Eritrean Liberation Front

This section of the chapter examines the role of women in both the first and second stages of the ELF's liberation struggle. The first stage, which relies heavily on alternative forms of female resistance and empowerment, is discussed in terms of three general strands of female participation in the struggle: a) The role of educated, exiled women who sought inclusion into the ELF on formal grounds; b) The undertakings of urban women within Eritrea, who possessed more tenuous links to the ELF than the previously mentioned group, but still provided active nonviolent resistance to Ethiopian rule, and c) The participation of predominantly rural women in nonviolent struggle who lived within the ethno-territorial zones demarcated by the ELF. The second stage briefly examines the period when a small number of women joined the fighting ranks of the ELF, and the impact this had on the Front and the women themselves.

A dominant discourse emphasizes the normative unity of African national liberation movements, linking this directly to emancipation from the perceived vicissitudes of 'difference' [Davidson, 1969, 1972; Ottaway and Ottaway, 1980; Young, 1982]. The ELF presents a troubling anomaly to these studies. Because it is an anomaly it has been consistently discredited, maligned and obscured, preventing serious analysis to this date. The ELF is predominantly portrayed as a feudal, ethnically divided and traditional body that unequivocally suppressed the rights of women. Commentators frequently focus on the largely Muslim composition of the ELF [Campbell, 1971; Gottesman, 1998], erroneously arguing that a large Muslim membership generated purely regressive or 'fundamentalist' beliefs.[3] Essentially, this approach perceives the central tenets of Islam as regressive and recalcitrant, with little understanding of the broader, theoretical issues surrounding Islam in a socio-political context [Eikelman and Piscatori 1996].

Most commentaries on the gender implications of the ELF posit that the presence of Islamic overtones in the ELF — stemming from what Wilson describes as a 'traditional semi-feudal culture' [Wilson 1991, 36] — led to the oppression of women. This 'oppression,' it is argued, manifested itself in the form of tradition and not only prevented female emancipation but prohibited them from participating fully in the resistance struggle. The 'women's arm' of the EPLF, the National Union of Eritrean Women (NUEW), for example, later maintained that the ELF espoused a

---

[2] Failed predecessors to the ELF were the Muslim League (ML) and the Muslim League of the Western Lowlands (MLWL). Both were infused with an Islamic ethos and imagined an Eritrean nation from this perspective. This was followed by another group, The Eritrean Liberation movement (ELM), which also failed to make any head way against the Ethiopian encroachment.

[3] I use the term 'fundamentalist' because it is the term employed by others in reference to the ELF and Islam and later the ISM. However, I find it an inaccurate and unhelpful term that is often used in conjunction with notions of an 'Islamic threat.' It is also too narrow to describe the diversity of Islamic thought in the ELF and ISM. I therefore direct readers to discussion of the term 'Islamism' which will be employed at times in this chapter: O. Roy [1994]; For an important commentary on Islam as a 'threat,' see J. Esposito [1992].

women-denigrating reactionary ideology, [and] prohibited them from performing their revolutionary duties... the participation of women in the armed struggle was thus greatly discouraged and limited until the 1970s, [However they were] active in preparing food for the fighters, propounding revolutionary music and other useful, even if *subordinate roles* (collecting and passing on to the Front information on enemy movements etc.) [author's emphasis] [NEUW, n.d.].

It is a view that is still held by the NUEW today as the NUEW president Luul Gebre-ab told me in early 1999:

In ELF villages, women prepared food but they were not allowed to join the ELF, not in armed struggle. They were therefore not allowed to fully develop and participate, leaving them trapped by traditional roles.

This is a revealing conversation, as it pinpoints the central issue of this chapter: resistance in the context of national liberation is understood in terms of militarized female equality within national liberation movements. Nonviolent resistance and refusal to take up arms was simply not considered 'resistance'. These women were viewed as weak and passive, allowing terrorism to dominate them while they failed to resist. More specifically, if a struggle is being waged, many commentators posit that women must 'fight' equally in order to be genuinely equal — therefore it assumes that an unarmed and non-combatant female is not 'fully liberated.' Examples of this discourse, are found in a great deal of the literature discussing the liberation struggles in Zimbabwe, Namibia, South Africa, Angola and Mozambique. Struggles in these regions have tended to highlight the 'equal' roles of men and women and downplay or overlook sexual abuse and other shortcomings within the liberation fronts [Bernstein 1994, 149]. Additionally, the less lauded nonviolent roles are obscured and underrated. Thus, a two-pronged process is taking place — one that undervalues nonviolent resistance and at the same time fails to examine detrimental activity occurring within the combatant sector [Cock 1991; Schwartz 1987].

In the case of Eritrea, resistance as a general strategy for liberation underwent a serious modification. The ELF emphasized female nonviolent resistance within the traditional and domestic spheres and through the nonviolent aspects of Islam. This approach also has much to offer in the realm of female liberation, as the interviews and discussions below demonstrate.

II. The ELF, Women and Resistance

As explained above, there were two main phases for women in the ELF. To put all these discussions in context, we will begin with an analysis of formal feminist nationalism in the first stage of ELF development (1961-1971).

'Formal' Feminist Nationalism in the First Stage of the ELF

The ELF germinated in an environment that included educated Eritrean women, particularly in Cairo. Amna Malikeen[4] and Zahra Jaber are representative of Eritrean women who became active in the ELF during this period. As a student, Amna was greatly influenced by the secular political developments taking place in Cairo as well as revolutions elsewhere in Africa and the Middle East [Author's Interview, Melbourne, Australia, 1999]. Egyptian feminists, such as Aminah al-Sa'id and other Arab and African revolutionaries such as Jamila Buhrayd (Algerian), were viewed with a great deal of respect [Author's Interview, Kaifa Hussein, Cairo activist during the early 1960s, Cairo, 1998]. Amna and Zahra, as with many of the educated, exiled female members of the ELF were Muslims, but Islam was not necessarily central to their quest. As one informant from the same era described the situation:

> We were educated and free during those days. I didn't wear the veil, there was no need. I was a revolutionary! [Author's Interview, M.I, Keren, Eritrea, 1998].

At first, in the early 1960s, women were members of the ELF but not part of its organizational structure. The 1965 ELF National Congress, in many respects, highlighted the absence of women from the ELF platform. Women were rarely mentioned and all the ELF office-bearers were male. Quite a few of the exiled, educated Eritrean women felt this was unrepresentative of Eritrea and in need of redress:

> There were women who were educated, like the men were, and they were aware of the liberation issues...but these women weren't included in the ranks of the ELF, well, not formally. Women had to take a stand to be included. [Author's Interview, Suad, Tessenei, Eritrea, 1999].

Part of a program to address the 'woman question' was the July 1967 establishment of the Cairo Branch of the General Union of Eritrean Women[5] (CB-GUEW). An active group of female students, including Amna and Zahra, who had already been keenly following the events and discussions of the ELF, were responsible for forming the CB-GUEW. It contained both secularly orientated women as well as Islamic feminists. Tension was minimal as the main cause was nonviolently putting the Eritrean question onto the world agenda. It focused on international support and publicity for the Eritrean cause. Members wrote articles for foreign publications [Author's Interview, M.I.L., Cairo, 1998], and visited countries such as Germany, Syria, Jordan, Iraq and Sudan to give presentations concerning the Eritrean struggle for independence and the status of women in Eritrea under Ethiopian terror. They highlighted mass rape by Ethiopian soldiers, sexual harassment, torture and the destruction of villages and infrastructure. This approach was largely to publicize the hardships and injustices of the war, especially its impact upon women, and also to secure foreign scholarships and training for Eritrean women. Through this, women became more directly involved in the ELF, with, for example, medical personnel trained in Iraq subsequently joining the medical division of the Front [GUEW, n.d.].

---

[4] Amna, for example, attended Halwan Boarding School in Cairo for her secondary studies and latter attained a degree in Social Work from Cairo University.

[5] The terminology used to describe the organization is misleading as by referring to it as a 'branch' implies there was another, central body, which there was not.

This small group of women who formed and publicized the CB-GUEW were addressing more than Ethiopian oppression. Many male members of the ELF did not approve of women being involved directly in the national struggle. The CB-GUEW believed that the ELF was a 'front' to be fought in its own right. The CB-GUEW argued that it constantly participated as much as it could in the national struggle but always 'in the face of the leadership's backward mentality [...] which found its manifestation in the Supreme Council [of the ELF]'[GUEW, n.d.]. With tension rising between male and female activists, the CB-GUEW needed to decide *how* it would work with men or at least in relation to them:

> We could not separate ourselves from men but at the same time, we were opposed to some of their ideas about women. We all wanted a free Eritrea, but the issue of 'free women,' be they Muslim or Christian, was controversial. It took many years to discuss and deal with these issues and women themselves were divided. Some, not many, wanted radical, secular feminism, others wanted to work within Eritrean culture and follow more religious Islamic lines. This second group was most influential and it was an approach accepted by the ELF more generally [Author's Interview, Zeinab, Keren, 1999].

It was at this juncture that many Eritrean Islamic feminists voiced their opinions strongly. By reading and reinterpreting (*ijtihad*) *Al-Qur'an*, many argued that violence was not necessary for Eritrean resistance. Many believed it was the antithesis of Islam and that terrorism must be fought *la 'unf* (without violence). They pointed out that this fitted in perfectly with Eritrean culture and society. As Khadija explained:

> Islam advocates peace. A large problem is the misinterpretation of concepts like *jihad*[6]. There were many of us who were not in favor of *jihad-i-ashgar* (literally: 'lesser jihad' or more violent struggle against others) but *jihad-i-akhbar* (literally 'greater *jihad*': such as struggle through the self for devotion to Allah spiritually). This meant we would resist with our protests, our minds, our bodies — even if it meant suffering sexual assault or death — but we would never resist Ethiopian terror ('*erhab*) through killing or violence [Author's Interview, Khadija, Tessenai, 1999].

I would argue that the ELF women under the auspices of the CB-GUEW did, to a large extent, build upon formations within women's communities and cultures that were pre-existent in Eritrean culture, rather than form new foundations [Hale 1996]. Openings for formal participation appeared in the national struggle, starting with the formation of the CB-GUEW and moving on to more extensive actions inside Eritrea, in urban regions. It is the internal actions of women within Eritrea to which we now turn.

III. Urban Eritrean Women and the Eritrean Struggle

Whispers and rumors concerning the activities of Eritrean women in exile filtered into the main urban centers of Asmara, Keren and Massawa in the early 1960s. As the struggle increased and world attention raised Eritrea's profile, women inside Eritrea became involved in the struggle in numerous ways. With support and encouragement from exiled female activists, a limited number of politicized 'women's cells' were formed in Asmara by 1965.

These cells were dominated primarily by educated women from the middle to upper classes of Eritrean society and tended to be situated in a domestic context. In terms of political affiliations, it is fair to say that some cells were more 'ELF orientated' than others but nearly all were linked to the ELF to some extent and nearly all were Muslim. This may have been through familial ties, with a cell member being related to a fighter at the front or in exile. At other times, cells were established by ELF members and any money raised was filtered back to the ELF through this initial contact. The 'women's cells' grew in number and importance. For those involved, the work was both covert and dangerous.

Underground activity was crucial to the liberation struggle and it was drawn from realms predominantly inhabited and indeed often controlled by Eritrean women. It was an area that could not easily be abandoned due to the presence of children and to do so would draw more attention to the family involved. Although extended families are a prominent part of Eritrean life, Ethiopian officials could become suspicious of a large family that obviously lacked the presence of parents. Due to the complex family issues incumbent upon women, cell activity was in essence an alternative strategy for overt activism. In this way, the household and women's role within it were politicized.

However, these more formal cells were only one of many strategies employed by Eritrean women during this period of the struggle. In Eritrea, routine and ordinary acts became acts of defiance and resistance. The everyday tasks of cooking bread, serving coffee, visiting family and friends were conducted against Ethiopian rule. Thus Jamila explained that by cooking bread and serving coffee to a large group of women — a fairly regular custom in Asmara — women were able to discuss the political situation, pass on news of fighters and relatives and raise money for nonviolent activities:

> A large group would gather, but not so large that it would bring attention, and we could do things together. It wasn't a formal group [an ELF cell] but a way of meeting to find out what was happening. There was so much secrecy outside and people spoke in hushed tones [that is, not in public]. Having *bunn* [coffee] together gave us time to discuss people who were fighting and things that we could do to help. Often, one person would collect money at these gatherings and people would give as much as they could afford. This money would go to help the struggle and we all felt that we were, even in small ways, helping to free Eritrea. We used the money to write pamphlets and smuggle them out and also to help poorer women whose husbands were fighting and they were without income [Author's Interview, Jamila, Sydney, Australia, 2000].

When I asked Jamila about these activities, she specified that she viewed them as not contributing to the killing and in Western terms, this meant she was firm that she was a nonviolent activist. Jamila also linked such activities to Eritrean culture and society. She viewed them as natural 'just as we are naturally peaceful people and will not be forced to take up arms. There are other ways, through Allah, to peacefully resist. We are proof' [Author's Interview, Jamila, Sydney, Australia, 2000]. These types of activities raise important issues about resistance to terror. As a general rule, in Eritrea, 'women and children' were not suspected or interrogated in the early stages of the struggle under the ELF. Nagel observes that in conflict situations

---

[6] For an excellent and comprehensive discussion of the concept and complexities of 'jihad,' see Bonney (2004).

women are less likely to be seen as dangerous or 'up to something', and so can serve as escorts for men or messengers for men who are sequestered inside houses. Similarly women are more successful at recruiting support for nationalist efforts *because they are seen as less threatening and militant*...[Nagel 1998, 253].

I would re-work Nagel's approach.[7] Since women in Eritrea were already pervasive in the domestic sphere, they extended their various roles, building upon them in order to resist Ethiopian domination, and carved their own spaces in respect of Eritrean men at the same time. Women who passed messages, sequestered fighters, fed and nursed them and raised money, support and awareness were extending, therefore, an already existing but limited agency. However, they did not see this as a violent reaction to Ethiopian terror but part of Eritrean culture, society and hospitality. They saw themselves as fighting Ethiopia by caring for male fighters, rather than joining them. The question still remains, however, is this support totally nonviolent? By 'helping' male fighters they inadvertently continued the killing by the ELF cadres. However, I would argue that because they believed it was nonviolent — and that was made clear in interviews — then it was nonviolent resistance to terrorism in their own minds and actions. They rarely linked the two issues, they just believed they were helping the wounded, hungry, and persecuted as Islam requires.

Many ELF women felt a similar disquiet about extending their roles beyond those traditionally occupied by them. For many, this fitted into an Islamic ethos:

In Islam, men and women fulfill different roles, and both are worthy to God. In the ELF, these roles were expanded but the differences between men and women remained the same, each was allocated different tasks according to their own ability. My role was as a nurse not a fighter, and I would never have wanted to fight and nor would it have been my role. My role was to care for anyone, be they Eritrean or Ethiopian. It often allowed us to build trust with captured Ethiopian soldiers and talk them out of the war [Author's Interview, Fatima, Keren, 1999].

It is this subaltern access to power that needs to be emphasized since it eludes so many who write about the role of women within nonviolent national liberation struggles [See seminal work of Spivak 1988]. There is not a clear active/passive dichotomy in relation to women's participation but variants and multifarious loci that provide small glimpses and maneuverings of female (and male) power. Foucault's work on power is instructive in this regard, since he recognized that 'power is exercised from innumerable points' [Foucault 1990, 94]. Nonviolent resistance, then, can be found in many places, often those least suspected or prioritized in the greater scheme of social organization and structure [Abu-Lughod 1985; Foucault 1990].

IV. Women in the *Wiliyat*

Female experiences of the ELF struggle in the rural areas of the *wiliyat* (ELF divided 'zones' of rural Eritrea), where the bulk of Eritrean women reside, were markedly different

---

[7] See also commentary of Taylor [2000] on female terrorists utilizing female roles to make strategic gains.

from those of urban and educated Eritrean women and those in exile. Women were expected to provide support for the roaming ELF cadres and as such, these women interpreted their acts of caring for wounded or hungry men as nonviolent resistance to Ethiopian oppression. This, as Leila explained, was simply part of the hospitality policy to anyone who came to a village, which she believed was inherent in Islam:

> I would collect more wood than usual to build several fires — then the food could be prepared for the fighters, depending on how many there were. Sometimes we looked after only a small amount so that attention would not be directed to the village...we would send another group on to the next small village. I would cook and then prepare supplies that could be taken with them to eat. I saw them as human beings not fighters. I am Muslim, it is our way...[Author's Interview, L.B., Tessenei, 1999]

The ELF attacks greatly embarrassed the Ethiopian government who were keen to banish any threats of 'Balkanization' in their territory. This meant that groups of Ethiopian cadres were sent out to find the 'Eritrean *shifta*' (bandits) and either kill or arrest them. Women were in a vital position. They were often free of suspicion and also able to utilize 'domestic,' everyday acts to assist in the liberation struggle. One informant describes a method used to hide ELF cadres:

> On several occasions we would hide a few fighters because the Ethiopians were looking for them and we knew they would kill them. We would even disguise them and put them inside [wrapped up] like a sick old man. We weren't really suspected at this stage of doing anything, so they [the Ethiopians] didn't really question us very much or even look too hard for fighters. Often we even fed Ethiopian fighters and even talked to them. After all, they were suffering as well...[Author's Interview, A. M., Barentu, 1998].

Women also devised ways to take food and supplies to fighters if they were not in the village. Said one: 'I bundled up some food like a baby under my clothes and found fighters to feed them...I also took traditional medicine and clothes' [Author's Interview, L.A.Z., Keren, 1998].

In summary, this first ('traditional') stage of ELF development fostered the participation of women within their own *ethnie* as primarily carers, service providers and messengers and other resistance acts. It is not disputed that these roles existed within masculinized and violent contexts, but to see such activities *only* in this way obfuscates their value as alternative avenues of female empowerment and invaluable nonviolent extensions of domestic roles for women. As a result, we cannot view the notion of what is and is not 'acceptable' as belonging to the realms of men since many ELF women also used and developed the same indices for behavior and participation. This leaves us with a vital and problematic example of female resistance that forces us to reassess conventional understandings of female power, liberation and nonviolent resistance.

V. Elf Women as Fighters

Very few ELF women fought violently, most seeing it as against Islamic edicts for women and therefore used nonviolence, as described above. However, those that did fight alongside male cadres faced a whole new set of problems besides Ethiopian terrorism. ELF women who did fight or participate in frontline activities were often the subject of male harassment and intimidation:

> There was a problem with high-ranking men seeking sexual relations with women in the ELF. If a woman refused, the man could make trouble for her, often in subtle ways. She might later need new trousers, and because he is her superior, she would apply through him and he would refuse her and then make it look like the refusal was related to a rule, not her sexual rejection of him [Author's Interview, Hidit, Asmara, 1998].

Certain women, faced with this situation, chose to have sexual relations in order to secure supplies or alternative postings. Frequently, this was not viewed by either the women involved or indeed the ELF as sexual assault:

> Although it was not traditional for a Muslim woman to have [sexual] relations prior to marriage, the situation was different during the struggle. I needed medical supplies, serious supplies, and I knew a high-ranking officer could get them for me. I guess, he needed something too, he longed for female company and intimacy. I felt Allah and my family would forgive me under the circumstances. I was really sick at the time and there was no chance of getting to medical supplies myself in time. The officer felt it would improve his morale if we were together, as well as mine, but I really just needed the medicine. So that is how it happened, it wasn't pleasant for me but being sick out there in the heat and dust was worse [Author's Interview, Aisha, Higaz, 1999].

Only if consent was *grossly breached*, and in reality this would have meant male witnesses or evidence of extreme violence towards a woman, would a man have been punished for sexual assault under the ELF. One way of analyzing this is to understand that fighting women were frequently viewed in terms of the notion of *fitna* (temptation, enticement). This was tied to the issue of sexual relations between male and female cadres in the ELF and Islam itself. However, the debate over sexual relations between cadres added to the view held by many ELF men that the women who joined the frontlines transgressed the acceptable boundaries of the 'feminine.' A candid interview with a former ELF male cadre from 1974-79 is important in these terms:

> If you want my opinion, women tempted fate by going to the frontlines with *jebha*[8] If they were Muslim, in particular, they were unveiled, unaccompanied and many of my compatriots thought this meant they were sexually available. No matter how much the ELF developed in its ideals, these views never left the frontlines. Women were taken [by force] in these frontlines, I knew about it but it was not my business to judge and as you know, it is not simple under Islam, since these [sexual] relations outside of marriage are tantamount to adultery. Many of these men were married, so it could have potentially been very serious for them [Author's Interview, Rahim, Melbourne, Australia, 1999].

To men, such as Rahim above, *fitna* explained and often justified the mistreatment of women. However, this is an internally contradictory approach, since as was discussed above, women in ELF controlled villages were also subject to sexual harassment and assault and they were not transgressing boundaries of perceived acceptable behavior. Thus, much of the

---

[8] Jebha is the local Arabic dialectic term for the ELF.

reasoning behind *fitna* serves to legitimate male sexual oppression and was not linked to Islam or ELF policy per se.

With all these complicated concepts and events in mind we now turn to the ELF's successor, the EPLF, which had a huge female fighting force, and did not use nonviolence as resistance to Ethiopian terror and eventually liberated Eritrea.

C. THE CASE OF ERITREA: THE ERITREAN PEOPLE'S LIBERATION FRONT

The EPLF defined itself in opposition to the Eritrean Liberation Front (ELF). The EPLF viewed its predecessor, the ELF, as traditional, feudal, and sectarian, and in contradistinction, deemed itself to be all that was modern, secular and unified. Unlike the ELF, there is a great deal of literature discussing the EPLF, especially its policies, structure and large female composition [See Firebrace and Holland 1984; Houtart 1980; Negash 1997; Iyob 1995; Wilson 1991; Killion 1997; and Zerai 1994]. As discussed in the previous section, very few women occupied rank-and-file positions in the ELF military wings. By contrast, commentators regularly record that women comprised between 30-35% of the EPLF's 'fighters' [Gottesman 1991, 53][9]. Moreover, there is an immense emphasis on women in the EPLF, particularly as combat fighters. Women in the EPLF discourse and in foreign accounts are perceived as the 'same' as men and reputedly equal in all respects during the EPLF struggle.

Additionally, and unlike the ELF's manifestos, there was an entire section in the EPLF's National Democratic Program devoted to women's rights. This section emphasized freeing women from 'domestic confinement;'assuring full *equality* with men in social, political and economic forums; marriage and family law reform; and the eradication of prostitution. The emancipation of women among all the Eritrean nationalities was expected to unify and solidify the fragmented communities of Eritrea.

The EPLF and NUEW argued that if men and women fulfilled the same tasks, equality would be achieved. Unlike the first stage of the ELF, the EPLF recruited women into the liberation struggle as fighters, mechanics, barefoot doctors, radio transmitters, truck drivers and any other task that was traditionally reserved for 'men.' A popular EPLF slogan encapsulated its approach to women and resistance:

Women, let us unite, get organized and armed
Lest we be found weaker than men
Only after this will men believe in our equality [*Eritrea in Struggle* 1978, 4].

This piece equates equality with fighting — an activity traditionally reserved for Eritrean men. Empowerment lay, according to the EPLF, in combat. Like Fanon's interpretation of the liberation of Algerian women [Fanon 1967], the ideology of the EPLF also posited that the liberation of Eritrean women could only evolve through violence. This violence, it was argued, truly transgressed gender boundaries. The emphasis on violent combat was in turn

---

[9] Firebrace and Holland distinguished between female members of the EPLF (30%) and female combatants (15%) [1984, 41].

closely linked to the symbolic nature of death, sacrifice and loyalty to the Eritrean nation. Women were symbols of sacrifice as well as representatives of national modernity. They were 'modern' because they had 'earned' the right to bear arms, and they were symbols of sacrifice because they were literally killed or 'torn apart' in a demonstration of their love for the nation. The fighting woman, as with other female symbols, was no longer 'passive' since '[i]t is her death and annihilation that makes her an active subject' [Rao 1999, 319]. A woman's death or disfigurement allows her to transcend boundaries and enter the male world of martyrdom.

D. THE REALITIES OF WOMEN IN/AT WAR

I. Sexual Harassment and Assault

Women, in becoming fighters, ran the risk of being stereotyped as 'loose' and wanton women. This became a way of defending and justifying male behavior even though ostensibly the EPLF maintained that men and women were equal, and many female ex-fighters have perpetuated this discourse [See Egensteiner 1995 and Wilson 1991]. It was apparent through my own research that the NUEW also perpetuates this approach and does not wish to discuss issues of sexual improprieties or misconduct against women.

Within the camps, as well as the frontlines, sexual harassment and assault, as with the ELF female fighters, took place. Within the ELF, there were fewer female cadres and such incidents were less frequent. Additionally, there was a greater segregation and division of revolutionary duties within the ELF, meaning that fighting remained predominantly in the male domain. In the EPLF, women occupied many more positions and as a result their interaction was far greater and in contradistinction to the 'traditional' roles of women in Eritrean history. The simple presence of women fulfilled an erotic fantasy for many male cadres:

> Most of my life, women were a separate entity to men — then suddenly [in the field], they were everywhere. They weren't like women at home, they were dressed in uniform and using weapons, smoking cigarettes, drinking *sewa* [alcoholic beverage] and often having [sexual] relations with men. It was like a different world, a fantastic world! [Author's Interview, Tekle, Massawa, 1998].

What Tekle was describing was a sense of the extraordinary. In the struggle, unusual measures were called for and to many male cadres, it was almost surreal. Tekle's words exemplify Degroot's fears:

> It is widely assumed that war is erotic. The precariousness of wartime life renders morality irrelevant. Young women, removed from parental control, and aroused by a range of erotic stimuli (danger, uniforms, guns, alcohol), offer themselves willingly to randy warriors. Or so it seems [Degroot 2000, 100-119].

Women in Eritrea and elsewhere were often perceived as promiscuous and therefore deserving of any untoward advances or greater violations that took place. Women who were sexually harassed or assaulted were, at times, viewed as the source of the problem in the

EPLF — it was easier for the victims to be labeled — 'they were too promiscuous,' 'too carefree' and 'too immoral' and this led to the incidents [Enloe 2000, 108-152].

Some male EPLF members convinced themselves such sexual violence against women was not happening. To admit it was occurring and was not due to any digression on the part of the victim was to admit that major gender problems and inequalities existed within the EPLF. Instead, there was a tendency to deny, and blame the victims.

II. The Reform and Strategic Use of Marriage

The issue of sexual relations was central to the EPLF. Initially a strict rule of celibacy was enforced among fighters. By 1977, however, the EPLF Marriage Law was promulgated advocating 'new democratic marriage' based on free choice, monogamy and equality of rights [Silkin 1989, 147-163]. As a result, polygamy, concubinage, child betrothals and the dowry were abolished on paper. More importantly, intimate knowledge of an intended partner was deemed central to informed consent to marriage.

More specifically, in order to truly undermine notions of 'family alliance' the EPLF actively sought to 'undermine the customary practice of marrying within one's ethnic, religious and social group' [Silkin 1989, 155]. Cross-ethnic marriages were therefore encouraged in an attempt to foster greater unity and a sense of 'Eritrean' identity as opposed to an allegiance to one's own *ethnie*.

However, this policy never stretched far beyond the fighter community. In fact, suggestions of cross-ethnic marriages 'were viewed with grave suspicion by those living in the liberated areas. Initiatives as radical as these [were not] ...carried forward into post-war society. Thus no mention is made in government documents' [Gruber 1998, 14]. In fact the curious disquiet surrounding the EPLF's marital reforms is at least partly do to the failure of the cross-ethnic program. While it would be fallacious to suggest that all cross-cultural marriages failed, it would be equally myopic to assume most succeeded.

As Gruber points out, the high divorce rate among ex-fighters (the main group involved in cross-ethnic marriage) remains 'unverified' and unresearched by the current government [Gruber 1998, 14]. It is likely the issue will continue to haunt the government for years to come.

E. 'FREE ERITREA' AND THE AFTERMATH FOR WOMEN

I. Post-Liberation for Elf Women

Women who were nonviolent participants in the ELF have faced different challenges in the liberated era, and it is interesting to assess these experiences by comparison to many women from the EPLF that will be detailed below. As explained, women fell into two broad groups in the ELF, the educated elite and the more traditionally focused rural majority.

The first group of educated elite women took various paths. Many, who had been abroad during parts of the struggle to raise awareness of the war and protest, migrated permanently to different countries for a variety of reasons. For example, many of these women had spent a long time campaigning in countries such as the United States and Australia and in Europe and had come to 'know' these new cultures and view the possibility of a new and better life outside of Eritrea for themselves and their families. Amna Malikeen, for example, moved to Australia, undertook higher education and secured well paid employment. This does not mean she stopped contributing to Eritrea. She continues to assist other Eritreans who move to Australia and refugees from the Horn of Africa. She also sustains her own family members remaining in Eritrea with financial sustenance they would not otherwise have, covering education, food and housing. Of those who stayed in Eritrea, a number of well known women went into business and other public service related positions. Examples known to the author are former elite ELF women now involved with family import companies and small businesses in Asmara, Keren and the port town of Massawa; employed by the various airline companies that fly into and out of Asmara; engaged in teaching; and working in medical fields and so forth. However, only a few women secured high positions within the new Government, the most prominent being Zahra Jaber who went on to become the Mayor of the city of Keren, the second biggest urban region in Eritrea. Also evident were two women [who wish to remain anonymous] who went to work for the NUEW, an arm that is part of, and closely monitored by, the current authoritarian government.

What is important overall is the respect and quality of lives these women lead after concluding their roles as nonviolent protesters and activists against Ethiopian terrorism. They are rarely, if ever, criticized for their roles by their families and friends. However, the main opposition they face, as with male ELF cadres, is persecution from the government, which is dominated by the former EPLF leaders. It is well known that most of the women spoken about above would not readily reveal they used to work for the ELF. As Rahima explained to me:

> I can talk to you because I trust you and you are not from the government. I really am happy in Eritrea, especially with our freedom, but I know I hide the fact I used to work for the ELF, especially in Germany. I also did a lot of underground work in Asmara at the beginning to motivate other women to oppose Ethiopian rule as well. However, the ELF and EPLF went to war, a civil war, as you know and the EPLF won and then it won the battle against Ethiopia, despite our hard work. So even now, we do not talk about the ELF. This saddens me greatly. However, I have a good life and a good job; I just do not talk about my past and neither does my family [Author's Interview, Asmara, 1999].

The second group of ELF women, the more traditional rural segments, tends to feel less disempowered and frustrated by the current political climate in Eritrea. Frequently, they distinguish themselves from the first group:

> Women who contributed nonviolently in the landed areas against Ethiopia are not so obsessed by being included in the government and politics generally. They are happy with their lives and their relationship with Allah. For many they feel closer spiritually because they did not harm or kill anyone, like the EPLF women did. They do not expect anything from the government and are happy the fighting is over and that they contributed in their own small way. Many women simply carry on with daily activities [Author's Interview, Amina, Afabet, 1998].

These same women are also inclined to see their social status as less affected by the war effort:

It is funny how things evolve. When I look at what is happening to some of those women who fought in the EPLF, I am glad I didn't select that option. We are more secure and protected now because we didn't fight. Society continues as we never left it and so we continue our lives as before but with more pride...[Author's interview, L.D., Keren, 1998].

Overall, ELF women fought Ethiopian terrorism nonviolently. The elite women did so differently; without the deep links to Islamic thought and principles that the rural based women demonstrated during this research. However, the outcome was largely the same in one aspect: their nonviolent resistance meant that the elite women from the ELF resistance movement integrated back into their families and society without the immense problems we are going to explore with relation to the women from the EPLF. However, their integration into society is very different to the relationship they have with the current Eritrean government. They are largely ostracized by the government and frequently do not talk about the ELF or deny any past history with the movement to protect themselves and their families [Connell 2005].

By contrast the rural women who participated nonviolently in the ELF resistance to Ethiopian terrorism did so largely based on Islamic principles and the traditional social customs of Eritrean society. As a result, this led to little or no negative ramifications for them, both during and after the war. They calmly continued their work and daily lives without great interference. They have a far greater marriage success rate since most did not leave the villages and waited for their husbands to return. Husbands and families were impressed at their resolve to work nonviolently in the spirit of Islam. Overall, Islam was a binding and sacred bond as it allowed the horrors of the war to be replaced by normality, not continued violence.

II. Post-Liberation for EPLF Women

Concurrently, whilst all nine *ethnie* were posited as equals, as were all Eritrean men and women, irrespective of ethnic, regional or religious differences by the new government, reality differs drastically for many of the former female fighters of the EPLF. This narrative of equality fails to recognize the persistent sexual harassment, assault, low ranking and sexualized context in which EPLF women existed in during the violent, masculinised environment of the EPLF resistance to Ethiopian terrorism. Moreover, gender-based reforms since independence have alienated and disenfranchised many women in Eritrea. A plethora of problems existed after independence. Ex-EPLF female fighters expressed mixed feelings about life after the liberation struggle. On one hand, the issue of civilian society was persistently raised as a hindrance to reintegration, since it was generally argued by ex-fighters that 'women in the EPLF changed more rapidly than society, which stayed traditional' [Author's Interview, Asgedet, Adi Teclesan, 1998]. Thus, when women returned from the frontline, their perceptions of the roles of women varied from societal perceptions. Many fighters now saw 'domestic' roles as a rejection of female liberation. Some research has also taken this approach, with a study by Egensteiner lamenting the fact that 'women were moving back into roles as *powerless* housewives and mothers'(author's emphasis) [1995]. This perception of domestic roles as powerless is, in itself, a substantial dilemma. In contrast, we have seen above that many ELF women saw it as a site of nonviolent resistance and power.

Many civilians, by the same token, found it difficult to accept former female fighters from the EPLF into the villages from which they originated [*The Economist* 1994, 64]. Informants were suspicious and unsure about the former fighters and some reactions were very harsh. Ruth described the events in her small village in relation to the small number of female ex-combatants that returned in the following words:

> They were cast out as prostitutes [*sharmuta*] and disobedient women. Some were even married to men from the same village who were also fighters, and even they left them. Forced to leave, several became prostitutes and others worked in bars or as cleaners — any work they could get. These women were peasant women when they joined the EPLF and they may have got a lot of new ideas and learned to read a little but they were still peasant women — the difference is they can fire a gun now. However, this has not enriched them in any way [Author's Interview, Ruth, Elabored, 1998].

Added to the unfamiliarity of Eritrean society was the lack of employment opportunities for female ex-combatants. External stereotypes, such as the ones alluded to in Ruth's narrative above, were exceedingly damaging and in many situations self-fulfilling. On numerous occasions, the author was directed to bars and brothels in order to find ex-combatants to interview, since many civilians believed this was the most suitable place to look. As one woman commented, 'those women [female fighters] defied custom to fight with men and they gave themselves freely to men while doing it. That's why they are all in bars and giving themselves to men even now' [Author's field notes, 1998]. Some informants had, in turn, internalized this perception of themselves and did indeed work in bars and brothels since it was impossible to find other work:

> I had no choice but to work here [as a prostitute in a bar]. I fought in the struggle but didn't marry or have children and I have no skills — just fighting, hiding in trenches, working for liberation. When we were free, I was so happy, but my family was uncomfortable. I knew I wasn't welcome in my village because it would bring shame on my parents. I had a relationship during the war and people knew about it, so my family would only see me away from... [the village]. I looked for work, but people think that we [female ex-fighters] are 'bad women,' that we are loose and free with men, disobedient and too head-strong. People are scared of us [Author's Interview, G.S., Asmara, 1998].

Sadly, there has been little solidarity among such ex-EPLF women and little resources or support for them. Additionally, this is not overtly encouraged or supported by either the Eritrean government or the NUEW, thus making progress more difficult.

Problems of employment and solidarity are further hampered by social issues of a personal nature among ex-combatants. Many ex-combatants have returned to find that their relationships with their family and husbands are not the same. The high rate of divorce between cadres, particularly in the case of inter-ethnic marriages within the EPLF, is controversial in light of the EPLF's emphasis on marriage and ethnic equality.

In Mehreteab's 1997 study of ex-combatants, it was apparent that marriage arrangements were altering in the newly independent state [Mehreteab 1997, 37]. Interestingly, of the twenty (20) male and female informants who indicated they were divorced, fifteen (15) were female. Additionally, of the eight (8) male and female informants who described themselves as 'separated' from their partners or husbands, seven (7) were female.

Are Mehreteab's conclusions fully satisfactory in this regard? If male fighters were so receptive to the gender and ethnic components of the EPLF's national liberation ideology, as the EPLF argues, then should they not have been able to resist the pressures supposedly put upon them by their family or village? It is the author's contention that 'village/family/religious/ethnic pressure' is but one component of the failure of relationships and the rejection of ex-fighter women in post-liberation society. As argued earlier, women were in fact subject to inequalities and indignities under the EPLF. As a result, marriages and relationships that were contracted within the EPLF must be understood in the context of high rates of sexual assault, harassment and generally lower status for women in all sections of the EPLF, except the NUEW. Since women did not attain equality in the EPLF and were often situated in a sexualized, violent and militarized context, they were subsequently perceived in negative ways, as described above. Men were complicit in this process rather than passive actors 'forced' to leave their EPLF wives under duress. In conclusion, it can be seen that the ELF and EPLF women who took up arms and accepted violent resistance suffered the consequences. Women engaged in violent resistance to terror and terrorism does not *solve* violence but creates more violence and hardship in the future; socially, politically and economically. All of this makes post-conflict peacebuilding basically impossible [Skjelbaek and Smith 2001; Sweetman 2005].

CONCLUSION

This study has demonstrated quite clearly that in Eritrea, Islam was a source of strength and a source of nonviolent resistance for ELF women against Ethiopian terrorism. This goes against the grain of so much media and literature that simply view Muslims and Islam as inherently violent and incapable of nonviolent resistance. It also demonstrates that in the aftermath of conflict, nonviolent female actors fit back into society without a militarised consciousness and with a deeper Islamic spirituality. This clearly demonstrates that nonviolence has a strong feminist component that can benefit women in long term peacebuilding in post-terrorist situations.

In contrast, the women who fought for the EPLF, and the few who bore arms for the ELF, suffered greatly both during the struggle against terrorism at the hands of their own cadres and the opposition, and this has continued long after the Ethiopian terror ended. They are largely rejected by society and neglected by the Eritrean Government. Quite simply, they are in a cycle of violence due to their decision to reject nonviolent alternatives.

ACKNOWLEDGEMENTS

Dr Christine Mason is a Lecturer in Peace and Conflict Studies at the University of Queensland, Brisbane, Australia. She spent two years in the Horn of Africa where she collated data for her doctoral dissertation, worked for the UNHCR and lectured in Political Science at Asmara University, Eritrea. She has published numerous journal articles and book chapters. Her forthcoming book is *Gender, Power and Resistance in East Timor: From Portuguese Colonization to Independence.*

REFERENCES

Abdalla, Amr. (2000/2001). 'Principles of Islamic Interpersonal Conflict Intervention: A Search within Islam and Western Literature.' *Journal of Law and Religion, 15* (1 and 2), 151-184.

Abu-Lughod, L. (1985). 'A Community of Secrets.' *Signs: Journal of Women in Culture and Society*, 10, pp. 637-657.

[Author Unknown.] (1994). 'Eritrea: The Kitchen Calls.' *The Economist.* 25 June.

Awde, N. (2000). *Women in Islam: An Anthology from the Qur'an and the Hadiths* [trans. and ed., Nicholas Awde]. Richmond, Vic: Curzon.

Bernstein, H. (1994). *The Rift: The Exile Experience of South Africans.* London: Jonathan Cape.

Bleiker, R. (2000). *Popular Dissent, Human Agency and Global Politics.* Cambridge: Cambridge University Press.

Bonney, R. (2004). *Jihād: From Qur'ān to bin Lāden.* New York: Macmillan Palgrave.

Boulding, E. (1995). 'Feminist Inventions in the Art of Peacemaking: A Century Overview.' *Peace and Change*, 20 (4), 408-438.

Campbell, J. (1971). 'Background to the Eritrean Conflict.' *Africa Report.*

Cock, J. (1991). *Colonels and Cadres: War and Gender in South Africa.* Cape Town: Oxford University Press.

Cook, A. and Kirk, G. (1984). *Greenham Women Are Everywhere: Dreams, Ideas and Actions from the Women's Peace Movement.* London: Pluto.

Connell, D. (2005). *Conversations with Eritrean Political Prisoners.* Trenton, NJ: Red Sea Press.

Davidson, B. (1961). *Black Mother: Africa and the Atlantic Slave Trade.* London: Penguin.

Davidson, B. (1969). *The Liberation of Guine: Aspects of an African Revolution.* London: Penguin.

Davidson, B. (1972). *In the Eye of the Storm: Angola's People.* London: Longman.

Degroot, G.J. (2000). 'Lipstick on Her Nipples, Cordite in Her Hair: Sex and Romance among British Servicewomen during the Second World War.' In G.J. Degroot and C. Peniston-Bird. (Eds.), *A Soldier and a Woman: Sexual Integration in the Military.* London: Longman (pp. 100-119).

Deming, B. (1982). *Two Essays: On Anger, New Men/New Women: Some Thoughts on Nonviolence.* Philadelphia: New Society.

Egensteiner, E.B. (1995). The Dream Becomes a Reality(?): Nation Building and the Continued Struggle of the Women of the Eritrean People's Liberation Front, unpublished Master of Arts (Visual Anthropology) thesis, University of Southern California.

Eikelman, D.F. and Piscatori, J. (1996). *Muslim Politics.* Princeton, NJ: Princeton University Press.

Elshtain, J.B. (1987). *Women and War.* New York: Basic Books.

Enloe, C. (2000). *Maneuvers: The International Politics of Militarizing Women's Lives.* Berkeley: University of California Press.

EPLF. (1978). *Eritreain Struggle*, II(4), 4.

Esposito, J. (1992). *The Islamic Threat: Myth or Reality?* New York: Oxford University Press.

Fanon, F. (1967). *A Dying Colonialism* [trans. H. Chevalier]. New York: Grove Press.

Feminism and Nonviolence Study Group. (1983). *Piecing It Together: Feminism and Nonviolence.* Buckleigh, PA: FNSG.

Firebrace, J. and Holland, S. (1984). *Never Kneel Down: Drought, Development and Liberation in Eritrea.* Nottingham: Spokesman.

Fisher, L. (1962). *The Essential Gandhi.* New York: Random House.

Foucault, M. (1990). *The Will to Knowledge: The History of Sexuality Vol. 1* [trans. R. Hurley]. London: Penguin Books.

Gandhi, M. (1938). *Harijan*, 31 December.

Gandhi, M. (1993). *Gandhi: An Autobiography – The Story of My Experiments with the Truth* [trans. M. Desai]. Boston: Beacon Press.

The General Union of Eritrean Women (GUEW) [The First Congress]. *The History of the Eritrean Women's Movement* [no date, no place of publication, no page numbers] [English/Arabic Script].

Gottesman, L. (1998). *To Fight and Learn: The Praxis and Promise of Literacy in Eritrea's Independence War.* Lawrenceville: Red Sea Press.

Gruber, J. (1998). *Gender Report.* UNICEF.

Holmes, R.L. (1990). *Nonviolence in Theory and Practice.* Prospect Heights, IL: Waveland.

Houtart, F. (1980). 'The Social Revolution in Eritrea.' In B. Davidson et al. (Eds.), *Behind the War in Eritrea* (pp. 208-266). Nottingham: Spokesman.

Iyob, R. (1995). *The Eritrean Struggle for Independence.* Cambridge: Cambridge University Press.

Killion, T. (1997). 'Eritrean Worker's Organization and Early Nationalist Mobilization: 1948-1958.' *Eritrean Studies Review*, 2(1), 1-59.

Martin, B. (1989). 'Gene Sharp's Theory of Power.' *Journal of Peace Research, 26*(2), 213-222.

Mason, C. (2001). 'Exorcising Excision: Medico-Legal Issues Arising from Male and Female Genital Surgery in Australia.' *The Australian Journal of Law and Medicine*, 9(1).

McCallister, P. (1982) (Ed.). *Reweaving the Web of Life: Feminism and Nonviolence.* Philadelphia: New Society.

McGuiness, K. (1993). 'Gene Sharp's Theory of Power: A Feminist Critique of Consent.' *Journal of Peace Research, 30* (1), 101-115.

Mehreteab, A. (1987). Assessment of Demobilization and Re-Integration of Ex-Fighters in Eritrea. Unpublished Masters Thesis, International Development Studies, University of Leeds.

Meyerding, J. (1982). 'Reclaiming Nonviolence: Some Thoughts for Feminist Womyn Who Used To Be Nonviolent and Vice Versa.' In P. McAllister, (Ed.), *Reweaving the Web of Life: Feminism and Nonviolence* (pp. 5-15). Philadelphia: New Society.

Nagel, J. (1998). 'Masculinity and Nationalism: Gender and Sexuality in the Making of Nations.' *Ethnic and Racial Studies*, 21 (2), 242-269.

National Union of Eritrean Women (NUEW). [nd] *Women in the Eritrean Revolution: Eye-Witness Reports and Testimonies*, Tipografia Moderna (held in the NUEW Resource Library, Asmara, Eritrea).

Negash, T. (1997). *Eritrea and Ethiopia: The Federal Experience*. New Brunswick, NJ: Transaction Publishers.

Ottaway, D and Ottaway, M. (1980). *Afrocomunism*. New York: Holmes and Meier.

Partner, P. (1997). *God of Battles: Holy Wars of Christianity and Islam*. Princeton, NJ: Princeton University Press.

Pateman, C. (1980). 'Women and Consent.' *Political Theory*, 8 (2), 149-168.

Pateman, C. (1988). *The Sexual Contract*. Cambridge: Polity Press.

Rao, S. (1999). 'Women-as-Symbol: The Intersections of Identity Politics, Gender and Indian Nationalism.' *Women's Studies International Forum*, 22 (3), 317-328.

Roy, O. (1994). *The Failure of Political Islam*. London: I.B. Tauris.

Said, E. (1981). *Covering Islam*. New York: Pantheon.

Said, J. (2000/2001). 'Law ,Religion and the Prophetic Method of Social Change' [trans. A. Jalabi]. *Journal of Law and Religion*, *15* (1 and 2), 83-10.

Salleh, K.M. (2001). Islam, Nonviolence and Women. In G.D. Paige et al. (Eds.) *Islam and Nonviolence*. Hawaii: Center for Global Nonviolence.

Schwartz, P. (1987). 'Redefining Resistance: Women's Activism in Wartime France.' In M. Higonnet, J. Jensen, S. Michel and M.C. Weitz (Eds.), *Behind the Lines: Gender and the Two World Wars*. London: Yale University Press.

Sharp, G. (1973). *The Politics of Nonviolent Action*. Boston, MA: Porter Sargent.

Shivers, L. (1982). 'An Open Letter to Gandhi.' In P. McAllister (Ed.), *Reweaving the Web of Life: Feminism and Nonviolence* (pp. 181-194). Philadelphia: New Society.

Silkin, T. (1989). '"Women can only be Free when the power of Kin Groups Is Smashed:" New Marriage Laws and Social Change in the Liberated Zones of Eritrea.' *International Journal of the Sociology of Law*, 17, pp. 147-163.

Skjelsbaek, I. and Smith, D. (1991). *Gender, Peace and Conflict*. London: Sage Publications.

Spivak, G.C. (1988). 'Can the Subaltern Speak?' In G. Nelson and L. Grossberg (Eds.), *Marxism and the Interpretation of Culture*. Chicago: University of Illinois Press.

Sweetman, C. (2005). (Ed.). *Gender, Peacebuilding, and Reconstruction*. Oxford: Oxfam Press.

Taylor, C. (2000). '"And Don't Forget to Clean the Fridge:" Women in the Secret Sphere of Terrorism.' In G.J. Degroot and C. Peniston-Bird. (Eds.), *A Soldier and a Woman: Sexual Integration in the Military*. London: Longman.

Tolstaia, S.A. (1985). *The Diaries of Sofia Tolstaya* [trans. C. Porter]. London: Cape.

[USIP] United States Institute of Peace. (2002). *Islamic Perspectives on Peace and Violence*. Washington, DC: USIP.

Wilson, A. (1991). *The Challenge Road: Women and the Eritrean Revolution*. London: Earthscan Publications Ltd.

Wolpert, S.A. (2002). *Gandhi's Passion: The Life and Legacy of Mahatma Gandhi*. Oxford: Oxford University Press.

Young, C. (1982). *Ideology and Development in Africa*. New Haven, CT: Yale University Press.

Zerai, W. (1994). 'Organising Women within a National Liberation Struggle: The Case of Eritrea.' *Economic and Political Weekly*, xxix(44), 63-68.

In: Nonviolence: An Alternative for Defeating...
Editors: S. Ram and R. Summy, pp. 131-142

ISBN: 978-1-60021-812-5
© 2008 Nova Science Publishers, Inc.

Chapter 8

THE *JAHILIYYA* FACTOR?: FIGHTING MUSLIMS' CULTURAL RESISTANCE TO NONVIOLENCE

Chaiwat Satha-Anand[1]

ABSTRACT

This chapter argues that Muslim societies are presently facing a new kind of *jahiliyya* (ignorance) regarding the Muslims'reluctance to employ the language of nonviolence in characterizing their own actions due to an inadequate understanding of both the concepts of power and nonviolent actions. Also there is a lack of nonviolent language to identify most present-day fighting against injustice. The end result means that Muslims bypass their own legacy of nonviolence. To redress this *jahiliyya* factor entails, among other things, overcoming the conceptual misunderstanding about non-

and replacing the historical absence of Muslims' legacy of nonviolence with accounts of another legacy that features nonviolence. All of this would be possible in the process of rediscovering the original meanings of the *jahiliyya* conducive to nonviolence in Islam.

INTRODUCTION

On April 28, 2004, a group of Muslims, many of them younger than twenty, armed primarily with machetes, attacked police posts and stations in ten different places in three Muslim-dominated Southern-most provinces of Thailand. A group of some thirty armed men occupied the ancient Kru-Ze mosque in the town of Pattani and fought a pitched battle with the Thai security forces. In the early afternoon, the military decided to storm the mosque and all 32 men inside it were killed. At the end of the day, there were 106 dead attackers, nine suspects were arrested and five policemen killed in the incident. Some local Muslim leaders said that the dead militants were '*jihad* warriors,' and most relatives of the dead attackers chose not to wash the bodies before burial, a sign indicating that local people considered their deaths as *shahid* (battle deaths in defense of Islam at the hands of non-Muslims) which requires no washing or praying before burial .

Earlier the militants themselves were said to have declared through the mosque's loudspeakers that they were doing God's work and they would sacrifice their lives in the path of *jihad* (struggle in the path of God, commonly misused as 'holy war'). A Thai field officer fighting at Kru-Ze told the press [*Bangkok Post* 2004b] that 'they would never surrender but fight to the end of their lives for God. They also said if they died they did not want their blood washed off because they had given their lives to God.' The families of fifteen people aged 17 to 25, who were all killed in front of the sub-district office in Yala, wondered why their children – healthy and good students – chose to die in violence [*Bangkok Post* 2004a]. Though their motives in choosing violence and preparing to die are difficult to ascertain, it is important to understand why violence with mortal self-sacrifice has become a preferred choice to other alternatives among some Muslims.

Elsewhere I have argued that there are strong religious grounds to substantiate the Islamic imperatives for Muslims to fight injustice with nonviolent actions based on Qur'anic injunctions as well as values emanating from the Prophet's examples [Satha-Anand 2001b, 195-211]. It could then be asked at this point, if there are such injunctions and examples for Muslims' nonviolent actions, why are these Islamic imperatives for nonviolence ignored, or generally relegated to marginal importance?

This question can best be addressed by exploring justifications used by some Muslims in their use of terror to realize their objectives, especially their understanding of the historical moment of *jahiliyya* (ignorance) which provided contexts for their struggles. I would argue that there is a need to reconceptualize this *jahiliyya* in terms of a lack of knowledge, particularly about nonviolent alternatives as a preferred method of struggle for Muslims. This chapter begins with a discussion of how some Muslim militants justify terror as their instrument in righting wrongs, based on a time of fighting when *jahiliyya* (ignorance) was rife. Then the notion of *jahiliyya* itself will be problematized with emphases on an inadequate understanding of both the concept of power and nonviolent actions, which contributes to a virtual bypassing of Muslims' own historical legacy of nonviolent pasts. Finally, a return to the original meaning of *jahiliyya* conducive to nonviolent alternatives as stipulated in both *Al-Qur'an* and the Prophet's practices will be advanced.

THE ABSENT PRECEPT AND THE STRUGGLE AGAINST *JAHILIYYA*

Less than ten days after the April 28 incident in Southern Thailand, Thai authorities announced that a 'New'version of the Koran (was) found [Headline of *Bangkok Post* 2004c]. Subsequently, the press reported that a 34-page book was found by the body of a dead militant. Written in Malay, the booklet titled *Ber Jihad di Patani* (*The Jihad of Patani*) urged '*jihad* warriors' to form troops to fight 'those outside the religion' for their religion, Allah and the glory of the Patani state, annexed by Siam at the turn of the twentieth century. Chapter 3 of the book tells the warriors to kill all opponents, even their own parents, and to sacrifice their lives to be in heaven with Allah. According to a news report: 'Chapter 7 quotes Chapter

---

[1] Based on a paper prepared for the Nonviolence Commission, IPRA, Sopron, Hungary, July 5-8, 2004, and revised in August 2006.

123 of the Koran as saying that: 'You must kill all of them, so they will know you, who have faith, are strong as well' [*Bangkok Post* 2004d]. The Thai prime minister commented on the discovered booklet by saying : 'It's an adapted version of the Koran being used to deceive Muslims....The Yawi version (in Malay) has much more violent content. Those reading it for seven days in a row could go crazy because it is completely distorted.' [*Bangkok Post* 2004d]. It goes without saying that for most Muslims, belief in the sacredness of *Al-Qur'an* is an article of faith (*Iman*) and therefore a revision or alteration of the Book is unthinkable. It should also be noted that though the holy book is much longer than '34 pages,' there are only 114 *Surah* (chapters) with 6,666 *Ayahs* (verses).

Seen as a call to use violence against those regarded as oppressors, this small book found in Southern Thailand is not unlike another written two decades ago in the ancient land thousands of miles away when President Sadat of Egypt was assassinated on October 6, 1981. It has been suggested that the major ideological statement of Sadat's assassins is to be found in a book entitled *The Absent Precept (Al Farida Al-Gha'eba)*, originally printed in a clandestine edition of five hundred copies, written by Abd al-Salam Faraj, a twenty-seven year old engineer [Sivan 1985, 103]. He was later tried and executed in 1982. He argued that the Muslims should first fight against their own rulers who were seen as turning against Islam because: 'Fighting the near enemy is more important than fighting the distant enemy....The cause of the existence of imperialism in the lands of Islam lies in these self-same rulers. To begin the struggle against imperialism would be...a waste of time.... There can be no doubt that the first battlefield of the *jihad* is the extirpation of these infidel leaderships...' [Quoted in Lewis 2002, 107-108]. Against these 'enemies,' violence is justified, and in fact prescribed, as *jihad* becomes incumbent upon all Muslims. Faraj writes:

> Despite its crucial importance for the future of our Faith, the *jihad* has been neglected, maybe even ignored, by men of religion of our age. They know, however, that *jihad* is the only way to reestablish and reenhance the power and the glory of Islam, which every true believer desires wholeheartedly. *There is no doubt the idols upon earth will not be destroyed but by the sword* and thus establish the Islamic state and restore the caliphate. This is the command of God and each and every Muslim should, hence, do his utmost to accomplish this precept, having recourse to force if necessary [quoted in Sivan 1985, 127; emphasis added].[2]

When asked to explain Faraj's motive, Khalid al-Islambouli, an officer who was the instigator and executor of the Sadat assassination, stated in the Egyptian investigation file record that: 'I did what I did, because the *Shari'a* (Islamic law) was not applied, because of the peace treaty with the Jews and because of the arrest of Muslim *Ulamaa* (religious scholars) without justification' [Guenena 1986, 44]. It could be said that the killing of President Sadat was perceived by the extremists as a necessity because he was a heretic since he did not rule in accordance with the traditions and laws of the Prophet; a traitor because he made peace with the 'enemy;' and an unjust ruler because he arrested Islamic scholars unjustly [Guenena 1986, 44].

---

[2] Ibn Taymiyyah is becoming increasingly popular among Muslims whereas a decade ago he would have only been known to a relatively small circle of Muslim scholars. Compared to Imam Abu Hanifa, his position regarding non-Muslims is much less liberal.

It is also interesting to note that for Faraj — following the thoughts of Ibn Taymiyya (1268-1328 who died in a Damascus jail) and Sayyid Qutb (1906-1966 who was executed in Egypt) — Sadat's Egypt had become something analogous to the Mongols who professed to being Muslims, yet failed to observe the *Shari'a* (Islamic rules based on law-like understanding of *Al-Qur'an* and the Prophetic traditions) concerning human behavior in society, both at the individual and collective levels [Sivan 1985, 103 and 127]. Failing to observe the rules of Islam in regulating human life in society means that something else other than God was being obeyed. In Islam, it is ignorance (*jahiliyya*) if a person serves not God but other things. *Al-Qur'an* says, 'Say: Is it some one other than God that ye order me to worship, O ye Ignorant ones?' [Al-Qur'an 1977, 39:64]. [3]

It is through the return to a pristine Islam that Muslims are allowed to realize their destined task of trying to put an end to the domination of humans by those who are seen as responsible for the corrupted order of the world. Influenced by Maudoodi's theory of modern *jahiliyya* (Modern Ignorance) developed in India since 1939, it could be argued that the influential Sayyid Qutb, an Egyptian modernist literary critic turned Muslim Brotherhood activist, considered the concept of *jahiliyya* central to his theory, since his aim was to show the wide gap between the rule of God and 'that of ignorance' to explain the consequences of such refusal to comply with God's law, and to establish 'an Islamic presence in the midst of *Ignorant* surroundings which are hostile to Islam...' [Qutb n.d., xv-xvi][4] He wrote *In the Shadow of the Koran*, outlining the danger of ignorance in the following words:

> *Jahiliyya* signifies the domination (hakimiyya) of man over man, or rather the subservience to man rather than to Allah. It denotes rejection of the divinity of God and the adulation of mortals. In this sense, *jahiliyya* is not just a specific historical period (referring to the era preceding the advent of Islam), but a state of affairs. Such a state of human affairs existed in the past, exists today, and may exist in the future, taking the form of *jahiliyya*, that mirror-image and sworn enemy of Islam. In any time and place human beings face that clear-cut choice: either to observe the Law of Allah in its entirety, or to apply laws laid down by man of one sort or another. In the latter case, they are in a state of *jahiliyya*. Man is at the crossroads and that is the choice: Islam or *jahiliyya*. Modern-style *jahiliyya* in the industrialized societies of Europe and America is essentially similar to the old-time *jahiliyya* in pagan and nomadic Arabia. For in both systems, man is under the dominion of man rather than of Allah [Quoted in Sivan 1985, 25-26].

What Qutb has done was to redefine the notion of *jahiliyya* commonly understood as a historical moment which existed before the rise of Islam in Arabia into 'a state of human affairs' freed from the chain of time, which is antithetical to the Way of God. Therefore Muslims everywhere need to choose between these two ways: Islam or *jahiliyya*. It goes without saying that the latter choice is un-Islamic. Muslims, therefore have to choose Islam and then fight 'the sworn enemy of Islam' to change the world in accordance with Islam [See for example Haddad 1983, 67-98]. In this sense, 'ignorance' becomes a malady that needs to be overcome because the choice is wrongly made without the capacity to distinguish 'the

---

[3] All citations from Al-Qur'an are from A.Yusuf Ali's Translation, The Glorius Qur'an. (US: Muslim Students Association, 1977).

[4] Muhammad Qutb is Sayyid Qutb's brother who taught at King Abdul Aziz University in Saudi Arabia.

True' from the false, or 'the Right' from the wrong when human thoughts are elevated to the status of a God. Such a state of affairs needs to be changed, with violence if necessary, as in the case of Faraj and some other advocates.

Philosophically, ignorance is taken to mean an absence or a lack of knowledge. In *The Republic*, Plato explicitly discusses the nature of ignorance (*agnoia*). He establishes that 'that which is' is the object of knowledge; 'that which is becoming' is the object of opinion, and 'that which is not' is the object of ignorance [Plato 1968, 159]. For Descartes, the emphasis is on the concept of 'error' when knowledge claims are made beyond the limit of understanding. Yet for David Hume, 'misperception' assumes paramount significance when a confused idea of the impression is imprinted on the mind [Wongwaisayawan 1983, 3]. In Islamic ethical teachings, *jahl* (folly or ignorance) — characterized by irascible temper or hasty and passionate anger when provoked — is antithetical to *aql* (intelligence) or wisdom in the sense of moral self-restraint and harmonious conduct in a communal context. Ignorance, in this sense, signifies 'all that is perverse and discordant in the person leading up to inner blindness,' and is responsible for social disorder and violence. To cultivate nonviolence in terms of character development from Islamic ethical practice, therefore, means to fight ignorance by strengthening intelligence with 'the moral transformation of the personality' through 'a process of grooming' [Crow 2001, 217-21; See also fn.24 on p. 225].

Taken together, it can be seen that ignorance occurs when something is understood for what it is not; the world is misperceived; and error takes place when knowledge claims do not recognize their limits. All this could result from 'an inner blindness.' Perhaps, an example of such blindness, or ignorance, in terms of nonviolent alternatives could be Faraj's assertion that '*There is no doubt the idols upon earth will not be destroyed but by the sword*' mentioned above. How then could this ignorance or blindness (*jahiliyya*) be accounted for in the area of nonviolence?

THE *JAHILIYYA* FACTOR: INADEQUATE LANGUAGE, CONCEPTUAL MISUNDERSTANDING AND HISTORICAL ABSENCE

Crow and Grant's [1990] groundbreaking book on nonviolence and Islam, *Arab Nonviolent Political Struggle in the Middle East*[5], points out at least six reasons why nonviolent actions are seen with some degrees of skepticism among Muslims. They are seen as: preventing legitimate self-defense; an imperialist ploy to pacify Muslims; non-existent in Arab history; without any contribution to the psychological health of the oppressed; inefficient political projects; and cannot mobilize world opinion against oppression [Crow and Grant 1990].[6] Almost a decade later at a conference on 'Islam and Peace' held at the American University on February 14, 1997, many delegates criticized nonviolence as an imported ideology lacking the requisite theological and cultural bases for true compatibility with Islam [Crow 1999, 10 and 17]. There seems to be a kind of cultural reluctance, if not

---

[5] This book was widely reviewed in scholarly journals and regarded as a pioneering work in the fields of nonviolence in the Middle East. See for example, reviews by Anthony Bing in *Middle East Journal*, Vol. 45 No.3 (Summer 1991), 511-512; and Sohail H Hashmi in *Journal of Third World Studies*, Vol. VIII No.1 (Spring 1991), 346-348.

[6] In this essay, the authors also try to argue against these six stereotypical reasons against nonviolence.

resistance, to accept nonviolent actions as an alternative in pursuing the causes of justice among Muslims. This 'blindness' or *jahiliyya* factor working against nonviolent alternatives is a result of a linguistic incompatibility when nonviolence is translated into Arabic, a lack of adequate understanding of the concept of nonviolence as power and fighting, and a refusal to accept an Islamic history of nonviolent actions.

LINGUISTIC INCOMPATIBILITY?

When the term 'nonviolence' is directly translated into Arabic, the sacred language of Islam for Muslims around the world, it becomes *la-unf*, which means 'no violence' or 'no vehement irascibility.' The term is problematic for at least three reasons. First, since it was introduced into Arabic before the middle of the last century in reference to Gandhi's method of nonviolence, the negative, or somewhat skeptical, ways in which Gandhi has been perceived by many in the Muslim world as someone who opposed the creation of the Islamic Republic of Pakistan may contribute negatively to the acceptance of the term. Second, for those Muslims who are oppressed and believe that violence could both contribute to their psychological freedom from the yoke of oppression and to their political liberation, *la-unf* connotes a denial of the only way they believe exists to alter their condition. Third, since *la-unf* mainly means 'no violence,' and not nonviolence, the term denotes not only 'no violence' but 'no action.' As a result, for Muslims taught repeatedly by *Al-Qur'an* that '(tumult and) oppression are worse than slaughter' [Al-Qur'an 1977, Surah II: 191; II: 217], to accept oppression without doing anything can be seen as un-Islamic. The notion of nonviolence is therefore generally considered negative and uninspiring. Hence it is not surprising to see that *la-unf* has become increasingly less popular among writers on nonviolence in Arabic. In fact, a scholar recently pointed out that the term is for the most past avoided, 'due to cultural preconceptions among Arab Muslims that it connotes passivity, weakness and lack of courage'[Crow 2000, 62].

Yet upon reflection, nonviolence can be appreciated as a positive concept, necessary for transforming societies without violence. For violence as such — direct, structural, or cultural — limits life in some form [Galtung 1996, 29-34]. Hence, it can be considered negative. The double negative form of the word thus renders 'nonviolence' a positive concept. As a result, for those in search of alternatives to violence, several terms are now used to translate 'nonviolence' into Arabic. They include: *al nidal al silmi* or 'peaceful struggle,' *al nidal al madani* or 'civilian struggle,' *al-muqawamat al-madaniyyah* or 'civil resistance,' or even *al-sabr* or 'long suffering perseverance.' In fact, one of the foremost Arab writers on the subject, Khalid al-Qishtayni who wrote *Nahwa l-la unf* (*Towards Nonviolence*) in 1984 has now been introducing the term *al-jihad al madani* or civil *jihad* in his recent book published in 1998: *Dalil al-muwatin li-l-jihad al-madani* (*The Citizen's Guide to Civil Jihad*) [Crow 2000, 62 and fn. 13 at p. 69]. It is interesting to note that, outside of these changing academic discourses, a political leader such as Sadiq al-Mahdi, since his release from prison in 1996 and subsequent exile, has been calling for 'civil *jihad*' against the Bashir government of Sudan [Crow 2000, fn. 15 at p. 69].

In addition, some Muslim scholars have argued that the terms 'violence' and 'nonviolence' are not *Qur'anic* terms. In 1986 at the first international conference on 'Islam and Nonviolence' held in Bali, Indonesia, the Egyptian theorist, Hasan Hanafi, for example, selected the term 'coercion' (*Ikrah*) to be used as a vehicle for discussing the origin of violence in Islam. But there are at least two problems here. First, if a term cannot indeed be found in *Al Our'an*, can it not be seriously discussed ? I believe that the term 'nuclear weapons' does not exist in *Our'an* and therefore not a 'Our'anic' term. But it is a part of human reality with a dangerous potential which could annihilate the whole human race. Should the Muslims be left out of the present discourse for world peace seeking nuclear disarmament simply because of the literal absence of a word? Second, judging from a sociological standpoint, coercion and violence are two distinctive concepts working at different levels. Violence will always be coercive, yet coercion can be violent or nonviolent [Satha-Anand 1993, 5]. This problem is a reflection of a lack of adequate understanding of the idea of nonviolence as power and fighting.

CONCEPTUAL MISUNDERSTANDING?

In *The Absent Precept*, Faraj maintained that 'An Islamic state cannot be reestablished without the struggle of a believing minority…,' then he divided the methods of struggle into two kinds: *jihad* and propaganda. He argued that the 'path' of propaganda, advocated by those who wanted to forsake the *jihad*, can not lead to the desired goal because 'all means of communication are in the hands of the infidels, of the morally depraved, and of the enemies of the Faith?' [Sivan 1985, 127]. Since for Faraj, *jihad* meant the path of 'the sword' or violence as indicated above, the alternative he saw as 'not violent' is, curiously enough, propaganda. Then due to the ways the media is controlled, this option turns out to be unavailable and the Muslims are left with no alternative, but violence. Faraj's juxtaposition is yet another example of how the path which is 'not violent' (*la unf* ?) is conceived, and consequently leads to the gross misunderstanding of nonviolence.

In a clever article written in the form of an imaginary exchange of letters between Mahatma Gandhi and Osama bin Laden, Bhikhu Parekh has bin Laden presented not as a real man but as an intellectual construct and a metaphor referring to a more generic, pro-terror radical Islamist, arguing that for him the struggle against the Soviets was a profound 'spiritual experience,' especially in reaffirming confidence in the success of violent methods. Bin Laden argued that violence is the only way to achieve the goals of getting the Americans out of Muslim lands — among other things, because it is the only language the US understands. Moreover, for him, violence is not inherently evil but should be judged on the basis of its goals and the results it produces [Parekh 2004].[7] In other words, violence is a weapon of choice for these Muslims because of its general power to deliver the desired results. Nonviolence is considered without power because it is seen as a weak and ineffective instrument. Therefore, it is not the language that could 'make the opponents understand.'

There is a conceptual problem with this understanding of the power of violence, however. In a speech at his trial in 1905, Trotsky pointed out that power has very little to do with violence because it resides not in the ability to kill others but in their readiness to die for something they believe [Schell 2003, 170]. Following the theorist Hannah Arendt, I would

---

[7] Originally a lecture delivered at Boston University, a longer version will appear in Anna Lannstrom (ed.), *The Stranger's Religion: Fascination and Fear*. (Indiana: University of Notre Dame Press, Forthcoming).

maintain that violence and power are opposites. Where there is violence, power is absent. This is because power is not exercised when people are forced to act but when they take action willingly [Arendt 1970, 56]. Here John Stuart Mill's answer to the question he raised in *Representative Government* is instructive. He pointed out that martyrs are more powerful than the authorities who put them to death [Schell 2003, 230-231]. In an odd way, I believe that this reasoning would be easily understood by the likes of people like Faraj or bin Laden.

It would be interesting, however, to confront a Faraj or a bin Laden with accounts of changes in the world brought about by the power of nonviolence. For example, nonviolence has been crucial in the fights against dictatorships in Latin America when from 1931 to 1961 eleven presidents were forced to leave offices in the wake of civic strikes [Parkman 1990].[8] But it is Peter Ackerman and Jack Duvall's *A Force More Powerful* which empirically addresses the myth of violence and power discussed above directly. They listed twelve significant cases of nonviolent conflicts during the twentieth century. Nonviolent conflicts were used in pursuit of power, as in 1905 Russia; to resist terror, as in the cases of Denmark and the Netherlands resisting the Nazis; and in the struggles for citizens' rights that occurred in the American South and the people's movement for democracy in the Philippines. The Ackerman and Duvall study seeks to dispel 'the greatest misconception about conflict' which maintains that violence is power — and, indeed, the ultimate form of power — by showing that ordinary Russians, Indians, Poles, Danes, Salvadoreans, African Americans, Chileans, South Africans, and Southeast Asians have not allowed themselves to be foreclosed by their opponents' use of violence and instead relied on primarily nonviolent alternatives to bring about great political changes in the last century [Ackerman and DuVall 2000, 9].

The *jahiliyya* factor responsible for the linguistic complexities and conceptual myths on nonviolence produce widely held beliefs about the absence of nonviolent resistance in Islam as well as in Arab history [Crow and Grant 1990, 76 and 78]. Sadly, due to this absence, many nonviolent actions undertaken by Muslims are not known, or accordingly labeled, and thus the tradition of nonviolence among Muslims has been further impoverished.

ISLAMIC HISTORY AND CULTURE OF NONVIOLENCE?

The more than 600-page volume, *Protest, Power and Change* is an encyclopedia of nonviolent action from *Act-Up* to Women's Suffrage. There are five issues related to nonviolence and Muslims/Islam. But most examples of Muslim nonviolent actions from the encyclopedia are only those related to Gandhi, Abdul Ghaffar Khan and the subcontinent. An item on Bosnian Muslims merely indicates their demographic and ethnic heritage, and another item refers to Burmese Muslims carrying green banners during mass demonstration for democracy in Burma. Other Muslim nonviolent actions elsewhere in the world are sadly absent [See Powers and Vogele 1997].

In the volume *Arab Nonviolent Political Struggle in the Middle East*, Khalid Kishtainy's essay uses injunctions from the Holy *Qur'an* and the *Hadiths* (Traditions of the Prophet) to paint a picture of Islam in history that is extremely conducive to nonviolence. He argues that violence was neither entrenched in Arab nor Islamic culture(s) and that, like others, the Arabs

---

[8] These 11 presidents were from Chile (1931), Cuba (1933), El Salvador (1944), Guatemala (1944), Haiti (1946), Panama (1951), Haiti (3 presidents in 1956-1957), Colombia (1957), Dominican Republic (1962).

only resorted to wars when they were forced to. It should be noted that most of the Arab 'generals' in the beginning of the Islamic era were either merchants or poets. Perhaps, Khalid bin Walid is the only one who dedicated his life to 'the arts of war,' and is therefore an exception. Moreover, unlike the Japanese Samurai or the Greek Spartans, the Arabs did not develop a warring caste. Culturally, the Arabs have no game of blood. They do not have bull fighting, or cock fighting, or boxing. Historically, the main contribution of the Arab Muslims to human civilization was in the field of arts, sciences and social sciences. They taught Europe the use of comfortable cushions and upholstered furniture instead of the hard, wooden chair, how to wear silk and dainty linen instead of coarse wool, and to drink from delicate glassware rather than heavy metal mugs. In fact, the world learns practically nothing from the Arabs in the field of warfare [Kishtainy 1990].

Kishtainy supported his radical reading of history with numerous examples. Among other things, he pointed out that the spread of Islam in Arabia did not succeed through the use of force. 'The Prophet applied skilful diplomacy and superb propaganda work in winning the tribes and villages. The bulk of Arabia was secured with peaceful negotiations and treaties, and not with the sword' [Kishtainy 1990, 14]. It should also be noted that especially in Southeast Asia, the conversion process to Islam took place in return for Muslims' bureaucratic, religious, and educational services. The advent of Islam in Southeast Asia was the story of Islam's continuity rather than conflict with previous cultures [Levtzion 1979]. Looking back at the history of Islamic expansion, it seems that the Muslims have lost much of what they have achieved through conquest and continue to retain most of what they have achieved through piety and trade.

In addition to Kishtainy's works, there are many other examples of Muslims' nonviolent actions both in history and at present. For example, in 1375, the religious scholar Ibn Qunfundh recorded the remarkable nonviolent story of Lala Aziza of Seksawa, Morocco. The general Al-Hintati set out with 6,000 men to conquer Seksawa. Aziza walked to the Marrakesh plain and stood alone before him and his army. She faced the general with her words and his faith. Listening to Aziza's words of God's command of justice and the wrong of harming God's creation, the general was overwhelmed. He later told Ibn Qunfundh that 'This one…is a wonder….She knew what was going on inside of me….I was not able to counter her argument, to reject her requests' [Combs-Schilling 1994, 17]. This is a clear case of the power of words, of courage, of a woman, and — perhaps most importantly here — of nonviolence that could send back an army of a would-be conqueror.

During the partition of India in 1948, there are examples of Muslims in South Asia who sacrificed their lives defending Hindus from the rage of violent crowds [See, for example, Satha-Anand 2001a]. In the last decade of the twentieth century, Kosovo Albanians, some 87% of Kosovo's two million residents in 1987 and most of whom are Muslims, used parallel institutions, a powerful form of nonviolent action, to noncooperate with Serbian authorities. In terms of discipline, strategies and scale, a scholar argues that it is the largest campaign of nonviolence since Martin Luther King Jr.'s civil rights movement [Salla 1995]. In contemporary Thailand, Muslim villagers in Songkhla have fought against the Thai-Malaysian Gas Pipeline Project using all kinds of nonviolent methods for the past six years [Janchitfah 2004]. These random examples are provided to make a simple point: there are many more Muslim nonviolent actions around the world, both in history and at present. Once the *jahiliyya* factor is overcome, alternatives to linguistic impasses can be found, misconceptions about nonviolence and power will be demythologized, and more examples of Muslim nonviolent actions will be seen.

CONCLUSION: REDEFINING *JAHILIYYA*

The *jahiliyya* factor advocated by Faraz, inherited from Maududi and Qutb, among others, is based on an understanding that ignorance is a state of affairs, and the present condition of the world is divided into two exclusive camps: between Islam and ignorance. The Muslims need to make a choice, and then fight to destroy ignorance with violence, if need be. In trying to overcome the *jahiliyya* factor, it may be useful to look back at the original meaning as it appeared in *Al-Qur'an* and the Prophetic traditions.

The clearest case of Islam fighting against *jahiliyya*, defined as practices common among Arabs before the rise of Islam due to ignorance, is female infanticide. *Al-Qur'an* is crystal clear about this practice in the age of ignorance.

> When news is brought to one of them of (the birth of) a female (child) his face darkens and he is filled with inward grief!
> With shame does he hide himself from his people because of the bad news he has had! Shall he retain it on (sufferance and) contempt or bury it in the dust? Ah! what an evil (choice) they decide on! [Al-Qur'an 1977, 16: 58-59].

Taking the position of the innocent child, God asked in *Al-Qur'an*: 'When the female (infant) buried alive is questioned for what crime she was killed…(then) shall each soul know what it has put forward' [Al-Qur'an 1977, 81: 8-9, 14].

There are several *Hadiths* against female infanticide. For example, Ibn Abbas reported God's messenger as saying, 'If anyone has a female child and does not bury her alive, or slight her, or prefer his children (i.e. the males) to her, God will bring him to paradise' (Abu Dawood) [Robson 1975, 1036]. In another place, Anas and Abdallah reported God's messenger as saying, 'All creatures are God's children, and those dearest to God are the ones who treat His children kindly' (Baihaqi) [Robson 1975, 1039].

Taken together, the 'authentic' Islamic tradition is saying that female infanticide is a violent practice, legitimized by accepted culture of the time of *jahiliyya*. The message of Islam is to stop killing the innocents and save lives by getting rid of cultural violence. The case against female infanticide in Islam as overcoming the *jahiliyya* factor is instructive for many reasons. First, the Islamic cosmology does have a place for the innocents and they do have rights. Second, killing the innocents, those who are the weakest link in the chain of the human family, is categorically wrong. Third, cultural violence, which exists to legitimize such an abominable act, needs to be called into question and considered unacceptable. The choice between Islam or *jahiliyya*, reconceptualized in accordance with the moral and historical roles of Islam, would be between killing and saving life, between violence and nonviolence. Using the injunctions against female infanticide as a guideline, choosing nonviolence is an Islamic imperative for Muslims facing an increasing acceptance of violence against the innocents.

ACKNOWLEDGEMENTS

Chaiwat Satha-Anand is Thailand Research Fund's Senior Scholar, teaching and conducting research on violence and nonviolence at Thammasat University in Bangkok. His latest book is *The Life of This World: Negotiated Muslim Lives in Thai* Society (Marshall Cavendish, 2005). He is working on a new book *Nonviolence and the Islamic Imperatives* to be published by the University Press of America.

REFERENCES

Ackerman, P. and DuVall, J. (2000). *A Force More Powerful: A Century of Nonviolent Conflict*. New York: St. Martin's Press.

Al-Qur'an (trans.). (1977). Ali, Y.A. *The Glorious Qur'an*. US: Muslim Students Association.

Arendt, H.. (1970). *On Violence*. New York: Harcourt, Brace and World, Inc.

Bangkok Post. (2004a). 1 May.

Bangkok Post. (2004b). 2 May.

Bangkok Post. (2004c). 4 June.

Bangkok Post. (2004d). 6 June.

Combs-Schilling, M.E. (1994). 'Sacred Refuge: The Power of a Muslim Female Saint.' *Fellowship*, vol. 60(5-6). May/June, 17.

Crow, K.D. (1999). (Ed.). 'Nonviolence in Islam: A round-table workshop' held February 14th 1997 at the American University, Washington D.C. Washington, DC: Nonviolence International.

Crow, K.D. (2000). 'Nurturing Islamic Peace Discourse.' *American Journal of Islamic Social Sciences*, vol. 17(3). Fall, 54-69.

Crow, K.D. (2001). 'Nonviolence, Ethics and Character Development in Islam.' In A.A. Said, N.C. Funk and A.S. Kadayifci (Eds.). *Peace and Conflict Resolution in Islam: Precept and Practice* (1st edition, 213-226). Lanham, NY and Oxford, UK: University Press of America.

Crow, R.E. and Grant, P. (1990). 'Questions and Controversies About Nonviolent Struggle in the Middle East.' In R.E. Crow, P. Grant, and S. Ibrahim (Eds.). *Arab Nonviolent Political Struggle in the Middle East* (75-90). Boulder, CO: Lynne Rienner Publishers.

Crow, R.E., Grant, P. and S.E. Ibrahim. (1990). (Eds.). *Arab Nonviolent Political Struggle in the Middle East*. Boulder, CO: Lynne Rienner Publishers.

Galtung, J. (1996). *Peace by Peaceful Means: Peace and Conflict, Development and Civilization*. Oslo: PRIO and London: SAGE.

Guenena, N. (1986). 'The 'Jihad': An "Islamic Alternative" in Egypt.' *Cairo Papers in Social Science*, vol. 9 (Monograph 2, Summer). Cairo: The American University in Cairo Press.

Haddad, Y.Y. (1983). 'Sayyid Qutb: Ideologue of Islamic Revival.' In J.L. Esposito (Ed.). *Voices of Resurgent* Islam (67-98). New York and Oxford: Oxford University Press.

Janchitfah, S. (2004). *The Nets of Resistance*. Bangkok: Campaign for Alternative Industry Network.

Kishtainy, K. (1990). 'Violent and Nonviolent Struggle in Arab History.' In R.E. Crow, P. Grant, and S. Ibrahim (Eds.). *Arab Nonviolent Political Struggle in the Middle East* (9-24). Boulder, CO: Lynne Rienner Publishers.

Levtzion, N. (1979). (Ed.). *Conversion to Islam*. New York: Holmes and Meier.

Lewis, B. (2002). *What Went Wrong?: The Clash Between Islam and Modernity in the Middle East*. New York: Perennial.

Parekh, B.. (2004). 'Why Terror?' *Prospect Magazine*, (April).

Parkman, P. (1990). *Insurrectionary Civic Strikes in Latin America 1931-1961*. Cambridge, MA: The Albert Einstein Institution.

Plato. (1968). *The Republic*. Allan Bloom (trans.). New York: Basic Books.

Powers, R.S. and Vogele, W. B. (1997). (Eds.). *Protest, Power and Change: An Encyclopedia of Nonviiolent Action from ACT-UP to Women's Suffrage*. New York and London: Garland Publishing, Inc.

Qutb, Muhammad. (n.d.). 'Introduction.' In S. Qutb (Ed.). *In the Shade of the Qur'an*. (vol. 30). Salahi, M.A. and Shamis, A.A. (trans.). New Delhi: Milat Book Centre.

Robson, J. (1975). *Mishkat al-Masabih* (vol.II) (trans.). Lahore: Sh. Muhammad Ashraf.

Salla, M. (1995). 'Kosovo, Non-violence and the Break-up of Yugoslavia.' *Security Dialogue*, vol. 26 (4), 427-438.

Satha-Anand, C. (1993). 'Introduction.' In G.D. Paige, C. Satha-Anand and S. Gilliatt (Eds.), *Islam and Nonviolence* (1-6). Honolulu: Center for Global Nonviolence Planning Project, Matsunaga Institute for Peace, University of Hawaii.

Satha-Anand, C. (2001a). 'Crossing the Enemy's Lines: Helping the Others in Violent Situations through Nonviolent Action.' *Peace Research: The Canadian Journal of Peace Studies*, vol. 33 (2), November, .

Satha-Anand, C. (2001b). 'The Nonviolent Crescent: Eight Theses on Muslim Nonviolent Action.' In A.A. Said, N.C. Funk and A.S. Kadayifci (Eds.). *Peace and Conflict Resolution in Islam: Precept and Practice* (1st edition, 195-211). Lanham, NY and Oxford, UK: University Press of America.

Schell, J. (2003). *The Unconquerable World: Power, Nonviolence and the Will of the People*. New York: Metropolitan Books.

Sivan, E. (1985). *Radical Islam: Medieval Theology and Modern Politics*. New Haven and London: Yale University Press.

Wongwaisayawan, S. (1983). The Buddhist Concept of Ignorance: With Special Reference to Dogen. Unpublished Ph.D. Dissertation, Department of Philosophy, University of Hawaii. May.

PART IV: NONVIOLENT ROLE OF EDUCATION, AESTHETICS AND UN POLICE

In: Nonviolence: An Alternative for Defeating...
Editors: S. Ram and R. Summy, pp. 145-168

ISBN: 978-1-60021-812-5
© 2008 Nova Science Publishers, Inc.

Chapter 9

A NONVIOLENT RESPONSE TO TERRORISM: WHAT CAN PEACE EDUCATION DO?

Donna McInnis

Our enemies are not man. They are intolerance, fanaticism, dictatorship, cupidity, hatred, and discrimination which lie within the heart of man. These are real enemies of humans, not humans themselves. In our unfortunate fatherland we are trying to plead desperately: do not kill man, even in man's name. Please kill the real enemies of man which are present everywhere in our very hearts and minds...

> Thich Nhat Hanh, in letter to Dr. Martin Luther King, Jr. dated June 1, 1965

The opinion of 10,000 men is of no value if none of them know anything about the subject.

> Marcus Aurelius

ABSTRACT

The way that people of the world are educated is dismally inadequate considering the enormous challenges that the threat of terror poses as we work towards a nonviolent future. 'An uninformed democracy is a weak and manipulable democracy' [Hastings 2003, 159]. A true democracy requires critical consciousness: the compassionate and considered participation of all its citizens. Yet in our current culture of violence with its pervasive manipulation of information, these citizens are paralyzed by fear and feel powerless to affect their world.

Fear is a very effective tool used by those in power to keep civil society in line. It is an interesting paradox. The very leaders whose fear-inducing rhetoric warns us of impending crisis and doom at the hands of the 'evil-doing terrorist enemies' are the very same leaders who then offer to protect us with the newest 'coolest' weapons that they recently added to the budget for our approval. They are not alone in the drive to disempower civil population. The media are happy to hype and pitch the message in order to get the headlines, increase their audience base, and maximize profits, while civil society for the most part sinks deeper and deeper into denial and despair.

Recognizing the many problems of violence with all their interrelated complexities, understanding where the deep roots of violence are leading the global society, and suggesting the outline of a nonviolent educational remedy are proposed in this chapter as the way to arrest and then reverse the spiral of self-imposed violence. A critical and humanely-based education program forms the long term solution to overcoming our paralysis of fear and containing terrorism at a tolerable societal level.

INTRODUCTION

What causes terrorism and what can be done to counter it? The extreme political violence that we label 'terrorism' is but one manifestation of the culture of war and injustice that pervades most societies and nations. How do we go about acknowledging, deconstructing, disarming, and countering the myths surrounding this culture of violence; and preparing global civil society to respond to any kind of threat with clear, informed vision and some kind of systemic analysis that favors nonviolence? Is it possible to break from fear's paralyzing grip?

Traditionally, the primary principle for organizing human relationships has been hierarchical — man over women; man over man; race over race; nation over nation; man over nature. Eisler [1987] refers to this as the Dominator Model. A different set of governing principles is called for which emphasize humanization and connection; realize democratic family and social structures which support gender equality and engage all members of civil society; result in a low level of violence and abuse; and nurture the environment which global civil society shares. In this Partnership Model [Eisler 1987], 'leadership is not based on the power to dominate, to control through fear or through force, it is not disempowering but empowering.' [Eisler 2002a, DVD]. In this time of regression towards ever more violent modes of human interacting, greater intentionality and vigilance are required to address the 'spectrum of terror' that ranges from gross poverty amidst conspicuous wealth, to various forms of economic and social injustice, to the expanding power of the state to torture or wage war whenever it has a notion to do so.

Education has a pivotal role to play in creating hope and a vision. We need desperately to develop in civil society a peace-oriented perspective that tackles terror by human intelligence [Elworthy 2005]. This calls for peace education in all its complexity to develop that intelligence and expose the inter-connectedness of the multiple kinds of violence. Not only do we need to know those who our governments label 'our enemies;' we must embrace and engage them, and understand the motivations for their actions. We must take responsibility for our complicity in and contribution to the way the world has been run. And finally we must do whatever it takes to discover the power within us to create a world in which all forms of violoence, including the terror perpetrated by governments in the name of 'security' and 'defense,' become outmoded and unacceptable.

TACKLING TERROR AT ITS ROOTS: UNDERSTANDING CAUSES OF THE CULTURE OF WAR AND VIOLENCE

If most people want peaceful nonviolent lives, as so many say they do, why is peace and nonviolence not happening on a massive scale and why is violence on the increase? Michael Lerner [2001, para. 4] asks, 'What is it in the way that we are living, organizing our societies, and treating each other that makes violence seem plausible to so many people?' The *Hague Agenda for Peace and Justice in the 21ˢᵗ Century* has identified five realities of our contemporary world that work to maintain the culture of war and violence: 'education that glorifies war while failing to teach about alternatives to violence; top-down globalization; unsustainable and inequitable uses of environmental resources; colonialism and neocolonialism that denies democracy; and discrimination and inequities such as racial, ethnic, religious, and gender intolerance' [Reardon and Cabezudo 2002, 27].

Terrorism is not 'a simple aberration unrelated to the political dynamics of a society' [Abou El Fadl 2001, para. 2]. It does not happen *out of the blue* as so many Americans thought immediately after the attacks of September 11, 2001. It is a calculated and premeditated act of extreme political violence perpetrated with the express intention of creating the maximum public disruption and response [Elworthy 2005]. Abou El Fadl [2001] explains that terrorism is the quintessential crime, an extreme act of frustration and deep despair, by those who feel powerless and humiliated seeking to undermine the perceived power of a targeted group. He points out that it is also a hate crime which relies on a polarized and aggressive rhetoric toward a particular group that is demonized and dehumanized to the point of being denied any moral value.

This being said, the motivations of the 'terrorists' do not seem to be a struggle to achieve clear-cut objectives but to awaken their perceived oppressors and create an environment in which these people are consumed with fear for their safety. It is psychological violence which deserves, in turn, a psychological response [Elworthy 2005]. Obviously, by declaring a 'war on terror' against an 'enemy' that is not acting on behalf of an ethnic group or nation constitutes what many would consider a less than intelligent response. Elworthy [2005] calls for an intelligent response that involves first and foremost avoiding more violence

At the outset, we need to define terror more broadly and realistically. By doing so, we can clearly identify a continuum of terror ranging from 'threats to individual security experienced by civilians whose airplanes have been hijacked to the global existential threat posed by the very existence of nuclear and other weapons of mass destruction' [Barash and Webel 2002, 81]. Accordingly, Barash and Webel acknowledge the existence of state terrorism and state-sponsored terrorism in addition to non-state terrorist groups, not to mention 'government-created counter- and anti-terrorist agencies and operations' [81] that also use so-called terror tactics. Clearly, 'who is or is not a terrorist and what may or may not be acts of terrorism depend largely on the perspective of the person or group' [81] doing the defining.

All violence is terrorism in one form or another. It is intentional harm done to people. In the current 'war between terrors' the MYTHS are being deconstructed right before our very eyes. The 'real' war system has been exposed, not as a system of honor which serves to protect but one which causes death and destruction; one which tortures; one which keeps secrets from the civil population in whose name they conduct previously denied or unmentioned atrocities. It is a system based on a plethora of fallacies. Reardon [1994] brings this point home when she states,

> Indeed, nations still think and behave in terms that give primacy to 'national security' over all other human concerns. Such a view of security has become dysfunctional and dangerous... Its heavy emphasis on the military not only results in the tragic social consequences of military expenditures, it results in many other system-damaging consequences that come from the competitive view nations or alliances of nations have taken of each other. Such a view, like the concept of national security itself, is based on a fundamental fallacy; that nations are separate, autonomous entities, systems unto themselves... [33].

The violence of the military system causes pain, anger, fear, humiliation, hatred, a whole spectrum of negative emotions and responses. None of these bring about peace and security. Michael Nagler reminds us [in Schoch 2001, para. 26] that, 'security comes from well ordered human relationships; not from bomb-sniffing dogs and high-tech spy satellites.'

UNDERSTANDING AND EXPOSING ENEMY IMAGE CONSTRUCTION

Enemy construction is an essential part of the culture of war that dominates human society. Enemy images are used to justify the violence of war and oppression and to justify the secrecy and hierarchical authority that characterize the culture of war and domination [Eisler 2002b; Lindner 2006]. The whole problem is exacerbated when the conflict becomes a *glorious cause* with great cosmic forces (God, destiny, history, morality) on our side that will solve all of our problems and bring lasting peace. In his essay 'Dehumanizing People and Euphemizing War, ' Bosmajian (1984) urges that

> Our political and religious leaders, as well as ordinary citizens, must be persuaded to refrain from dehumanizing people into viruses and cancers residing in an evil empire which Scripture admonishes us to destroy. The euphemisms of war must be exposed for what they are — words and phrases that fool us into accepting the unacceptable. Dehumanizing the "enemy" and euphemizing the weapons of war and war itself is a deadly combination that, unfortunately, has historically been successful in defending the indefensible [para. 21].

People who do *not* question destructive power structures; people who do *not* pose questions when their leaders tell them that they must go to war to keep the peace; people who do *not* question the injustice of the economic system that is squeezing the life out of 99% of the world's people; people who do *not* question rampant development and the destruction of the natural environment; and people who do *not* question government policies and media messages that dehumanize and make an enemy out of anyone who is not one of *us*, are the victims of a deficient educating process.

What we are witnessing now as a result of this kind of education is a polarization in societies, particularly in the US, where any kind of dialogue for creating goodness or community is perceived as an extreme threat to stability. Schmookler [2005] asserts that the surest way of preventing people from advancing goodness in this world is by dividing them. 'Goodness,' he believes, 'is about bringing things together, about harmony, about wholeness. Tearing things apart — turning one group against another, displacing cooperation with conflict, shredding structures of good order — manifests a spirit of an altogether different sort' [para. 13-14]. This seems to be the strategy of those now in power, to first divide rather than unite civil populations and then to divide rather than unite all peoples of this world. Rather than creating a global community, they are intensifying global divisions by keeping the world in a chronic state of fear and loathing of the 'other', creating enemies of just about everyone who does not kowtow to their whims for perverse power. Rather than resolving conflicts, this way of conducting affairs leads to deeper and deeper chasms, spiraling out of control towards hotter and more complex conflicts. Clearly, as Schmookler [2005, para. 6] warns, 'when people are focused on their conflicts, they're unable to build a more whole world based on their common humanity.' Elworthy and Rifkind [2005, 49] explain,

> Wars and violence rest on the presumption that the person or people being attacked are not human. The process of dehumanizing the enemy is a defense structure that does not allow space for taking responsibility. Fear shapes the process and allows it to continue massively reducing the capacity to think about and engage with the other side. With time, a desire for backlash builds up and can manifest itself through physical action. Thus, the question remains whether a balance can be struck between self-protection and preserving the humanity and integrity of the other side.

Susan Opotow has done extensive work on the sociology and psychology involved in moral exclusion — seeing others as outside the scope of justice and as eligible targets of discrimination, exploitation and violence. Her work examines the intersection of conflict, justice and identity as they give rise to moral exclusion. The processes that are manifest in moral exclusion enable enemy construction and aid in justifying behaviors that we would otherwise deem unacceptable and anti-social. Opotow identifies a whole range of exclusion-specific processes and ordinary processes that work to create the climate in which these behaviors might occur [Opotow 1990, 10-11; 2001, 102-109; reprinted in Reardon 1995, 171-172].

Exclusion-specific processes include:

- Biased Evaluation: The strong belief that one's own group is superior to another group in all aspects.
- Derogation: Regarding others as lower life forms or inferior beings — e.g. barbarians, vermin, animals, cockroaches, 'rats hiding in holes.'
- Dehumanization: The denial of others' humanity, dignity, ability to feel, deserving compassion.
- Fear of Contamination: The belief that contact with others presents a threat to one's own health and well-being.
- Expanding the target: Regarding an entire group as a legitimate target for attack, persecution, punishment, or mass incarceration.
- Open approval of destructive behavior and a general disregard for moral standards: Harm doing is condoned and praised and the pace of destructive and abhorrent behavior is often accelerated to reduce remorse and inhibitions against the infliction of harm.

- Blaming the victim: Projecting the blame for shameful actions on those who are harmed.
- Self-righteous comparisons: Justifying harmful acts by contrasting them with morally condemnable atrocities committed by the opponent.
- Desecration: Harm doing, often symbolic or gratuitous, to demonstrate disdain for others.

Ordinary processes include:

- Groupthink: Maintaining isolation from dissenting opinion that would challenge the assumptions, distortions, or decisions of the group in order to preserve group unanimity
- Transcendent ideologies: Feeling, believing, and experiencing oneself or one's group as particularly blessed and chosen, which condones and allows even harmful behavior as necessary to bring a better world to fruition.
- Deindividuation and/or moral engulfment: Experiencing anonymity within a group thereby weakening one's ability to maintain personal standards of behavior, morals and values, and/or replacing one's personal ethics with those of the group.
- Psychological distance: Others are perceived as objects or as nonexistent or the presence of others is not felt at all.
- Condescension: Patronizing others, regarding them as inferior, and with disdain.
- Technical orientation: Outcomes are ignored while efficiency becomes the focus; harm doing becomes a mechanical, routine process.
- Double standards: Moral rules and obligations are different for different categories or groups of people.
- Unflattering comparisons: Making unbecoming contrasts to reinforce one's superiority over others.
- Euphemisms: Using language which masks, sanitizes, and misrepresents cruel and reprehensible behavior.
- Displacing responsibility: Denying personal responsibility for harms or behaving in ways that run counter to one's own standards by blaming others, such as subordinates or higher authorities, for the consequences.
- Diffusing responsibility: Viewing harm done as the result of collective rather than individual behaviors and decisions.
- Concealing the effects of harmful behavior: Injurious outcomes are denied, ignored, distorted, disbelieved, or minimized.
- Glorifying and normalizing violence: Viewing violence as not only a sublime activity but as a legitimate form of human expression and as normal due to chronic exposure to it, compounded by societal acceptance of it while denying the harm to people, the environment, relationships, and efforts to resolve conflict nonviolently [Opotow, Gerson, and Woodside 2005, 307].
- Temporal containment of harm doing: Perceiving one's harmful behavior as an isolated occurrence happening this *one* time only

In related research, Leshan [2002] maintains that psychologically people have different modes of perceiving reality in times of peace and in times of conflict. In peacetime, people operate in *sensory mode*, and possess a realistic understanding of what is going on in the world and how the world operates [Leshan 2002; MacNair 2003]. In wartime, however, reason is clouded, and people's perceptions shift to a *mythic mode* of understanding that is commonly called *war hysteria* [MacNair 2003]. Since most people get most of their information about the world from the mainstream media, education for media literacy is essential to raise awareness of the effect of the media on our psyche. Civil society must be critically alerted to the process by which our governments, in collusion with the mainstream media, create the environment of fear which precedes enemy image construction, provokes the shift to a mythic perception of reality, and is manifest in moral exclusion. Leshan [2002, 114-116] has identified several warning signs to look out for which echo and complement Opotow's research. They include:

a. Devaluing of 'other' — dehumanizing, demonizing the entire 'enemy' group. All individual characteristics are completely ignored/denied and only a negative (media created) stereotype remains (terrorist, insurgents, tyrants...). This is very hard to resist in a competitive Dominator Culture [Eisler 1987] where winning and *power-over* are valued.

b. Reasons for differences — reasons for the conflict in the first place are denied. The root causes of the problem are not even considered. Differences are perceived as irreconcilable because of the propaganda campaign that has taken place convincing us that we are good, civilized, lovers and promoters of freedom and THEY are evil, barbaric, heathens who beat and eat their children. That we are a human family is considered to be naïve rhetoric. Discussion concerning the root causes of anger or resentment is ignored primarily because that would be acknowledgement of the 'other' as a human being with feelings and needs the same as our own.

c. Subversion is demonized. Those who do not fall into lock-step with the prevailing (status quo) orthodoxy [LeShan 1992, 115] are shunned, labeled naïve, traitorous, and a danger to 'our nation's security.' Contrarians are discouraged from voicing their views for fear of dangerous repercussions in the form of character assassination at best, physical harm or death at worst to self and to family. The threat of violence serves quite nicely to silence or discourage dissent, and this is accepted in the Dominator System [Eisler 1987].

d. Moral and ethical standards which we uphold as sacred are discarded. Human rights standards become bothersome. Civil liberties are denied to those who happen to be a part of the 'enemy' group. It is acceptable to detain or imprison them without trial, do violence against them, torture them. This is perhaps the most sinister effect of dehumanization of the 'other.' Years of work to create standards for creating peace culture are ignored, seen as 'not applicable at this time' of danger to our national security. And because civil society has been educated into complacency, there are very few voices raised in opposition to the bending and shaping of International Human Rights Laws and Covenants.

e. Our actions are not barbaric or ruthless — their actions are. Deconstructing this distinction is necessary when we define terror. We need to do away completely with the distinction that what we do is for a worthy goal; what they do is simply evil. 'Re-humanization' and truly engaging with those who are either committing acts of terror or supporting those who are doing the terrorizing is necessary to understand what is needed to stop the cycle of violence and retaliation.

If we are conscious of these processes and warning signs, we will be well on our way to countering their negative effects and making informed decisions based on human rights and justice and grounded in empathy and respect for the dignity of all sentient beings.

PEACE EDUCATION: TRANSFORMING HUMAN HEARTS

Hate and prejudice are learned. Education for 'othering' is a major obstacle to peace and it could be argued that this is the fuel that enflames 'terrorism', the cycle of violence, and retaliation. 'If terrorism is to be prevented,' Elworthy asserts, 'it is at a human level that it must operate, because the origins of the cycle can only be dismantled within the individual mind and heart' [2005, 3-4]. We need to remember that young people are resilient and that unlearning hate and prejudice is not such an impossible task.

Michael Nagler [2001, 206] tells the story of Jan Øberg, head of the conflict mitigation team of Sweden's Transnational Foundation for Peace and Future Research. He conducted a series of 'reconciliation seminars' in Eastern Slavonia with 120 Croatian and Serbian gymnasium students. For the majority of the young people, it was the first time that they had the opportunity to meet 'the other side.' The students got to know each other, make friends, make music together, cry about hurt and pain, and most importantly envision together a peaceful future, for Croatia, Eastern Slavonia, and Vukovar. Øberg remarked that, 'It took Croat and Serb students less than an hour to find out that they have a lot in common, in contrast to what they have been told by their government, the media and, often, their parents since 1991.' This humanizing of the 'other' is powerful. Initiatives such as this are taking place all over the world. What we need to do is continue to create the conditions for it to happen on a grander scale. And we need a media that reports when, where, and how it is happening! Nagler urges that it is not different individuals in power that we need, so much as we need a different kind of power in individuals!

Education happens in a social and historical context and clearly serves a social purpose. The social purposes of peace education include the elimination of social injustice and the renunciation of all forms of violence [Reardon and Cabezudo 2002]. Peace educators have a critical role to play in helping learners 'commit to changing the ways that humans treat each other and the natural world' [Harris and Morrison 2003, 192]. A strategy which aims for a nonviolent response to terror needs to locate its base in peace education by actively engaging people in humanizing all aspects of their lives. Humanization serves to break down enemy images or damaging stereotypes. When conflicting parties regard each other as fellow human beings deserving moral consideration rather than evil monsters deserving annihilation, it becomes very difficult to rationalize violent tactics and blatant disregard for human rights norms [Maiese 2003]. Hastings 2004 writes

Challenging our social norms toward humanizing all of humanity is one of our sacred duties as educators. Keeping this perspective even through the aftermath of a terrorist attack is an even greater challenge, but one that is made more possible each time we educate and transform one human heart [2004, 168].

Reardon and Cabezudo (2002) stress that the changes necessary for peace will not be achieved by peace education alone. Rather peace education encourages learner-citizens to explore possibilities for their *own* contributions to achieving a peace culture. It prepares them to resolve problems and achieve the necessary changes by cultivating in them awareness of social and political responsibilities; and guiding and challenging them to determine their own views on the issues of peace and justice. An emphasis on the development of critical capacities ensures that 'learners are sensitized to nationalistic, competitive values hidden in 'neutral' teaching about critical issues and are prepared to question and challenge the existing structures, norms, and values of the war system...' [Reardon and Cabezudo 2002, 20].

By educating people in this way we prepare them to maintain or sustain hope throughout the numerous challenges ahead. When people become aware of the many forms of violence and perverse injustice that exist, they naturally want to know what choices they have to do something about it. Too often, they are 'told' that this is the 'way of the world' and there is nothing that will change that. We often lament that people feel powerless or that they have become apathetic, that no one really cares. What I think happens is that when people are not educated to realize the choices they have, they withdraw, retreat, and lose hope. Hopelessness and despair in our young is unacceptable. Hopelessness and despair in the entire global population is unbearable. By preparing people to be both constructively and hopefully critical, to envision and perceive possibilities, and to construct ways to make these possibilities a reality, we instill in learner-citizens the energy to 'keep on keeping on' [Reardon 2006b].

CONCLUSION: TOWARDS A PEDAGOGY OF ENGAGEMENT AND A CULTURE OF HUMAN RIGHTS

No matter how we work towards social and cultural change, we do so in time. We need to insure a place for both ancient wisdom and new knowledge which involves linking the past, present, and future in our efforts to shape a nonviolent world [Loeb 1999, 310-349]. Dismantling the prevailing system seems at first glance an overwhelming task. Elise Boulding reminds us however that

> After all, we are not inventing peace from scratch. People have been at it for centuries and centuries. And to talk about the 200-year present as something we are present in – you and I – means that we have these colleagues and co-workers who link us to experiences larger than our own lifespan [1996, 38].
> By this, I don't mean some utopian image of a peaceful world, but a realistic way of achieving the goal of nonviolence and culture of peace... we cannot do just one thing at a time. We cannot do just peace; we cannot do just human rights; we cannot do just the environment; we cannot do just development. We have to move in all these spheres at once [1996, 39].

Fortunately, there is a solid foundation of knowledge, research, and practice to guide us towards creating positive possibilities and futures. What we need to do is implement and continue to build upon the existing frameworks and blueprints that have been created by the peace education community. We need to take note of strategies that work short-term and long-term and things that do not work so well and go from there. 'We have the knowledge, technology, and organizational capacity to create the world we choose. We need only the vision to see the possibility of a caring and compassionate Earth Community and choose to live it into being.' [Korten 2002]. And we need leaders. A great deal more energy needs to be spent on educating people to lead towards peace rather than the ever continuing/never ending cycle of violence.

Columbia University's Teacher College Peace Education Program has made a significant contribution towards building a clearly articulated and comprehensive approach to Peace Education. Reardon and other peace educators insist that a pedagogy of engagement is crucial to capacitate learner-citizens to engage in transformative public action in order to become *agents* of social transformation. By guiding students through a process of learning toward personal growth and social change, the potential for transformative learning is enhanced. Learners engage through study, reflection, analysis and action on several levels, from internal, individual reflection to community and global involvement focusing on relevant issues that lead toward the achievement of change — Awareness, Knowledge, Action. Through this process which begins from an initial arousal or awakening of concern, transformative change develops

> as the learning process itself is extended to the larger community through dialogues that constructively challenge unexamined assumptions, values, policies or systems that impede the full realization of human rights of all community members... The institutionalization of the changes and the evolution of consequent, new social norms constitute, in very practical terms, a social transformation. Clearly, nothing short of such a transformation can eliminate the religious discrimination, intolerance and persecution which characterize our current world society [Reardon 2006a, 18-19]

At this time the individual, 'voice in the wilderness' peace educator is up against the entire system of war and violence. Creating and connecting educators and people whose energy is entirely devoted to transforming our culture of violence to one of peace is crucial. Peace Education must continue to inform and be informed by work being done in the areas of Human Rights Education; Holistic Education; Cooperative Education; Partnership Education; Conflict Resolution Education; Education for Social Responsibility; Environmental Education; Nonviolent Action Education; Nonviolent Communication Education, Futures Education — to name a *few*. Actively and continually uniting people within these areas of thought and practice will empower our base and accelerate movement towards a peace culture.

In *The Hague Agenda for Peace and Justice for the 21st Century* (2000, 6) we read:

> A culture of peace will be achieved when citizens of the world understand global problems, have the skills to resolve conflicts and struggle for justice non-violently, live by international standards of human rights and equity, appreciate cultural diversity, and respect the Earth and each other. Such learning can only be achieved with systematic education for peace.

The Hague Agenda for Peace and Justice for the 21st Century reflects the four major strands of the Hague Appeal for Peace: (www.haguepeace.org)

1. Root Causes of War/Culture of Peace,

2. International Humanitarian and Human Rights Law and Institutions,
3. Prevention, Resolution, and Transformation of Violent Conflict,
4. Disarmament and Human Security.

The *Declaration and Programme of Action on a Culture of Peace* (adopted by the United Nations General Assembly in 1999) promotes:

*   Understanding, tolerance, solidarity,
*   Peace education,
*   Sustainable economic and social development,
*   Human rights,
*   Equality between men and women,
*   Democratic participation,
*   Free flow of information and knowledge,
*   International peace and security.

What follows is by no means an exhaustive list of peace education resources which aim to systematically advance *The Hague Agenda for Peace* and *The Program of Action on a Culture of Peace*, but the list represents a sampling of works that would be useful additions to the library of any peace-minded person.

The Global Campaign for Peace Education of the Hague Appeal for Peace

Resources
Levitas, G. (Ed.) *Peace and Disarmament Education.* Available from www.haguepeace.org
Libresco, A.S. and Balantic, J. (2005). *Peace Lessons from Around the World.* Produced in cooperation with the International Advisory Committee of the Global Campaign for Peace. Available from www.haguepeace.org
Reardon, B.A. with Cabezudo, A. (2002). *Learning to Abolish War: Teaching toward a Culture of Peace.* New York: Hague Appeal for Peace. Available from www.haguepeace.org
Tyler, J. and Berry, A. (2005). *Time to Abolish War. A Youth Agenda for Peace and Justice.* Available from www.haguepeace.org

Culture of Peace/General Peace Education

Resources
Adams, D. and True, M. (1997). 'Unesco's Culture of Peace Programme: An Introduction.' *International Peace Research Newsletter*, 35 (1), 15-18.
Adams, D. (2002). 'Moving from a Culture of War to a Culture of Peace.' *Fellowship of Reconciliation Magazine (FOR)*, September/October. http://www.forusa.org/fellowship/sep-oct_02/cultureofpeace.html
Boulding, E. (1988). *Building a Global Civic Culture: Education for an Interdependent World.* New York: Teachers College, Columbia University.

Boulding, E. (1996). 'Toward a Culture of Peace in the 21st Century'. *Social Alternatives*, 15 (3), 38-39. St. Lucia, QLD: The University of Queensland.

Boulding, E. (2000). *Cultures of Peace: The Hidden Side of History.* Syracuse, NY: Syracuse University Press.

Boulding, E. (2002). 'Peace Culture.' In M. Afkhami (Ed.), *Toward a Compassionate Society.* Bethesda, MD: Women's Learning Partnership. Also available from www.learningpartnership.org.

Eisler, R. and Miller, R. (Eds.). (2004). *Educating for a Culture of Peace.* Portsmouth, NH: Heinemann

Harris, I. and Morrison, M.L. (2003). *Peace Education.* Jefferson, NC: McFarland and Co.

Hutchinson, F. (1996). *Educating Beyond Violent Futures.* London: Routledge.

Reardon, B.A. (1988a). *Comprehensive Peace Education: Educating for Global Responsibility.* New York: Teachers College Press.

Reardon, B.A. (1988b). *Educating for Global Responsibility: Teacher Designed Curricula for Peace Education, K-12.* New York: Teachers College Press.

Teaching Tolerance

Tolerance is essential to the realization of human rights and the achievement of a culture of peace [Reardon 1997a, 14]. Thus, 'the overriding goal of education for tolerance is an appreciation of and respect for the human dignity and integrity of all persons' [19]. Hastings reminds us that,

(P)ublic education is a mirror and a molder of public opinion and public policy. Without intervention by teachers, without correction of racist and stereotyping texts, without teaching tolerance to the youngest schoolchildren, the likelihood of peace diminishes and the chances of more terrorism increase [2004, 162].

In its *Declaration on the Principles of Tolerance*, UNESCO defines tolerance as

respect, acceptance, and appreciation of the rich diversity of our world's cultures, our forms of expression and ways of being human. Tolerance is harmony in difference.

Teaching Tolerance (www.teachingtolerance.org) — a pioneer in anti-bias education — views tolerance 'as a way of thinking and feeling — but most importantly, of acting — that gives us peace in our individuality, respect for those unlike us, the wisdom to discern humane values and the courage to act upon them.'

Resources

Chappelle, S. and Bigman, L. (1998). *Diversity in Action.* Hamilton, MA: Project Adventure.

Declarations of Principles on Tolerance. Proclaimed and signed by the Member States of UNESCO on 16 November 1995. http://www.unesco.org/tolerance/declaeng.htm#article1.

Derman-Sparks, L. (1989). *Anti-bias Curriculum: Tools for Empowering Young Children.* Washington, DC: National Association for the Education of Young Children.

Hooks, B. (2003). *Teaching Community: A Pedagogy of Hope.* New York: Routledge.
Reardon, B.A. (1997). *Tolerance — The Threshold of Peace. Units 1-3.* Paris: UNESCO Publishing.

Human Rights Learning

Human Rights are the backbone of peace education. Human rights learning prepares people to actively engage in social transformation to achieve a culture of human rights in which people truly know and understand human rights, internalize the fundamental principles and ethics of human rights, and diligently act to apply and fulfill them so that human rights for all becomes the reality rather than the exception to the rule [Reardon 2006a, 18-19].

Books and Organizations
Andreopoulos, G. and Pierre Claude, R. (Eds.). (1997). *Human Rights Education for the Twenty-First Century.* Philadelphia, PA: University of Pennsylvania Press.
Peoples Movement for Human Rights Education http://www.pdhre.org/ Excellent resource!
Reardon, B.A. (1995). *Educating for Human Dignity: Learning about Rights and Responsibilities.* Philadelphia: University of Pennsylvania Press.
Reardon, B.A. (2006). *Freedom of Religion and Belief: An Essential Human Right.* A 59 page companion guide to a set of videos on the Human Right to Freedom of Religion and Belief. Produced by IARF and PDHRE in collaboration. http://www.pdhre.org/IARF-manual.pdf.

Nonviolence/Nonviolent Action

Resources
Akerman, P. and DuVall, J. (2000). *A Force More Powerful: A Century of Nonviolent Conflict.* New York: St. Martin's Press. Video and teaching materials available from http://www.aforcemorepowerful.org
Cortright, D. (2006). *Gandhi and Beyond: Nonviolence for an Age of Terrorism.* Boulder, CO: Paradigm Publishers.
Hastings, T. (2004). *Nonviolent Response to Terrorism.* Jefferson, NC: McFarland and Co.
Hastings, T. (2006). *The Lessons of Nonviolence: Theory and Practice in a World of Conflict.* Jefferson, NC: McFarland and Co.
Kennedy-Cuomo, K. (2003). *Speak Truth to Power: Human Rights Defenders Who Are Changing Our World.* New York: Umbrage Editions, Inc. www.speaktruthtopower.org for teaching materials (*Speak Truth To Power* Education Packet available from Amnesty International or Umbrage Editions (www. umbragebooks.com). Video available from http://shop.pbs.org/teachers).
Nagler, M. (2004). *The Search for a Nonviolent Future: A Promise of Peace for Ourselves, Our Families, and Our World.* San Francisco: Inner Ocean Publishing. (Formerly entitled, *Is There No Other Way?*).
Schell, J. (2003). *The Unconquerable World: Power, Nonviolence, and the Will of the People.* New York, NY: Metropolitan Books.

Sharp, G. (1973). *The Politics of Nonviolent Action*. (3 vols.). Boston: Porter Sargent.

Sharp, G. (2003). *There are Realistic Alternatives*. Boston: The Albert Einstein Institution.

Sharp, G. (2005). *Waging Nonviolent Struggle: 20th Century Practice and 21st Century Potential*. Boston: Porter Sargent.

Steger, M. and Lind, N. (Eds.). (1999). *Violence and Its Alternatives*. New York, NY: St. Martin's Press.

Social Responsibility/Democratic Participation/Restoring Hope

Books

Berman, S. (1990). *ESR Journal: Educating for Social Responsibility*. Cambridge, MA: Educators for Social Responsibility.

Berman, S., Lafarge, P. (Eds.). (1993) *Promising Practices in Teaching Social Responsibility*. Albany: SUNY Press.

Berman, S. (1997). *Children's Social Consciousness and the Development of Social Responsibility*. Albany: SUNY Press.

Diamond, L. (2001). *The Peace Book: 108 Ways to Create a More Peaceful World*. Bristol, VT: The Peace Company. www.ThePeaceCompany.com

Jones, E., Haenfler, R. and Johnson, B. (2001). *The Better World Handbook*. Gabriola Island, BC, Canada: New Society Publishers.

Krieger, D. (2003). *Hope in a Dark Time*. Santa Barbara, CA: Capra Press.

Krieger, D. and Ong, C. (Eds.). (2005). *Hold Hope, Wage Peace*. Santa Barbara, CA: Capra Press. *Hold Hope, Wage Peace Supplemental Study Guide* can be downloaded from The Nuclear Age Peace Foundation website http://www.wagingpeace.org/ holdhopewagepeace/.

Lappé, F.M. and Lappé, A. (2003). *Hopes Edge*. New York: Tarcher/ Penguin.

Lappé, F.M. and Perkins, J. (2004). *You Have the Power: Choosing Courage in a Culture of Fear*. New York: Tarcher/Penguin.

Lappé, F.M. (2006). *Democracy's Edge: Choosing to Save Our Country by Bringing Democracy to Life*. San Francisco, CA: Jossey-Bass.

Loeb, P. (1999). *Soul of a Citizen: Living with Conviction in a Cynical Time*. New York: St. Martins Press.

Loeb, P. (2004). *The Impossible Will Take a Little While: A Citizens Guide to Hope in a Time of Fear*. New York: Basic Books.

Websites

The Peace Company. http://www.thepeacecompany.com/.

The Better World Handbook. www.betterworldhandbook.com.

Organizations

Educators for Social Responsibility. 23 Garden St., Cambridge, MA. 02138. http://www.esr.org.

The Nuclear Age Peace Foundation. http://www.wagingpeace.org/

Nonviolent Conflict Resolution/Peacebuilding

Resources

Deutsch, M. and Coleman, P. (Eds.). (2000). *The Handbook of Conflict Resolution: Theory and Practice.* San Francisco: Jossey-Bass.

Fisher, S. et al. (2000). *Working with Conflict: Skills and Strategies for Action.* London: Zed Books.

Fisk, L. and Schellenberg, J. (Eds.). (2000). *Patterns of Conflict: Paths to Peace.* Ontario, CA: Broadview Press.

Kreidler, W.J. (1984). *Creative Conflict Resolution.* Glenview, IL: Scott, Foresman and Co.

Kreidler, W.J. (1990). *Elementary Perspectives: Teaching Concepts of Peace and Conflict.* Cambridge, MA: Educators for Social Responsibility.

Kreidler, W.J. (1994). *Teaching Conflict Resolution Through Children's Literature.* New York: Scholastic.

Kreidler, W.J. (1995). *Adventures in Peacemaking: A Conflict Resolution Activity Guide for School-Age Programs.* Cambridge, MA: Educators for Social Responsibility.

Kreidler, W.J. (1997a). *Conflict Resolution in the Middle School.* Cambridge, MA: Educators for Social Responsibility.

Kreidler, W.J. (1997b). *Early Childhood Adventures in Peacemaking: A Conflict Resolution Activity Guide for Early Childhood Providers.* Cambridge, MA: Educators for Social Responsibility.

Lantieri, L. and Patti, J. (1996). *Waging Peace in Our Schools.* Boston, MA: Beacon Press.

Lederach, J.P. and Jenner, J.M. (Eds.). (2002). *Into the Eye of the Storm: A Handbook of International Peacebuilding.* San Francisco, CA: Jossey-Bass.

Lederach, J.P. (2005). *The Moral Imagination: The Art and Soul of Building Peace.* New York: Oxford University Press.

Mertz, G. and Miller-Lieber, C. (2001). *Conflict in Context: Understanding Local to Global Security.* Cambridge, MA: Educators for Social Responsibility.

Miller-Lieber, C. (1998). *Conflict Resolution in the High School: 36 Lessons.* Cambridge, MA: Educators for Social Responsibility.

Humiliation Studies/ Reducing Enmity/Moral Inclusion/Media Literacy

To achieve mutually enhancing, respectful, and empowering human interactions and relations involves critical thinking and media literacy. We need to create a civil society that is resistant to the constant barrage of negative images of those deemed our 'enemy' by the current power holders. Opotow [2001, 109] stresses that

although moral exclusion, direct and structural violence, and social injustice are ubiquitous, they are not inevitable. Inclusionary thinking is fostered by valuing one's connections to and interdependence with others, while seeing the mutually constructive possibilities of those connections as beneficial.... peace is an inclusionary process. In the long run, cultures of peace, characterized by human rights, tolerance, democracy, free flow of information, nonviolence, sustainable development, peace education and equality of men and women will depend upon moral inclusion.

Books

Fabick, S. (Ed.). (2004). *Enemy Images: A Resource Manual.* Washington, DC: Psychologists for Social Responsibility. http://www.psysr.org/Enemyimagesmanual.pdf).

Friedrich, S. (2004). *Enemy Images.* Excellent Power Point presentation! Washington, DC: Psychologists for Social Responsibility. http://www.psysr.org

LeShan, L. (2002). *The Psychology of War: Comprehending its Mystique and its Madness.* Watson-Guptill Publications.

Lindner, E.G. (2004). Humiliation in a Globalizing World: Does Humiliation Become the Most Disruptive Force? New York, NY: Paper prepared for the "Workshop on Humiliation and Violent Conflict," November 18-19, 2004 at Columbia University.

Lindner, E. (2006a). *Making Enemies: Humiliation and International Conflict.* Westport, CT: Prager Security International.

Lindner, E. G. and Wyatt-Brown, B. (Eds.). (2006b). 'Humiliation and History in Global Perspectives.' *Social Alternatives*, 25 (1), 2-60.

Articles

Opotow, S. (1990). 'Moral Exclusion and Injustice: An Introduction.' *Journal of Social Sciences*, 46 (1), 1-20.

Opotow, S. (2000). 'Agression and Violence.' In M.Deutsch and P. Coleman (Eds.), *The Handbook of Conflict Resolution: Theory and Practice* (pp. 403-427). San Francisco: Jossey Bass.

Opotow, S. (2001). 'Social Injustice.' In D.J. Christie, R.V. Wagner and D.D. Winter (Eds.), *Peace, Conflict and Violence: Peace Psychology for the 21st Century* (pp. 102-109). Upper Saddle River, NY: Prentice Hall.

Opotow, S., Gerson, J., and Woodside, S. (2005). 'From Moral Exclusion to Moral Inclusion: Theory for Teaching Peace.' *Theory into Practice*, 44(4).

Websites

Media Ed Foundation. www.mediaed.org

Propaganda Posters from WWI and WWII can be downloaded from http://www.earthstation1.com/American_Propaganda_Posters.html

For a comprehensive look at propaganda leading up to the war in Iraq, see the following websites. They provide plenty of lessons and ideas to build either a full course or a mini-workshop. This is a very good resource for examining how people are manipulated to support and maintain the culture of war.

http://www.classroomtools.com/prop.htm
http://www.classroomtools.com/faces.htm
http://www.classroomtools.com/iraq_war.htm
http://www.classroomtools.com/armyprop.htm
http://www.classroomtools.com/wartax.htm

Moveon.Org – Selling the War in Iraq

Links are quite extensive
http://www.moveon.org/moveonbulletin/bulletin4.html

Propaganda Critic
http://www.propagandacritic.com/
http://www.propagandacritic.com/articles/about.html

Video - Faces of the Enemy
This award-winning program suggests that conflicts can be resolved by discarding symbolic images of our so-called enemies and meeting them as human beings. The DVD version includes a bonus program that discusses post-September 11th applications to terrorism and the Middle East. (Available from Social Studies School Services www.socialstudies.com).

Reporting America At War
http://www.pbs.org/weta/reportingamericaatwar/teachers/

Gender and Peace/Partnership/Gender Equality

Women and men need to join together in partnership in order to create a more just and peaceful world. Without gender equality — a process which involves and respects the contributions of BOTH men and women — democracy is a myth and comprehensive peace will not happen.

Books
Afkhami, M. (Ed.). (2002). *Toward a Compassionate Society.* Bethesda, MD: Women's Learning Partnership. Also available from www.learningpartnership.org

Bucciarelli, D. and Pirtle, S. (2001). *Partnership Education in Action.* A *Companion to Tomorrow's Children* by Riane Eisler. Tucson, AZ: Center for Partnership Studies.

Connell, R.W. (2003). *The Role of Men and Boys in Achieving Gender Equality.* Prepared for the United Nations Division for the Advancement of Women (DAW) in collaboration with International Labour Organization (ILO), Joint United Nations Programmes on HIV/AIDS (UNAIDS), United Nations Development Programme (UNDP) Expert Group Meeting on 'The role of men and boys in achieving gender equality.' 21-24 October, Brasilia, Brazil.

Connell, R.W. (2000). *The Men and the Boys.* Berkeley: University of California Press.

Eisler, R. (2000). *Tomorrow's Children: A Blueprint for Partnership Education in the 21st Century.* Boulder, CO: Westview Press.

Eisler, R. (2002). *The Power of Partnership.* Novato, CA: New World Library.

Korten, D. (2006). *The Great Turning: From Empire to Earth Community.* Co-published by San Francisco: Berret-Koehller Publishers, Inc. and Bloomfield, CT: Kumerian Press.

Reardon, B.A. (1993). *Women and Peace: Feminist Visions of Global Security.* Albany, NY: SUNY Press.

Reardon, B.A. (1996). *Sexism and the War System.* Syracuse, NY: Syracuse University Press.

Reardon, B.A. (2001). *Education for a Culture of Peace in a Gender Perspective.* New York: UNESCO Publishing/The Teacher's Library.

Video

   Tomorrow's Children : Partnership Education in Action, DVD featuring Riane Eisler. Available from Media Education Foundation (http://www.esr.org) and The Center for Partnership Learning (http://www.partnershipway.org/). Located at

   Partnership Center
   The Center for
   Partnership Studies
   P.O. Box 51936
   Pacific Grove, CA 93950
   USA
   Phone 831-626-1004
   Fax 831-626-3734
   center@partnershipway.org

Nonviolent Communication/Language and Peace/From Dehumanizing to Humanizing Education

   Awareness of the power of language to hurt or to heal relationships is crucial as is instilling people with the skills they need to communicate with others in a healthy, nonviolent, respectful, life-affirming way. This involves not only communication skills, but also intrapersonal skills, interpersonal skills, intercultural skills and conflict processing skills [Reardon 2001]. When people are able to recognize the feelings, needs, concerns, fears, hopes and values of self and other, they can avoid the frustration and anger that so often triggers violence, hostility, and conflict, therefore increasing the potential for them to identify the root causes of problems and to find creative solutions to them. [See Reardon 2001; Rosenberg 2003a].

Resources

Bosmajian, H. (1984). *Dehumanizing People and Euphemizing War.* http://www.religion-online.org/showarticle.asp?title=1442.

Brennan, W. (1995). *Dehumanizing the Vulnerable: When Word Games Take Lives.* Chicago, IL:Loyola University Press.

Gorsevski, E. (2004). *Peaceful Persuasion: The Geopolitics of Nonviolent Rhetoric.* Albany, NY: SUNY Press.

Reardon, B.A. (2001). *Education for a Culture of Peace in a Gender Perspective.* New York: UNESCO Publishing/The Teacher's Library.

Rosenberg, M.B. (2003a). *Life-Enriching Education.* Encinitas, CA: Puddledancer Press.

Rosenberg, M.B. (2003b). *Nonviolent Communication: A Language of Life.* Encinitas, CA: Puddledancer Press.

Rosenberg, M.B. (2005). *Speak Peace in a World of Conflict: What You Say Next Will Change Your World.* Encinitas, CA: Puddledancer Press.

Schaeffner, C. and Wenden, A. (Eds.). (1995). *Language and Peace.* Brookfield, VT: Dartmouth Publishing Co..

Caring

In her work on caring, Nel Noddings has demonstrated the significance of caring and relationship both as an educational goal and as a fundamental aspect of education. Noddings' work has become a fundamental reference point for those wanting to reaffirm the ethical and moral foundations of teaching, schooling and education more broadly. Noddings recommends teaching themes of care: caring for self, for intimate others, for global others and strangers, for non-human life and the environment, for the human-made world and its artifacts, and for ideas. She writes:

> Time spent in helping students to learn about matters of central importance to human flourishing should enhance the study of human life in all its fullness; they should not be set up as the point of life or used to distract students from what really matters to their own growth and happiness [Quoted in Eisler 2000, x].

Reardon beautifully points out that

> Caring is an active investment and kind of twin to hope. Both elements are essential to the abilities to be socially responsible, to act toward the effectuation of change, to move against injustice, to protest against and intervene in the degradation of the environment. We hope to help learners develop those abilities. We hope to help learners become responsible, having the capacity to respond actively and effectively, to live out a commitment to the common future [1994, 40].

Resources

Noddings, N. (1984, 2003). *A Feminine Approach to Ethics and Moral Education.* Berkeley: University of California Press.

Noddings, N. (1992). *The Challenge to Care in Schools: An Alternative Approach to Education.* New York: Teachers College Press.

Noddings, N. (2002a). *Educating Moral People: A Caring Alternative to Character Education.* New York: Teachers College Press.

Noddings, N. (2002b). *Starting at Home: Caring and Social Policy.* Berkeley: University of California Press.

Noddings, N. (2003). *Happiness and Education.* Cambridge, UK: Cambridge University Press.

Noddings, N. (2005). *Educating People for Global Awareness.* New York: Teachers College Press.

Environmental Sustainability

Resources

Clayton, S. and Opotow, S. (Eds.). (2003). *Identity and the Natural Environment: The Psychological Significance of Nature.* Cambridge, MA: MIT Press.

Orr, D. (2004a). *The Last Refuge: Patriotism Politics, and the Environment in an Age of Terror.* Washington, DC: Island Press.

Orr, D. (2004b*). Earth in Mind: On Education, Environment, and the Human Prospect.* 10th Anniversary Edition. Washington, DC: Island Press.

Reardon, B.A. and Nordland, E. (Eds.). (1994). *Learning Peace: The Promise of Ecological and Cooperative Education.* Albany, NY: SUNY Press.

Shiva, V. (2005). *Earth Democracy: Justice, Sustainability, and Peace.* Cambridge, MA: South End Press.

Smith, G. and Williams D. (Eds.). (1999). *Ecological Education in Action.* Albany, NY: SUNY Press.

Psychology of Peace and Violence

Psychology has important contributions to make in understanding ways to reduce violence in the world and to foster cooperative, caring relationships within and between groups. MacNair [2003, 57] stresses that 'solving the problems of violence, then, involves not only understanding its causes and removing them. It also involves understanding the causes of behavior that counters violence, and determining how this can be encouraged.' Clearly, 'positive effects can be a cause of behavior because people seek those effects' [MacNair 2003, 94]. By examining the positive impact of nonviolence, the hope is to determine the experiences that people need to be exposed to in order to continue practicing and 'doing' nonviolence as a way of life and a way of affecting change.

Books and Organizations

Adams, D. (1995). *Psychology for Peace Activists.* See David Adams website: http://www.culture-of-peace.info/ppa/title-page.html.

Christie, D., Wagner, R. and Winter, D. D. (2001). *Peace, Conflict, and Violence: Peace Psychology for the 21st century.* Upper Saddle River, NJ: Prentice-Hall.

LeShan, L. (2002). *The Psychology of War: Comprehending Its Mystique and Its Madness.* New York: Watson-Guptill Publications.

MacNair, R. (2003a). *Gaining Mind of Peace: Why Violence Happens and How to Stop It.* Xlibris Corporation: www.Xlibris.com.

MacNair, R. (2003b). *The Psychology of Peace.* Westport, CT: Praeger Publishers.

The American Psychological Association. 'Raising Children to Resist Violence: What You Can Do.' http://www.apa.org/pubinfo/apa-aap.html.

Psychologists for Social Responsibility. http://www.psysr.org/.

Contemplative Practice

Incorporating some kind of contemplative practice into people's education and lives will ensure that future generations are clearly able to see and act upon what needs to be done to reconnect, to heal, and to lead the way towards peaceful nonviolent futures. In "Being Peace", Thich Nhat Hanh says

What we are, what we do every day has much to do with world peace. If we are aware of our lifestyle, our way of consuming and looking at things, then we know how to make peace right at the present moment. If we are very aware, then we will do something to change the course of things. [1986 reprinted in Wink 2000, 156]

Books and Organizations

Kabat-Zinn, J. (1994). *Wherever You Go There You Are: Mindfulness Meditation in Everyday Life*. New York: Hyperion.

Kabat-Zinn, J. and Kabat-Zinn, M. (1997). *Everyday Blessings: The Inner Work of Mindful Parenting*. New York: Hyperion.

Kabat-Zinn, J. (2005). *Coming to Our Senses: Healing Ourselves and the World Through Mindfulness*. New York: Hyperion.

Nhat Hanh, T. (1986). 'Being Peace.' Originally appeared in *Fellowship Magazine*, July-August. Reprinted in *Peace Is the Way* (2000) pp. 153-158 edited by Walter Wink. Maryknoll, NY: Orbis Books.

Nhat Hanh, T. (1991). *Peace is Every Step: The Path of Mindfulness in Everyday Life*. New York: Bantam Books.

Nhat Hanh, T. (1996). *Being Peace*. Berkeley, CA: Parallax Press.

Nhat Hanh, T. (2003). *Creating True Peace*. New York: Free Press.

The Center for Contemplative Mind in Society
199 Main Street, Suite 3
Northhampton, MA 01060 USA
+1- 413-582-0071
www.contemplativemind.org

Peace Education, Peace Studies, and Civilian Peace Building Training Programs

The action component in a comprehensive peace education program is key. A few of the active and 'in the field' institutions where a humane peace is promoted include:

Australian Centre for Peace and Conflict Studies
The University of Queensland
Brisbane, Qld. 4072, Australia
acpacs@uq.edu.au

Austrian Study Center for Peace and Conflict Resolution
International Civilian Peace Keeping and Peace Building Training Program
Stadtschlaining, Austria
http://www.aspr.ac.at/ipt.htm

Columbia University
Teachers College Peace Education Center
New York, New York USA
http://www.tc.columbia.edu/PeaceEd/philosophy.htm

European University for Peace Studies
Stadtschlaining, Austria
http://www.aspr.ac.at/epu/index.htm

United Nations University for Peace
Costa Rica
http://www.upeace.org/contact.cfm

University of Massachusetts Department of Psychology
Psychology of Peace and Prevention of Violence Program
http://www.umass.edu/peacepsychology/

Elise Boulding [2002, 12] maintains that 'people who cannot imagine peace will not know how to work for it. Those who can imagine it are using the same imagination to devise practices and strategies that will render war obsolete. Imagination is the key that can unlock the possibility of future peace.' *Making all forms of terror obsolete* is a possibility which we must work towards with an ever increasing urgency, vigilance, and diligence. What is needed to accomplish this is imagination, engagement, and constructive action fueled, informed and guided by an education for peaceful nonviolent futures, operating within a cultural framework of human rights.

The works mentioned above and below provide life-affirming insight into the role that education is playing in our journey towards a caring, humane, whole culture which respects the fragile variety, interdependence, and integrity of all living beings on this precious earth of ours.

ACKNOWLEDGEMENTS

Donna McInnis is a Professor in the Department of Humanities at Soka University in Hachioji, Japan where she teaches and develops courses in Nonviolent Communication, Conflict Resolution, Gender and Security, Human Rights, and the Psychology of Peace and Nonviolence. She has been a member of the Soka University Peace Research Institute since 1993.

REFERENCES

Abou El Fadl, K. (2001). 'Islam and the Theology of Power.' *Middle East Report 221Online*, (Winter). Available from: http://www.merip.org/mer/mer221/221_abu_el_fadl.html
Barash, D. and Webel, C. (2002) *Peace and Conflict Studies.* Thousand Oaks, CA: Sage.
Bosmajian, H. (1984). 'Dehumanizing People and Euphemizing War.' Available from: http://www.religion-online.org/showarticle.asp?title=1442. This article first appeared in the *Christian Century* December 5, 1984, p. 1147.
Boulding, E. (1996). 'Toward a Culture of Peace in the 21st Century.' *Social Alternatives,* 15(3)*, 38-39.* St. Lucia, Qld: University of Queensland.

Boulding, E. (2002). 'Peace Culture.' In M. Afkhami (Ed.), *Toward a Compassionate Society.* Bethesda, MD: Women's Learning Partnership. (Also available for download at www.learningpartnership.org).

Declaration and Programme of Action on a Culture of Peace. Adopted by the United Nations General Assembly in 1999. Available from http://decade-culture-of-peace.org/resolutions/resA-53-243B.html.

Eisler, R. (1987). *The Chalice and the Blade: Our History, Our Future.* San Francisco: Harper Collins.

Eisler, R. (2000). *Tomorrow's Children: A Blueprint for Partnership Education in the 21st Century.* Boulder, CO: Westview Press.

Eisler, R. (2002a). *Tomorrow's Children: Partnership Education in Action.* DVD. Media Education Foundation: www.mediaed.org

Eisler, R. (2002b). *The Power of Partnership.* Novato, CA: New World Library.

Elworthy, S. (2005). *Tackling Terror by Human Intelligence.* Available from http://www.transnational.org/SAJT/forum/meet/2005/Elworthy_TacklingTerror.pdf

Elworthy, S. and Rifkind, G. (2005). *Hearts and Minds: Human Security Approaches to Political Violence.* London: Demos.

Harris, I. and Morrison, M.L. (2003). *Peace Education.* Jefferson, NC: McFarland and Co.

Hastings, T. (2004). *Nonviolent Response to Terrorism.* Jefferson, NC: McFarland and Co.

Korten, D. (2002). 'Beyond War: What Kind of America?' Keynote Address delivered by David C. Korten at the Earth Charter Community Summit, Seattle, WA, September 28. From *YES! Online, http://www.yesmagazine.org/article.asp?ID=1038.*

Lerner, M. (2001). 'A World out of Touch with Itself: Where the Violence Comes From.' *Tikkun Magazine,* September 12. (http://www.paxchristiusa.org/ news_events_ more.asp?id=105).

LeShan, L. (1992). *The Psychology of War: Comprehending Its Mystique and Its Madness.* Chicago: Noble Press.

Lindner, E. (2006). *Making Enemies: Humiliation and International Conflict.* Westport, CT: Prager Security International.

Loeb, P. (1999). *Soul of a Citizen: Living with Conviction in a Cynical Time.* New York: St. Martins Press.

Maiese, M. (2003). 'Humanization.' In G. Burgess and H. Burgess (Eds.), *Beyond Intractability.* University of Colorado, Boulder, CO: Conflict Research Consortium. Posted: July. (http://www.beyondintractability.org/essay/humanization/).

Mayor, F. (1999). 'Toward a New Culture of Peace and Nonviolence' http://www.gppac.net/documents/pbp_f/intros/a6_towar.htm (Introduction to *People Building Peace: 35 Inspiring Stories from around the World.* Utrecht, The Netherlands: European Centre for Conflict Prevention online at http://www.gppac.net/documents/ pbp_f/content.htm)

Nagler, M. (2001). *Is There No Other Way? : The Search for a Nonviolent Future.* Berkeley, CA: Berkeley Hills Books.

Nhat Hanh, T. (1965). In Search of the Enemy of Man (addressed to Rev. Martin Luther King). In Nhat Hanh, T. et al, *Dialogue,* pp. 11-20. Saigon: La Boi.

Nhat Hanh, T. (1986). 'Being Peace.' Originally appeared in *Fellowship Magazine, July-August 1986.* Reprinted in *Peace Is the Way* (2000) pp. 153-158 edited by Walter Wink, Maryknoll, NY.: Orbis Books.

Opotow, S. (1990). 'Moral Exclusion and Injustice: An Introduction.' *Journal of Social Sciences*, 46 (1), 1-20.

Opotow, S. (2000). 'Agression and Violence.' In M. Deutsch and P. Coleman (Eds.), *The Handbook of Conflict Resolution: Theory and Practice* (pp. 403-427). San Francisco: Jossey Bass.

Opotow, S. (2001). 'Social Injustice.' In D.J. Christie, R.V. Wagner and D.D. Winter (Eds.), *Peace, Conflict and Violence: Peace Psychology for the 21st Century* (pp. 102-109). Upper Saddle River, N.Y.: Prentice Hall.

Opotow, S., Gerson, J., and Woodside, S. (2005). 'From Moral Exclusion to Moral Inclusion: Theory for Teaching Peace.' *Theory into Practice,* 44(4), 303-318.

Reardon, B.A. and Nordland, E. (Eds.). (1994). *Learning Peace: The Promise of Ecological and Cooperative Education.* Albany: SUNY Press.

Reardon, B.A. (1995). *Educating for Human Dignity: Learning about Rights and Responsibilities.* Philadelphia: University of Pennsylvania Press.

Reardon, B.A. (1997a). *Tolerance - The Threshold of Peace.* Unit 1. Paris: UNESCO.

Reardon, B.A. (1997b). 'Human Rights as Education for Peace.' In G. Andreopoulos and R. Pierre Claude (Eds.), *Human Rights Education for the Twenty-First Century.* Philadelphia, PA: University of Pennsylvania Press.

Reardon, B.A. (2001). *Education for a Culture of Peace in a Gender Perspective.* New York: UNESCO Publishing/The Teacher's Library.

Reardon, B.A. with Cabezudo, A. (2002). *Learning to Abolish War: Teaching toward a Culture of Peace.* New York: Hague Appeal for Peace.

Reardon, B.A. (2006a). *Freedom of Religion and Belief: An Essential Human Right.* (59 page companion guide to a set of videos on the Human Right to Freedom of Religion and Belief.) Produced by IARF and PDHRE in collaboration. http://www.pdhre.org/IARF-manual.pdf.

Reardon, B.A. (2006b). Perceptions of Religious Conflict. (One day workshop offered at Teachers College Peace Education Program, May 13). Tokyo, Japan.

Rosenberg, M.B. (1999). *Nonviolent Communication: A Language of Compassion.* Encinitas, CA: Puddledancer Press.

Rosenberg, M.B. (2003a). *Life-Enriching Education.* Encinitas, CA: Puddledancer Press.

Schmookler, A.B. (2005). *By Their Fruits Ye Shall Know Them.* (January). Available from: *http://www.nonesoblind.org/blog/?page_id=17.*

Schoch, R. (2001). *A Conversation with Michael Nagler.* Available from: http://www.alumni.berkeley.edu/Alumni/Cal_Monthly/December_2001/QA A_Conversation_with_Michael_Nagler.asp

The Hague Agenda for Peace and Justice for the 21st Century (2000). The Hague Appeal for Peace, http://www.haguepeace.org/resources/HagueAgenda Peace+Justice4The21st Century.pdf

In: Nonviolence: An Alternative for Defeating...   ISBN: 978-1-60021-812-5
Editors: S. Ram and R. Summy, pp. 169-186   © 2008 Nova Science Publishers, Inc.

Chapter 10

ART AGAINST TERROR: NONVIOLENT ALTERNATIVES THROUGH EMOTIONAL INSIGHT[1]

Roland Bleiker

ABSTRACT

The terrorist attacks of September 2001 highlight a fundamental paradox. While security issues are becoming increasingly complex and transnational, our means of understanding and responding to them are still based primarily on strategic expertise and corresponding militaristic ways of articulating defense policy. Nonviolent alternatives are rarely explored, even though they offer important ways of understanding and dealing with terrorist threats. Pursuing such a line of inquiry, this chapter seeks to provide new insight by examining aesthetic reactions to the terrorist attacks of 11 September 2001. Focusing on literature, visual art, architecture and music, the chapter demonstrates that aesthetic sources are particularly suited to capture emotional aspects of security threats.

INTRODUCTION

The aim of this essay is to show how art, as an inherently nonviolent engagement with the world, can shed new and revealing light on the problem of global terrorism. In doing so, the chapter addresses a fundamental paradox that became apparent with the terrorist attacks of 11 September 2001 on the World Trade Center and the Pentagon. While security threats are becoming increasingly complex and transnational, our means of understanding and responding to them have remained largely unchanged. They are still based primarily on strategic expertise and corresponding militaristic and state-centric ways of articulating defense policy.

[1] This chapter draws upon my article (2005). 'Art After 9/11'. *Alternatives: Global, Local, Political*, vol 30/4, 77-99. Copyright (c) by Lynne Rienner Publishers, Inc. Used with permission of the publisher. I am grateful to Stephen Chan, Alex Danchev, Toby Ganley, Ian Hunter, Emma Hutchison, Brian Martin, Martin Leet and Oliver Richmond for comments on an earlier draft. I would also like to acknowledge the generous support of a fellowship from the Centre for Research in the Arts, Social Sciences and Humanities at Cambridge University.

Military defense will undoubtedly remain a crucial element of security policy, but the problem of terrorism is far too complex and far too serious not to employ the full register of human intelligence and creativity to understand and deal with it. This is particularly the case because the potential use of weapons of mass destruction amplifies the dangers of terrorist threats [Laqueur 1999]. One of the key intellectual and political challenges today thus consists of legitimizing a greater variety of approaches to and insights into the phenomenon of terrorism.

Art has the potential to contribute to this broadening process. It can help us deal with dimensions of security challenges that cannot easily be understood through conventional forms of policy analyses. The essay draws attention to this potential by examining some of the artistic reactions to 9/11. The ensuing endeavor lays no claim to comprehensiveness, for surveying the astonishing outpouring of artistic creativity that followed the tragic events would be doomed from the start. The objective, then, is limited to two specific tasks 1) to draw upon a few select examples, stemming from literature, visual art, architecture and music, in order to demonstrate the relevance of art to the process of coming to terms with 9/11; and 2) to engage some of the more fundamental epistemological puzzles that are entailed in understanding the links between art and politics. Both aspects reveal the potential – and limits – of art to offer suggestions about how to create nonviolent alternatives to the type of military-based responses that have characterized the fight against terrorism. Can fiction, for instance, express certain aspects of terrorism better than a straightforward factual account? Can we see things through visual art that we cannot express through textual analyses? Can music make us hear something that we cannot see? If aesthetic engagements are indeed qualitatively different from others, what is the exact political content and significance of this difference? And how can the respective insights be translated into concrete policy recommendations without loosing the essence of what they capture?

Artistic engagements, the chapter argues, have the potential to capture and communicate a range of crucial but often neglected emotional issues. Prevailing scholarly analyses and policy approaches to global security certainly pay no attention to the role of emotions, even though terrorism is a highly emotional issue. Various recent studies in philosophy, aesthetics and ethics have shown how emotions are not just subjective and irrational reactions, but do in fact contain insights that can be as revealing and as important as conventional knowledge forms, such as those emanating from social scientific inquires. This is why our knowledge of global security threats, and our practical abilities to counter them, would greatly improve if we found ways of legitimizing both emotional knowledge and a range of alternative, artistic ways of expressing them.

The fact that art is an inherently nonviolent practice is an essential element of its ability to break through existing and often violent approaches to dealing with terrorism. Nonviolent means are much more likely to create and sustain the type of respectful communities that are essential for dealing with the legacy of pain and death. But it also needs to be stressed that the form of nonviolence expressed through art, works in fundamentally different ways than the resistance practices that are most often theorized by scholars who explore the relevance of nonviolence. The latter tend to see nonviolence as a strategic form of action, one that can bring about social and political change by interfering in the power relationship between ruler and ruled. Or so at least stipulate works conducted in the wake of key thinkers, such as Mohandas Gandhi and Martin Luther King. Gene Sharp's still influential work on nonviolent action from the 1970s is the most illustrative contemporary articulation of this approach to nonviolence [Sharp 1972].

Art operates in different, more subtle but no less effective ways than this strategic operation of nonviolence. It does not tap into power relationships directly. It does not seek to uproot rulers or change laws. But it can have a major impact on social and political dynamics by shaping the manner in which people view, represent and judge the issues at stake. No direct principles of action can be derived from such an engagement. The target is not to change people's actions, but their mode of thinking. But the long-term transformations that can be engendered in this manner may be as effective, and perhaps even more enduring, than those triggered by more direct actions – or so at least this chapter will seek to demonstrate.

9/11: FROM A BREACH OF SECURITY TO A BREACH OF UNDERSTANDING

The terrorist attacks of 11 September 2001 undoubtedly mark a key turning point in international politics. The death toll alone would not necessarily render the event so central, for many other recent conflicts, from Bosnia to Rwanda, produced far more casualties. 9/11 is significant because it fundamentally questioned the prevailing sense of security and the political structures that had been established to provide it. Or so at least argue most scholarly commentators.

The shock experience of 9/11 was thus linked to a fundamental breach of security, for security had come to be associated with the integrity and sovereignty of the nation state. There is a well established body of literature that examines the relationship between states as security machines and states as war machines. The most influential perspectives on foreign policy, those shaped by realist ideas, stress the need for states to protect peace and order at the domestic level by promoting policies that maximize the state's military capacity and, so it is assumed, its external security. That this very practice only increases everyone else's insecurity is evident, not least through extensive realist attempts to theorize the respective dilemmas.

But the significance of 9/11 goes beyond a mere breach of state-based security, which is dramatic but can still be understood through existing conceptual means. The terrorist attacks also engendered a more fundamental breach in human understanding, which remains largely ignored by security experts. 9/11 displays all features that Susan Neiman identifies as key elements of major turning points: moments in history when certain events defy 'human capacities for understanding' and trigger a 'collapse of the most basic trust in the world' [Neiman 2003, 1-2].

Aesthetic insights into 9/11 have the potential to identify and shed light on this fundamental breach of understanding. It is no coincidence that one of the most remarkable but often overlooked reactions to the terrorist attacks is the astonishing outpouring of artistic creativity. Countless artists around the world have tried to deal with both the nature of the tragic event and its implications for the future. They painted and filmed, they wrote poems and novels, they composed and performed music. This wave of aesthetic creativity may be comparable to the reactions Immanuel Kant described when faced with a powerful object, such as a storm or erupting volcano. The prevalent faculties, including reason, are confronted with their limit, for they are unable to grasp the event in its totality [Kant 1974, 184-9]. The result is incomprehension, pain, and fear, which express the gap between what was experienced and what can actually be apprehended by existing conceptual and descriptive means. This is particularly the case for survivors of major traumas, who tend to find that there are no words to convey what happened [Edkins 2003, 111; Scarry 1985, 279]. But even people who are only indirectly affected by the events can feel distressed by their inability to comprehend them through existing conceptual means.

Artistic representations may capture certain emotional dimensions that remain out of reach for prevalent forms of communication and analyses. They are an essential element of how the tragic events are viewed, interpreted and remembered. But while offering insight into the nature and meaning of terrorism, these aesthetic reactions have had no influence on the making of security policy, which continues to be dominated by prevalent techno-strategic assessments of threats. Although presented as 'new ways of thinking and new ways of fighting [Rumsfeld 2002, 21], the US response is above all characterized by a strong desire to return to the reassuring familiarity of dualistic thinking patterns that dominated foreign policy during the Cold War. Once again the world is divided into 'good' and 'evil,' and once again military means occupy the key, if not the only role in protecting the former against the latter. This has the unwelcome effect of representing the wars of response - Afghanistan and Iraq - as moral crusades, obscuring a deeper understanding and threatening to evoke the atavistic logic of religious war. Such an approach may make sense in the context of the shock that followed the events of 9/11, but it creates more difficulties than it solves. The rhetoric of 'evil madmen,' one commentator stresses, 'advances neither understanding of [terrorist] horror nor, for that matter, the capacity to combat or prevent it' [Euben 2002, 4]. Even high-ranking military commanders now question the usefulness of the wars of response, admitting that 'defeating terrorism is more difficult and far-reaching than we have assumed' [Clark 2004].

The tendency to resort to old thinking patterns in times of crises is as entrenched in international relations scholarship as it is in the domain of policy making. Most approaches to the study of world politics remain dominated by social scientific principles. This is even the case with many authors who seek to open up new perspectives. Alexander Wendt, for instance, one of the leading constructivist contributors to scholarly debates, stresses that 'poetry, literature and other humanistic disciplines are not designed to explain global war or Third World poverty, and as such if we want to solve those problems our best hope, slim as it may be, is social science [Wendt 1999, 90]. The resulting tendency to marginalize alternative insights, such as those emanating from aesthetic sources, is particularly prevalent in the specific domain of security studies. This tendency is exacerbated by the fact that art is an inherently nonviolent way of engaging political issues – a mode of engagement that tends to be considered far too 'soft' to be relevant to scholars and practitioners working on security. They still rely almost exclusively on military-based forms of defense and deterrence, even if these practices of defense generate as much new conflict as they provoke old ones.

While major crises initially tend to reinforce old thinking and behavioral patterns, they also allow societies to challenge and overcome entrenched habits, thereby creating the foundations for a new and perhaps more peaceful future. Major traumas have, indeed, always played a central role in redefining political communities [Edkins 2003, 42]. Questioning the key assumptions that guide security thinking should therefore be an essential element of coming to terms with 9/11. And it should entail fundamental discussions about the nature and meaning of security in a rapidly changing world - discussions that include the use of a range of hitherto neglected sources of insight, such as aesthetic ones. The latter are essential not least because aesthetic factors have made 9/11 into a major global event in the first place. What haunted the world more than anything were the images and sounds of the crumbling twin towers, of human suffering and death, being instantaneously and repeatedly televised around the world.

QUESTIONING REPRESENTATION

A series of aesthetic questions thus need to be posed with regard to 9.11. These questions revolve to a large extent about the issue of representation, about how one can understand major political events in a way that does justice to both their complexities and the need to find adequate ways of responding politically. The chapter now raises some of these questions by focusing on four specific aesthetic domains: literature, visual art, architecture and music. My ambition is not to map how artists in these aesthetic fields have engaged 9/11. There have been far too many artistic engagements to even attempt a comprehensive survey, at least in an essay length exposé. I am merely showing how paying attention to artistic and inherently nonviolent activities allows us to pose questions that are central for the study of security and international relations in general.

The potential and problems of literature's contribution to the study of political phenomena is well illustrated through a recent book by the French philosopher Bernard-Henri Lévy. Entitled *Who Killed Daniel Pearl?*, the book engages the regional political context of the US invasion of Afghanistan, which was the initial military response to 9/11. Lévy examines the death of Daniel Pearl, an American journalist who, in early 2002, was kidnapped in Karachi and then decapitated. The latter act was captured on video and linked with a range of political demands. Lévy's book, which became a best-seller both in Europe and North America, mixes investigative journalism with fiction, a style he calls *romanquête*. Since many facts regarding the case are not known, Lévy simply uses his literary imagination to provide a coherent narrative. The later include speculation about events and motives and about Pearl's emotional response to being captured and tortured [Lévy 2003].

Whether or not Lévy's book constitutes literature is an open question. Clearly, however, it has caused a great deal of controversy. One prominent commentator, writing for the *New York Review of Books*, dismissed Lévy's research as 'amateurish,' drawing attention to his 'shaky' knowledge of South Asian geography, his 'deep ignorance' of the corresponding political situation and his stereotypical representation of 'fanatical Orientals' [Dalrymple 2003]. This comes in the wake of years of critique by prominent philosophers such as Gilles Deleuze or Pierre Vidal-Naquet, who accused Lévy of gross factual errors and intellectual mediocrity [Deleuze 2003; Vidal- Naquet 1979]. Levy's latest best-seller may well be 'ill-informed and simplistic,' as the above commentator stresses, but it also triggered a number of more generic, more fundamental controversies, which are well worth investigating. They have to do with the author's stylistic transgressions, with his attempt to blur journalistic inquiry and fictional creativity. Many reviewers were far more disturbed by these transgressions than by Lévy's lack of investigative competence and literary flair. They worry primarily about 'a more unsettling doubt raised by the fusion of genres,' [Wood 2003], about occasions when the author 'distorts his evidence and actually invents the truth' [Dalrymple 2003; see also Halimi 2003].

What are the exact political and ethical dangers of crossing factual and fictional accounts? Can literature, as Proust once claimed, provide certain insight into human beings and their emotions that other accounts fail to capture [Nussbaum 2003]. Can literature's appeal to the imagination generate political and social change in a way that factual accounts can not [Levinson 1998]. Or is not today's opposition between 'fact and fancy' a historical product, replacing earlier intellectual traditions that provided space for a range of different truth claims, including those 'that could be presented to the reader only by means of fictional techniques of representation?' [White 1978]. Needless to say, an essay-length survey cannot spell out the exact policy relevance of literary readings of 9/11. But the potential of such engagements can nevertheless be identified. A brief example:

Fictional accounts of reactions to terrorist threats can offer insight into the psychological, political and cultural motives that underlie our reactions to them. They may capture emotional dimensions that a purely analytical account cannot. That is one of the main assets of literature: to provide detailed descriptions of situations, including emotional states that would otherwise remain beyond our personal experiences [Rorty 1989, xvi]. An approach that takes such insights into account could, for instance, help us understand a puzzle that many commentators, including Michael Ignatieff and William Pfaff, identify: why the actual threat – and impact – of terrorism is often grossly exaggerated in comparison to many other problems, such as poverty or crime [Ignatieff 2004, 44; Pfaff 2005, 50]. A better understanding of the emotional reactions to terrorism can also facilitate understandings of the conditions under which public support emerges for a state of exception: that is, when and how the government authorities should suspend existing rights, such as civil liberties, to increase their effectiveness in preventing terrorist threats [Agamben 2005; Butler 2005; Hersch 2004].

A focus on visual art helps to illuminate the potential and problems of such aesthetic engagements. There have been an unusually high number of painters, from leading artists to amateurs, seeking to deal with various aspects of 9/11. The diversity of websites devoted to representing these activities is in itself astonishing. Various internet-based projects, such as the 'WHY Project,' the 'ARTproject,' 'Rhizome,' or 'Arts Healing America' display literally thousands of art works that deal with the terrorist attack and its aftermath. They stress the importance of art in the process of 'coming to terms with what has happened,'[2] in the 'healing, recovery and rebuilding of self and community.'[3] They seek to 'function as a dialogue for those who wish to communicate through images.'[4] They want to 'open up avenues of discussion and expression... through cultural intervention.'[5] Such artistic and cultural engagements are not limited to local people, reacting directly to the events in New York. One of the most prominent websites, the WHY Project, was established on the day of the attacks. It featured instructions in several languages, inviting artists around the world to submit their work as part of a collective effort to address the aftermath of the events.[6]

Many visual artists throughout the world did, indeed, feel the need to deal with the event in the medium they know best. Look at the indigenous Australian painter Gordon Bennett. As

---

[2] '9-11 Show: Artists Respond,' Kentler Gallery, http://kentlergallery.org (accessed Jan 2004).

[3] 'Arts Healing America,' http://www.americansforthearts.org (accessed Jan 2004)

[4] 'TheARTproject,' http://www.theartproject.net (accessed Jan 2004).

[5] 'Rhizome,' http://www.rhizome.org (accessed Jan 2004).

[6] 'The WHY Project,' http://www.whyproject.org/ (site no longer active). For a commentary see 'Why addressing the September 11 Event,' Coral Coast Art Gallery, http://coralcoast.com/art (accessed Jan 2004).

an extended aesthetic dialogue with the African-American artist Jean-Michel Basquiat, Bennett produced a series of paintings that dealt directly with the events of 9/11 [Ward 2002]. On one level, the paintings are relatively figurative, with tumbling buildings, airplanes, flames and suffering people clearly visible. But they also represent the events in ways that place emphasis not on external appearances but on the emotional reaction to them. Can such artistic engagements provide insights that language-based accounts cannot? If so, what is their exact content and can they be translated back into language based representations and brought to bear upon the formulation of security policy?

PUBLIC DEBATES ABOUT THE AESTHETIC RECONSTRUCTION OF GROUND ZERO

Some of these difficult questions also entered debates about the rebuilding of Ground Zero, the space in New York where the twin towers of the World Trade Center used to stand. Consider, for instance, the work of Daniel Libeskind, who has chief responsibility for overseeing the rebuilding process, and a range of other architects and artists, such as Michael Arad, whose design was chosen for the memorial at Ground Zero. Debates about the highly symbolic rebuilding process led to heated disagreements, both among the architects involved and in the public at large. The very existence of these debates demonstrates that architecture has the potential to generate discussion about political and moral issues. 'Architecture is communication,' Libeskind argues [2004a], it is 'poetry in stone and in light and in gravity' [WNBC 2003]. And he goes on to stress that 'contrary to public opinion the flesh of architecture is not cladding, insulation and structure, but the substance of the individual in society in history' [Libeskind 2004b].

Structural elements did, however, generate considerable tension. This was the case, for instance, with disagreements about the so-called Freedom Tower, the centerpiece of the rebuilding process. Libeskind's master plan foresaw a building with a slanting roof that holds a spire reaching up to 1,776 feet in total, symbolizing the year of the Declaration of Independence. David Childs, the architect chosen by the developer, planned a much more massive structure with a facade that is twisted as it rises. A compromise between these two architectural approaches produced a hybrid-design that retains elements of Child's basic structural ideas while adding Libeskind's notion of an asymmetrical summit and a symbolic height of 1,776 feet [Pitzke 2003; Muschap 2003]. The latter would make it the world's tallest building when completed in 2008, thus symbolizing, in the words of Governor George Pataki, that 'the world of freedom will always triumph over terror.' [Cited in Dunlap 2003b].

Debates over the memorial at Ground Zero offer particularly revealing glimpses into the relationship between aesthetics and politics. The purpose of the memorial is to commemorate the 2,982 lives lost in the attacks on the World Trade Center. A thirteen-member jury was set up to oversee the selection process. Rather than choosing politicians for the process, it consisted mostly of people from the arts and cultural professions, including Maya Lin, the designer of the Vietnam War Memorial, and Vatan Gregorian, the president of the Carnegie Corporation. The main aim of the Jury was to 'find a design that will begin to repair both the wounded cityscape and our wounded souls, to provide a place for the contemplation for both loss and new life' [WTC 2003]. Besides this broad goal there were very few official rules, but they included that the memorial 'make visible the footprints of the original World Trade Center towers' and that it 'recognize each individual who was a victim of the attacks' [Dunlap 2003a].

After examining a total of 5,201 submissions the jury announced eight finalists in November 2003. The respective designs were far more abstract and minimalist than, say, Bennett's figurative rendering of the event. In some sense they continued a tradition of abstract memorialization that was initiated twenty years earlier by Maya Lin's Vietnam War memorial. 'Everywhere abstraction and minimalism became the unavoidable language of the monument,' stresses one commentator. 'We have become uncomfortable with the idea of literal representation when we make monuments' [Sudjic 2003]. Arad's design reflected a very conscious aesthetic choice made by the Jury which, as mentioned, included Lin. 'We resisted the idea of the literal,' said one of the jurors [Collins and Dunlap 2004a]. The basic idea was to choose a memorial that could provide a living memory by allowing 'for the change of seasons, passage of years and evolution over time' [WTC 2003]. The initial public reaction was rather negative. A survey conducted by the Municipal Art Society found that the most frequent criticism of the designs, including that of the subsequent winner, were 'too cold, bleak and angular' [Dunlap 2004; Feuer 2003]. A leading New York architect spoke of 'a public-relations disaster' [Sudjic 2003]. One commentator aptly summarized these critical voices by stressing the designs were too remote and sanitized to 'capture the destruction and injustice' of the event, to 'speak of the cruelty and the horror, of the vulnerability and desperation, of the valor and sacrifice.' To remember what 'really happened' on September 11, he stressed, one needs to be more figurative, one needs monuments that 'capture the drama, images that haunt us and objects that carry the scars of their survival' [Fischl 2003]. Others strongly defended the choice of finalists, insisting they 'make the strongest possible case for simplicity as the most suitable aesthetic for ground zero' [Muschamp 2003b].

The eventual winner of the competition, Michael Arad's memorial 'Reflecting Absence,' perfectly captures these aesthetic tensions. Revised in collaboration with Peter Walker, a prominent landscape architect, Arad's memorial consists of an open plaza with pine trees. In the middle of it, and submerged thirty feet below street level, is a pair of enormous reflective pools marking the space where the two twin towers used to stand. These 'voids can be read as containers of loss, being close-by yet inaccessible,' Arad observes. He describes the descent into the memorial as follows:

> This descent removes [visitors] from the sights and sounds of the city and immerses them into a cool darkness. As they gradually proceed, step by step, the sound of water falling grows louder, and more daylight filters in from below. At the bottom of their descent, they find themselves behind a thin curtain of water, staring out at an enormous pool that flows endlessly towards a central void that remains empty [Arad 2003].

Disputes arose about several aspects of the design, including the manner in which the dead are individually remembered. Arad's original design foresaw that the two central and massive pools be surrounded by a ribbon of names that indicated the victims of the attack. Key was that the names appear in no discernible order, so that they 'reflect the haphazard brutality of the death' [Arad 2003]. But many relatives of victims found the plan 'too impersonal and generic,' demanding a more specific acknowledgement. Some family members of officials who died in the attack went as far as threatening to remove the name of their relatives from the memorial in case they are listed together with civilians [Collins 2003; Keenan 2003]. As a compromise, the revised version of Arad's and Walker's memorial designated individual shields for the names of police officers, fire-fighters and other officials [Collins and Dunlap 2004b].

How can such memorial and architectural features, and the discussions about them, contribute to our memory of 9/11? Can artistic representation express forms of memory that the more linear representations of verbal narrative cannot? Jenny Edkins provides an excellent discussion of this theme [see 2003]. Prevalent political reactions to 9/11, for instance, generated a patriotic movement that led to considerable cultural and racial stereotyping, particularly vis-à-vis people of an Arabic origin. On the other hand, aesthetic representations of traumas, such as memorials, are much less linked to cultural prejudices or boundaries of sovereignty. They thus contain the potential to offer sources that could be used to re-articulate notions of community and security in a transnational and culturally sensitive way.

POLITICS BETWEEN TEXT AND MUSIC

Radical change of scenery: from the hard bricks of architecture the chapter examines the soft rhythm of musical tunes. But the change is not as abrupt as it seems, for music does, in similarly nonviolent ways, epitomize the questions and dilemmas entailed in aesthetic engagements with politics.

Music, at least in its 'pure' instrumental form, does not seem to represent anything outside itself — certainly no concrete and straight-forward political message. But musical activities are among the most widespread and intensive engagements with 9/11. The domain of popular music alone has produced countess songs about the event. Some musicians are explicitly political. DJ Shadow, for instance, composed a song that is highly critical of the US military campaign in Afghanistan. His rationale for doing so is that 'artists, be they painters, actors, writers or musicians, have a responsibility to reflect and interpret the world around them.' Or, expressed in the lyrics accompanying his music: 'I was born with the voice of a riot, a storm lightening the function, the form, far from the norm... I'm back in the cipher my foes and friends, with a verse and a pen against a line I won't toe or defend' [Shadow 2004][7].

Other musicians focus less on the explicitly political and more on the purely emotional sides of coming to terms with 9/11. Look, for instance, at an album by Bruce Springsteen, which contains songs such as 'My City of Ruins' or 'Into the Fire.' The latter spoke of how 'I need you near, but love and duty called you someplace higher, somewhere up the stairs, into the fire' [Springsteen 2003]. Some commentators endow Springsteen's music with central importance, elevating it to a semi-official 'requiem for those who perished in the sudden inferno, and those who died trying to save them' [Loder 2002]. Others see it above all as a

---

[7] Other examples of musical engagements, representing a variety of political positions, include 'We Saw The Best In You! A Gift of Songs Musical Tribute Inspired by September 11, 2001,' various artists, 2002 (ASIN: B00006B0UJ); 'The Concert for New York City,' various artists (Sony: 2001 / ASIN: B00005S83H); 'Straight From The Heart/Tribute to the Families, Victims & Heroes of September 11, 2001,' Bonita C. Ruff (2002 / ASIN: B00006K01L); 'One Nation Under God - Remembering 9.11,' Frog & Scorpion / various artists (Frog & Scorpion Records, 2003 / ASIN B00007J5UE); 'Freedom / From a Lover to a Friend,' Paul McCartney (Capitol: 2001 / ASIN: B00005T7IX); 'Home of the Brave, Emergency Rations,' Mr Lif (Def Jux, 2002); 'Know Your Enemy, Turn Off the Radio,' Dead Prez; and 'Down with U.S.' S.T.O.P. Movement.

patriotic celebration of New York's heroic fire-fighters [Obst 2003] or critique him for not mentioning anything about the state of the country or, for that matter, the far more problematic war of response [see Kurtz 2004]. Entering these debates is not my task. I am interested in the more generic nonviolent relationship between music, text and politics.

The independence of musical content from the lyrics that may accompany them becomes evident if one examines an earlier song by Bruce Springsteen. The title track of his 1984 album 'Born in the USA' is often cited as the most misinterpreted song in the history of rock music. But a closer looks reveals less of a misinterpretation than an inherent tension between text and music. The textual message Springsteen wanted to communicate was one of protest. It was meant to critique how American society treated its working class veterans from the Vietnam War. Two representative stanzas from the song:

- Got in a little hometown jam
- So they put a rifle in my hand
- Sent me off to a foreign land
- To go and kill the yellow man
- Born in the USA...
- Down in the shadow of the penitentiary
- Out by the gas fires of the refinery
- I'm ten years burning down the road
- Nowhere to run ain't got nowhere to go
- Born in the USA... [Springsteen 2003]

While designed as a protest against American society, 'Born in the USA' had mostly the opposite effect. It became a widely recognized and uncritically employed hymn for the celebration of patriotic pride and duty. 'Born in the USA' was even used as a theme song in Ronald Reagan's republican presidential campaign in 1984. A conservative columnist, George Will, perfectly captured the logic of this appropriation:

> I have not got a clue about Springsteen's politics, if any, but flags get waved at his concerts while he sings songs about hard times. He is no whiner, and the recitation of closed factories and other problems always seems punctuated by a grand, cheerful, affirmation: 'Born in the USA!' [Cited in Cullen 1997, 2].

Springsteen is said to have been horrified by this political appropriation of his music. But the death of the musician is as prominent a theme as the much discussed death of the author. Once composed, a piece of music takes on its own life, independently of the intention its creator bestowed upon it. The political nature of a song thus has as much to do with the musical content as with the lyrics that accompany it. Eliminate the text of Springsteen's song for a moment, or assume a listener who does not understand English, and the appropriation of 'Born in the USA' suddenly looks far less surprising. One commentator hit the nail on its head:

> If you set your troubled examination of Vietnam's after-effect to the sort of declamatory fanfare last heard when an all-conquering Caesar returned to Rome, bellow it in a voice that suggests you are about to leap offstage and punch a communist, then package it in a

sleeve featuring the Stars and Stripes and a pair of Levi's, it's no good getting huffy when people seize the wrong end of the stick [Patridis 2002].

'Born in the USA' shows how the sound of music itself can carry a message, either in the absence of words or in combination (or contraction) with them. From a political point of view this may well be the most significant aspect of music. A move from popular music back to theoretical debates can help to clarify the issue.

MUSIC AND EMOTIONAL KNOWLEDGE

The role of emotional insights into 9/11 illustrates how even purely instrument music may contain political content, and thus the potential to add to our understanding of security issues. Prevalent scholarship on international relations pays little to no attention to emotions, which are considered purely subjective and irrational, involving neither thought nor meaningful knowledge. This is in many ways paradoxical, for terrorism is a highly emotional phenomenon. The motives and means of terrorists are usually presented in emotional terms, as 'fanatical,' 'irrational' or simply 'evil.' Reactions to terrorist attacks are equally emotional. They involve dealing with the memory of death, suffering and trauma, leading to emotional calls for political action, often involving feelings of retribution that go far beyond the mere need to provide security. Political leaders do not shy away from drawing upon emotional appeals, such as nationalist rhetoric, to win support for their positions. And yet, the actual policy analyses of terrorist threats are advanced in a highly detached and rationalized manner [Cohn 1987]. The very presentation of contemporary warfare, from sanitized video-images of satellite guided missiles to the abstract language of defense experts (exemplified through terms like 'collateral damage' or 'clean bombs') not only eliminates suffering from our purview, but also fails to take into account emotional issues when assessing threats and formulating policy.

Although unacknowledged by experts in security studies, there is an extensive body of literature that deals with emotional insight. Martha Nussbaum's impressive study on the topic is particularly significant here, for she demonstrates that emotions do not just highlight our vulnerability towards events that lie outside of control, such as terrorist attacks. They are also important forms of knowledge and evaluative thought. Literature, music and other works of art offer possibilities to express these emotional insights in ways that cannot easily be achieved through conventional accounts of events. This is why, Nussbaum stresses, emotional intelligence and aesthetic ways of representing them should be accepted, alongside more conventional sources, as legitimate elements in the formulation of ethical and political judgments [Nussbaum 2003, 1-2].[8]

Music exemplifies the potential and limit of gaining emotional insights into political puzzles. It is not based on the idea of representing a specific object in the political world. But

---

[8] The literature on emotions and politics is highly complex and diverse, featuring heated debates between the type of cognitive approaches advocated by Nussbaum and more affect-oriented alternatives. This chapter is far too short to enter these debates but see, for instance, Jack Barbalet (ed), *Emotions and Sociology*. (Oxford, Malden, MA: Blackwell, 2002); Gillian Bendelow and Simon J. Williams (eds), *Emotions in Social Life: Critical Themes and Contemporary Issues*. (London: Routledge, 1998); Thomas J. Scheff, *Microsociology: Discourse, Emotion, and Social Structure*. (Chicago: University of Chicago Press, 1990).

music does, at the same time, relate to aspects outside itself, to a state of mind, an attitude, a feeling, or an emotion [Budd 1985, x]. Music is unique in a variety of ways, including its performative and rhythmic nature and the fact it can be perceived simultaneously from all directions, which is not the case with visual or textual sources [Ong 1982, 72]. These are some of the reasons why several writers and philosophers, including Schiller, Schopenhauer and Nietzsche, believed that music is particularly suited to express emotions, that, the effects of music are more immanent and profound than those emanating from other arts, for 'these speak only of the shadow, but music of the essence' [Schopenhauer cited in Nussbaum 2003, 259-60; see also Friedrich Nietzsche 1972].

Can music thus offer insights that other forms of knowledge cannot? Mahler, for instance, was only interested in composing music about experiences that cannot be expressed in words [Nussbaum 2003, 255]. As with other aesthetic insights, the challenge here consists of locating the precise political content and communicating it in non-musical terms. Prevalent linguistic conventions are inadequate to capture musical knowledge. Consider, for instance, how I reluctantly but, for lack of alternatives, inevitably had to refer to musical 'insight,' or to the possibility of music 'illuminating' political phenomena. Both of these terms are inherently visual, reflecting a deep seated assumption that our ideal experience, as Nussbaum stresses, 'must be a visual experience, that its illumination must be accounted for in terms of the eye' [Nussbaum 2003, 640]. But to communicate aural experiences through visual metaphors is problematic. To express musical experiences appropriately one would need to replace concepts like 'insight' and 'illuminating' with 'inhearing' or additives such as 'musicate' or 'aurate.'[9] Some languages are already better equipped for such sensitivities than English is. For Aboriginal people in the Western desert of Australia, for instance, 'the metaphor for thought and memory is the ear' [Lieberman 1985, 60 and 169]. But even if equipped with more appropriate metaphorical tools, language would still not be able to capture the unique representational style of music, or, rather, music's refusal to engage in representation at all. 'Music has to be listened to and nothing can replace this experience,' as Gordon Graham would point out [1997, 80].

THE CHALLENGE TO APPRECIATE ARTISTIC
KNOWLEDGE ON ITS OWN TERMS

The main methodological challenge consists of legitimizing musical and other artistic insights on their own terms, rather than through the conceptual framework of social scientific conventions. But how is one to legitimize approaches to knowledge and evidence that contradict many established principles that guide international relations scholarship? And how can one communicate aesthetic insights in ways that retain their uniqueness and integrity? Knowledge that is communicated through artistic and philosophical insights cannot always be verified, as Gadamer stresses, by methodological means proper to science. Indeed, the significance of aesthetic knowledge is located precisely in the fact that it 'cannot be attained in any other way' [Gadamer 1999, xxii].

---

[9] The latter two are suggestions by Alex Danchev, to whom I am indebted for discussions about the challenge to expand our conceptual and linguistic repertoire not only with 'visual literacy' but also with 'musical literacy.'

I do not pretend to offer answers to these difficult questions here. Debates about them go back at least to Kant. By examining how the beautiful and the sublime generate an inherent tension (rather than a smooth link) between imagination and reason, Kant sought to find ways for allowing each faculty to cultivate its unique insights and passions [Deleuze 1974, 136-7 and 146; Kant 1974]. Many contemporary commentators are more pessimistic than Kant, at least about the practical possibilities of conveying clear emotional issues through music. Gordon Graham, for instance, admits that music is an unusually powerful means for expressing emotions. But he is very skeptical about music's possibility to say anything concrete, or at least anything that goes beyond very broad sensations, such as sadness or happiness. Graham thus believes that 'very few other states or conditions can be ascribed to music without a measure of absurdity creeping into the discussion' [Graham 1997, 69].

Reading concrete emotional messages into (or out of) music is, indeed, a difficult, perhaps even an inherently problematic endeavor. But it is not quite as impossible as Graham holds. Nussbaum's study shows why. While acknowledging the difficulty of describing connections between music and our emotional life, Nussbaum stresses that part of this difficulty has less to do with music and more with our lack of conceptual insight into the issue of emotions in general [Nussbaum 2003, 249]. Reaching a systematic understanding of the importance of emotional insight is thus central. And so is the need to recognize the limits of what can be conveyed through music. Nussbaum, for instance, admits that music cannot communicate clear and authentic emotional messages. Any persuasive account of the emotional content of music, she argues, is intrinsically linked to the experiences of listeners [Nussbaum 2003, 151]. This, in turn, requires recognizing that the links between music and emotions are culturally specific. Indian or Japanese music, Nussbaum illustrates, is not immediately accessible to the untrained Western ear. This is why an appreciation of music, as well as its emotional content, requires a certain level of 'education and attunement' [Nussbaum 2003, 253 and 263].

Music in this sense is a form of representation, even though it does not represent anything outside of itself. Its attempt to capture and express emotions may well be broader and less demarcated, but in other ways it is not much different than language. Both mediums, language and music, cannot capture the world as it is. Whenever we use language to convey meaning, we say as much about our values and prejudices, which are embedded in specific linguistic structures and cultural norms, as we say about the actual objects and phenomena we seek to describe. Nussbaum thus stresses that

> Music is another form of symbolic representation. It is not language, but it need not cede all complexity, all sophistication in expression, to language. So it is not obvious why we think that there is a greater problem about expressing an emotion's content musically than about expressing it linguistically. We think this way because we live in a culture that is verbally adept but (on the whole) relatively unsophisticated musically [Nussbaum 2003, 264].

In a highly insightful and inspiring dialogue about music, society and politics, Daniel Barenboim and Edward Said stress a similar point. They lament the increasingly marginalized role that music plays in society, and ascribe this marginalization to the larger modern process of splitting up life and knowledge into ever more specialized subfields. The ensuing practices have led to impressive advances of knowledge, but they have come at a certain price. Music, for instance, is now treated as separate not only from politics, but also from the other arts. Most people today no longer receive a basic education in music. But precisely such an education would be necessary, as Nussbaum already indicated, to appreciate the various dimensions of music, including its intertwinement with politics and society [Barenboim and Said 2003, 44-45]. Without that knowledge music is simply dismissed as irrelevant to the political, even though the careful and informed listening necessary to correct that image requires no more and no less education than, say, the specialized skills necessary to read a defense studies manual. The result is that we know more and more about increasingly specialized topics, but hardly ever explore the promising linkages between them.

Barenboim and Said advance a passionate claim for making music more central again to societal and cultural life, and thus to politics too. They draw attention to the benefits that could emerge from such a renewed appreciation and reintegration of music. They have done so in a very practical way, by bringing together a group of young Israeli and Arab musicians in the German cultural centre of Weimar. Named after Goethe's *West-Eastern Divan*, the project used music as a way of promoting cross-cultural communication, understanding and tolerance [Barenboim and Said 2003, 6-11]. Although pre-dating the events of September 11, this musical dialogue represents precisely the type of cultural engagement that many critics find missing in the official policy response to the terrorist attacks [see Parekh, 270-83].

Said stresses the need for a 'common discourse,' a type of broad understanding of society that replaces the current specialization of knowledge, where only a few fellow experts are still capable to communicate with each other. For Said the danger of this tendency is that we no longer take on the most challenging problems, for the fragmentation of knowledge and its corresponding institutionalization makes it easy to avoid responsibility for decisions regarding the overall direction of society [Barenboim and Said 2003, 149-50]. Barenboim, likewise, emphasizes that music is 'one of the best ways to learn about human nature.' Learning here means far more than the mere accumulation of knowledge. It means retaining the ability to question some of the problematic assumptions that are often taken for granted, even though they cause a great deal of conflict in the world. The elevation of realist power politics to a virtually unchallenged mantra of foreign policy behavior is a case in point. The key political challenge, then, consist of searching for new perspectives (i.e., listening capabilities), rather than new facts. This challenge is perfectly expressed by Barenboim, who wants to make listeners forget what they know, so that they can experience the world anew and thus open up to possibilities that are foreclosed by intellectual and practical conventions that are so entrenched that they are uncritically accepted as common sense [Barenboim and Said 2003, 24, 53 and 80]. Music may well be better suited for this task than many other forms of expression, for, as Nussbaum contends, 'it is not the language of habit' [Nussbaum 2003, 268]. It may thus be able to offer us a fundamentally different take on some of the key political challenges, thereby opening up possibilities that stay foreclosed within conventional policy deliberations.

CONCLUSION

This chapter has examined the role of art as a nonviolent way of engaging questions of terrorism. It has taken a different route than most studies of nonviolence do. Nonviolence here is not seen as a practice of resistance that interferes directly with power relationships. Art, as nonviolence, is rather a way of engaging the manner in which people perceive and judge political issues. Such forms of resistance can be just as effective, but they can generate change only in a slow and largely ineffable manner.

Artistic insights are not necessarily better or more authentic than prevalent interpretations of security dilemmas. They certainly do not replace the need for technical expertise and social scientific inquires into security dilemmas. But aesthetic insights offer the opportunity to reach a broader understanding of the emergence, meaning and significance of key political challenges, such as global terrorism. By generating new insights, art demonstrates what Ekkehart Krippendorff once noted: that politics is far too important a domain to leave to politicians, or to political scientists for that matter.[10] While writers, painters, musicians and philosophers, such as Barenboim, Said and Nussbaum, have long made this point, international relations scholarship has so far paid far too little attention to knowledge that can emerge from drawing upon alternative sources, including aesthetic ones.

It is reasonable to assume that art can provide only limited or no input on purely technical and strategic issues, such as decisions with regard to weapons systems or strategic deployment of troops. But security policy is, and always has been, about far more than military policy. Although presented as a pragmatic response to external threats, security is just as much about defining the values and boundaries of political communities, about separating a safe inside from a threatening outside. It is about sustaining national identity and legitimizing the use of violence for political purposes [Shapiro 1997; Dillon 1996]. In short, security is about the political imaginary as much as it is about facing threats. And it is in this realm that art can become politically relevant: it can contribute to discussions about the nature of threats and their impact on political communities, about the memory of trauma and its shaping of future policies, about the fundamental definition of security and the ensuing relationship between inside and outside.

ACKNOWLEDGEMENTS

Roland Bleiker is a Professor in Peace Studies and Political Theory at the University of Queensland in Australia. He is the author of *Popular Dissent, Human Agency and Global Politics* (Cambridge University Press, 2000); *Divided Korea: Toward a Culture of Reconciliation* (University of Minnesota Press, 2005) and essays on political theory, social movements, aesthetics, international relations and Asian politics. He has had a long interest in nonviolence. He spent a year at Harvard University's Program on Nonviolent Sanctions and regularly taught a course on the Politics of Nonviolent Change at the University of Queensland, where he has been since 1999. Currently he is finishing a book for Palgrave on *Aesthetics and World Politics*. He has also started a follow-up project that engages key dilemmas in global security, such as terrorism and health, through a range of aesthetic sources of insight.

---

[10] Krippendorff, Die Kunst, nicht regiert zu werden, p. 8.

REFERENCES

Agamben, G. (2005). *State of Exception.* Chicago: The University of Chicago Press.

Arad, M. (2003). 'Reflecting Absence: A Memorial at the World Trade Center Site' in Finalists' Statements. *The New York Times*, 19 Nov.

Barenboim, D. and Said, E.W. (2003). *Parallels and Paradoxes: Explorations in Music and Society.* London: Bloomsbury.

Budd, M. (1985). *Music and the Emotions: The Philosophical Theories.* London: Routledge.

Butler, J. (2005). *Precarious Life: The Powers of Mourning and Violence.* London: Verso.

Clark, W.K. (2004). 'Winning Modern Wars: Iraq, Terrorism and the American Empire.' *Public Affairs.*

Cohn, C. (1987). 'Sex and Death in the Rational World of Defense Intellectuals.' *Signs*, 12 (4).

Collins, G. (2003). '8 Designs Confront Many Agendas at Ground Zero.' *New York Times*, 20 Nov.

Collins, G. and Dunlap, D.W. (2004a). 'The 9/11 Memorial: How Pluribus Became Unum.' *New York Times*, 19 Jan.

Collins, G. and Dunlap, D.W. (2004b). 'Unveiling of the Trade Center Memorial Reveals an Abundance of New Details.' *New York Times*, 15 Jan.

Cullen, J. (1997). *Born in the USA: Bruce Springsteen and the American Tradition.* New York: Harper Collins.

Dalrymple, W. (2003). 'Murder in Karachi.' *New York Review of Books*, 50 (19).

Deleuze, G. (1994). *Difference and Repetition*, trans. P. Patton. New York: Columbia University Press.

Dillon, M. (1996). *Politics of Security: Towards a Political Philosophy of Continental Thought.* New York: Routledge.

Rumsfeld, D.H. (2002). 'Transforming the Military.' *Foreign Affairs*, May/June.

Dunlap, D.W. (2003a). 'Seeking the Sublime in the Simple to Mark 9/11.' *New York Times*, 27 Nov.

Dunlap, D.W. (2003b). '1,776-Foot Design Is Unveiled for World Trade Center Tower.' *New York Times*, 20 Dec.

Dunlap, D.W. (2004). 'Ground Zero Jury Adheres to a Maxim: Less is More.' *New York Times*, 7 Jan.

Edkins, J. (2003). *Trauma and the Memory of Politics.* Cambridge: Cambridge University Press.

Euben, R.L. (2002). 'Killing (for) Politics: Jihad, Martyrdom, and Political Action.' *Political Theory*, 30 (1), Feb 2002, p. 4.

Feuer, A. (2003). 'On World Trade Center Memorial, Criticism Outstrips Praise.' *New York Times*, 23 Nov.

Fischl, E. (2003). 'A Memorial That's True to 9/11.' *New York Times*, 19 Dec.

Gadamer, H-G. (1999). *Truth and Method.* New York: Continuum.

Gilles D. (2003). *Deux Régimes de Fous - Textes et Entretiens (1975-1995).* Paris: Minuit.

Graham, G. (1997). *Philosophy of the Arts: An Introduction to Aesthetics.* London: Routledge.

Halimi, S. (2003). 'Romanquête ou Mauvaise Enquête?' *Le Monde Diplomatique*, 11 Dec.

Hersch, S.M. (2004). *Chain of Command: The Road from 9/11 to Abu Ghraib*. Middlesex: Penguin.

Ignatieff, M. (2004). *The Lesser Evil: Political Ethics in an Age of Terror*. Princeton, NJ: Princeton University Press.

Kant, Immanuel. (1974). *Kritik der Urteilskraft*. Frankfurt: Suhrkamp.

Keenan, T. (2003). 'Making the Dead Count, Literally.' *New York Times*, 30 Nov.

Kurtz, S. (2004). 'Those 9/11 Songs,' *National Review* Online, http://www.natinalreview.com/kurtz (accessed Jan 2004).

Laqueur, W. (1999). *The New Terrorism: Fanaticism and the Arms of Mass Destruction*. London: Phoenix Press.

Levinson, J. (1998). 'Introduction to Levinson' (Ed.). *Aesthetics and Ethics: Essays at the Intersection*. Cambridge: Cambridge University Press.

Lévy, B-H. (2003). *Qui A Tué Daniel Pearl?* Paris: Grasset and Fasquelle. Trans. J.X. Mitchell. (2003). as *Who Killed Daniel Pearl?* South Yarra, Victoria: Hardie Grant Books.

Libeskind, D. (2004a). 'Catching on Fire.' www.daniel-libeskind.com (accessed Feb 2004).

Libeskind, D. (2004b). 'Proof of Things Invisible.' www.daniel-libeskind.com (accessed Feb 2004).

Lieberman, K. (1985). *Understanding Interaction in Central Australia: An Ethnomethodological Study of Australian Aboriginal People*. Boston: Routledge.

Loder, K. (2002). 'Bruce Springsteen: The Rising.' *Rolling Stone*, 22 Aug. http://rollingstone.com./reviews (accessed Jan 2004).

Muschamp, H. (2003a). 'A Skyscraper Has a Chance to be Nobler.' *New York Times*, 20 Dec.

Muschamp, H. (2003b). 'Amid Embellishment and Message, a Voice of Simplicity Cries to be Heard.' *New York Times*, 20 Nov.

Neiman, S. (2003). *Evil in Modern Thought: An Alternative History of Philosophy*. Melbourne: Scribe Publications.

Nietzsche, F. (1972). *Die Geburt der Tragödie aus dem Geiste der Musik*. Berlin: Walter de Gruyter.

Nussbaum, M.C. (2003). *Upheavals of Thought: The Intelligence of Emotions*. Cambridge: Cambridge University Press.

Obst, A. (2003). 'Liebeslieder an den Feuerwehrmann.' *Frankfurter Allgemeine Zeitung*, 3 Aug, p. 37.

Ong, W. (1982). *Orality and Literacy: The Technologizing of the World*. London: Mehtuen.

Parekh, B. 'Terrorism or Intercultural Dialogue?' in K. Booth and T. Dunne (eds). *World in Collision: Terror and the Future of Global Order*. Houndmills, UK: Macmillan, 270-83.

Patridis, A. (2002). 'Darkness on the Edge of Town.' *The Guardian*, 26 July.

Pfaff, W. (2005). 'What We've Lost: George W. Bush and the Price of Torture.' *Harper's*, Nov.

Pitzke, M. (2003). 'Schlanker Kompromiss am Ort des Terrors.' *Der Spiegel*, 19 Dec.

Rorty, R. (1989). *Contingency, Irony and Solidarity*. Cambridge: Cambridge University Press.

Scarry, E. (1985). *The Body in Pain: The Making and Unmaking of the World*. New York: Oxford University Press.

Shadow, DJ. (2004). 'March of Death,' lyrics by Zack de la Rocha, plus commentary, at http://www.marchofdeath.com/lyrics.html (accessed Jan 2004).

Shapiro, M.J. (1997). *Violent Cartographies: Mapping Culture of War*. Minneapolis: University of Minnesota Press.

Sharp, G. (1973). *The Politics of Nonviolent Action*. 3 vols.. Boston: Porter Sargent.

Springsteen, B. (2003). *The Rising*. Sony Music Entertainment.

Sudjic, D. (2003). 'Is There a Hero for Ground Zero?' *The Observer*, 7 Dec.

Vidal-Naquet, P. (1979). *Le Nouvel Observateur*, 18 June.

Ward, P. (2002). 'Graffiti at Ground Zero: Gordon Bennett Responded to September 11 in the Only Way He Knew How.' *The Australian*, 6 March, p. 17.

Wendt, A. (1999). *Social Theory of International Politics*. Cambridge: Cambridge University Press.

White, H. (1978). 'The Fiction of Factual Representation.' *Tropics of Discourse: Essays in Cultural Criticism*. Baltimore: Johns Hopkins University Press.

WNBC. (2003). 'Daniel Libeskind Discusses the Plan for Memorializing the World Trade Center.' 3 June. www.wnbc.com (accessed Feb 2004).

Wood, G. (2003). 'Je Suis un Superstar.' *The Observer*, 15 June.

WTC. (2003). 'World Trade Center Site Memorial Competition Jury Statement.' *New York Times*, 19 Nov.

In: Nonviolence: An Alternative for Defeating...   ISBN: 978-1-60021-812-5
Editors: S. Ram and R. Summy, pp. 187-210   © 2008 Nova Science Publishers, Inc.

Chapter 11

THE ROLE OF UN POLICE IN NONVIOLENTLY COUNTERING TERRORISM

Timothy A. McElwee

'The UN is the only fire brigade in the world that has to acquire a fire engine after the fire has started.'

Secretary-General Kofi Annan

ABSTRACT

Over the course of the past 50 years, United Nations peacekeepers have been called upon to function as police agents, primarily charged with enforcing agreed-upon rules to minimize continued armed conflict and to protect the innocent. On occasion, UN peacekeeping operations have become, in essence, military actions. This study emphasizes the importance of distinguishing between military and police actions on the part of UN peacekeepers. It suggests that peacekeepers, employing non-military, even nonviolent means of law enforcement designed to alleviate human suffering and counter terrorist threats, would strengthen peacebuilding efforts and lend much-needed support to constructing political systems grounded in the rule of law. Adopting this approach is dependent upon the commitment of the international community to reduce its reliance on military aspects of UN peacekeeping operations and pursue instead efforts to strengthen the effectiveness of UN civilian police units functioning as nonviolent police agents. A summary presentation based on four brief case studies illustrates the importance of UN peacekeeping operations remaining focused on nonviolent responses to crises, and to maintaining and building peaceful societies.

INTRODUCTION

Regardless of our age or cultural upbringing, many of us can easily call to mind scenes from the 'Old West' in the United States. Depictions of cowboys fighting in small town saloons, and of sheriffs trying to maintain civil order, serve as focal points in many of the movies or television shows that conveyed these images. In many such stories, chaos reigned supreme and violence dominated society before the sheriff came to town. An important though seldom appreciated aspect of these accounts is that once the town leaders — often including the 'outlaws' as well as the up-standing citizens — consented to comply with the rule of law, life greatly improved for the majority of the citizens of the town. Once the sheriff was accepted as the legitimate civil authority, and respect for the rule of law was generally embraced, the village progressed in a more peaceful manner and with greater justice and prosperity for everyone involved. The widespread violence and instability in our war-torn world — fraught with terrorist attacks by state and non-state actors[1] — often resemble the lawless violence and chaos of a 'wild west town' in early US history. As this illustration reveals, and as countless historical records confirm, humanity has discovered and embraced nonviolent means to counter terrorism for centuries. A United Nations rapid response, nonviolent civilian police service could function similarly to that of an Old West sheriff. It, too, could enable 'violence-ridden societies' to become 'rule-of-law societies' [Johansen 2004, 44]. Even, or perhaps especially, in the face of terrorist threats, if such a service were adopted on a global scale, it could greatly enhance the prospects of a more peaceful, just, and stable international community.

Of course, civil order in Old West towns was not always maintained in a consistent and equitable manner. Every societal institution, whether it functions within domestic jurisdictions or executes its duties on the international level, is staffed by fallible and corruptible human beings. At times the civil authority of an Old West village succumbed to dishonest or unlawful behavior. On occasion laws that were perceived as biased were forced upon the populace without the consent of the citizenry. Sometimes legal disputes were not settled in a timely fashion, nor in a fair and impartial manner. In some instances, families or groups of families manipulated village life through undue power and influence. True as well, there have been instances in which police have enforced unethical social and political orders. In some cases, police have moved beyond their assigned protective role and have engaged in aggressive, even offensive assaults. When police cross the line from defensive to offense, their effectiveness is greatly compromised, as societal trust erodes and authorized violence in turn provokes unauthorized, revengeful violence.

Nonetheless, despite these obvious shortcomings and failures, what has been called a 'culture of compliance'[2] [Johansen 1996, 304] was eventually established in the small towns and villages of the Old West and it became possible for citizens to enforce norms grounded in the pursuits of civil order, peace and justice, all of which were based on the rule of law. In short, the citizens of the Old West learned to settle disputes through nonviolent and juridical means. They made peace through peaceful means.

The world community continues to aspire to these goals. However, when attempting to counter terrorism, the prevailing assumption within many nation-states tends to be heavily biased toward attempts to secure peace and bring about justice through coercive military

---

[1] For purposes of this analysis, terrorism is defined as 'the deliberate threat or use of violence for political, religious, or ideological purposes against innocent civilians by either states or non-state actors' (Johansen 2004, 31). Despite several attempts, the United Nations has been unable to agree on a definition of terrorism. For an important and clearly stated call for a definition as well as an appeal for a multinational anti-terrorism convention, see 'A More Secure World: Our Shared Responsibility,' Report of the High-Level Panel on Threats, Challenges and Change (United Nations, 2004), 47-52. This volume also provides a suggested definition of terrorism (paragraph 164.d).

[2] In a subsequent writing, Johansen describes a culture of compliance as a society in which 'most people obey most laws most of the time without being forced to do so at the point of a gun' (2004, 41).

might. If terrorism were instead viewed as criminal behavior — whether practiced by states or non-state actors — and if it were addressed through nonviolent and juridical means, and through the efforts of a professional police force, many lives would be spared, the rule of law would be advanced, and the affected community would be much more able to embark on effective peacebuilding endeavors.

IN PURSUIT OF A NONVIOLENT FUTURE

For centuries, scholars and international theorists have pondered the requirements necessary to construct an international civil society able to attain lasting peace with justice on a global scale. While the metaphor of the sheriff's impact on the prototypical Old West town is not entirely applicable to the world stage, there are nonetheless many pertinent applications of domestic legal instruments to international institutions. These lessons are particularly germane to efforts intended to confront terrorism. Their potential effectiveness is enormous. More than four decades ago renowned political theorist Inis Claude urged consideration what he referred to as the 'domestication of international relations.' It is increasingly clear that the global community would benefit to a much greater extent than did the small towns of the Old West if international leaders collectively agreed to transcend their hesitations and embrace a global peace system[3] based in part on multilateral and non-military means of enforcing the law and maintaining peace.

Beyond traditional military means of responding to international and intrastate conflicts, the international community is in need of alternative means of peacefully resolving deadly conflicts. Once hostilities have ended and a peace accord has been enacted, the global community is equally in need of maintaining peace and pursuing justice in a manner that builds respect for and confidence in the rule of law. An old aphorism suggests, 'If the only tool in your toolbox is a hammer, all of your problems start looking like nails.' We need many more tools in our collective toolbox if we are to successfully address urgent international concerns such as global terrorism, provide life-enhancing alternatives to wars of aggression such as we have witnessed in the US-led war against Iraq, and overcome protracted intrastate conflicts such as the genocide underway in Darfur, Sudan. Former United States UN Ambassador, Adlai Stevenson, suggested in 1961, 'We do not envision a world without conflict; we do envision a world without war. This inevitably requires an alternative security system for dealing with human conflict' [Quoted in Johansen 1978, 1]. Nearly 25 years ago, peace scholars Robert Johansen and Saul Mendlovitz wisely observed:

> The central problem of international relations is the willingness of governments to threaten or use violence to settle disputes. This willingness is unlikely to diminish until nonmilitary means for defending and advancing group interests become more reliable and common [Johansen and Mendlovitz 1980, 307].

---

[3] The term 'global peace system' is adapted from the work of Robert C. Johansen. In his book, *Toward a Dependable Peace* (1978), Johansen defines the concept as a global system through which 'conflict is resolved through nonviolent, political, social, and judicial processes. There are no expectations of war and no national military arsenals. There is a widespread sense of solidarity with the rest of the human species' (16).

This sagacious observation is as relevant to causes of international war as it is to efforts to sustain peace and build civil societies within communities suffering from internal or civil wars. Member states of the United Nations, and specifically the membership of the Security Council, must be further convinced that reliable non-military means are available to advance civilian police actions within authorized peacekeeping operations. Although non-military yet coercive means of law enforcement hold great promise for promoting international conflict transformation,[4] little research and even fewer financial resources have been committed to its pursuit by the world community. According to the Stockholm International Peace Research Institute (SIPRI) the world spent $1.11 trillion in 2005 in pursuit of military solutions to terrorist threats or other national and international conflicts. If only a fraction of the financial resources currently devoted to military expenditures were committed instead to non-military enforcement actions, the global community would benefit greatly from the effective use of these new tools of conflict transformation. Such a shift in resource allocations, and the successful application of non-military enforcement actions, would also generate a concomitant increase in international confidence that conflict can be nonviolently and effectively transformed.

UN PEACEKEEPING AND THE QUEST FOR A GLOBAL NONVIOLENT POLICE SERVICE

The advancement of world peace and international security is the raison d'être of the United Nations. Nonetheless, the concept of multilateral peacekeeping as practiced by the United Nations over the last 60 years or so is not to be found in the UN Charter. Rather, the idea and procedures of UN peacekeeping operations came into being as a practical necessity based upon the operating experiences of the UN during the Cold War. In broad strokes, UN Peacekeeping Operations can be defined as an amalgam of three proposed routes to international peace: peaceful settlement, collective security, and preventive diplomacy. As of 30 June 2006, the UN had established 60 peacekeeping operations. At the time of writing, 15 UN sponsored operations were underway, employing 62,811 troops, 7,242 police, and 2,671 military observers [United Nations, 2006]. Projections call for as many as 100,000 troops and police to be deployed by the end of 2006, which will represent the largest number in the history of the United Nations [Lynch]. Each of the previous and current peacekeeping operations had or has unique missions, and among these efforts, no consistent pattern is found regarding the authorized use of force or coercion. In some instances UN peacekeeping personnel served solely as unarmed observers; in other cases they functioned as police units,

---

[4] I use the term conflict transformation intentionally in this chapter. It is preferred over more common terms such as conflict resolution (which often implies that conflict is somehow 'bad,' short term, and can be permanently ended), and conflict management (which tends to objectify people and social groups and suggests that those caught-up in volatile conflicts can be controlled). For further elaboration of the term conflict transformation, see the writings of John Paul Lederach, e.g. his work, 'Conflict Transformation: The Case for Peace Advocacy,' in *NGO's and Peacemaking: A Prospect for the Horn*, (Ed.). Menno Wiebe (Waterloo, Ont.: Conrad Grebel College, 1989), or *Building Peace: Sustainable Reconciliation in Divided Societies* (Washington, DC: United States Institute of Peace, 1997). Further application of the term conflict transformation will follow.

or as humanitarian aid distributors. Regrettably, some peacekeeping operations have descended into aggressive military actions.

When UN peacekeeping personnel become party to a conflict, and one side in the dispute is perceived as the enemy, not only does the operation sacrifice one of its most important attributes, i.e., its impartiality, but worse, the possibility that the operation will be able to build and sustain requisite trust levels from within the affected community is seriously jeopardized. Ideally, UN peacekeeping operations should aim to enter a conflict-torn society and function in the manner described by former United Nations Under Secretary-General Brian Urquhart, viz:

> A peacekeeping force is like a family friend who has moved into a household stricken by disaster. It must conciliate, console, and discreetly run the household without ever appearing to dominate or usurp the natural rights of those it is helping [1987, 248].

Of course, a family friend is likely to enter such a conflict setting with presuppositions about the relative guilt or innocence of the disputing parties. Such is often the case, of course, with UN peacekeeping personnel as well. The degree to which they are able to remain neutral, however, is fundamental to the potential effectiveness of the operation. Even if this goal is attained, some analysts argue that the further one enters a conflict setting, the more difficult it becomes to remain neutral.[5] Others argue that if a peacekeeping force 'freezes the status quo' in a conflict in which one side is clearly dominant, the peacekeeping operation has in effect joined the conflict on the side of the party most interested in maintaining its preeminent position [Weber 1996, 8]. These problems notwithstanding, a nonviolent police force would clearly be much more able to maintain a balanced approach to the conflicting parties, minimize violence, and build communal trust if for no other reason than the reduced sense of threat that accompanies unarmed international police units.

The idea of pursuing global justice through the rule of law is certainly not new. Since 1923, with the creation of the International Police Commission (Interpol), the vast majority of nations have collaborated in efforts to investigate and bring to justice criminals whose illegal conduct crossed international borders. A nonviolent UN rapid response civilian police force, similar in scope and purpose to what has been termed a 'UN Emergency Peace Service' (UNEPS),[6] would be equipped and authorized to function under a UN Security Council mandate and through an established UN peacekeeping operation. It would be charged with enforcing agreed upon rules designed to minimize armed conflict and build a sustainable civil society. However, whereas many previous UN peacekeeping operations and some of the proposed UNEPS forces are designed to include military personnel, a rapid response, nonviolent UNCIVPOL (an abbreviation for 'United Nations civilian police') operation would be structured along the lines of the customarily non-military and nonviolent characteristics on which CIVPOL operations are based.

This concept was commended by the first UN Secretary-General, Trgvye Lie, and advocated by Secretary-General U Thant several years later. Indeed, even classical realist

---

[5] See, e.g., Johan Galtung and Helge Hveem, 'Participants in Peacekeeping Forces,' in *Essays in Peace Research*, Vol. 2, War, Peace and Defence, 1976.

[6] Regarding this concept, see, A United Nations Emergency Peace Service: To Prevent Genocide and Crimes Against Humanity, published by the Institute for Global Policy, a program of the World Federalists Movement, 2006. Available at: http, p.//www.globalactionpw.org/uneps/index.htm.

theorists such as Lincoln Bloomfield suggested that a preferred international security system would be based not on means of effectively waging war, but through 'police work' [quoted in Johansen 1998, 4]. Secretary-General Kofi Annan revealed similar convictions regarding the role of international intervention in pursuit of Charter goals. During a 1998 lecture presented in the United Kingdom, Annan asserted, 'the most effective interventions are not military. It is much better, from every point of view, if action can be taken to resolve or manage a conflict before it reaches the military stage' [1999a, 8].

UNCIVPOL operations have evolved considerably since the initial application in the Congo in 1964 and the success story of the 1989 United Nations Transition Assistance Group in Namibia (UNTAG). In the former case, Secretary-General Dag Hammarskjold introduced the concept of a peacekeeping force to assist the Congolese government in maintaining the rule of law. In the Namibia case, the UN effectively ensured free and fair elections in an emerging democracy. As of 31 December 2005, UN police personnel represented approximately 12% of all UN peacekeeping staff, i.e. 7,241 police among a total of 69,838 uniformed UN peacekeepers [United Nations 2005, 28].

With some exceptions, the generally accepted criteria for UNCIVPOL operations stipulate that personnel will be multinational, unarmed, without executive power (i.e., not equipped with arms nor the authority to arrest suspects), responsible to a single head of mission, and committed to the 'SMART' concept.[7] The latter refers to a set of guidelines first established through a 1995 UN Department of Peacekeeping trainers' guide. The concept stipulates that UNCIVPOL personnel should: (1) Support human rights and provide humanitarian assistance, (2) Monitor the performance of local police and judicial officers, (3) Advise local police on humane and effective law enforcement standards, (4) Report on potentially illegal incidents, and (5) Train local law enforcement personnel in best practices for police work and the maintenance of human rights standards [Hartz, 31; Perito, 88]. The essential qualifications of UNCIVPOL personnel were established during a 1996 seminar co-sponsored by the United Nations Department of Peacekeeping Operations and the Lester B. Pearson International Peacekeeping Training Center in Canada. The criteria as summarized by Robert Perito, a career US foreign service officer and special advisor to the Rule of Law program at the United States Institute of Peace, are as follows:

1. Citizenship of the sending country.
2. Sworn member of the police force.
3. Five and preferably eight years of active community policing experience.
4. Ability to meet the UN health standards.
5. A valid 4 X 4 driving license.
6. Speaking and writing ability in their native language and the mission language.
7. Competence in the use of firearms.
8. Impeccable personal and professional integrity [Perito, 95].

Over the years UNCIVPOL operations have generally been quite effective whether the source of the dispute was international or intrastate, and whether the mission was to arrest and bring to justice war criminals, or to assess a host government's compliance with human rights

---

[7] For additional information see United Nations Civilian Police Principles and Guidelines, available through United Nations publications at: http, p.//www.un.org/depts/dpko/training/tes_publications/list_publi.htm.

standards. Because UN peacekeepers are not well-suited for combat missions — a notion that is further explored below — and because a nonviolent police service would be much more able to achieve genuine peacebuilding within the context of violence-torn societies, a nonviolent UNCIVPOL service holds great promise in achieving a nonviolent counter to terrorism.

Just as the pursuit of global justice through the rule of law is not a novel concept, the idea of creating an international nonviolent 'peace army' has a long history as well. Thomas Weber has provided one of the best historical overviews of these efforts in his book, *Gandhi's Peace Army*, which traces the evolution of the Shanti Sena (a Gandhian peace brigade), founded by Gandhi's spiritual heir, Vinoba Bhave. The Shanti Sena, as Weber explains, was proposed by Gandhi in his lifetime, but not established until nearly ten years after his death. It functioned consistently, if sporadically, for the next 35 years. The peace army was 'unarmed, nonviolent, and its members preferred to die rather than kill when fulfilling their peacekeeping duties' [xix]. Weber traces the evolution of the idea through, inter alia, the early twentieth century writings of William James, and his famous essay, 'The Moral Equivalent of War,' to Abdul Ghaffar Khan's founding of the Khudai Khidmatgar (Servants of God, a Pathan application of Gandhi's Shanti Sena), to Maude Royden's 1932 call for a Peace Army, to the modern formation of Peace Brigades International.[8]

Most relevant to the present study is the proposal to internationalize and make permanent such a peace army. It should be stated that while the agency proposed in this study is not precisely the same concept as a peace army, it is instructive to consider the potential parallel between these efforts and that of a nonviolent UNCIVPOL service. The most eloquent and compelling declaration of this idea was crafted at a conference that concluded in January 1950 in Sevagram, India — Gandhi's ashram and headquarters. The gathering was attended by Vinoba Bhave and US peace scholar/activist A.J. Muste, the latter drafting the stirring concluding statement. It reads:

> We propose that serious and sustained attempts should be made to establish Satyagraha units in different countries. These units will be composed of those individuals who have full faith in the superiority of non-violence and moral force over violent methods and who are prepared to discipline their own lives for becoming true satyagrahis...Unlike the military forces, Satyagraha units will be fully active during peace time by tackling the roots of violence in social, educational and administrative spheres. Non-violent defence has to lay great emphasis on preventive actions, as illustrated in Mahatma Gandhi's Constructive Programme. The Satyagraha units will also try to meet crisis situations non-violently in their respective localities or regions. They will not quietly wait for a conflagration to break out, but will, from day to day, try their utmost to create conditions which would nip conflicts in the bud. This could be made more effective if they are able to cultivate intimate personal contacts with people inhabiting those areas. In organizing non-violent defence we will have to stress quality rather than quantity, and, unlike military officers, the leaders will be required to be in the front rather than in the rear. There can be no policy of secrecy in such an organization because non-violence and truth are integrally related [quoted in Weber 1996, 53].

---

[8] See also, Nonviolent Intervention across Borders: A Recurrent Vision (2000), Yeshua Moser-Puangsuwan and Thomas Weber, Eds.(Honolulu, HI: Spark M. Matsunaga Institute for Peace).

More than twenty years later, through the efforts of two Quaker leaders, A. Paul Hare and Charles Walker, another effort was made to internationalize Gandhi's Shanti Sena through the Cyprus Resettlement Project. Through this endeavor, Walker later crafted 'a detailed model for a World Peace Guard' designed to eventually replace the UN peacekeeping forces on the island nation [Weber, 30]. Walker's ultimate goal, along with that of his supporters, was to convince the United Nations to create a nonviolent standing peace brigade based on the Charter provision found in Article 43(1), which stipulates that

> All Members of the United Nations, in order to contribute to the maintenance of international peace and security, undertake to make available to the Security Council, on its call and in accordance with a special agreement or agreements, armed forces, assistance, and facilities, including the rights of passage, necessary for the purpose of maintaining international peace and security.

A similar effort was proposed several years later by Raymond Magee, the founder of Peace Brigades International [Weber 1996, 33].

While Walker and Magee would have celebrated the creation of a nonviolent peace army under the auspices of the United Nations, they also suggested that running parallel to these proposals of a top-down approach should be peace armies established on the local level, comprising people from the conflicted region itself. This emphasis was also central to the Sevagram declaration in its call to 'cultivate intimate personal contacts with people inhabiting those areas' [Muste quoted in Weber 1996, 53]. This approach to peacebuilding stands at the very core of organizations such as Peace Brigades International, Witness for Peace, and Christian Peacemaker Teams — the latter an agency organized through and supported by the historic peace churches.[9] Each of these organizations train and support unarmed bodyguards and nonviolent human rights monitors.

The idea of discovering and calling forth peacebuilding principles from within strife-ridden societies is also a fundamental tenet of John Paul Lederach's 'elicitive' approach. Lederach distinguishes his approach from the more common 'prescriptive approach' which assumes that all conflicts share certain common characteristics and that universal techniques can be prescribed and/or taught by trained experts to successfully overcome the conflicts. Lederach's work in numerous countries convinced him that this approach often fails. Instead, he recommends the use of the elicitive approach to conflict transformation through which a volunteer, serving as both catalyst and co-learner, endeavors to elicit from the participants their own social and cultural knowledge pertaining to previous efforts to address and nonviolently overcome conflicts [1995, 1997]. As Lederach explains, the elicitive approach builds from knowledge within the given conflict setting. Therefore, 'unlike the prescriptive approach, it cannot bracket culture' [1995, 62].

The guiding question for persons engaged in conflict transformation is: 'How do we end something that is not desired, and together build something we do desire?' These conceptual guidelines undergird the essential goals of conflict transformation which can be summarized as: (1) to increase justice; (2) to reduce violence; (3) to restore broken relationships

---

[9] For more information about Peace Brigades International, see Liam Mahony and Luis Enrique Eguren, *Unarmed Bodyguards: International Accompaniment for the Protection of Human Rights* (1997). For a helpful narrative of the efforts of Christian Peacemaker Teams, see Tricia Gates Brown, Ed., *Getting in the Way: Stories from Christian Peacemaker Teams* (2005).

[Lederach, 1995, 23]. Rooted in an appreciation for mutuality and interdependency, the attainment of these goals depends to a great extent upon successfully restructuring broken relationships.

To pursue this path, the work must begin with new perceptions of 'the other.' UNCIVPOL officers are already much better trained for entering war-ravaged societies and building mutually respectful relationships than are military forces. A permanent, well-trained nonviolent UNCIVPOL would be even more effective. Were these and other fundamental principles of conflict transformation theory included in the training of a permanent UN civilian police service, the nonviolent pursuit of peace with justice would be greatly enhanced, the work of post-conflict peacebuilding would be strengthened, and the likelihood of terrorism taking root or expanding its appeal within a given society would be greatly diminished.

Through such training, the underlying goal of consolidating the bases of positive peace would also greatly reduce the likelihood of a return to violence. If such an emphasis had been included in even the more successful UN peacekeeping operations, such as ONUSAL or UNMIK (both of which are described in further detail below), civil society in these settings would also have been much more firmly grounded in respect for the rule of law. When UNCIVPOL operations have been most successful, UN personnel have pursued similar ambitions. A global nonviolent police service would be particularly well-suited for building trust and developing relationships within conflictive societies. These strengthened relationships could, in turn, more effectively facilitate the discernment of indigenous principles and methods of countering terrorism and transforming conflict.

BEYOND TRADITIONAL MILITARY ENFORCEMENT EFFORTS

For reasons too numerous to recount in this brief chapter, nation-states are much more reluctant than citizens of the prototypical Old West town to entrust their legitimate security needs to a central authority such as the UN Security Council. States are generally unwilling to sacrifice national sovereignty in the name of international cooperation. Seeking to overcome this widespread orientation is indeed a daunting challenge, one that is compounded further when the proposed global central authority intends to deploy non-military or non-lethal[10] means of enforcement through UN-sponsored international civilian police forces. Despite this pervasive reluctance, we have extensive historical evidence to suggest that when national leaders become convinced that national interests can be secured through international law, compliance with the rule of law on the world stage becomes a reality. In fact, as human rights scholar Jack Donnelly has suggested, 'international law can be seen as the body of restrictions on sovereignty that have been accepted by states through the mechanisms of custom and

---

[10] Non-lethal weapons, such as stun guns, pepper spray and tasers (electroshock or kind of 'stun gun') have been promoted for several years. Many of these may prove to be effective for UN peacekeeping operations. However, some modern versions of non-lethal weapons pose serious questions. For example, the Pentagon recently announced plans to consider the use of a high- tech megaphone the size of a satellite dish capable of emitting an extremely loud, piercing tone that produces the equivalent of a migraine headache, and could result in loss of hearing in extreme cases. See William M. Arkin, 'The Pentagon's Secret Scream,' published in the *Los Angeles Times*, March 6, 2004.

treaty' [2003, 157]. This sentiment was perhaps best captured in Secretary-General Kofi Annan's now-famous declaration:

> A new, broader definition of national interest is needed in the new century, which would induce states to find greater unity in the pursuit of common goals and values. In the context of many of the challenges facing humanity today, the collective interest *is* the national interest [1999b, emphasis author's].

This new conception of national interest conforms with an important new understanding of sovereignty as it pertains to humanitarian concerns and multinational responses to terrorism. The highly regarded 2004 report of the UN Secretary-General's High-Level Panel on Threats, Challenges and Change concisely summarized this new perspective in its assertion that, '[t]here is growing recognition that the issue is not the "right to intervene" of any State, but the "responsibility to protect" of *every* State when it comes to people suffering from avoidable catastrophe' [United Nations 2004, 65, emphasis author's].[11] A nonviolent global police service represents a promising means for the world body to honor our collective responsibility to protect, and to do so in a manner that is much less likely to inflame national or religious passions due to the nature of its principles and methods. Sensitivities to local cultural traditions, as well as a clearly perceived neutral posture, make a nonviolent UNCIVPOL operation much more likely to successfully quell violence and, over time, facilitate peacebuilding initiatives. As suggested by the Secretary-General's High-Level Panel on Threats, Challenges and Change, when a sovereign state is unable or unwilling to protect its citizens, 'that responsibility should be taken up by the wider international community' [United Nations 2004, 66]. Particularly in instances such as these — i.e. when a United Nations sponsored peacekeeping operation enters a sovereign state without consent — the least provocative approach holds the greatest promise for attaining peace through peaceful means.

It is increasingly clear that it will not be possible to overcome current deficiencies of the UN's capacity to meet its Charter mandate of saving succeeding generations from the scourge of war without the expanded use of UNCIVPOL.[12] Indeed, this is precisely what Under Secretary-General for Peacekeeping Jean-Marie Guehenno had in mind when he formally issued his call for a standing civilian police capability [Johansen 2006, 69]. The benefits would be as enormous as the needs are expansive. As Chuck Call and Michael Barnett have concluded,

> From Gaza to El Salvador, from Mozambique to Rwanda to Bosnia, the transition from civil war to civil society is inextricably linked to the development of civilian, apolitical

---

[11] In completing its report, the High-Level Panel made extensive use of volume, *The Responsibility to Protect: Research, Bibliography, Background: Supplementary Volume to the Report of the International Commission on Intervention and State Sovereignty, International Commission on Intervention and State Sovereignty* (2001). See also, Johansen, *A United Nations Emergency Peace Service* (24-25); Francis Deng, *Protecting the Dispossessed: A Challenge for the International Community* (Washington, DC: Brookings Institution, 1993); and Francis Deng, *Sovereignty as Responsibility* (Washington, DC: Brookings Institution, 1995).

[12] For a review of the concept of UN-based rapid deployment operation, two key sources are H. Peter Langille's Bridging the Commitment-Capacity Gap: A Review of Existing Arrangements and Options for Enhancing UN Rapid Deployment (2002)., and Durch, et al., The Brahimi Report and the Future of UN Peace Operations (2003).

police forces that are composed of different political contingents and ethnic groups, and who will protect citizens, uphold the rule of law and help to maintain order with a minimum of force. The ability of these forces to be both representative and effective in combating common crime will be a key factor in whether peace and, in many cases, democracy can be consolidated. And if military troops are not well suited to the public-security tasks of peacekeeping, then they are particularly inappropriate for building permanent civilian police forces [2000, 44].

In addition to the virtues of its nonviolent and multinational structure, if such a United Nations civilian peace service were also established on a permanent basis, as well as designed for rapid response — as has been suggested for the proposed United Nations Emergency Peace Service — the prospects for achieving a nonviolent counter to terrorism would be greatly enhanced. Regrettably, not only does the military mindset describe US efforts in the waging of war on terrorism, in several unfortunate cases UN peacekeeping operations have also demonstrated a preference for the use of military force rather than the pursuit of nonviolent means of dispute resolution. Prior to examining specific UN peacekeeping cases illustrative of these approaches, it is useful to clearly distinguish between the pursuit of peace and justice through police action and through military action. These differing roles are concisely summarized in a brief report entitled, 'Nonviolence and Humanitarian Intervention.' As noted in this report, the key distinctions between police and military action can be summarized as follows:

1. Law enforcement, in intent, avoids killing rather than seeking it, as is the case with military combat.
2. Law enforcement focuses upon individuals suspected of guilt; military combat tends to dehumanize an enemy people, not distinguishing between the innocent and the guilty.
3. Law enforcement, when just, seeks to protect, without prejudice, individual rights and interests for the benefit of the whole; military action usually protects special (national) interests.
4. Domestic police in democracies operate ideally under clearly defined laws made and agreed to by the community, to which all parties, including officers, are subject; war, on the other hand, in spite of instruments such as the Geneva Conventions, is essentially lawless.
5. Police roles may include community service functions such as linking people with help and offering mediation in conflict, such as family interventions; military action has no such aim.[13]

These criteria are pertinent for the comparison of police action with traditional combat operations, and each of these five points of distinction are also applicable to UN peacekeeping operations — albeit some are more instructive than others.

The distinctions were recast and similarly summarized by Perito as he reflected on his responsibilities with the UN peacekeeping and post-conflict operations in Bosnia, Kosovo,

---

[13] In addition to the author of the present chapter, the other editors of this study were: Dale Aukerman, Kenneth Brown, Celia Cook-Huffman, Robert Johansen, Kimberly McDowell, (1996).

and East Timor. During a presentation to the Pentagon's Defense Planning Board in February 2003 regarding the US invasion of Iraq, Perito noted:

> [T]here's a major difference between military and police. Soldiers are trained to deal with soldiers. They're trained to deal with opposition armies. They're not trained to deal with civilians. There's a different ethos here. Police are trained to deal with civilians. They're trained to interact on a whole different basis. So while soldiers are trained to, as one officer said, 'shoot people and break things,' police are trained to preserve and protect [PBS 2003].

These sentiments were echoed by General Wesley Clark, the former NATO Supreme Allied Commander, who acknowledged that 'Experience in peace operations has proven that good soldiers, no matter how well equipped, trained and led, cannot fully perform police duties among local populations' [quoted in Perito 2003, 84]. Perhaps Don Kraus captured this perspective most concisely when he wrote, 'The aftermath of the Iraq War has shown us that good soldiers are not always good cops' [2003, 1].

No better cases can be found to illustrate the futility of attempting to overcome terrorism through military might than the US-led wars in Iraq and Afghanistan. In the case of the so-called 'war on terror' launched by the Bush administration, the failures of seeking a military solution to terrorism is increasingly evident. Approaching terrorism as criminal activity, and directing enforcement action toward guilty individuals would achieve vastly different results. Indeed, one of the tragic consequences of the US-led wars in Iraq and Afghanistan is that after enduring several years of devastating war, Iraqis and Afghanis appear to be nearly unanimous in the view that the vast majority of them have been dehumanized as an enemy people rather than judged individually and fairly as innocent until proven guilty.

The 2006 US National Intelligence Estimate confirms what many analysts have posited for several years, viz. that these wars are fueling rather than thwarting Islamic radicalism and serving as catalysts for future terrorist actions. The estimate, which was completed in April 2006 and is based on a consensus of the sixteen US intelligence agencies, asserts: 'Jihadists, although a small percentage of Muslims, are increasing in both number and geographic dispersion.' This finding certainly came as no surprise to Robert Pape, a former professor at the US Air Force's School of Advanced Airpower Studies and current University of Chicago professor. Pape conducted the most comprehensive demographic assessment of suicide terrorism, beginning in 1980 and concluding in 2005. Based on his investigation of more than 460 suicide attacks, Pape concludes that 'spreading democracy at the barrel of a gun in the Persian Gulf is not likely to lead to a lasting solution against suicide terrorism' [146]. Moreover, in an interview with Scott McConnell for *The American Conservative* magazine, Pape asserted: 'Since suicide terrorism is mainly a response to foreign occupation and [is] not [due to] Islamic fundamentalism, the use of heavy military force to transform Muslim society over there, if you would, is only likely to increase the number of suicide terrorists coming at us' [McConnell, 2].

How different might the results have been had the US allowed the UN to address the purported threat from Iraq? Furthermore, how different might the results have been had the UN placed a nonviolent UNCIVPOL service in Afghanistan in response to the brutal rule of the Taliban regime? The widespread anti-US hostilities perpetuated through this war effort are starkly contrasted with much more promising results that could be achieved through a

UN-sponsored multinational nonviolent police service. Brigadier Michael Harbottle illustrates well this potential in his description of the qualities a peacekeeper needs, namely, 'patience, restraint, advocacy skills, approachability, tact, fairness, persuasiveness, a broad perspective of the situation, impartiality, flexibility, and humor, [none of which are] traditionally part of a soldier's makeup' [quoted in Weber 1996, 10]. Instead of coercive military power to counter terrorism and to enforce the rule of law, the world is in need of an alternative approach. Nonviolent international police operations can be as effective in international settings as are police on domestic levels. By eschewing unnecessary violence and focusing police efforts on guilty individuals rather than militarily targeting entire populations, a nonviolent UNCIVPOL represents one of the most hopeful instruments for reducing instances of international terrorism.

Indeed, the US military appears to be close to embracing a new appreciation for the value of such an approach. A draft Army and Marine field manual due to be released in late 2006 stresses the 'importance of safe-guarding civilians and restoring essential services, and the rapid development of local security forces' [Gordon, A1]. The manual further emphasizes 'the importance of minimizing civilian casualties,' and notes, 'the need to interact with the people to gather intelligence and understand the civilians' needs' [Gordon, A19]. According to Jack Keane, a retired four-star general and former acting chief of staff for the US Army, the new manual will change the Army's 'entire culture as it transitions to irregular warfare' [quoted in Gordon, A19]. These sweeping changes, apparently viewed as not only sweeping and unorthodox, but as nearly unintelligible, are considered by some US military officers as the equivalent of 'the graduate level of war.'

The new insights are captured in what the new field manual refers to as 'nine paradoxes.' Each of them reflects fresh thinking on the part of the US military, and also illustrates well many of the essential attributes of a nonviolent UNCIVPOL operation. For the purposes of this study the four most revealing are summarized below.

1. The more you protect your force, the less secure you are. If military forces stay locked up in compounds, they lose touch with the people, appear to be running scared and cede the initiative to insurgents.
2. The more force used, the less effective it is. Using substantial force increases the risk of collateral damages[14] and mistakes, and increases the opportunity for insurgent propaganda. Sometimes doing nothing is the best reaction. Often an insurgent carries out a terrorist act or guerrilla raid with the primary purpose of causing a reaction that can then be exploited.
3. The best weapons for counterinsurgency do not shoot. Often dollars and ballots have more impact than bombs and bullets.
4. The host nation's doing something intolerably is better than the occupier doing it well. Long-term success requires the establishment of viable indigenous leaders and institutions that can carry on without significant foreign support [Gordon, A19].

---

[14] The term is a US military euphemism used to refer to unintended death and destruction.

CASE STUDIES IN UN PEACEKEEPING

It is beyond the scope of this inquiry to thoroughly critique the widely varied UN peacekeeping operations that have taken place over the past fifty years. Nor is it possible to fully consider those peacekeeping operations that engaged in military actions. Suffice it to say that one of the most telling examples of the latter is the February 1992 to March 1995 UN peacekeeping mission in the former Yugoslavia known as UNPROFOR. At the height of military escalation in March 1995, UN authorized personnel included 38,599 military personnel, but a mere 803 civilian police. Initially established in Croatia, UNPROFOR's mandate expanded to support efforts by the United Nations High Commissioner for Refugees to achieve the following three goals: (1) ensure delivery of humanitarian relief throughout Bosnia and Herzegovina, (2) monitor the 'no-fly zone' which banned all military flights in Bosnia and Herzegovina, and (3) protect the Security Council's established 'safe areas' around five Bosnian towns and the city of Sarajevo.

This effort has been described by many observers, such as Ramesh Thakur, Assistant Secretary-General, as a 'peacekeeping operation in a theater where there was no peace to keep' [2006, 40].

Indeed, the mission was established for the express purpose of creating the conditions of peace and security that could lead to a negotiated solution to the conflict. The effort, however, failed miserably. Not only was the mandate unrealistic, the fighting was complicated by the fact that each of the three warring parties, i.e. the Serbs, the Croats, and Muslims, used unorthodox and often brutal — and therefore quite unpredictable — combat methods in their fight to control Bosnia. Although UN personnel returned fire and in some instance engaged in offensive military action, the UN-imposed safe havens and no-fly zones became simply unenforceable. As Thakur explains, UNPROFOR 'offered neither safety to the local people, solace to the displaced and dispossessed, nor even consolation to the international community of having done the job to the best of their ability' [40].

In its struggling and often failed attempts to deliver humanitarian aid, the UN eventually negotiated the delivery specifications with the Bosnian Serbs. Not surprisingly, the authorized shipments were consistently well below the needs of the war-weary survivors. Regarding this decision and its deadly impact on the people of Sarajevo, Richard Holbrooke, then US Assistant Secretary of State for European and Canadian Affairs and chief negotiator of the 1995 Dayton Peace Accords, later asserted, 'It was as if the U.N. were negotiating with the city's chief executioners as to whether Sarajevo's death would be by starvation or freezing, slow or fast' [quoted in Thakur 2006, 48].

One can certainly argue that the 167 fatalities (3 military observers, 159 other military personnel, 1 civilian police, 2 international civilian staff and 2 local staff) suffered by UNPROFOR represents less loss of life than might have occurred had a nonviolent UNCIVPOL operation been used. However, it is equally plausible to suggest that a UN peacekeeping operation comprised of CIVPOL personnel trained in nonviolent methodologies, rooted in conflict transformation theory and praxis, and equipped with non-lethal weapons, could have achieved more positive peacebuilding results while sustaining fewer fatalities.

An additional case that clearly illustrates the limitations of UN peacekeeping operations functioning as a military force is seen in the 1992-93 UN peacekeeping operation in Somalia, known as UNOSOM II. The effort, authorized under Chapter VII of the UN Charter, was fraught with problems from the very beginning. Many analysts have noted the lack of planning prior to the on-site arrival of the UN commander. Most troubling, however, is the fact that the operation was granted authority to employ coercive force over a much more expansive territory than had been the case in previous efforts. Complicating matters further, when the mandate was revised on 5 June 1993 through UN Security Council Resolution 837, it included a specific proviso authorizing what many rightly understood to be a call for the arrest of Somali militia commander Mohammad Farrah Aideed and key officers in his Somali National Army. Had an UNCIVPOL operation been foremost in the planning and implementation of this action, rather than further flaming national and factional passions — as was the case when coercive military force was employed in an attempt to bring combatants to justice — a nonviolent UN police force would have enhanced trust within the strife-ridden communities and produced much less political volatility.

In addition, had a UN police force monitored operations in a clearly impartial manner that underscored the promise and efficacy of a 'rule-of-law society,' it likely would have resulted in the safe provision of needed humanitarian aid for the millions of Somalis on the brink of starvation. The International Peace Academy concluded that the failures in UNOSOM II are primarily attributable to the fact that the operation, 'was led by former and serving officials from the US military establishment and the US National Security Council' [quoted in Johansen 2004, 43].

The dominance of US military objectives diminished both the reputation as well as the effectiveness of the UN operation. As one observer of this tragic intervention notes:

> The military objective to marginalize and eliminate General Aidid after the attack on Pakistani peacekeepers on 5 June 1993 stripped the UN of the impartiality that it required to perform a useful role in civilian peacebuilding efforts. By the time these military objectives changed in October 1993, UNOSOM II had become too discredited to be seen as an honest broker in the political process [Jan 1996, 4].

At the heart of these unfortunate developments is the fact that UN leadership and members of the Security Council had been encouraged to address the Somali conflict from a markedly different perspective. Regrettably, however, they failed to heed the counsel of Mohamed Sahnoun, Special Representative of the Secretary-General to Somalia from April to November 1992. In a manner strikingly similar to Lederach's elicitive approach, Sahnoun had argued that UN personnel should work in concert with local tribal clan leaders in seeking to implement ancient and proven means of enforcing societal norms and procedures to address the crisis and more equitably distribute the humanitarian aid. These procedures, if they had been pursued, would have provided opportunities for UN staff to learn from, collaborate with, and support indigenous means of enforcing the rule of law and building a system of justice on the foundation of Somali customs and tradition. Indeed, objectives such as these lie at the very heart of the UNCIVPOL mandate, which is, 'to create a safer environment where communities will be better protected and criminal activities will be prevented, disrupted and deterred' [United Nations Department of Public Information 2006].

Sahnoun's approach also closely conforms to one of the essential objectives of CIVPOL, viz., supporting the capabilities and effectiveness of local law enforcement agencies. Despite the fact that lawlessness reigned throughout much of Somalia at the time of the UN intervention, in the northern third of the state, where traditional approaches to societal problems were applied through tribal clan leaders and local custom, less violence occurred and improved systems of justice produced more equitable distributions of humanitarian aid. Despite these failings of UNOSOM II, little progress has been made to learn from the wisdom of seasoned diplomats such as Sahnoun. As Lederach has noted, 'We persist in relying on traditional statist diplomacy, despite its inadequacies in responding to the nature of conflicts today' [1997, 16]. Sadly, this tendency is often as pervasive within the UN as it is within the leadership of its member states.

In contrast to the above cases, the 1992 UN-brokered peace agreement in El Salvador serves as a sterling example of the effectiveness of an UNCIVPOL operation when staff members are actively engaged in promoting lawful behavior and in providing on-site training of local police forces in the aftermath of a bitter and extremely deadly civil war. The 1989 UN observer mission in El Salvador, referred to as ONUSAL, played a critically important role in monitoring the protection of human rights and eventually in bringing about much needed judicial and police reform measures. At the heart of the peace accords, known as the Chapultepec Agreement, lays the creation of the National Civilian Police (PNC), an entity that made possible the dismantling of several branches of military police forces that were guilty of countless human rights violations throughout the decade-long war.

In addition, the PNC also provided a means for former rebels of the Farabundo Marti National Liberation Front (FMLN) to move peacefully back into society while restoring a sense of trust and respect for the political rights of the Salvadoran people. The distinction that was crafted between the roles and responsibilities of the El Salvadoran police and their national military provided a solid basis for affirming and preserving the fragile peace accord. As William Stanley has noted, the plan to develop the civilian police force was the product of a breakthrough compromise that allowed members of the FMLN to gain access to the new police without discrimination [2000, 116]. The UN provided the expertise in developing 'a detailed proposal for a professional, apolitical, civilian-controlled police force...that would exclude the armed forces from internal security, giving the civilian police a monopoly over that role' [116].

A final case that reveals the effectiveness and potential of an expanded use of UNCIVPOL is the on-going effort known as the United Nations Interim Administration Mission in Kosovo, or UNMIK. Authorized in 1999 under UN Security Council Resolution 1244, the operation was designed from the outset to provide an international civil and security presence. The resolution further stipulated that the mission will 'provide a transitional administration, while establishing and overseeing the development of provisional democratic self-governing institutions to ensure conditions for a peaceful and normal life for all inhabitants of Kosovo' [UN Security Council 1999, 3]. At the heart of the operation is the responsibility to 'maintain civil law and order and to establish local police forces, through the deployment of international police personnel' [4].

With funding in the range of a mere $200 million, and within only a few months of the launch of the operation, UNMIK supervised the creation of the Kosovo Police Service (KPS) and an international police training academy. Law enforcement officers, primarily from the Organization for Security and Cooperation in Europe (OSCE), have now trained more than 7,000 police officers who are, quite literally, keeping the peace in this formerly war ravaged nation-state. In addition, the UN continues (as of 30 June 2006) to employ an additional 1,928 uniformed police officers who work collaboratively with the KPS.

Even more impressive than the number of trained police officers are the statistical indicators of the effectiveness of the KPS. For example, from 2000 to 2002 the murder rate in Kosovo dropped from 245 to 68 [UNMIK 2002]. It must be acknowledged that while the KPS has been effective, it also represents one of the few CIVPOL operations in which UN personnel were granted executive power, i.e. the police officers were armed with light weapons, and were authorized to arrest suspects. UNMIK police continue to work closely with the Interpol Liaison Office, and the 178 police agencies from its member states, but the foundation of their service remains the commitment to community policing. As Johansen has suggested of UN police operations, at their best they are able,

> to nurture an 'us-us' relationship of helping local communities sort out their problems, gradually *increasing reliance on their own nationals* for impartial enforcement of international norms of peace and human rights [2004,49, emphasis author's].

Although UNMIK functions with one of the lowest annual budgets of any UN peacekeeping operation, its performance and effectiveness in peacebuilding is perhaps unrivaled.

THE LEGACY AND PROMISE OF A NONVIOLENT GLOBAL CIVILIAN POLICE SERVICE

The effectiveness of the community based police units that are functioning well in Kosovo serve as an excellent example of the power that can be derived from a police operation that has established the trust of its citizenry. If the United Nations had at its disposal a permanent volunteer police force, able to respond quickly to conflict settings, similarly successful peacebuilding enterprises could be realized. A rapid response to domestic or international conflict would, as Johansen has suggested, 'enable the international community to discharge its responsibilities at the time when it can do the most good with means that exact the least moral cost' [2006, 30]. The precedent for a rapid response operation was established with the very first fully functioning UN peacekeeping operation. The first UN Emergency Force (UNEF I), which was instrumental in resolving the 1956 Suez Crisis, was deployed within eight days of Secretary-General Dag Hammarsjold's request. Even during the Cold War, when superpower rivalries frustrated countless opportunities for collective security measures, the UN Security Council authorized UNEF II within seventeen hours after having received the request [Urquhart, cited in Johansen 2006, 7]. The operation was organized to preserve a cease-fire between Egypt and Israel following what has been called the 1973 'Yom Kippur War.'

Johansen has provided a concise summary of the significant advantages afforded through a permanent UN civilian police force when he writes:

> Because it would be dedicated to UN causes, such a force could be specially trained in a way ad hoc forces cannot be. Within the force, specialized units could be highly trained for different missions (e.g., unarmed monitoring, patrolling with executive or enforcement authority, tension-diffusion and crowd control, police training, investigating, witness protection, accompaniment, or arresting indicted war criminals). Its command

structure could function more dependably because it would be an integrated force not drawn from national contingents. It could be more rapidly deployed because it would be a standing force, ready at all times, not an ad hoc force to be created after a conflict erupts and moves into stages in which police enforcement becomes far more difficult. Deployment would be more dependable because the decision about whether to deploy would not be held up by national political reluctance to call for deployment that would obligate their own nationals to be placed at risk [1998, 14].

A similar call was issued through the Secretary-General's High-Level Panel on Threats, Challenges and Change. The panel recommended that the UN

have a small corps of senior police officers and managers (50-100 personnel)[15] who could undertake mission assessments and organize the start-up of police components of peace operations, and the General Assembly should authorize this capacity [United Nations, 2004, 70-71].

Perito identifies another compelling reason to make UNCIVPOL operations permanent when he notes that '[p]oliticians and senior police official are reluctant to release officers for international service...[Moreover,] police forces find it particularly difficult to part with their best and most experienced officers and those with special skills' [2004, 90].

Clearly, a permanent nonviolent UN police force would not be a panacea. No doubt there would be instances in which such police units would be unable to achieve an effective reduction in hostilities or to create lasting peace out of the fires of a terrorist incident or a protracted conflict. Of course, similar limitations are also widely evident when attempting to construct peaceful relations through military action — whether under UN auspices or through individual or regional military operations. Regarding the relative effectiveness of a permanent UN civilian police force, the insightful observations of Nobel Laureate John Polanyi are instructive. As he explains:

Fire departments and police forces do not always prevent fire or crime, yet they are now widely recognized as providing an essential service. Similarly, a rapid reaction capability may confront conditions beyond its capacity to control. This should not call into question its potential value to the international community. It is a civilized response to an urgent problem [quoted in Johansen 1998, 15].

In the same way, a UN rapid response permanent police service, especially a UNCIVPOL operation committed to nonviolence, may confront conditions beyond its capacity to control. As with the inability of fire departments to prevent all fires, this concern should not call into question the potential value of such a police service to the international community.

Under present conditions, the challenges the world faces are even more severe. As Secretary-General Annan has stated, 'the UN is the only fire brigade in the world that has to acquire a fire engine after the fire has started' [quoted in Johansen 2006, 9]. The reasons for making UN peacekeeping and CIVPOL operations permanent are myriad. Interestingly, these potential benefits appear obvious to a majority of people within the United States even while

---

[15] This number pales in comparison to the recommendation issued through the Brahimi Report that calls for a police force of 4,000-8,000 officers [Durch, et. al, xxvii]. Even more ambitious is the UNEPS recommendation that calls for a standing rapid response force of 12,000 to 15,000 personnel [Johansen 2006, 22].

(or perhaps because) their country was plummeting further into the quagmire of simultaneous wars of aggression in Afghanistan and Iraq at the time they were queried. These insights were revealed through a 2004 comprehensive poll conducted by the Chicago Council on Foreign Relations. Among several encouraging indicators, the poll found that 75% of those surveyed 'favored the creation of a standing UN peacekeeping force, selected, trained, and commanded by the United Nations' [Joseph 2007, 236-37].

One of the most authoritative summaries of the necessary means to improve multilateral peace enforcement mechanisms is the Report of the Panel on UN Peace Operations. Secretary-General Annan convened this distinguished panel in March 2000 'to undertake a thorough review of the United Nations peace and security activities, and to present a clear set of specific, concrete and practical recommendations to assist the United Nations in conducting such activities better in the future.' The statement, often referred to as the 'Brahimi Report,' (in honor of Lakhdar Brahimi, the former Algerian Minister of Foreign Affairs and Chair of the Panel) was disseminated on August 21, 2000. Among the many pertinent recommendations provided by the report, perhaps most significant is the call for a 'doctrinal shift' to expand the use of civilian police, judicial personnel, and human rights monitors toward the goal of strengthening respect for and adherence to the rule of law. Among the more innovative recommendations included in the report is the call for a 'team-based approach to the rule of law' [Durch et al 2003, 29].

In addition, the following major findings are also instructive for the purposes of this essay:

Civilian police personnel:

a.   Member States are encouraged to each establish a national pool of civilian police officers that would be ready for deployment to United Nations peace operations on short notice, within the context of the United Nations Standby Arrangements System (UNSAS);

b.   Member States are encouraged to enter into regional training partnerships for civilian police in the respective national pools, to promote a common level of preparedness in accordance with guidelines, standard operating procedures and performance standards to be promulgated by the United Nations;

c.   Members States are encouraged to designate a single point of contact within their governmental structures for the provision of civilian police to United Nations peace operations;

d.   The Panel recommends that a revolving on-call list of about 100 police officers and related experts be created in UNSAS to be available on seven days' notice with teams trained to create the civilian police component of a new peacekeeping operation, train incoming personnel and give the component greater coherence at an early date;

e.   The Panel recommends that parallel arrangements to recommendations (a), (b) and (c) above be established for judicial, penal, human rights and other relevant specialists, who with specialist civilian police will make up collegial 'rule of law' teams.

The Panel Report argued that, 'force alone cannot create peace; it can only create the space in which peace may be built' [Panel Report Executive Summary 2000]. If the force employed is non-military — or even more promising, multilateral and nonviolent in nature — the prospects for transforming international disputes and for creating enduring peace will be greatly enhanced.

Promising as the above recommendations are, considerable concerns have emerged regarding the Panel's appeal for 'more robust UN operations.' Such language led some member states to recall NATO's 1999 aerial bombardment against Serbia. The Secretary-General sought to allay such fears by pointing out that such uses of force 'should always be seen as a measure of last resort' [quoted in Durch et al 2003, 22]. Annan stated further:

> I therefore do not interpret any portions of the Panel's report as a recommendation to turn the United Nations into a war-fighting machine or to fundamentally change the principles according to which peacekeepers use force [quoted in Durch et al 2003, 22].

Disavowal of the intent to emphasize military force within UN peacekeeping operations is certainly heartening. Even more encouraging would be indications that the international community is committed to investing in a permanent, well-funded, UN civilian police service trained in the nonviolent pursuit of peace and justice. As William Durch *et al* have pointed out:

> [I]nconsistent national attention to civilian policing roughly matches the inconsistent quality that CivPol contributed to UN operations and suggests that there is still a long way to go before the United Nations can expect consistent and timely contributions of well-trained and well-qualified police for its operations [2003, 81].

Fundamentally, of course, it will not be possible to create and support an entity such as a nonviolent UN permanent civilian police force without a dramatic shift in thinking. As long as traditional military means are considered the only reliable means of ensuring national security in the face of terrorist aggression or other security concerns, i.e. as long as violent forces are viewed as the only effective 'tools in the toolbox,' countless lives and massive amounts of the world's resources will continue to be squandered in pursuit of peace through war.

Similarly, until UN leadership and key member states recognize and affirm the value of a permanent UN civilian police service trained in nonviolence, it is also unlikely that adequate progress will be made in this pursuit. What is required is a concerted and well organized global educational effort to build the requisite support and to bring about sweeping attitudinal changes regarding effective and law-enforcing responses to terrorism, as well as concerns pertaining to human rights and human needs.

CONCLUSION

Many people world-wide are understandably concerned about terrorist threats from state and non-state actors. Most remain, however, as ill-equipped to deal with these concerns as were the aforementioned Old West villagers before the sheriff came to town. For the international community to successfully confront and eventually overcome a challenge as pervasive as global terrorism new tools are needed. Because innovative tools are generated through creative thoughts, it is imperative that global citizens, and our leadership, look beyond traditional approaches. As these much-needed alternatives pertain to security concerns, it is particularly imperative that citizens and global leaders look beyond efforts with extremely low utility such as aggressive and costly military campaigns. As Lederach has suggested,

> Much of our current system for responding to deadly local and international conflict is incapable of overcoming cycles of violent patterns precisely because our imagination has been corralled and shackled by the very parameters and sources that create and perpetuate violence. Our challenge is how to invoke, set free, and sustain innovative responses to the roots of violence while rising above it [2005, 172].

Although it is daunting to consider the challenge of generating such substantial adjustments to our collective thinking, it is helpful to recall that sweeping attitudinal change has taken place throughout human history. Just as the widely accepted system of slavery was essentially overcome, so the war system can also be abolished in place of nonviolent, multilateral means of conflict transformation and peacebuilding. Such change, of course, will not take place quickly. Nor will it become possible without a great deal of determined effort on the part of an engaged global citizenry. Yet every step in the direction of nonviolent law enforcement brings the world community closer to the promise of a global peace system. Indeed, the domestication of international relations, to which Inis Claude referred decades ago, is already taking root within the norms of the global community. Heinous violations of human rights such as genocide are no longer countenanced on either the domestic or the international levels.

For centuries, scholars and international theorists have pondered what it might take for civil order, and with it the concomitant attainment of peace with justice, to be created within the global community. Through broad support for a permanent UN civilian police service, trained in nonviolence and conflict transformation theory, the world community can devise the means to transform even the most intractable international disputes and overcome the challenges of terrorism. Despite the current reluctance of many international leaders to entrust national security concerns to a central authority such as the UN Security Council, as the global community grows more interdependent, it becomes increasingly clear that global threats such as terrorism can only effectively be addressed through collaboration grounded in respect for the rule of law.

ACKNOWLEDGEMENTS

Timothy A. McElwee is Plowshares Associate Professor of Peace Studies, and Director of the Peace Studies Institute at Manchester College (Indiana). He holds a Ph.D. in political science, with an emphasis in international relations, from Purdue University. His current research focuses on the role of media and nonviolent social change.

REFERENCES

Annan, K. (1999a). *The Question of Intervention: Statements by the Secretary-General*. New York: United Nations Department of Public Information.

Annan, K.(1999b). 'Two Concepts of Sovereignty,' *The Economist*, 18 September.

Arnson, C.J. (1999). (Ed.). *Comparative Peace Processes in Latin America*. Washington, DC: Woodrow Wilson Press and Stanford, CA: Stanford University Press.

Brown, T.G. (2005). *Getting in the Way: Stories from Christian Peacemaker Teams*. Scottdale, PA: Herald Press.

Call, C. & Barnett, M. (2000). 'Looking for a Few Good Cops: Peacekeeping, Peacebuilding and CIVPOL.' In T.T. Holm & E.B.Eide (Eds.), *Peacebuilding and Police Reform*. London: Frank Cass Publishers.

Claude, I. (1984 [1956]). *Swords into Plowshares: The Problems and Progress of International Organization* (4th edition). New York: Random House, Inc.

Deng, F. (1993). *Protecting the Dispossessed: A Challenge for the International Community*. Washington, DC: Brookings Institution.

Deng, F. (1995). *Sovereignty as Responsibility*. Washington, DC: Brookings Institution.

Donnelly, J. (2003). *Universal Human Rights in Theory and Practice*. Ithaca, NY: Cornell University Press.

Durch, W., Holt, V.K., Earle, C.R., & Shanahan, M.K. (2003). (Eds.). *The Brahimi Report and the Future of UN Peace Operations*. Washington, DC: The Henry J. Stimson Center.

Galtung, J. & Hveem, H. (1976). 'Participants in Peacekeeping Forces.' In J. Galtung (Ed.), *Essays in Peace Research*, Vol. 2, War, Peace and Defence. Copenhagen: Christian Ejlers.

Gordon, M.E. (2006). 'Military Hones A New Strategy On Insurgency.' *The New York Times*, October 5, pp. A1 and A19.

Hanson, W.L. (2004). 'Police Power for Peace.' *Friends Journal*. August, pp. 6-7 and 34-35.

Harbottle, M. (1978). (Ed.). *Peacekeeper's Handbook*. New York: International Peace Academy.

Hartz, H. (2000). 'CIVPOL: The UN Instrument for Police Reform.' In T.T. Holm & E.B.Eide (Eds.), *Peacebuilding and Police Reform*. London: Frank Cass Publishers.

Holbrooke, R. (1999). *To End a War*. New York: Random House, Inc.

Holm, T.T. (2000a). 'CIVPOL Operations in Eastern Slavonia, 1992-98.' In T.T. Holm & E.B.Eide (Eds.), *Peacebuilding and Police Reform*. London: Frank Cass Publishers.

Holm, T.T. & E.B.Eide. (2000b). (Eds.). *Peacebuilding and Police Reform*. London: Frank Cass Publishers.

International Commission on Intervention and State Sovereignty. (2001). *The Responsibility to Protect: Research, Bibliography, Background*: Supplementary Volume. *Report of the International Commission on Intervention and State Sovereignty*. Ottawa: International Development Research Centre.

Jan, A. (1996). *Peacebuilding in Somalia*. New York: International Peace Academy.

Johansen, R C. (1978). *Toward a Dependable Peace: A Proposal for an Appropriate Security System*. New York: Institute for World Order.

Johansen, R.C. (1996). 'The Future of United Nations Peacekeeping and Enforcement: A Framework for Policymaking.' *Global Governance*, Vol. 2, 299-333.

Johansen, R.C. (1998a). 'Enhancing United Nations Peacekeeping.' In C. F. Alger (Ed.), *The Future of the United Nations System: Potential for the Twenty-first Century*. New York: United Nations University Press.

Johansen, R.C. (1998b). Overlooked and Underutilized: International Enforcement by United Nations Civilian Police. Unpublished manuscript prepared for the International Studies Association 39th Annual Convention, March 17-21, 1998.

Johansen, R.C. (2004). 'Reviving Peacebuilding Tools Ravished by Terrorism, Unilateralism, and Weapons of Mass Destruction.' *International Journal of Peace Studies*, Vol. 9, 31-55.

Johansen, R.C. (2006). (Ed.). *A United Nations Emergency Peace Service to Prevent Genocide and Crimes Against Humanity*. New York: World Federalist Movement-Institute for Global Policy.

Johansen, R.C. & Mendlovitz, S.H. (1980). 'The Role of Enforcement of Law in the Establishment of a New International Order: A Proposal for a Transnational Police Force.' *Alternatives*, Vol. 6, 307-337.

Joseph, P. (2007). *Are Americans Becoming More Peaceful?* Boulder, CO: Paradigm Press.

Kraus, D. (2003). *The Need for UN Police*. www.fpif.org

Langille, H.P. (2000). 'Conflict Prevention: Options for Rapid Deployment and United Nations Standing Forces.' *International Peacekeeping*, Vol. 17, 219-53.

Langille, H.P. (2002). *Bridging the Commitment-Capacity Gap*. Wayne, NJ: Center for UN Reform Education.

Lederach, J.P. (1995). *Preparing for Peace: Conflict Transformation across Cultures*. Syracuse, NY: Syracuse University Press.

Lederach, J.P. (1997). *Building Peace: Sustainable Reconciliation in Divided Societies*. Washington, DC: United States Institute of Peace Press.

Lederach, J.P. (2005). *The Moral Imagination: The Art and Soul of Building Peace*. Oxford: Oxford University Press.

Lynch, C. (2006). 'Peacekeeping Grows, Strains UN: Group's Troop Numbers across Globe to Hit New High.' *The Washington Post*, September 17, p. A17.

Mahoney, L. & Equren, L.E. (1997). *Unarmed Bodyguards: International Accompaniment for the Protection of Human Rights*. West Hartford, CT: Kumarian Press.

Mani, R. (2000). 'Contextualizing Police Reform: Security, the Rule of Law and Post-Conflict Peacebuilding.' In T.T. Holm & E.B. Eide (Eds.), *Peacebuilding and Police Reform*. London: Frank Cass Publishers.

McConnell, S. (2005). 'The Logic of Suicide Terrorism: It's the Occupation, Not the Fundamentalism.' July 11. *The American Conservative*. http://amconmag.com/2005_07/article.html.

Moser-Puangsuwan, Y. & Weber, T. (2000). (Eds.). *Nonviolent Interventions across Borders: A Recurrent Vision*. Honolulu: Spark M. Matsunaga Institute for Peace.

Pape, R. (2005). *Dying to Win: The Strategic Logic of Suicide Terrorism*. New York: Random House.

Perito, R.M. (2004). *Where is the Lone Ranger When We Need Him? America's Search for a Postconflict Stability Force*. Washington, DC: United States Institute of Peace Press.

Public Broadcasting Company. (2003). 'Truth, War and Consequences: Interviews with Robert M. Perito.' *Frontline*, October.

Stanley, W. (2000). 'Building New Police Forces in El Salvador and Guatemala: Learning and Counter-Learning.' In T.T. Holm & E.B. Eide (Eds.), *Peacebuilding and Police Reform*. London: Frank Cass Publishers.

Stockholm International Peace Research Institute. (2006). *SIPRI Yearbook 2006: Armaments, Disarmament and International Security.* http://www.sipri.org/contents/publications/pocket/pocket_yb.html.

Thakur, R. (2006). *The United Nations, Peace and Security.* Cambridge: Cambridge University Press.

United Nations. (1990). *The Blue Helmets: A Review of United Nations Peacekeeping* (2nd edition). New York: United Nations Department of Public Information.

United Nations Security Council. (1999). *Resolution 1244.* New York: United Nations. http://www.un.org/Docs/scres/1999/sc99.htm.

United Nations. (2000). *Report of the Panel on United Nations Peace Operations, Executive Summary.* New York: United Nations. http://www.un.org/peace/reports/peace_operations/ docs/summary.htm

United Nations Interim Administration Mission in Kosovo. (2002). http://www.unmikonline.org/civpol.reports

United Nations. (2004). 'A More Secure World: Our Shared Responsibility.' *Report of the High-Level Panel on Threats, Challenges and Change.* New York: United Nations.

United Nations. (2005). *United Nations Peace Operations: Year in Review 2005.* New York: United Nations.

United Nations. (2006). The Department of Public Information, in Consultation with the Department of Peacekeeping Operations. http://www.un.org/dpko.

Urquhart, B. (1987). *A Life in Peace and War.* New York: Harper & Row Publishers.

Urquhart, B. (1998). 'Looking for the Sheriff.' *The New York Review of Books*, Vol. 45, July 16.

Weber, T. (1996). *Gandhi's Peace Army: The Shanti Sena and Unarmed Peacekeeping.* Syracuse, NY: Syracuse University Press.

Weiss, T., Forsythe, D. & Coate, R. (2001). *The United Nations and Changing World Politics* (3rd edition). Boulder: Westview Press.

PART V: NONVIOLENT RESPONSES TO TERRORISM

In: Nonviolence: An Alternative for Defeating...
Editors: S. Ram and R. Summy, pp. 213-220
ISBN: 978-1-60021-812-5
© 2008 Nova Science Publishers, Inc.

Chapter 12

NONVIOLENT RESPONSE TO TERRORISM: ACTING LOCALLY

Tom H. Hastings

ABSTRACT

In the aftermath of 9.11.01, more and more researchers have looked at what a nonviolent response to terrorism might look like. Elements are varied and interlocking, ranging from the humanitarian to the legal, from the trade policy to the Security Council sanction policy and far beyond. This chapter is a simple account of how one group of local actionists in Portland, Oregon have woven a nonviolent response to terrorism into their struggle against the terrorism of war and occupation launched from their own nation-state. Ultimately, our lessons learned from such campaigns will help inform the next generation of thinking on an effective, disciplined nonviolent response to terrorism from any quarter.

INTRODUCTION

I looked toward the chief's lodge and saw that Black Kettle had a large American flag tied to the end of a long lodgepole and was standing in front of his lodge, holding the pole, with the flag fluttering in the gray light of the winter dawn. I heard him call to the people not to be afraid, that the soldiers would not hurt them; then the troops opened fire from two sides of the camp [George Benet, Native American survivor of the Sand Creek Massacre, quoted in Brown 1970, 88].

On 29 November 1864 Colonel John Chivington commanded the Sand Creek Massacre of peaceful, coöperating Cheyenne. While there had been fighting previously between the Cheyenne and the US armed forces, a ceasefire had been in effect and Black Kettle thought peace had been achieved. His belief in the integrity of the US commanders was solid — and tragically misplaced. Almost all the innocents encamped and slaughtered were women, children, and elders — the men having been told by a Major Anthony to hunt buffalo to feed their village. The Cheyenne men, and some Arapaho, were many miles to the east, totally unaware of what was about to transpire. Civilians were targeted and killed without quarter or mercy by US soldiers, the Colorado Volunteers.

In the aftermath of 9.11.01, in the US, more than 1,200 people — mostly men of Middle Eastern descent — were rounded up and detained for varying time periods [Bruce 2003, 436]. Aside from Zacharias Moussawi, nothing was proven against any of them (and he was in custody before 9.11.01). These people were taken from their lives, and their lives, in many senses, were taken from them, by this hysterical government reaction. In Portland, we gathered at the Immigration and Naturalization Service (INS) and Homeland Security offices to protest and we protested one Somali imam's incarceration in particular until he was released to a jubilant crowd. When immigrants are seized — especially when they are from nations which would likely prove lethal to them if they were returned — this amounts to a form of terrorism. We responded in Portland as best we could, with some successes and some failures. We strongly felt that stripping people of their freedom and dignity was hardly the way to fight terrorism, and in fact that the opposite was imperative [True 1992, 116].

On 20 March 2003 the US unleashed 'Shock and Awe,' the attack upon Iraq, a nation that had not fired a single bullet at the US, had not participated in any sense in the attacks on 9/11/01, had been stripped of all its WMD by the UNSCOM inspections and enforced WMD destruction, had not been seeking nuclear capability, and had been consistently weakened in every way by a combination of sanctions and UNSCOM intrusions. The overwhelming propaganda blitz on each of these points was 180 degrees opposite the truth, which apparently convinced the American people that their troops and war matériel were somehow liberating Iraqis. With Shock and Awe plus over three years of occupation, more than 100,000 Iraqi civilians have been killed. The US government knew, by the use of missiles, rockets and other bombs that civilians would be killed and still they used those weapons. It was an offensive attack with overwhelming military force of foreign dominators with foreknowledge that civilians would be killed. This meets all salient criteria under the definition of terrorism, and no doubt felt exactly like terrorism to many Iraqis.

Indeed, this is the lead from CBS News far in advance, from 24 January 2003:

> They're calling it 'A-Day,' A as in airstrikes so devastating they would leave Saddam's soldiers unable or unwilling to fight.
> If the Pentagon sticks to its current war plan, one day in March the Air Force and Navy will launch between 300 and 400 cruise missiles at targets in Iraq. As CBS News Correspondent David Martin reports, this is more than the number that were launched during the entire 40 days of the first Gulf War.
> On the second day, the plan calls for launching another 300 to 400 cruise missiles.
> 'There will not be a safe place in Baghdad,' said one Pentagon official who has been briefed on the plan.[1]

There are many forms of terrorism, all of them involving the killing of civilians. We are reminded by the terrorism experts that the irregular terrorism — that practiced by revolutionaries, guerrillas, fanatical irredentists or religious fundamentalists is a spectacular but minor portion of the problem of terrorism. The vast majority of terror acts and campaigns are committed by nation-states against their own people, and against people from other lands [White 1992, xx]. It is cynical yet understandable, if not justifiable, and the state terrorists are

---

[1] http://www.cbsnews.com/stories/2003/01/24/eveningnews/main537928.shtml, retrieved 26 June 2006.

usually clandestine arms of death squads acting cheaply, quickly and outside media, judicial and transparent budget envelopes [Griset and Mahan 2003, 48]. Indeed, the von Clausewitzian concept of total war is terrorism writ chaotically large by nation-states.

APPLYING NONVIOLENCE TO A SIEGE OF TERROR

The claim for *satyagraha* is that through the operation of nonviolent action the truth as judged by the fulfillment of human needs will emerge in the form of a mutually satisfactory and agreed-upon solution [Bondurant 1965, 195].

And so, we operate against terrorism using nonviolence at whatever level we can, if we would prefer a nonviolent response to terrorism. The first responsibility, then, is probably for the entity which acts in our names. For those of us in Portland, Oregon, this would be the US government. If we believe our government is conducting a terror operation, we are called to act as effectively as we can to mitigate and preferably help eliminate such actions by our government.

Some of the strategic considerations in preparing to do nonviolence include assessment (issues, subsystems, strengths and weaknesses of parties, apply counterfactuals to various potentially targeted opponent's source of power, potential roles of externals) and examination of potential outcomes of potential actions [Sharp 2003, 26].

In December 2005 I proposed to the local group of peace rally organizers that we begin to incorporate nonviolent resistance into our rallies, beginning with the next major rally planned for March 19, to coincide with the end of the third year of war, invasion and occupation of Iraq. Only one or two people were receptive to the idea, as the image in Portland of the resister in the context of a large demonstration is the black-masked, booted youth, full of profanity and expressed hatred, smashing and dashing. This is precisely what had occurred during the ramp-up to the announcement that the White House was planning to invade Iraq, so the fear was not entirely misplaced. Indeed, that is the reason I had held off so long; I felt as though Portland needed to right itself toward nonviolence before it could assimilate and support nonviolent resistance. After more than three years of successfully doing so, it was long past time to move to the next level of organizing and nonviolently responding to terrorism.

I set up a list-serve to discuss the idea and began to pitch it at local peace meetings, drawing in about 75 subscribers and we began meetings in January 2006. We quickly decided we needed to nonviolently invade and occupy a federal politician's office (see how they like it) [Merton 2000, 43]. After some deliberation, we agreed to do so at US Senator Ron Wyden's office and decided further to do so the day after the main peace rally, since that was the first business day and since we did not want to foster fear of police reprisals in the hearts and minds of the big rally organizers.

We chose Senator Wyden because we had the most hope for his transformation from quiet Democrat backbencher to leader for peace. We wrote up a petition that informed the Senator that we would insist that he commit to writing legislation that would mandate a US troop withdrawal in months, not years, and would see to funding reconstruction and a peace process for Iraq. We assured him that any peace process must be predicated on complete Iraqi self-determination [Kazak 1994, 218]. The petition also assured him that, if he would not commit to these ideas, a delegation of us would offer nonviolent resistance.

For our first meeting with his staff, I prepared a leaflet with an image of Dr. Martin Luther King, Jr., in Birmingham jail in 1963, with the header, 'Nonviolence is Negotiation.' While the staff did not seem to understand that we meant to offer nonviolence in that spirit of reconciliation and negotiation, the point was made again and again. Senator Wyden responded in writing that he would not meet with us further as long as we were 'threatening to interfere with the legitimate business of my office.'

We gathered some 1,800 signatures and prepared for nonviolent action with a series of trainings for ourselves, our supporters, and for a team of nonviolent security, or Vibeswatchers. The peace rally in Portland on 19 March 2006 was the largest in the US, showing that our base was strong, and we organized a press conference with spokespeople that would occur at a city park directly across the street from the federal building in downtown Portland, in which our Senator had his office.

The tone of the action, the press conference, and the small support rally were carefully prepared to be the actions of mainstream Americans in anguish over this unjust, illegal, terrorist attack and occupation of other people's lands. I argued against costumes, street theater or any actions that would potentially detract from the image of working Americans finally grappling with their consciences. Three years of endless stories of US violations of human rights at home and abroad [Weiss et al 2004, 115], along with an ongoing death toll, conspired to produce a *raison d'resistance* that mainstream Americans could understand and possibly support.

There were nineteen who committed to, trained for, and showed up to engage in the nonviolent resistance. We entered the federal building in small groups and reassembled at 11:30 a.m. at the Senator's office on the 5th floor and all entered. We were eventually greeted by the Senator's chief of staff, who reasserted that we were not going to negotiate with the Senator using these methods. We had carefully chosen spokeswomen and avoided all responding to him at once, in order to maintain our civil and respectful stance from a place of intersubjective truth [Gier 2004, 78]. We acknowledged the Senator's good vote in October 2002, when he refused to join the majority who ceded massive warmaking power to George W. Bush. We did so in the spirit of Gandhian generosity in assuming the best motives of the opponent [Alexander 1984, 9]. We continued to express our intention to talk and he left us. We attempted Gandhian *satyagraha*, which is an exercise not just in nonviolent resistance, but in elicitive mutual education and a strengthening of civic culture, not an attack on it [Boulding 1990, 152].

While we were inside occupying the Senator's office, our speakers addressed both the small support rally and local media. An Iraqi woman journalist, a United Church of Christ minister, a rabbi and others spoke and the media were given a packet of background information, including short statements of our reasoning and intentions. We heard later that the Iraqi journalist was especially cogent, reminding all that the Iraqi people simply wanted foreign occupiers out. All the rhetoric about democracy notwithstanding, people in the Middle East, Northern Africa and Central Asia are extremely chary of US action designed to spread democracy. From the US-backed French intervention in the elected Islamic government of Algeria in 1989 — an intervention that directly led to a war that cost in excess of 100,000 lives [Noah 2003, 5] — to the US role in Iran, in Saudi Arabia, in Jordan, in Egypt, Kuwait and more, the US-announced intentions have rarely matched the results on the ground. Actual

Iraqis pointing out that the citizens there were better off under Saddam helped to strengthen our nonviolent resistance. US occupation inspires terror in the Iraqi citizenry and is thus perceived as a regime of terror in the classic sense of the temporary rule by might with no real commitment to civil society-building [Walter 1969, 294]. Many US citizens now understand that replacing one regime of terror with another is scarcely in line with our self-image as Americans.

We had done outreach to the Portland Police Bureau beforehand, and I had obtained a permit for the press conference and rally from the Federal Protective Services. All were assured that we would be absolutely nonviolent, and that, in the immortal words of Dr. King, we would meet any *physical force with soul force* [King Jr. 1963, 48]. The permit required approval from Homeland Security, who ultimately became our arresting officers. At each step along the way, we were gentle but insistent in our message and outreach, and that behavior was reciprocal. We were proving to Portland and its large peace movement that nonviolent resistance was a robust yet peaceful way to offer our peace message. In my comments to the Senator's staff, I stressed that 15,000 or more of us had just rallied for peace the day before and that we were the Senator's natural constituency.

At 5 p.m. the Wyden staff left and Homeland Security moved in to arrest us, very courteously. We were charged and released. While we discussed all the legal implications and tactics, we were ultimately informed by the federal prosecutor that if we pled either guilty or *nolo contendre* that we would be sentenced to ten hours of community service, no fines and no jail time. We all signed up for that and continued working for peace and feeding the hungry and regard that sentence as an invitation to offer more nonviolent resistance.

What are the benefits of such an action? How does it fit into a notion of nonviolent response to terrorism?

A possible set of sequelae to this action:

- more nonviolent resistance to the militarism at the heart of terrorism by the US
- larger nonviolent actions that actually clog and burden the system enough to directly interfere with acts of terror
- sympathetic media coverage and word-of-mouth opinion that further delegitimates the terror policies of the US government
- encouragement to other nonviolent actionists in other US cities, other locales in coalition countries, and, ultimately, even to nonviolent Iraqi groups seeking to express dissent in their country to US occupation
- movement by the targeted politicians toward peace
- movement of other politicians toward peace to avoid our nonviolent attention
- actual negotiation sessions with Congressional staff and/or members toward peace legislation

And in fact some of these follow-on phenomena have occurred and continue to develop. The very day after the arrest, Wyden's chief of staff called me to essentially say he wasn't going to call me. I listened to his complaints, really listened, and acknowledged them, which was a natural extension of our nonviolent witness [Rosenberg 1999, 91]. He also announced that there was no chance for a meeting — 45 minutes later (at the end of our conversation during which I talked about his service to us and our desire to serve the public good too) we had a meeting scheduled. Framing our campaign and our politicians' life in terms of service seems to bring out the best leadership and spirit [Kyi 1997, 194]. While 'nonviolent struggle is not magic,' [Sharp 2005, 435] it is a fresh approach and can yield new openings if we practice it and watch for them.

Working with such officials was deemed impossible by Tolstoy but desirable by Gandhi, so we chose the Gandhi nonviolent path in that regard [Naess 1965, 103]. We went to work on promoting a Pacific Northwest Exit Strategy and Peace Process forum, bringing in experts and mixing them with the lawmakers and their staffers. The meeting — held on 10 June after many delays — was a full eight hours and the staffers became angry. We offered evidence and testimony that an exit strategy was imperative and that nonviolence capacity-building was one of the most important components of any realistic and humanitarian peace process [Karatnycky 2005, 7]. They left pleased and ready to continue, which is where we are at now.

This has also led to further discussions with the United States Institute of Peace and one high-level advisor to the Iraq Study Group (ISG), which is composed of prominent emeriti such as Sandra Day O'Connor, Vernon Jordan, Edwin Meese, James Baker III, and Lee Hamilton. The ISG has the ear of the White House, so that is an interesting track. We are simply following paths that our nonviolence has shown us, which contrasts, as Dr. King reminded us, with the passivity of watching lawyers or politicians fight for us [King Jr. 1967, 20].

We are making progress where we were assured at many points by many observers and players that there was no chance to go forward. This is also the nature of nonviolence [Ackerman 2000, 495].

Other correlatives include our Senator, who had shown no leadership on the question of Iraq previously:

- The day after our arrest in his office, his website contained his antiwar position, which had previously been conspicuously absent.
- Three weeks after our arrest, Senator Ron Wyden stood on the floor of the US Senate and challenged his colleagues to begin acting like a co-equal branch of government again.
- Senator Wyden was one of only 13 to initially vote for a US troop pullout date.

The Senator continues to act much more strongly on questions all around this basic Iraqagmire issue and we seem to be calling his office weekly to thank him. We are going to take it to the next level in cooperation with the National Campaign for Nonviolent Resistance as we head into the Bring the Troops Home Fast, the Peace Voter pledge and the Declaration of Peace campaign. Our goal had been to shift the political sensibilities from the 'wait-until-after-the-midterm-elections' to 'come out for peace if you hope to remain in or gain office.'

CONCLUSION: LESSONS LEARNED

Recognizing that this is but one locale responding to but one form of terrorism, what lessons have we taken from this process so far?

- Nonviolent resistance can be a part of a nonviolent response to terrorism [King Jr and Washington 1986, 528].
- Demonstrating sincerity and non-hostile nonviolent resistance can strengthen rather than destroy relationships and can foster dialog where some assume only hostility [Malick and Hunter 2002, 248].
- Focusing locally and regionally can provide a template for national action and can dovetail with it well.
- Bringing nonviolence into a good dialog with those in power sometimes 'can reverse that entropic drift by receiving energy from outside itself' [Nagler 2001, 207]. We the people often have better ideas than we fully realize, and those ideas can sometimes gain purchase if borne on the shoulders of good nonviolent action.
- Hearts and minds naturally belong to nonviolent actionists if we offer ourselves in some kind of sacrifice demonstrating humility and sincerity.
- Building the large peace movement is extraordinarily helpful in gaining the ear of the politicians.

ACKNOWLEDGEMENTS

Tom H. Hastings is Coordinator of Peace and Nonviolence Studies track in the Portland State University, Conflict Resolution MA/MS program. His books include: *The Lessons of Nonviolence* (2006), *Power* (2005), *Nonviolent Response to Terrorism* (2004), *Meek Ain't Weak: Nonviolent Power and People of Color* (2002), and *Ecology of War and Peace: Counting Costs of Conflict* (2000). With Seattle writer Geov Parrish, he wrote the 2002 War Resisters League calendar datebook, *52 True Stories of Nonviolent Success*. He edits *The PeaceWorker* and *Candles*, two peace publications. He is a nonviolent peace, justice and environmental activist, a Plowshares nonviolent veteran of three prisons and has done nonviolence trainings for more than twenty years across the US. He is national co-chair of the Peace and Justice Studies Association, on the National Coordinating Committee of the National Campaign for Nonviolent Resistance, and on the Boards of Directors of the Peace and Conflict Studies Consortium and the Oregon Peace Institute. He lives in the Portland Catholic Worker community Whitefeather House, and hikes and bikes for fun and transport — he owns no automobile.

REFERENCES

Ackerman, P. and DuVall, J. (2000). *A Force More Powerful: A Century of Nonviolent Conflict*. New York: St. Martin's Press.

Alexander, H.. (1969). *Gandhi Through Western Eyes*. Philadelphia: New Society Publishers.

Bondurant, J. V. (1965). *Conquest of Violence: The Gandhian Philosophy of Conflict* (rev. ed.). Berkeley, CA: University of California Press.

Boulding, E. (1988). *Building a Global Civic Culture*. Syracuse, NY: Syracuse University Press.

Brown, D. (1970). *Bury My Heart at Wounded Knee*. New York: Henry Holt.

Feldman, N. (2003). *After Jihad: America and the Struggle for Islamic Democracy.* New York: Farrar, Straus and Giroux.

Gier, N. F. (2004). *The Virtue of Nonviolence: From Gautama to Gandhi.* Albany, NY: SUNY Press.

Griset, P.L. and Mahan, S. (2003). *Terrorism in Perspective.* Thousand Oaks, CA: Sage Publications.

Karatnycky, A. (2005). *How Freedom Is Won: From Civic Resistance to Durable Democracy.* New York: Freedom House.

Kazak, A. M. (1994). 'Belief Systems and Justice without Violence in the Middle East.' In P.

Wehr, H. Burgess, and G. Burgess (Eds.), *Justice without Violence.* Boulder, CO: Lynne Rienner.

King, Jr., M.L. and Washington, J.M. (Eds.). (1986). *A Testament of Hope: The Essential Writings and Speeches of Martin Luther King, Jr.* New York/San Francisco: Harper.

King, Jr.,M.L. (1963). *Strength to Love.* New York: Harper and Row.

King, Jr., M L. (1968). *Where Do We Go From Here: Chaos or Community?* New York: Bantam Books.

Kyi, A.S.S. and Clements, A.. (1997). *The Voice of Hope,* New York: Seven Stories Press.

Mallick, K. and Hunter, D. (Eds.). (2002). *An Anthology of Nonviolence: Historical and Contemporary Voices.* Westport, CT: Greenwood Press.

Maxwell, B. (2003). *Terrorism: A Documentary History.* Washington, DC: CQ Press.

Merton, T. (2000). 'Blessed Are the Meek.' In W. Wink (Ed.), *Peace Is the Way: Writings on Nonviolence from the Fellowship of Reconciliation.* Maryknoll, NY: Orbis Books.

Naess, A.. (1965). *Gandhi and the Nuclear Age.* Totowa, NJ: Bedminster Press.

Nagler, M. (2001). *Is There No Other Way? The Search for a Nonviolent Future.* Berkeley, CA: Berkeley Hills Books.

Rosenberg, M. B. (1999). *Nonviolent Communication: A Language of Compassion.* Encinitas, CA: PuddleDancer Press.

Sharp, G. (2003). *There Are Realistic Alternatives.* Boston: The Albert Einstein Institution.

Sharp, G. (2005). *Waging Nonviolent Struggle: 20th Century Practice and 21st Century Potential.* Boston: Extending Horizon Books.

True, M. (1992). *To Construct Peace: 30 More Justice Seekers, Peace Makers.* Mystic, CT: Twenty-Third Publications.

Walter, E.V. (1969). *Terrorism and Resistance: A Study of Political Violence.* New York: Oxford University Press.

Weiss, T.G., Crahan, M.E. and Goering, J. (2004). (Eds.). *War on Terrorism and Iraq: Human Rights, Unilateralism, and U.S. Foreign Policy.* New York: Routledge.

White, J.R. (1998). *Terrorism: An Introduction* (2nd edition). New York: West/Wadsworth Publishing.

In: Nonviolence: An Alternative for Defeating...
Editors: S. Ram and R. Summy, pp. 221-234
ISBN: 978-1-60021-812-5

Chapter 13

DISSOLVING TERRORISM AT ITS ROOTS

Hardy Merriman and Jack DuVall

ABSTRACT

This chapter explains that as nonviolent resistance is used to fight oppression, which terrorists exploit to mobilize support, and as it models a new, more effective way of representing grievances and opposing injustice, the perceived need for and legitimacy of terrorists as liberators will be marginalized. When civilian-based, nonviolent forces are able to come to the fore and produce decisive change in a society, the demand for terrorism as a form of struggle will subside. To further this end, we propose that support should be given to specific groups that are waging nonviolent struggles for rights, freedom, and justice, and that a new discourse be developed about the effectiveness of strategic nonviolent action compared to terrorism or other forms of insurrectionary violence.

INTRODUCTION

When groups in political conflict feel that their fundamental rights are denied or their deepest interests are threatened, they are likely to oppose such abuses by the strongest means with which they are familiar. For many people in history, this has meant waging a conventional military struggle or guerrilla warfare. For others, this means a violent uprising or terrorism. Terrorism, therefore, is a means of conducting a political conflict and is a response to the belief that some form of oppression must be fought.

Despite this fact, many discussions about non-military responses to terrorism focus on judgments that the United States' 'war on terror' has been conducted in ways that are amoral or wrong, that Western countries are using the 'war on terror' as an excuse to further their own geopolitical or economic agendas, or that a violent response to terror will result in more violence. Whatever the merits of these claims, when they become the primary points of discussion, the rationale for non-military responses to terrorism loses its pragmatic content and often fails to identify concrete alternatives. Therefore, our goal here is to address how, pragmatically, non-military policies and responses can be designed to deal with transnational and local political actors who are willing to use extreme violence against civilians in an attempt to achieve their ends. For the purposes of this chapter, we focus primarily on Islamist terrorism because it is a pressing worldwide concern that has spawned significant debate about how nations and organizations should respond to it.

REDUCING TERRORISTS' SOURCES OF POWER

Our ideas for a nonviolent response to terrorism are designed to diminish the ability of terrorists to rely on two of their primary sources of support, which are authoritarian regimes and disaffected or alienated peoples living in oppressed societies. If such regimes and peoples no longer support terrorism or believe in its efficacy, the capacity of terrorists to function will be seriously degraded.

There are three forms of action that are required to do this. They are:

1. Address oppressive conditions that terrorists exploit
    Authoritarian regimes provide significant, if sometimes indirect and unintentional, support for terrorists by creating oppressive conditions (such as the suppression of rights, horrendous economic inequality, and lack of educational and employment opportunities) that terrorists exploit and claim to be able to solve. Some of these regimes also support terrorists directly by providing them with resources and sanctuary. To make it difficult for terrorists to rely indefinitely on these sources of power, people who are living under oppression and who want to obtain self-rule, justice, and human rights should be identified and provided with the knowledge of how to do this nonviolently.

2. Provide a realistic alternative form of mass struggle
    Marginal or deeply alienated groups in many societies may offer support, particularly in the form of young people for recruitment, to terrorist organizations because they come to see terrorism as the most vigorous way to wage struggle against a potentially existential threat, such as foreign occupation or cultural annihilation. Therefore, one way to decrease the adoption of extreme violence in these situations is to offer a realistic alternative form of struggle that has the promise of being more effective than terrorism. Strategic nonviolent action can and should be promoted and taught as such an alternative.

3. Develop a new discourse about nonviolent power
    As a means to further these first two objectives, developing a new discourse about comparative advantages of different ways of fighting for higher causes, for use in education and also in the media in these societies, is essential. This reformed discourse would have the theme of explaining past successes and future potential of civilian-based rather than military struggle as well as the comparative costs of the two forms of struggle — thus countering the implicit belief that terrorism is the most effective form of expressing militancy or fighting for a cause. This theme would then be adapted to specific societal contexts.

Following discussion of these three elements of how to dissolve the roots of terrorism, we address how they may be implemented in practice.

ADDRESS OPPRESSIVE CONDITIONS THAT TERRORISTS EXPLOIT

Authoritarian regimes indirectly provide support for terrorists by creating political, economic and social conditions that make members of their publics more receptive to terrorist recruiting. Furthermore, some severely repressive regimes directly provide resources for terrorist groups that are willing to collaborate with them in attacking their perceived enemies. For example, Iran subsidized non-Iranian terrorist organizations that bombed U.S. military facilities in Lebanon and Saudi Arabia. But if the resources and reach of authoritarian regimes were to be significantly contracted, so too would the likelihood of these governments serving as foils or funders of terrorism.

The invasion and occupation of Iraq suggests that military intervention (whether pre-emptive or reactive), as a way to accomplish 'regime change' in the case of an authoritarian government, is unlikely to be a frequent occurrence in the future, given the enormous human, economic and political costs imposed on an invader or occupier. The fact that there are almost no instances in the past hundred years in which violent insurrection has displaced an authoritarian regime and led the way to a sustainable and stable democratic order suggests that armed internal resistance is also unlikely to diminish the problem of authoritarian oppression as a cause or support of terrorism.

In contrast to the high cost or futility of organized violence as a strategy to displace authoritarian rule, nonviolent resistance has been a powerful form of struggle that has been used increasingly over recent decades on behalf of a wide variety of geographical, political, social, and cultural causes and movements. From struggles for woman's suffrage, minority rights, economic justice, and labor organizing to anti-corruption campaigns, human rights campaigns, and large-scale pro-democracy movements, nonviolent action is a proven and effective way for ordinary people to fight for government, based on the consent of the governed and equality under the law.

The potential for nonviolent power is created when people withdraw their obedience and cooperation from an oppressive system. It involves using methods of protest and persuasion (such as rallies and marches), noncooperation (such as economic boycotts and strikes), and intervention (such as sit-ins or civil disobedience) to gain leverage in a contest with an institutional or armed opponent. Over the course of a struggle, a nonviolent movement raises the cost of maintaining a ruler's system of oppression, calling into question the system's sustainability and dividing the loyalties of its defenders. Ultimately, because of the pressure generated by the nonviolent movement, the oppressive system must reform or face collapse.

The nonviolent movements that are most successful are those that, formally or informally, have represented a proposition to the public about a better vision for the future. In order to motivate people to overcome their inertia, a movement's vision should incorporate the goals and aspirations of many groups from the existing society. This 'vision of tomorrow' for the movement helps to co-opt a regime's main supporters, such as the military and police, to transfer their support from the regime to the nonviolent movement. This has been seen most dramatically in the fall of autocratic rulers at the hands of pro-democratic campaigns in Ukraine (2004), Serbia (2000), Chile (1988) and the Philippines (1986). In each of these cases, military forces refused in a crisis to obey corrupt or criminal rulers, who thereafter had no choice but to surrender power to democratic successors.

Beyond these four examples, a major new study by Freedom House, published in July 2005, found that in 50 of the 67 transitions from authoritarianism to democracy in the past 33 years, nonviolent civic resistance was a 'key factor' — but that, in contrast, when opposition movements used violence, the chances for liberation were greatly reduced. What is more, not only was nonviolent action demonstrated to be an effective means of struggle against oppression, it was also shown that it is far more likely to result in a freer, fairer society. In 20 of the 67 transitions from authoritarian rule covered in the study, violence was used at some point by political oppositions—but in only four of those nations do people have full political rights today. Yet, in 31 of the 47 nations where no opposition violence occurred during the transition, the people now enjoy full political rights [Freedom House 2005].

The logical conclusion to draw from this evidence is that nonviolent action needs to be considered and applied far more frequently and in a broader variety of oppressive situations than it has been. Consequently governments, nongovernmental organizations, and other groups should identify civilian groups that are in authoritarian-ruled countries and that want to fight for political change or reform. If and when these civilian groups ask for help, governments and nongovernmental organizations should provide the skills training and know-how to teach these groups how to engage in nonviolent struggle. The goal of this assistance would be the lifting of oppression or transformation of authoritarian systems, which would deny terrorists the opportunity to exploit the popular antagonism that these systems produce, and therefore reduce their ability to recruit and maintain their legitimacy. In addition, all the forms of assistance that such regimes directly provide to terrorists, such as sanctuary, legitimacy, material support (equipment, finances, weapons), training grounds, and schools, would then be denied to them.

MODEL: A REALISTIC ALTERNATIVE FORM OF STRUGGLE

One useful way to understand why terrorism enlists support is to imagine that there is a market for terror — a supply of terrorists, obviously, but also a demand for their services. The West's military response to terror has the effect of reducing the supply of terrorists by finding and killing or imprisoning them. While that has undeniably deprived terrorist organizations of certain key operatives and complicated their operations, it is not claimed that that has degraded their capacities to the extent that they are no longer regarded as a grave threat. Moreover, military action in multiple countries has fueled worldwide antiwar-based opposition to the effort against terrorism and some have argued that it has backfired by enabling terrorists to portray the effort as part of an alleged 'crusade' to subordinate such societies. Regardless of the merits of these arguments, one thing is clear: the military option attempts to address only the supply side of the market for terror without noticeably lowering the demand.

As stated in the opening paragraph of this chapter, terrorism represents a protagonist position in a political conflict, on behalf of the claim that some form of oppression must be fought. The demand for terror has political roots, and therefore lowering the demand for terror should more logically require a form of political action than military strikes or moral exhortations not to use violence.

Waiting for foreign governments or third parties to remove the grievances or correct the specific injustices that terrorists bemoan presumes that those capable of intervening will understand and agree that this would be effective, have the means and will to intervene when necessary, and that collateral damage will be minimal. But since indigenous energies and strategies have almost always been the predicate for successful resistance to oppression, stealing the thunder of terrorists by invoking an alternative method of resistance does not require waiting for the *deus ex machina* of third party remedies. What is required is that a proffered alternative to violent struggle be persuasively presented and modeled as a pragmatic choice.

The aim of promoting and representing this alternative would not be to convert terrorist leaders who embrace violence for ideological or religious reasons. Instead, it would be to cut off their support by appealing to large segments of various societies' populations that see no other way to be liberated. There is already evidence that many people in these societies are uncomfortable with terrorism and would embrace realistic alternatives if they were presented. News coverage, especially in Iraq, Jordan and Egypt, has been replete with interviews of bystanders to terrorist incidents who are appalled by the devastation to innocents caused by terrorism and who deplore the idea of suicide bombings. Yet some of these same people may still reluctantly support terrorist groups because they feel that in the face of oppression, doing something is better than doing nothing — that violence is the strongest form of resistance.

Reducing market demand for a product or service is typically accomplished when a competing product or service captures more buyers. So nonviolent insurrection must be promoted so as to show its advantages in satisfying the needs of those 'buyers' — that it can succeed in situations where terrorism has so far failed, and can do so at far lower cost to participants and would-be beneficiaries. The general failure of terrorism is an historical fact. Insurrectionary violence has typically led to the worst oppressive governments.

Therefore, the heart of a non-military response to terrorism involves convincing aggrieved people, who may be attracted to terrorist groups, that nonviolent movements can aggressively represent their aspirations and yield results. Groups that are receptive to this logic should be educated and indeed trained in the practical know-how required to organize and apply nonviolent power. As the latter becomes the driving force in a society's fight against oppression, it will begin to reduce the demand for terror, which in turn will deny to ideologically committed terrorists the support that they need from a society, in the form of material resources, sanctuary, new recruits, and legitimacy. As the terrorists lose their putative base, the society will be gaining a far more constructive means of liberation.

DEVELOP A NEW DISCOURSE ABOUT NONVIOLENT POWER

The third component of a non-military response to terrorism must be a large-scale new global educational campaign to universalize a new kind of discourse about how societies struggle and achieve change. This discourse would be culturally-specific and infused with creativity, but the central theme of it would be the same wherever it was used: political violence and terrorism stall or destroy the causes they attempt to advance, and civilian-based, nonviolent struggle is a far more effective alternative.

This new discourse would recognize that the chief weakness of terrorism is the ideas and assumptions that support it. Theatrical rhetoric and spectacular terrorist acts, if not followed by political results, reveal the flaws that will cause terrorism to collapse from its own contradictory arguments: that people's lives can be liberated through death, and that better societies can be built by triggering armed conflict on a national or global scale. In the meantime, a nonviolent response to terrorism can expedite this collapse by targeting terrorism's vulnerabilities. To do this, new arguments should rebut the efficacy of terror and promote nonviolent struggle on every level: religious, psychological, political, cultural, and linguistic.

Religion

Regarding religion, a robust new set of arguments must be developed in conjunction with moderate Muslims and academics to demonstrate that targeting and killing innocent civilians is not consistent with the highest traditions of Islam. The people to make these arguments are those who are respected in the societies in which terrorist rhetoric is most prevalent. There are clear exhortations in all major religions that life is sacred, and this heavily challenges the use of terror.

Simultaneously, arguments also need to be made for why nonviolent action is an appropriate response to oppression that is within the scope of Islam. As Professor Stephen Zunes writes:

> One of the great strengths in Islamic cultures that makes unarmed insurrections possible is the belief in a social contract between a ruler and subject. This was stated explicitly by the Prophet Muhammad's successor Abu Bakr al-Siddiq when he said 'Obey me as long as I obey God in my rule. If I disobey him, you will owe me no obedience.' Successive caliphs reiterated the pledge; Imam Ali, for instance, said, 'No obedience is allowed to any creature in his disobedience of the Creator.' Indeed, most Middle Eastern scholars have firmly supported the right of the people to depose an unjust ruler. The decision to refuse one's cooperation is a crucial step in building a nonviolent movement [Zunes 2002].

Psychology

Beyond defining religious reasons for the legitimacy of nonviolent action, the psychological truth must be driven home that extreme violence goes against most human instincts. The language of terrorists employs constant re-justification of the use of violence, because terrorists otherwise encounter reflexive resistance to killing as a routine tactic of struggle.

Another psychological vulnerability of terrorist methods is that their application is predicated on elite-based, non-participatory ideological (if not tactical) decision-making. This reveals terrorism as a tool of those who wish to control the actions of, instead of empower, the people they claim to represent. By joining a terrorist cause, you get to put your life at risk, but you have no say in the ends or means of the movement. You are expected to make enormous sacrifices — indeed the commitment of your entire life — but you do not get to contribute your ideas or perhaps even see the results of your work.

In contrast, nonviolent struggle is participatory, expects contributions from ordinary activists, uses means that are proportionate in scale and quality to the ends, and holds out the prospect of success before the end of the lifetimes of those engaging in the struggle. Indeed, the *gestalt* of a nonviolent struggle mirrors and anticipates that of the outcome which is sought: the reification of the people's own decision-making and empowerment. Terrorists, on the other hand, have nothing to say about how extreme violence helps build the future society that is attractive to most people. How do secret societies, suicide bombings, and targeting civilians help create a society that most people want to live in? They don't.

Politics

One political argument that deserves special emphasis in this new discourse is that by taking up arms against an oppressive power, resisters are confronting their oppressor where he is strongest: his military force. In contrast, nonviolent action creates a genuinely asymmetric conflict, in which the means of struggle are categorically different than those easily available to an authoritarian opponent. In comparison, the world has not entered an era in which non-state violent actors numbering in the thousands can challenge major state actors and defeat them on any battlefield defined by the ability to deliver and apply violent force.

Culture

Specific cases in Muslim and Middle Eastern countries can be cited and publicized to combat the contention that civic resistance does not work or cannot happen in these societies because of special cultural factors. History bears out the opposite[1]:

- In Egypt, from 1919-1922, Egyptians used methods such as demonstrations, strikes, boycotts, and other means of noncooperation to help win their independence from the British.
- In 1929, Abdul Ghaffar Khan founded the *Khudai Khidmatgar* (Servants of God) movement to resist British rule in what is now Pakistan. The *Khudai Khidmatgar* wore uniforms, trained themselves as a nonviolent army, and set up a code of behavior that stressed discipline, community service, and bravery. Anyone who committed an act of violence was immediately removed from the movement. Their methods consisted of creating alternative institutions (mostly schools), organizing work projects, picketing and strikes.
- In 1978-79, a combination of strikes, boycotts, protests, tax refusal and other forms of non-cooperation in Iran withstood enormous repression (it is estimated that as many as 20,000 resisters may have been killed) by the US-backed Shah and his well-trained armed forces. This broad civic resistance paved the way for the flight of the Shah in 1979.

---

[1] These cases draw from: Zunes (2002) and Bennet (1990).

- In December 1981, Druze in the Golan Heights began a nonviolent struggle against forced Israeli citizenship. The Druze used a general strike, demonstrations, and courted arrest by defying certain restrictions. After 15,000 Israeli soldiers imposed a 43-day siege in which homes were destroyed, some resisters were shot, and hundreds were arrested, the Israelis dropped their demand that the Druze accept Israeli citizenship. The Druze were also promised a pardon from military conscription, the right to have economic relations with Syrians, and non-interference with their civil, water, and land rights.
- In March 1985, after protest riots were put down by police, the struggle against Sudanese president Ja'far Numeiri took a nonviolent turn. Doctors, lawyers, teachers, and other professionals leafleted and called for a general strike and civil disobedience campaign. Some sectors of the police and judiciary joined the opposition. Labor leaders joined the strike. By early April, the army took over the government in a bloodless coup, but the nonviolent resisters continued to demonstrate to ensure that the new army-led government would disband the national security forces and arrest the former dictator's supporters. The military acquiesced.
- In 1987-88, the first Palestinian Intifada had major elements of nonviolent action and consisted of demonstrations, strikes, boycotts, refusals to pay fees, and building alternative institutions such as schools. Although not totally nonviolent, the Intifiada impressed many Israelis with the determination of ordinary Palestinians to struggle for their own homeland, pushed the Jordanians to endorse Palestinian self-determination, and indirectly led to Oslo negotiations between the Palestinian Liberation Organization (PLO) and Israel and the United States.
- In February 2005, in response to the suspected Syrian assassination of former Lebanese prime minister Rafik Hariri, Lebanese took to the streets in the so-called Cedar Revolution. After massive demonstrations, 14,000 Syrian troops in Lebanon withdrew and the pro-Syrian Lebanese government was disbanded.

These and other cases (such as the overthrow of the brutal Suharto dictatorship in 1999, and the ongoing nonviolent struggle in Western Sahara) show that nonviolent action can gain traction in these societies, that it can succeed even under situations of harsh repression, and that it is not a culturally-specific phenomenon that somehow cannot occur in Middle Eastern or Muslim countries. These cases need to be re-told and publicized as examples of the militant character and effectiveness of this form of struggle.

Linguistics

Linguistically speaking, part of the effort to re-tell these historical cases and to present nonviolent action as a realistic alternative to terrorism involves creating new terminology that makes the underlying ideas and concepts come alive for people who are otherwise bombarded with the view that violence is the most powerful sanction. Without this new terminology, some will not recognize nonviolent action as a powerful, pragmatic form of political struggle and may confuse it with pacifism or religious or moral forms of nonviolence (which can also be powerful and political, but are not the same as nonviolent action). As Zunes writes about nonviolent resistance movements in the Muslim world:

The term 'nonviolent action' is not highly regarded among those in unarmed Islamic resistance movements, in part because its Arabic translation of the term connotes passivity. Yet while the term understandably may not have widespread acceptance, and while few may explicitly refer to these movements as largely nonviolent campaigns, in practice many such actions fall under the rubric of nonviolent action [Zunes 2002].

A similar example is given by American theologian Walter Wink, who interviewed participants in the anti-apartheid movement in South Africa. Wink writes: 'What we found most surprising is that a great many of the people simply do not know how to name their actual experiences with nonviolence.' When asked about using nonviolent action as a form of resistance to apartheid, he was told 'We tried that for fifty years and it didn't work.... violence is the only way left.' Yet, when Wink asked the South Africans what resistance methods had been most effective in the previous two years,

> They produced a remarkably long list of nonviolent actions: labor strikes, slow-downs, sit-downs, stoppages, and stay-aways; bus boycotts, consumer boycotts, and school boycotts; funeral demonstrations; noncooperation with government appointed functionaries; non-payment of rent; violation of government bans on peaceful meetings; defiance of segregation orders on beaches and restaurants, theaters, and hotels; and the shunning of black police and soldiers. This amounts to what is probably the largest grassroots eruption of diverse nonviolent [methods]... in a single struggle in human history! Yet these students, and many others we interviewed, both black and white, failed to identify these tactics as nonviolent and even bridled at the word [Cited in Schock 2005, 11].

Examples such as these show that the terminology to describe accurately pragmatic nonviolent struggle does not yet exist in some societies. Any new discourse to advance nonviolent struggle must take this into account and find or create effective new terms to frame what nonviolent action is.

What all of these religious, psychological, political, cultural, and linguistic arguments show is the need for a new discourse to rebut the spurious claim of terrorism's effectiveness and to introduce and dramatize the historical reality that civilian-based nonviolent conflict is a powerful and realistic alternative. This discourse would have great appeal if it could help articulate not just what people are willing to abjure (terrorism), but also what they believe will work better (nonviolent 'people power'). We can see evidence of groups that could be receptive to this discourse in the recent opposition party boycott of elections in Egypt, in the fledgling movements for rights and justice in Tunisia and other North African countries, and in the still-resilient student and labor-driven opposition in Iran. All those presently active in civic resistance in Muslim countries are already far more numerous than terrorists. What they need is a new public recognition of their bravery, an informed appreciation of the results that their methods have had earlier in history, and, to support all this, a new public discourse about 'people power' that reflects its actual dynamics.

IMPLEMENTATION

The initiatives proposed in this chapter would have greatest impact if adopted or represented in the work of local, regional, national, and international groups. This would include both governments and nongovernmental organizations, pursuing a comprehensive strategy to support — but not interfere with — civilian-based movements in parts of the world where terrorism thrives or is threatening, by:

1. Underwriting independent efforts to furnish tools, equipment and training in strategic nonviolent action to civic groups resisting oppression;
2. Defending the rights of nonviolent resisters;
3. Promoting accurate media coverage of nonviolent struggles; and
4. Promoting the new underlying discourse through educational and public-informational programs

1. Underwriting Independent Efforts to Furnish Tools, Equipment and Training in Strategic Nonviolent Action

There are two elements that groups need to wage nonviolent struggle successfully. The first is generic knowledge of how nonviolent struggle works, and the second is specific knowledge of a situation that is used to identify and map the opportunities and constraints facing nonviolent resistance in particular conflicts and circumstances.

The international community can do a great deal to help transfer generic knowledge to oppressed people about how nonviolent struggle works — through identifying reformers or change agents within a society and providing them with translated materials (books, videos and other learning tools) about the dynamics of nonviolent action, how it can be strategically planned, and how it has been used around the world. The goal of this assistance would be to support the development of a self-reliant nonviolent struggle capacity in these societies. How the recipients of this assistance choose to apply their new knowledge in their own contexts would be entirely up to them. No-one will know the situation on the ground in these countries better than the people living there. International groups should not and do not need to involve themselves in trying to tell these movements what to do.

We can see an example of the value of such assistance in the case of Serbia. Through the 1990s the United States tried to rely mainly on diplomacy with Slobodan Milosevic to end his aggression in the Balkans, but it declined to provide much support to his democratic opponents inside Serbia when they were using nonviolent action to oppose him. When Milosevic began ethnic cleansing in Kosovo, NATO bombed Serbia until he stopped, but he remained in power. Finally, in 1999, US and European institutions gave modest but well-targeted support to nonviolent pro-democracy groups in Serbia, which brought Milosevic down in a year. The leader of one group famously remarked in 2001 that if Serbs had known in the mid-1990s how, for example, Chileans had forced out Pinochet, there never would have been ethnic cleansing in Kosovo, because Milosevic would have been removed before he started that genocide.

The lesson of this example is that, when properly directed, foreign assistance focused on transferring knowledge and skills in civic resistance can help to accelerate a burgeoning nonviolent movement — the goals, terms and modalities of which will still be developed by indigenous groups. This is not to say, however, that foreign support was the decisive factor in the Serbian or other cases. These broad-scale movements cannot be spawned or orchestrated by international actors, nor can such assistance ever be a substitute for the development of a genuine mass movement which only native political activists will know how to galvanize. It is therefore the role of international groups and institutions to try to assist, not control or create, indigenous movements whose message, strategy, and organization must be self-originated to resonate and unite people who are facing oppression.

2. Defending the Rights of Nonviolent Resistance Groups

The right to undertake the specific action that takes the form of nonviolent resistance is enshrined in the Universal Declaration of Human Rights in a number of articles, but it is particularly clear in Article 19[2] (freedom of expression) and Part 1 of Article 20[3] (freedom of assembly). By clearly endorsing the people's right to resist nonviolently if their rights are being trampled, and then taking efforts vigorously to promote and protect this right, members of the international community can go a long way towards 'incentivizing' this form of resistance against oppression.

Furthermore, if the underlying right to rise up nonviolently is already implied by the Universal Declaration of Human Rights, more explicit international norms defending this right should be developed. For example, when a government is oppressing its citizens, and these citizens begin to organize and act nonviolently to protect their rights, an international norm could be framed and invoked whereby it would be considered legitimate for certain kinds of assistance to be given to the civilians taking this action. This promulgation of new norms could strengthen the rationale for assistance.

3. Promoting Accurate Media Coverage of Nonviolent Struggles

Media coverage can be crucial in alerting people to the power of nonviolent struggle in overcoming oppression. Yet, much of the media's current reporting and analysis tends, subtly or obviously, to reinforce unintentionally the belief that extreme violence is a logical default response to oppression, while also propagating misconceptions about nonviolent action. This happens for several reasons.

First, many journalists have no real understanding of the political dynamics in a nonviolent conflict in which civilians are engaged. That is usually true because foreign correspondents pay attention to leaders and diplomats and unthinkingly assume that they have

---

[2] *Article 19*: Everyone has the right to freedom of opinion and expression; this right includes freedom to hold opinions without interference and to seek, receive and impart information and ideas through any media and regardless of frontiers.

[3] *Article 20*: (1) Everyone has the right to freedom of peaceful assembly and association.

decisive influence over events, rather than paying attention to less visible civic action that often ends up driving those events.

Second, because many journalists lack understanding of the sources of nonviolent power, most news stories reinforce the belief that violence is the most propulsive, certainly the most concussive, methodology for challenging oppression. This, of course, is the same justification that is constantly expressed in terrorist rhetoric. (Even the most admired news reporters rarely question the assumptions behind that rhetoric.) While we have already explained why history contradicts this claim, and noted that violence, and especially terrorism, have a relatively poor record in ending oppression, it is important to realize that the arguments that continue to form the conventional wisdom in most analysis and reporting have serious consequences in terms of the messages they convey to people about what is possible in the world of political power. Certain beliefs may be invalid but they can still impel people to make disastrous choices or preclude other people from making productive choices. It is difficult to create a new discourse while the mass media continues to peddle the old discourse.

Finally, when media coverage does appear about nonviolent action, it often attributes its success to factors that are not the most pivotal in these struggles. For example, media coverage of the 'color revolutions' emphasized foreign support for resistance groups, which had nevertheless rallied most of their own support and money on the basis of their own political propositions and strategies. Earlier media coverage of the people power revolution in the Philippines and the rise of Soldarity in Poland tended to emphasize the charisma of their movements' leaders rather than the intelligence of their strategies, the content of what they said, or the concrete action taken by tens of thousands of their supporters, which divided the loyalties of defenders of the regimes they were challenging.

There are numerous other factors that are also cited erroneously in the media to explain the success of nonviolent movements. Among these is the belief that the regime being fought with nonviolent action was 'soft' and that such strategies would never work against a 'hard' regime (which overlook stories about the brutality of Milosevic in Serbia, Videla in Argentina, Pinochet in Chile, or even the British in India). Another misconception is seen by the way some stories emphasize the supposed enlightened action of a few elites who, at the critical moment, supposedly chose to grant concessions to a nonviolent movement (ignoring, of course, how those decisions may have actually been constrained, or forced, by the power of the nonviolent movement). Other popular misconceptions are the belief that this form of resistance can only work in countries that have reached a certain level of economic development or that nonviolent strategies can only be adopted by certain cultures, or by people with a certain educational level. Again all of these supposed factors or explanations that members of the media cite as pivotal serve to de-emphasize the power of what ordinary people can do when they are organized, united, and have a strategic plan. While it is beyond the scope of this chapter to rebut each of these misconceptions in detail, more work needs to be done to publicize and teach the real operation of nonviolent movements to members of the media.[4]

Nongovernmental organizations can play a crucial role in doing this. First, they can, through their own reporting, accurately depict and analyze nonviolent struggles in their own media sources (such as newsletters, websites, articles monographs, reports, books and other literature). Second, they can make efforts to explain to members of the media how nonviolent

---

[4] Two excellent sources that address popular misconceptions are Schock (2003) and Schock (2005).

action works, what its record is, and how to identify signs that it is occurring in countries around the world right now. Coordinated attempts to do this could create a significant impact, because disproving the efficacy of terrorism and highlighting the impact of nonviolent struggle must be driven home to everyone who is otherwise in a position to be attracted by the false claims of those who push extreme violence.

4. Promoting the New Underlying Discourse through Educational and Public-Informational Programs

A greater effort needs to be undertaken to promote this discourse in schools and other public-informational programs. New curricula need to be created for primary, secondary, college, and university education that question the historical assumption that violence is the most powerful sanction and that explore other, more powerful, forms of force that people can bring to bear in political conflicts.

Specifically, historical examples of nonviolent movements should be taught and analyzed in history classes, with particular emphasis on understanding the strategies that such movements have employed. The results of historical violence and terrorism should also be compared to those of nonviolent movements in history. Humanities classes should emphasize works that show forms of power other than violence. Current events should be discussed that illustrate the widespread use of nonviolent methods in countries around the world. These and other ideas need to be developed and incorporated into classroom and informal learning settings at all levels for all ages.

CONCLUSION

As arguments supporting the supposed supremacy of violence saturate many oppressed societies, it is clear that a new and coherent counter-voice needs to emerge. This voice needs to challenge terrorism and address its political roots. History makes clear that nonviolent action has long been a more effective strategy for dissolving oppression. What remains is teaching the world that this is true.

As nonviolent struggle is promoted and modeled more conspicuously, authoritarian regimes that support terrorists can be transformed; the social, economic, and political conditions that terrorists exploit can be alleviated; and the perceived necessity of terrorism as a strategy for liberation will recede. As civilian-based forces begin to come to the fore and produce decisive change, the appeal of and demand for terrorist-driven resistance will subside.

Violence is no longer the ultimate sanction available to oppressed people. John F. Kennedy said: 'The wave of the future is not the conquest of the world by a single dogmatic creed but the liberation of the diverse energies of free nations and free men.' The new work of nonviolent civic power can represent the arrival of that future.

ACKNOWLEDGEMENTS

Hardy Merriman is a former Director of Programs and Research at the International Center on Nonviolent Conflict (ICNC) in Washington, DC. He contributed to *Waging Nonviolent Conflict: 20th Century Practice and 21st Century Potential* (Extending Horizons Books, 2005) by Dr. Gene Sharp and previously worked at the Albert Einstein Institution in Boston, Massachusetts.

Jack DuVall is the co-author of *A Force More Powerful: A Century of Nonviolent Conflict* (Palgrave, 2001), was executive producer of the documentary film series of the same name, and is now president of the International Center on Nonviolent Conflict. Since 1980, he has been a political speechwriter in national campaigns, vice president of a public television station, and frequent speaker and writer.

REFERENCES

Bennet, B. (1990). 'Arab-Muslim Cases of Nonviolent Struggle.' in R.E. Crow, P. Grant, and S.E. Ibrahim (Eds.), *Arab Nonviolent Political Struggle in the Middle East* (pp. 41-57). Boulder, CO: Lynne Rienner Publishers, Inc.

Freedom House. (2005). *How Freedom Is Won: From Civic Resistance to Durable Democracy.* Washington, DC: Freedom House. Online access at: http://www.freedomhouse.org/ uploads/special_report/29.pdf

Schock, K. (2003). 'Nonviolent Action and Its Misconceptions: Insights for Social Scientists.' *PS: Political Science and Politics*, 36(4), 705-712.

Schock, K. (2005). *Unarmed Insurrections: People Power Movements in Nondemocracies.* Minneapolis: University of Minnesota Press.

Zunes, S. (2002). 'Nonviolent Resistance in the Islamic World.' *Nonviolent Action*, (January-February).

In: Nonviolence: An Alternative for Defeating...
Editors: S. Ram and R. Summy, pp. 235-256

ISBN: 978-1-60021-812-5
© 2008 Nova Science Publishers, Inc.

Chapter 14

TERRORISM: VIOLENT AND NONVIOLENT RESPONSES

Kevin P. Clements

ABSTRACT

This chapter argues that terrorist tactics and strategy challenge all 'legitimate' politics and that those who utilize or are toying with the use of such tactics need to be dissuaded in the most energetic and imaginative ways possible. In terms of behavioral modification, however, it is argued that most of the existing coercive or violent tactics for dealing with this problem are having exactly the opposite effect. Far from de-legitimating terror the violent responses to terrorism are generating more 'blowback' than positive results, and are unintentionally legitimating the use of violence as an acceptable tool of politics. The messages being sent to terrorist organizations are that might equals right; the militarily powerful set political agendas, and more worryingly is the fact that democratic politics are set aside in the face of 'exceptional emergencies.' Since the US has now decided that the 'exceptional emergency' of terrorist threats is going to last decades, this is a very deliberate challenge to those seeking more collaborative problem-solving orientations to the issues generating terrorist tactics. Unless the course of the war on terror is changed, there will be pathological consequences for years to come.

In this chapter I argue for a general de-legitimation of all violence — except in self-defense — and for effective controls on state power (especially executive power). I want to argue that war and violence have no place in contemporary geo-politics and that no state has the right to pursue a war of choice. Only when courageous political leaders start de-legitimating the use of all violence, pursue non-offensive defense policies and only use the military in self-defense will the right signals be sent to terrorist organizations. Only then will citizens be empowered to constrain the use of violence and marginalize those who choose violent political means over more nonviolent political methods.

The anxiety I am referring to is now being echoed by many military leaders as well. Colin Powell, for example, in mid September 2006 announced that 'The world is beginning to doubt the moral basis of our war against terrorism' [2006, 6].

INTRODUCTION

The argument throughout this chapter focuses on the need to rethink current responses to terror and terrorism. We need to be much more imaginative, creative and nonviolent in our approach and only when these tactics have been exhausted and only when we see real threats emerging that cannot be contained by nonviolent means is it permissable to use force. Of course many would say that this is the situation we are currently facing. I would like to argue otherwise. If we do not think of viable alternatives, then we are in for a very bleak future, indeed. From the point of view of constitutional democracy, for example, far from advancing the cause of pluralist democratic politics, the Global War on Terror is generating worrying undemocratic dynamics as advanced Western democracies cede inordinate powers to the executive at the expense of national parliaments, and as these executives in turn challenge the independence of the judiciary and the independence of the rule of law by attacking fundamental constitutional principles.

By declaring a 'Long War' against extremists, the message being sent is that terrorism is not fundamentallty a criminal and political problem but a military one. The military response to terrorism justifies the terrorist commitment to violence. Each over-reaction to a terrorist threat and incident generates more disenchanted youth willing to utilize such tactics. The fact is that terrorism is an extremely blunt instrument for achieving political objectives, and current counter-terrorism tactics are an equally blunt and ineffective instrument, both militarily and politically. It is time to rethink. Top down state-sponsored terrorism or terror tactics cannot be justified pragmatically any more than bottom up terrorism. Moreover, there is no ethical justification for either the 'top down' or 'bottom up' variant.

There are, therefore, four different kinds of challenges facing analysts of terrorist behavior. The first is to understand what drives particular states, individuals, groups and social movements to contemplate using terrorist tactics? The second is to discern what messages are being communicated and what objectives are being sought through such activity? The third is to work out what sort of policies and processes might prevent terrorist action from taking place in order to protect innocent lives? The fourth is an assessment of just how important the terrorist threat is nationally, regionally and globally.

THE REAL THREAT TO LIBERAL DEMOCRACY

It is somewhat ironic that it took a terrorist attack in New York and Washington to highlight the challenges of terrorism. Scores of other countries had been dealing with terrorist actions for many years prior to 9/11. Because of the hegemonic position of the US and its continued control of the media, the terrorist threat has progressed close to the top of most western and non-western defense and security concerns. I would like to argue, however, that even though such threats are challenging to all political systems, terrorism has assumed a political significance far out of proportion to its actual incidence or capacity to generate lethal political consequences.

This is not to diminish the real threat that terror and terror tactics pose to all political authority but to argue that its existence has been used by a variety of political leaders (and by groups who lack other means to gain recognition of their concerns) to generate fear, paralysis and docility in citizens. Certainly, it has been used to justify a very deliberate arrogation of power by political leaders as they initiate far reaching anti-terrorist legislation, challenge taken-for-granted constitutional rights and civil liberties, undermine global commitments against torture, and now declare a 'long' and never ending global war against terror. Philip S Golub in an excellent article states that

> The will to power was there before the events of 11 September 2001... [but] after the attacks the president was transfigured into an American Caesar; dissent was silenced by fear and the mobilisation of nationalist sentiment....[T]he usual domestic constraints in a democratic society on the arbitrary use of coercive state power were lifted. ...[as was] apparent in the torture memos drafted in 2002 by Alberto Gonzales...which affirmed the constitutional power of the president to use whatever means necessary in wartime, including acts overriding international law, in the accomplishment of his mission as commander-in-chief [2006, 5].

'On this reasoning,' wrote the jurist David Cole, 'the president would be entitled by the constitution to resort to genocide if he wished. This process negates the founding principles of classic liberalism: the diffusion of power and the establishment of constitutional safeguards protecting the individual from arbitrary coercive action by the state' [2006, 6].

The current President of the United States, George W Bush, continues to try and win electoral advantage by playing the security card. He does it by reminding American citizens of their vulnerability, reactivating grief for their 2001 loss and stimulating high levels of anxiety about a generalized menace from 'extremists.' While it is entirely appropriate to mourn innocent loss of life, there is something quite cynical about the rhetoric that dominated the media just six weeks before the November 2006 Congressional elections. Proclaimed the President:

> We face an enemy determined to bring death and suffering into our homes. America did not ask for this war, and every American wishes it were over. So do I. But the war is not over, and it will not be over until either we or the extremists emerge victorious. If we do not defeat these enemies now, we will leave our children to face a Middle East overrun by terrorist states and radical dictators armed with nuclear weapons. We are in a war that will set the course for this new century and determine the destiny of millions across the world. This struggle has been called a clash of civilisations. In truth, it is a struggle for civilisation. We are fighting to maintain the way of life enjoyed by free nations. And we are fighting for the possibility that good and decent people across the Middle East can raise up societies based on freedom, and tolerance, and personal dignity [Cited in AP Reuters 2006].

A detailed analysis of this text raises all sorts of important political questions. What is the Global War on Terror (GWOT)? Who declared it on whom? What are its parameters? How is it being waged and by whom? Who are the 'extremists' and 'radical dictators' referred to in the text and and whose civilization is being advanced by a global war on terror? How are the concepts of tolerance, pluralism, dignity and freedom challenged by such statements? What is it doing to the very concept of liberal democracy? The recent conflict within the Republican Party over the legitimacy of coercive interrogation or torture is the latest indication of the ways in which discussions of 'terror' and 'terrorism' have managed to subvert some precious human rights principles.

DEFINING TERROR(ISM)

There are high levels of subjectivity in the definition of who is an extremist and who is a terrorist — just as there is a high degree of uncertainty about what are terrorist acts. Many of the attempts at definition have been made in the context of groups which specific governments consider politically threatening rather than in terms of clearly defined or specific terrorist acts. Thus the United Nations has been unable to develop a satisfactory definition of terrorism, even though it has been trying to do so for the last seven years.

The Oxford English dictionary defines a terrorist as

Anyone who attempts to further his views by a system of coercive intimidation [as] a member of a clandestine or expatriate organisation aiming to coerce an established government by acts of violence against it or its subjects.

The FBI regards terrorism as

The unlawful use of force or violence against persons or property to intimidate or coerce a government, the civilian population, or any segment thereof, in furtherance of political or social objectives [See Barnaby 2002, 13].

Paul Wilkinson in his 1986 book on the subject says, 'What distinguishes terrorism from other forms of violence is the deliberate and systematic use of coercive intimidation' [Cited in Barnaby [2002, 15].

The British Government in its attempt to define terrorism officially in the British Terrorism Act 2000 saw terrorism as

The use or threat of action where the use or threat is designed to influence the government or to intimidate the public or a section of the public, and the use or threat is made for the purpose of advancing a political, religious or ideological cause. Action falls within the Act if it involves serious violence against a person, involves serious damage to property, endangers a person's life other than that of the person committing the action, creates a serious risk to the health or safety of the public or a section of the public, or is designed seriously to interfere with or seriously to disrupt an electronic system [2000, 25].

Rich Rubenstein defines terrorism as follows:

Terrorism is violence by small groups claiming to represent massive constituencies and seeking by 'heroic' provocative attacks to awaken the masses, redeem their honour, and generate an enemy over reaction that will intensify and expand the struggle [2001].

As Ambassador Philip C Wilcox put it:

This problem of a definition masks a deeper problem of the need to resolve the grave conflicts that give rise to terrorism. We need an international consensus on definition in order to isolate and eliminate all sympathy and support for terrorism but we can't reach this definition unless we work harder to deal with the underlying conflicts. Let's face reality. So as long as there are weak, oppressed and aggrieved people and groups who can find no redress, there will be terrorism, and what for one man is a terrorist, will continue to be another's freedom fighter. Of course, there will always be terrorists whose causes have no merit and who must be defeated. I do not recommend, however, that we give up trying to win a consensus that terrorism is an unacceptable political weapon under any circumstances. In the search for a more peaceful, humane and civilized world, we need to keep trying to absolutely delegitimize terrorism in favor of more civilized forms of political action [2002].

Irrespective of what definition of terrorism is employed, it is clear that terrorist threats and acts do have a capacity to induce fear within communities and states. It is important, however, for analysts and scholars to focus calm attention on issues of their probability and lethality if we are to develop a realistic assessment of the dangers posed by terrorist activity. It is also important that we do not just accept western definitions of terror. Individuals in a variety of non-western states have quite different concepts of terror.

There is, for example, the daily existential terror faced by those without food, shelter, or basic security. Then there are the unpredictable cries of anguish generated by those who feel powerless and marginalized because of the particular kind of political regime they are living under. Such people are likely to utilize violent tactics against more powerful entities in order to create some space for the expression of their own grievances and to probe for vulnerabilities. This gives rise to asymmetric warfare. Then there is the terrorism of those resisting what they consider the illegal occupations of their homelands. All of these are examples of bottom up terror. As well, there is pathological criminal terror inflicted simply to gratify the sadistic or psychopathic inclinations of severely disturbed individuals, although this explains very little modern political terrorist activity which is normally performed by rational political actors.

Finally, there is the terror inflicted by State systems on their own citizens or the citizens of other countries. When citizens fear arbitrary arrest, torture, imprisonment and death they are experiencing top down terror. Powerful military machines generate terror when they inflict suffering on innocent civilians in pursuit of military objectives. The possession of nuclear weapons or other weapons of mass destruction have their own distinctive capacities to generate terror. Think of all the global anxieties about nuclear warfare during the Cold War? Each one of these conceptions of terror generates its own distinctive politics as individuals seek to avoid and/or challenge what they perceive to be the sources of their own terror.

BACKGROUND OF TERRORISM AND COPING IN THE MODERN ERA

The use of terror to achieve different objectives dates back to antiquity. Between 66 and 73 AD, for example, Jewish zealots used terrorist violence to fight the Romans in occupied Judea. They assassinated individuals, poisoned wells and food stores and sabotaged Jerusalem's water supply [Barnaby 2002, 12]. Between 1090 and 1272 AD a Muslim Shi'a group called the Assassins attacked Christian crusaders throughout the Middle East [Barnaby 2002, 12].

The words terror and terrorism assumed popular currency during the French Revolution. In this context terrorism referred to state-sponsored top down efforts to rule and govern through terror. It is important to remember this original understanding of terrorism —

because, states can and do terrorize their own citizens and those of other nations when it suits them. If, as many argue, terrorism is the deliberate targeting of civilian populations for political or ideological purposes, then it is clear that states are just as likely to engage in terrorist acts as non-state actors.

The problem is that individuals and political movements who believe they cannot realize their political objectives through nonviolent political means will always have violence as an option. The challenge facing the world community, national governments and civil society organizations interested in nonviolent problem solving, therefore, is how to:

1. discourage states from using their military for anything other than defensive purposes under the rule of the United Nations,
2. set limits on the kinds of weapons and on the defense expenditures necessary for protecting state systems and their citizens,
3. defend the principles of international humanitarian law and not resort to the tactics of those who have no respect for such principles,
4. ensure that disaffected groups do not embrace terrorism for political or any other purpose,
5. deny them the means for pursuing such action,
6. stimulate collaborative nonviolent activities that boost civil society resilience and negate the impact of terrorist initiative,
7. create national, regional and global institutions that are responsive to expressions of grievance and capable of addressing them, and
8. establish effective international mechanisms that will ensure the arrest, trial and imprisonment of perpetrators of terrorist acts according to acceptable international legal principles.

Very few of these objectives have anything to do with an open ended, never ending 'war on terror.' As argued above, using military language in response to terrorist threats has the unintended consequence of generating over reactions that justify and expand terrorist struggle. While we have to take terrorist threats seriously, it is important to do so in ways proportionate to the problem; that are effective in methodology and implementation and most likely to reincorporate those who have chosen to pursue violent options against legitimate political frameworks. There is a lot of growing evidence which suggests that the language currently used in the war on terror generates communications that encourage terrorism. The rhetoric of 'the war on terror' generates contradictory sets of messages. Using military language in response to terrorism, for example, disempowers crucial civil society actors from assuming responsibility for de-legitimating terror and terrorist tactics. Indeed, militarized language and military responses to terrorism tend to perpetuate militarized and violent resistance with higher levels of violence and terror.

The 'war on terror' — despite being oxymoronic because you cannot fight an abstract noun — rests on a Manichaean division of the world into good and evil, civilized and barbarian, Muslim and non-Muslim, terrorist and counter-terrorist. It has also resulted in an extreme dehumanisation of the 'other' on both sides. This creates a very adverse climate for rational discussion about needs, interests, positions and grievances. It also means that critical statements on either side are filtered into an echo chamber that makes calm reflection difficult, if not impossible.

In an analysis of editorial cartoons following September 11th 2001, for example, communication specialists discovered that al-Qa'ida, Osama Bin Laden and Muslims generally, were dehumanized and demonized. They were depicted variously as 'animals, aggressors, abstractions, barbarians, enemies of God, faceless, desecrators of women and children, or as criminals and death' [Hart and Hassencahl 2002, 146-47]. This divisive discourse creates the divisions that need to be bridged if collaborative problem solving is to occur. It certainly makes it difficult for civil society organizations and political leaders to highlight connections rather than divisions, bridges rather than fault lines, and inclusive rather than exclusive concepts of both national and global community. It also creates a very real division between idealists interested in collaborative nonviolent problem solving and realists interested in coercive power politics.

COMMON MISCONCEPTIONS ABOUT TERRORISM

It is becoming increasingly clear that many of the statements about and explanations for terrorism are quite wrong. Terrorism, for example, is often described in globalist terms. The proponents of this view argue that there are terrorist networks based in one country or region plotting violence against others across national borders. While there are some that are engaged in transnational plotting, this is far from the norm.

The reality is that Islamic fundamentalism has not created a monolithic terrorist threat against the US or any other Western country. Each terrorist movement has to be contextualized and understood in its own terms. Most are motivated by essentially nationalist goals to compel removal of foreign troops or foreign influence or to change particular regimes. Some have more diffuse aims such as changing values or cultural priorities. In Asia, for instance, there is little evidence of centralized co-ordination of Jamaah Islamaya in South East Asia with Hamas, Hezbollah, or al-Qa'ida. In Pakistan, groups such as Lashkar-e-Toiba, Harku-ull-Ansar, and Jaish-e-Mohammed may have links to al-Qa'ida but the foci of their political and military interests also seem to be more national and regional than global. There may be some general links, some common training programs and a disposition to engage in copy cat activity, but this is very different from a tightly knit integrated terror network. It is very important, therefore, that each threat or actual incidence of terrorist activity be contextualized and understood on its own terms if it is to be understood and dealt with effectively.

Far from being a global phenomenon terrorism is in fact largely national in origin with national targets. Global transnational terrorism is the exception rather than the rule. Monty Marshall and Ted Gurr make an interesting distinction between national and international terrorism [2005, 25]. National terrorism is where a single country provides the actors, the target and the location. International is where persons from more than one country are involved in the event and the targets are normally outside of the country. In an analysis of all terrorist events for ten years from 1991 to 2001 they discovered that 91% of all terrorist incidents were national in origin and target and accounted for 94% of the 32,264 fatalities

This trend seems to continue. While individual terrorists may have had some contact with groups based in other countries, they tend to be nationals of the country that they wish to attack; their targets tend to be national in origin, and the locations are also national.

International terrorism, defined in terms of a well integrated global network and straddling a variety of national borders, does not seem to be the primary source of political fatality. Nevertheless, theorists and policy makers talk primarily in terms of international terrorism or the global reach of international terrorists.

The reasons for this are obvious. Post 9/11, the United States persuaded its allies and the United Nations of the importance of condemning terrorism in all its forms. Each ally or friend of the United States was expected to join 'Operation Enduring Freedom' and the never ending war on terror. Later they were asked to join the 'Coalition of the Willing' in Iraq and to sign and ratify all twelve UN Anti-Terrorism conventions and the different Security Council resolutions on terrorism. This was all aimed at developing a united response in meeting the terrorist threat globally and regionally. The US and its allies managed to do this without any 'reflective' analysis of terrorist behavior or threat or any universally agreed definition of terrorism.

In fact there was no particular need to define terrorism in detail; 9/11 was all the justification needed for changing the world according to the United States. It was enough simply to cite terrorism as the major threat facing the world and therefore the overwhelming justification for a massive increase in global intelligence and military expenditure.

World military expenditure in 2004, for example, was $1.4 trillion. This was the sixth year in a row that it had increased in size. The US defense budget in 2005 was $415 billion. This figure excluded the Iraq supplementals expected to top $90 billion in 2006. The 14% increase to 2006 US defence budget was $49 billion which is over half of what the entire world spent on Overseas Development Assistance which in 2005 was just $79 billion.

The US defense budget is larger than the combined total of the next nine biggest defense spenders. The US is responsible for 47% of the world's military spending. It is in its interests, therefore, to assert the unpredictability of global terrorism as a major justification for such massive defense expenditure. Terrorists have, to a large extent, replaced the Soviet Union as the major justification for Western military expenditure.

The sad fact, however, is that the numbers of people killed in terrorist incidents — while tragic— do not begin to compare to those killed in other kinds of political violence. Adding the numbers of people killed in terrorist incidents since 2001 to the 32,264 killed between 1991 and 2001 brings the total to approximately 38,800 in the 15 years to the present. This number can be compared with the 27,000 plus who have lost their lives in Afghanistan since Operation Enduring Freedom began; or the 100,000 plus who have lost their lives in Iraq since the occupation[1]; the 200,000 who lost their lives in the Sierra Leone conflict; the hundreds of thousands already killed or at risk of death in Dafur in the Sudan; or the 3.8 million persons who have lost their lives either directly or indirectly as a result of the conflict in the Eastern Congo since 1985. These figures indicate very clearly that most political death occurs in internal armed conflict between military forces and rebel movements; they do not occur in terrorist activity. To mobilize the whole world in a war on terror utilizing worst case scenarios and conflating these with other anxieties about nuclear proliferation, and nuclear terrorism is generating a political pathology far out of proportion to the real risk of violent death.

---

[1] Other analysts cite even higher casualty figures. According to the John Hopkins Bloomberg School of Public Health, for example, 655,000 Iraqi civilians have lost their lives since the occupation. This figure does not include the military deaths — for the US almost 3,000 deaths [*Guardian Weekly* 2006, 15].

To put those killed in terrorist incidents in perspective, for instance, it is important to provide some comparative statistics. Those killed by gun violence in the United States every year far exceeds those killed in terrorist activity over a fifteen year period. As J. Zulaika and W.A. Douglass point out,

> *The Journal of the American Medical Association* in its June 1995 issue stated that firearms kill 40,000 and harm another 240,000 each year in the United States; the direct and indirect costs surpass 14 billion annually. ...yet this is not really viewed as abnormal or to pose a threat to national security or provoke any major debate [1996, 188].

ENGENDERING PATHOLOGIES OF FEAR AND POWER

One has to wonder, therefore, whether the resources dedicated to combating terrorism since 2001 are justifiable in terms of all those who have lost their lives in other political conflicts (or in normal criminal violence) in the late 20th century and into the 21st.

It is clear that terror and terrorism in the 21st century have demonstrated a capacity to engender fear. This fear in turn generates its own responses including very specific political distortions and pathologies. There is growing evidence, for example, that terrorism and terrorist threats are being cynically manipulated by political leaders in a number of countries for a wide variety of political and military purposes, many of which are far from positive and some of which are making the risk of a terrorist attack more, rather than less, likely. In the United Kingdom and Australia, for example, new draconian anti-terrorist legislation challenges taken-for-granted freedoms and rights, creating a climate of fear and generating a deep division between Muslim and non-Muslim communities (as epitomized by the Cronulla race riots in Sydney, Australia and by all the current debates initiated by Prime Minister Howard about Australians accepting 'Australian values' and condemning terrorism in all its forms).

The carefully manipulated fear of terrorism in the West is by and large dealing with symptoms rather than causes. It is rare for any political discussion of terrorism to address its statistical probability or lethality. This alone makes it all the more important to understand the underlying dynamics of terrorism so that it can be dealt with effectively and nonviolently.

ANALYZING THE CORRELATES OF TERRORISM

The United States Department of State and the National Security Agency commissioned a special investigative team (*The US Political Instability Task Force*, 2004) to try and identify the underlying sources of all kinds of national and international terrorism. This task force analyzed a huge number of sophisticated data sets and developed the following correlates of incidents of terrorism and other types of political violence. These correlates while not causes of terrorism were present in all terrorist incidents. The correlates identified were as follows:

- Poverty, underdevelopment and maldistribution of resources
- Weak regimes and poor governance
- Poor regional integration

- Bad neighborhoods.

At a structural level, therefore, these are the issue areas that need to be addressed if we are to deal with some of the underlying conditions conducive to terrorist activity. They do not explain specific terrorist acts but are part of the macro-environment within which terrorist activity takes place.

What is interesting and depressing is that very few of these issue areas are being addressed specifically by countries that are most at risk of terrorist threat. On the contrary many of the resources that could be directed to these problems are being diverted into the war on terror or the wars in Iraq and Afghanistan or into the expansion of national security services all around the world.

Terrorism is being used, increasingly as the primary justification for an expansion of concepts of hard state power. Instead of working to create conditions conducive to human security, the United States and its allies are producing conditions which are generating new kinds of insecurity. At the Millenium Plus Five Summit in New York in September 2006, for example, the United States delegation tabled 750 amendments to the emerging consensus document two weeks before the Summit began, thereby sabotaging global efforts to develop much more holistic analyses and policies which might have brought the security, development and human rights agendas closer together.

The result of this was that the human security aspirations spelled out in Koffi Annan's *In Larger Freedom* of the previous year were not given the political support needed to develop detailed policy prescriptions and action plans for the UN and its members. This is a pity as Koffi Annan's report was aimed at developing conditions that would make terrorism less, rather than more, likely. As he put it,

> In the 21st century, all states and their collective institutions must advance the cause of larger freedom by ensuring freedom from want, freedom from fear and freedom to live in dignity. In an increasingly interconnected world progress in the areas of development, security and human rights must go hand in hand. There will be no development without security and no security without development. And both development and security also depend on respect for human rights and the rule of law [2005, 3]

More recently Robert A Pape, in his book *Dying to Win: The Strategic Logic of Suicide Terrorism* has established some new ways of thinking about suicide terrorism (which he considers the deadliest and most destructive of all terrorist behavior). Pape is careful not to generalize from this type to all other forms of terrorism but since he has done an analysis of all suicide terrorist events since 1980, I want to summarize his arguments in order to see how they complement the recommendations that flow from the conclusions of *The US Political Instability Task Force*.

His analysis is important also to discussions of pro-active nonviolent responses to terrorist threats aimed at moving us beyond punishment, denial or capitulation. While Pape's analysis is made in the context of a new kind of coercive response, he develops an important framework for thinking of a range of nonviolent options as well. I think that these nonviolent options need to be considered and exhausted before the application of more coercive solutions.

Pape identifies three different kinds of terrorism:

1. 'demonstrative terrorism,' which is aimed at generating publicity in order to recruit activists, publicize grievances and win over third parties;
2. 'destructive terrorism' aimed at coercing opponents through threat of injury or death (irrespective of whether or not they win support in the process); and
3. 'suicide terrorism,' which he argues is the most aggressive form. This is aimed at coercing opponents even if it means angering potential supporters [2005, 9-10].

He then explores suicide terror through history and develops what he calls his 'causal logic' of suicide terrorism. This operates at three levels: strategic, social and individual. To some extent it complements *The US Political Instability Task Force* (PITF) report.

At the strategic level, Pape's thesis is that suicide terrorists exert coercive power against democratic states in order to get them to cease occupation of territory which the terrorist groups consider their legitimate homeland. This is an important source of political grievance which plays on the poverty, marginalization, bad governance, lack of regional integration and bad neighborhoods identified in the US PITF report. Thus when seeking solutions to questions of terrorism it is vital that states ask themselves whether or not they are illegally or unjustifiably occupying land which belongs to someone else. If they are, then Pape argues, there is a high probability that violent terrorist action will be considered a legitimate response to illegal occupation.

At the social level, Pape argues that suicide terrorism will only be sustained and legitimated if it receives the popular support of local communities and, at the individual level, is motivated by altruism rather than despair or egotism. (He uses the classical Durkheimian suicide typology arguing that although this might be a slight perversion of what Durkheim understood by altruistic suicide [since it causes the death of others], it can be be justified as altruistic because suicide terrorist groups are communally organized and the terrorists, themselves, claim to be acting on behalf of aggrieved communities.

Pape [2005, 19-23] argues that the major strategic purpose of all the terrorist groups he explores (Hezbollah, al-Qa'ida, The Tamil Tigers [LTTE], Sikhs from Babbar Khalsa International, the PKK Parti Karkaren Kurdistan, and others) is the elimination of foreign occupation. Foreign occupation is defined in terms of control of territory (not military occupation alone) [2005,46]. This means that some suicide terrorist groups are not objecting to direct military occupation (although this is a very potent mobilizing factor) but also to what is considered inordinate political and military influence. In this analysis, for example, the Gulf States of the Arabian peninsula would be considered possible targets because of the presence of foreign bases and or external military and political influence. Similarly, in Pakistan, Pape's arguments suggest that groups engaged in terrorist action there might be motivated more by a perception of inordinate US influence over domestic and foreign policy rather than any particular religious animus, although this might be an accelerant in the equation.

In Australia, groups which might be interested in violent politics are this way inclined largely because of perceived domestic inattention to their grievances and Australian support for US foreign and defense policies in the Middle East and other parts of the world. Very few are adopting violent tactics to advance particular religious causes.

All of the terrorist groups Pape investigates tend to be part of much larger popular political campaigns. Their goals are secular and political rather than religious (although religion in many of the cases is a powerful means of distinguishing the invader from the resister). Thus when seeking to understand terrorist threats, it is vital to understand something of the issues/grievances and mobilizing capacity of the movements that terrorists claim to be acting on behalf of. It is vitally important to know whether or not the 'occupier' is willing to negotiate with terrorists and how flexible they are likely to be. This is important for both the wider political movement and for its terrorist associates. It will also determine whether or not nonviolent tactics and strategies are relevant.

Pape argues that democracies (including the United States) despite their rhetoric of not negotiating with terrorists have made important concessions to suicide terrorists, thereby fuelling further terrorist activity because terrorists have learned that suicide tactics are effective. In fact there has been a long tradition in the West of official rejection of negotiations with terrorists accompanied by back channel discussions — when and as necessary — in response to particular events. Pape and most other observers of terrorist action, however, underline that such tactics are overwhelmingly the tactics of the weak.

Pape's book also explores the community legitimation of martyrdom which is absolutely critical to justifying terrorist tactics and suicide. And it is martyrdom, in turn, which gives a powerful causal logic to extra social and community approval. The central argument that Pape advances is that suicide terrorism (far from being the irrational acts of deluded individuals responding to Islamic fundamentalism) is strategic; it has a plausible and legitimate logic and this needs to be understood if we are to address it at its source. He does this very systematically, by analyzing the movements, the leaders, the ideologies and the individual bombers.

In relation to al-Qa'ida he thinks that the movement has been reified far too much. It has been deliberately misunderstood in order to justify a wide range of political behavior. He wishes to demystify the movement and in doing so he unconsciously confirms the arguments of Marshall and Gurr. He sees al-Qa'ida as 'less a transnational network of like-minded ideologues … than a cross-national military alliance of national liberation movements working together against what they see as a common imperial threat' [2005, 104]. If he is right, it is important to start asking questions about the nature of current imperial threats as well as the assumed threat from al-Qa'ida or any of the other terrorist groups that have emerged in the last twenty years or so.

In his analysis of terrorist movements in areas other than the Middle East, e.g. Sri Lanka which has had more terrorist fatalities from suicide bombing than any other part of the world, or in relation to Sikh terrorism, what becomes clearer and clearer is that it is not religious difference that tips the balance in favor of violent politics but resistance to political occupation. In the Sri Lankan and Sikh cases, the resistance movements flow from perceptions of illegitimate national occupation rather than foreign occupation, but the dynamics remain the same.

If most suicide terrorist behavior can be explained in terms of resisting what is perceived as unacceptable imperial or national occupation, this is an extremely important finding in terms of devising a range of political solutions. It also provides some important openings for those interested in nonviolent options.

The final question that Pape explores has to do with the demographics of terrorist actors (particularly those that choose suicide tactics). He effectively rebuts all the pathological explanations for suicide bombers.

In general, suicide attackers are rarely socially isolated, clinically insane, or economically destitute individuals, but are most often educated, socially integrated, and highly capable people who could be expected to have a good future [2000].

In relation to Hezbollah he notes that neither were they primarily religious fundamentalists. Pape writes that Hezbollah suicide bombers in the period 1982-1986, for instance, were 71% Christian, 21% Communist/Socialist, and only 8% Islamist [204-07]. Most were in their early 20s, and most were male.

Pape did not discover mental illness or personal pathology in any case of suicide terrorism although there were 16 cases of personal trauma (e.g. the loss of a loved one) which certainly fuelled some of the Chechen suicide bombers [209-210]. Overall Pape argues that Arab suicide terrorists are in general better educated than average and are from the working or middle classes. '[T]hey resemble the kind of politically conscious individuals who might join a grassroots movement more than they do wayward adolescents or religious fanatics' [210]. He finishes his analysis with detailed portraits of three different suicide bombers all of whom were well integrated personally, socially and politically and all of whom could have had full and illustrious careers had they chosen a different path.

Because Pape is a security specialist he proposes a largely military strategy for responding to the strategic logic of suicide terrorism and the individuals and groups that fuel it. His conclusions are as follows: Because suicide terrorism (and arguably quite of lot of other terrorism) is essentially a rejection of national or foreign occupation of what is considered 'sacred' homeland, Pape argues that a major part of the solution lies in changing the military and political direction of United States policy, especially in the Middle East. He suggests that the US should identify what 'victory' might look like and what strategy might deliver it. He asserts that the US should define victory as the separate objectives of 'defeating the current pool of terrorists' and 'preventing a new generation from arising' [238-39]. His argument directs attention away from any arguments based on the clash of civilizations or dialogue between religions. On the contrary he argues that '...the taproot is American military policy' [240].

This is somewhat at variance with the basic military strategy against terrorism which is containment, search and arrest and/or destruction of terrorists or potential terrorists. This is now accompanied in the US, UK and Australia, by what is described as a 'Battle of the Minds' which are political efforts to engage 'moderates' while isolating and separating them from 'extremists.' Pape raises some questions about the wisdom of these strategies. He argues for a military withdrawal from Iraq as soon as possible, a settlement of the Palestine/Israel problem as soon as possible and what he calls 'off-shore balancing,' which is establishing local military alliances while maintaining the capacity for rapid deployment of military forces [247-250]. He also argues strongly that any attempt by the West to force Muslim societies to transform 'is likely to dramatically increase the threat we face' [245]. All of these proposals are responses to direct and indirect military political occupation which he sees as fuelling insurgency and terrorism.

I agree on the necessity to withdraw foreign troops from the Middle East as soon as is practically feasible. I also agree with the necessity to cease imperial interference in the domestic affairs of states in the region. I think that the idea of 'off shore balancing,' however, is not likely to be as successful as the assertion of a quite different non-instrumental relationship between both states and peoples in the Middle East and the West and between the

West and other sites of national terrorism. In the final analysis if we are to deal with the root causes of terrorism we need to think of some quite different strategies.

SOME NONVIOLENT RESPONSES TO TERROR AND TERRORISM

1. Reframing the Problem

In the first place it is important to rethink and reframe the problems of terror and terrorism and current responses to them. In particular it is vital that the West ceases using the oxymoronic term 'war on terrorism' or the 'global war on terror' even if it does have a long pedigree in US politics.

President George W Bush was not the first US president or senior official to declare a war against terrorism. Two decades ago Secretary of State George Schultz outlined the Reagan administration's strategy in the 'war against terrorism' [See Luck 2004, 83]. Similarly, when President Bill Clinton authorized unilateral cruise missile attacks against Bin Laden's training camps in Afghanistan and a Sudanese pharmaceutical company suspected of producing chemical weapons, these were described as 'a new war on terrorism' [Luck 2004, 85]. It is important to acknowledge, therefore, that the United States rhetoric in relation to the war against or on terrorism has been around for some time. What made September 11th 2001 different was that President George W. Bush declared that he would

> direct every resource at our command, every means of diplomacy, every tool of intelligence, every instrument of law enforcement, every financial influence and every necessary weapon of war to the disruption and to the defeat of the global terror network [Cited in Luck 2004, 88].

In other words terrorism moved right to the top of the United States Foreign and Defense policy agendas. At a stroke terrorism was framed as a 'threat to world peace' and therefore primarily a military and security rather than a criminal problem.

This particular framing of the problem is not helpful and does not address the primary sources of terrorism. These are much more likely to be domestic rather than global in source and, if Pape is right, more about resistance to occupation or external political and cultural influences than the promotion of particular religious views. Terrorism should be seen for what it is, namely a failure of politics rather than a military or security threat. It represents a failure of national, regional and global mechanisms and institutions. Most terrorism occurs where political institutions are not robust enough to hear and respond to deep grievances and to contain vigorous political differences.

The United Nations is partially responsible for this perspective and it, too, needs to take a lead in its reframing. In response to 9/11, Security Council Resolution 1368 (September 12th 2001) recognized 'the inherent right of individual and collective self defense' as a legitimate response to terrorism. This resolution resulted in some 68 countries providing support to the United States as it contemplated military action against Afghanistan. Not content with this degree of support, however, the US and the UK decided to harness energy behind combating terrorism at national levels.

Security Council Resolution 1373 (2001), for example, required all member states to develop or amend national legislation against terrorism and report progress under such legislation to the newly formed Counter Terrorism Committee. Boulden and Weiss note that these two resolutions generate an astonishing dichotomy.

> The Security Council chooses to exercise no control or oversight on the use of military force in response to terrorism but is vigilant and arguably intrusive when it comes to dealing with terrorism through national mechanisms and controls [2004, 11].

The direct consequence of the first resolution was (i) the overthrow of the Taliban regime in Afghanistan, and later (ii) UK/US efforts to develop links between 'terrorism' and the regime of Saddam Hussein in order to generate international legitimacy for regime change in Iraq. When these links seemed tenuous, political leaders in the UK and the US argued their case on the basis of preventing weapons of mass destruction falling into the hands of terrorists. Both of these arguments failed to convince most of the countries that had supported the initial invasion of Afghanistan and the arguments have subsequently been proved quite false.

The right to self defence against terror has resulted in a willingness to collapse and conflate many diverse and different terrorist movements into a single 'global terror network.' This has been used to engage in a very rapid expansion of state security institutions, especially intelligence and military institutions. While this makes for simplified politics, it distorts reality. There is no single global terror network. It is vital, therefore, to spend much more time on highlighting the grievances and contextual differences of each specific group.

This right to self defense against terrorism, for instance, has been used by Russia to justify military actions against Chechens; by China to justify coercive action against Muslims in Xinxiang; by the Philippines government against separatist movements in Mindanao; and by the former Nepalese government against the Maoist insurgency in Nepal. Other states have invoked this resolution to justify and heighten internal surveillance, and in many instances illegal mistreatment of 'aliens.' Conflicts, which in other circumstances might have been viewed as legitimate acts of self determination or resistance against arbitrary and dictatorial rule have also fallen under the terrorist rubric.

The global war on terror and the way in which it is manifesting itself nationally, regionally and internationally, therefore, is having adverse and deleterious effects on the capacity of civil society organizations and communities all around the world to work with and across a range of political movements (both legitimate and illegitimate) in order to prevent violent conflict and to develop institutional mechanisms that make the resort to terrorist violence less likely.

2. Use of 'Soft Power'

Second (after reframing the problem so that terrorism is seen primarily as illegitimate politics, i.e. a criminal activity rather than a military threat to national security) it is important that states and peoples focus more attention on the enhancement of 'soft power' [See Nye 2004, 4-5], and nonviolence as a real alternative to 'hard' coercive responses to terrorism. Pape, Marshall, Gurr and others agree that coercive responses to terrorism as we have seen in

Iraq and elsewhere have in fact exacerbated the problem. When President Bush stated just prior to the 2004 Presidential election that the 'war on terror is a never ending and probably unwinnable war [2006, 5] he compounded these problems. Civil society actors, faced by the prospect of the US and its allies waging a never ending, unwinnable war against terror have to counter some extremely powerful dynamics in order to focus attention on non-militarized ways of dealing with terrorist acts. Much of the national legislation dealing with terror, for instance, has resulted in a draconian tightening of immigration laws and procedures, increased use of surveillance mechanisms, infringements of privacy, challenges to civil liberties and the rule of law, and a deepened division of the world into 'them and us.' The measures have made 'ordinary politics' more difficult.

The fact that most of these measures are not having a particularly positive impact on the incidence of terrorist activity is further cause for concern. In fact the West's pursuit of security at the expense of the rule of law and liberty is resulting in severe challenges to democratization and human rights processes. Prison abuse at Abu Ghraib, and Guantanamo Bay, coupled with doctrines of 'extraordinary rendition,' (i.e the US process of detaining potential terrorist suspects and transferring them to countries with weak or lax proscriptions on the use of torture for interrogation), the widespread use of torture, and legislation which removes basic legal rights such as habeas corpus, has severely damaged the West's assumption of 'moral superiority' in relation to international relations and domestic politics.

To develop effective nonviolent alternatives to terrorism means focussing on the consolidation of relationships between peoples as well as states; on the development of human as opposed to national security; on collaborative problem solving rather than adversarial competition; and on the expansion of international legal and institutional regimes. Nonviolence is about building positive relationships with all human beings — relationships that are based on love, compassion, mutual respect, understanding and appreciation. It is also about the development of a new ethical basis for politics, a capacity to forgive and a willingness to pursue reconciliation when confronted by deeply divided and broken relationships.

None of these aspirations are naïve or unrealistic. They do demand, however, a change in the way in which we do social and political analysis. As Gandhi said, 'We must become the change we wish to see in the world.' In particular it is important to enhance a personal and political capacity to imagine ourselves in an inclusive and expandable web of human relationships, which includes those who might wish to harm us or those whom we fear or feel a strong ambivalence toward. In relation to terrorists it is important that we start asking some fundamental questions about how they relate to us and we to them and what would be our preferred outcome or optimal solution in relation to them. Isolation, marginalization, imprisonment, and or violence and destruction of those who might wish to harm us represents a certain failure of human imagination. In other words, if we are to defeat terrorism, we need to pay as much attention to the anger and rage that fuels it as we do to controlling and containing it. To do this effectively means that we also need to sustain a problem-solving curiosity that embraces complexity without reliance on dualistic polarity — that is, either/or decision making. If we engage in a crass Manichaean division of the world or its constituent parts, we will never be able to see its infinite complexity and devise nuanced and proportionate responses to difficult problems. In particular it is important that there be political leaders all over the world who are willing to reject cultures of violence in favor of cultures of peace and who are willing to stand up for communitarian principles against atomising and individualizing principles. The whole world may have to confront the fact that advanced industrial capitalism may be unsustainable in the long term and is having destructive consequences in the short to medium term.

3. Need to Breakdown Big Power Politics

Third, it is important that the world community acts to constrain the most powerful military powers in the world from pursuing unilateralist and national exceptionalist policies and focus much more attention on regional and multilateral solutions to problems. It is important to change the atmospherics justifying 'national exceptionalism' by focussing attention on the politics of trust rather than the politics of fear, on confidence and bridge building rather than on paranoia and division. It is also time to acknowledge that 19th and 20th century divisions of states into big powers, imperial powers, superpowers, middle and insignificant powers has to be transcended. The reality is that large powers are vulnerable and small powers sometimes resilient. What is more important is whether states are effective or ineffective global citizens, macro actors capable of solving the common problems confronting humanity. Whether they are small or large is not as important as whether they are committed to values of human betterment or the naked advancement of self interest.

4. Time to Exit from Iraq

Fourth, it is absolutely crucial that a clear exit strategy be enunciated for withdrawing all foreign troops from Iraq. The War in Iraq has diverted resources that might have been directed to dealing with the root causes of terrorism and its specific manifestations. It has certainly done huge reputational damage to the United States and its closest allies in Europe and in the Middle East. All members of the coalition of the willing are now considered legitimate targets for *jihadists*. The war on terrorism and the war in Iraq have generated a major trans-atlantic rift on this subject [See Benjamin et al 2004]. When the Head of the British Army, General Sir Richard Dannatt, stated that the 'UK must withdraw from Iraq soon or risk serious consequences for Iraqi and British society' [*The Guardian* 2006, 1], he was confirming Pape's argument that uninvited occupying forces generate military resistance and create an impossible military situation for the occupiers.

The war has resulted in a very significant battering of the United Nations as the legitimate global agency for managing global threats to peace. None of this is helpful to addressing the root causes of the problems in terms of creating more space for international negotiations, mediation and adjudication, for UN and citizen-based sanctions, cross-cultural communication initiatives, citizen initiatives, the development of effective international treaties and greater use of the World Court and the International Criminal Court — all of which are arguably going to deliver more long term solutions to terrorism than prolonged forceful occupation ever will.

5. Politics of Fear and Loss of Liberties

Fifth, it is absolutely important that human rights and freedoms in the West not be compromised by anti-terrorist legislation and by a radical division of the world into Islamic and Non-Islamic peoples. The terrorist threat in the United States (but also in Australia, the United Kingdom and elsewhere) has resulted in fearful publics willing to cede some personal liberty in return for an Executive promise of security. (This has occurred despite the statement of one of the Founding Fathers of America, Benjamin Franklin, who said that 'They that can give up essential liberty to obtain a little temporary safety deserve neither liberty nor safety'). The second election victory of President Bush is testimony to the powerfulness of the politics of fear.

6. Failure of Media and Governance

Sixth, it is necessary that the media become much more robust in challenging taken-for-granted perspectives on terror and terrorist threats. States have been able to sacrifice liberty for state security because of a compliant media, extensive and well-targeted governmental information campaigns, and the specific privileging of 'official' intelligence, executive and administrative perspectives. When the full power of the State is harnessed behind the promotion of military and coercive orientations to security it is extremely difficult for more pacific, non-state citizen's voices to be heard. This inevitably has had a slightly chilling effect on proposals and activities which involve civil society and non-military political actors. It has certainly resulted in a marginalization of the concept of 'Human Security' which is a concept that addresses both the presenting and the underlying problems of a terrorist threat with its twin emphases on 'Freedom from Fear' and 'Freedom from Want.' The monopolization of security discourse by security specialists and the executive branches of government has also made it difficult for proponents of a 'Culture of Peace' to make much headway against those whose professions rest on 'Cultures of Violence.'

7. Enabling Process for Peacemakers

Seventh, it is important that conflict prevention and peacebuilding organizations work out ways in which they can continue doing their work without fear or favor with groups on all sides of the terrorist divide. They need to be able to do this without falling foul of specific pieces of anti-terror legislation. If civil society groups cannot communicate with warring parties, provide safe spaces for difficult discussions, and if they cannot help individuals and groups frame and reframe their problems in creative ways (without fear of state surveillance and repression), the international community loses important insights into ways in which the needs and interests of terrorists or potential terrorists might be satisfied nonviolently.

In particular it is important that we work hard to break down global stereotypes and meet 'the other.' This means much more attention is paid to people, to people exchanges, and to a recognition that, if you really want peace, you do not talk to friends; you talk to your enemies. It also means that we need to pay much more attention to the ways in which the 'voiceless' might be heard so that they do not have to resort to terrorist threats to attract attention. It also means a simultaneous assault on the glorification of war and violence without intentionally or unintentionally condoning oppression and injustice.

Joseba Zulaika and William A Douglass [1996] suggest that we need to develop a clear understanding of the role of terror and terrorism as a substitute for political debate about development, security, and more constructive ways of generating structural stability and order. In a brilliant analysis (published five years before 9/11) they argue that;

> Terrorism discourse singles out and removes from the larger historical and political context a psychological trait (terror), an organizational structure (the terrorist network) and a category (terrorism) in order to invent an autonomous and aberrant realm of gratuitous evil that defies any understanding [22].

This then becomes an absorbing narrative for politicians, the military, the media and academics who use hypothetical as well as actual threats to generate passive and frightened citizens. Indeed, there is a very symbiotic relationship between the terrorists, politicians, the military and those who research and write about terrorism. Each one has a vested interest in ensuring the threat continues and is seen to be personally threatening. While the threat may be real it may also be imagined. For the purposes of terrorist discourse, however, this is immaterial.

8. Nonviolently 'Draining the Swamps'

Eighth, in order to change the logic that justifes top down or bottom up terror, it is important to remind ourselves of other equally compelling narratives. The United Nations Development Program (UNDP) has some very sobering statistics on violence most of which have nothing to do with terrorism. Every day, for example, more than 30,000 children around the world die of preventable diseases; 2.8 billion of the world's population live on less than $2.00 per day with 1.2 billion of them subsisting on less than $1.00 per day. An estimated 815 million people are undernourished. Every year there are 300 million cases of malaria. More than 500,000 women die each year as a result of pregnancy and childbirth [See UNDP 2002]. This is the daily existential terror faced by the vast majority of humankind. Against these kinds of statistics the number of those killed in terrorist activity is relatively modest. It is important, therefore, that civil society groups working for conflict sensitive development assistance, humanitarian relief, and long term conflict prevention join forces with regional and global organizations in reminding everyone of some of the basic conditions that might generate terrorism. These matters are as — if not more — important than dealing with shadowy terrorist networks whose raison d'etre is to generate bottom up fear instead of workable solutions.

To do this effectively requires a robust well-funded United Nations which is capable of spearheading regional and global responses to some of these problems. This is not an optional extra and it requires the UN to work out ways in which it can combine the activities of the Security Council, its Counter Terrorism Committee, and the Committee on Human Rights and the Human Rights Commission, alongside all the diverse development agencies of the UN, in order to drain the swamps within which terrorists and terrorist grievances thrive.

It also means paying much more attention to some very basic but negative dynamics that fuel terrorist activity. It is vital that much more attention be directed, for instance, to halting the arms trade and militarism, and certainly stopping arms flow to terrorists. These disarming measures then need to be coupled to the development of sustainably just economies, aid to the poor, the reduction of privileged overconsumption, education in peace and conflict studies, the repatriation of refugees, and listening and responding to those who feel 'colonized,' 'occupied' and marginalized.

As Zulaika and Douglass suggest: 'Terrorism is the latest embodiment of an old theme — civilization locked in deadly struggles with wildness....wildness invoked in the name of order' [150]. For those groups concerned with conflict prevention, justice and long term peacebuilding it is vital that they do not succumb to a struggle with wildness in the name of order. On the contrary, it is important that the fields of conflict prevention and peacebuilding maintain their commitment to a radical humanism in which no individual or group is dehumanized and demonized, and no one is assumed to be unreachable or incapable of conversation, and where (given the right conditions) everyone is capable of engaging in positive transactions. In particular it is important that the world is not divided into good and evil, the saved and unsaved, the blessed and the cursed.

The next five to ten years are going to be critical for the humanist enterprise. In an age of insecurity and extremes, there is a disposition to gravitate to authoritarian government and rule, and to cede personal and collective responsibility to the state. Ceding such authority may be necessary in the face of an imminent and direct major threat to national security but it is not necessary or useful in relation to relatively random small scale acts of intimidatory terrorist violence.

It is imperative that those of us concerned with generating realistic responses to deal with ruthless enemies work out ways of identifying and separating the really ruthless from those who have political agendas that are capable of being satisfied with enlightened and well-resourced social and economic development policies. For those who are caught in an orgy of violence the onus on civil society actors is not to capitulate all responsibility for dealing with such people to the security actors alone. To deal with the highly intractable terrorists requires heroic individuals who are willing to cross boundaries of violence and open up difficult dialogues. The challenge is to confer respect and humanity on those who are unwilling to do this to others. This is not a task for the faint hearted but equally it is not a task for the marines either. It is a task for enlightened civil society actors working in concert with politicians and others in conjunction with regional and global organizations. If this does not happen, the prospects for effectively handling terrorist violence, using existing methods, are very poor indeed. As one of the world's finest exponents of nonviolence, Martin Luther King, stated:

- Darkness cannot drive out darkness,
- Only light can do that.
- Hate cannot drive out hate,
- Only love can do that.
- Hate multiplies violence,
- And toughness multiplies toughness
- In a descending spiral of destruction...
- The chain reaction of evil,
- Hate begetting hate,

- Wars producing more wars
- Must be broken,
- Or we shall be plunged into
- The darkness of annihilation.

ACKNOWLEDGEMENTS

Kevin P Clements is the Professor of Peace and Conflict Studies and the Foundation Director of the Australian Centre for Peace and Conflict Studies at the University of Queensland, Brisbane Australia. He comes to this position from International Alert (IA) where he was its Secretary-General from January 1999 to September 2003. IA has made major contributions to the mainstreaming of conflict prevention within European Foreign and Development Ministries, the EU and a variety of UN institutions. During his time there he was on the Board of the European Centre for Conflict Prevention and past President of the European Peace Building Liaison Office in Brussels. Previously Professor Clements held the Vernon and Minnie Lynch Chair of Conflict Resolution and the Directorship of the Institute for Conflict Analysis and Resolution (ICAR) at George Mason University, Fairfax, Virginia, 1994-99. His career has been a combination of academic analysis and practice in the areas of peacebuilding and conflict transformation. He was formerly Director of the Quaker United Nations Office in Geneva and Head of the Peace Research Centre at the Australian National University in Canberra. Born in New Zealand, he has been an advisor to the New Zealand, Australian, British, Swedish and Dutch governments on conflict prevention and peace, defense and security issues. He was a member of the New Zealand Government's Defence Committee of Enquiry in 1985, President of the International Peace Research Association (IPRA) from 1994-1998, President of the IPRA Foundation from 1995-2000, and Secretary-General of the Asia Pacific Peace Research Association in the early 90s. He has written or edited six books and over 140 chapters /articles on conflict transformation, peacebuilding, preventive diplomacy and development.

REFERENCES

Annan, K. (2005). *In LargerFreedom*. New York: United Nations Publications.

AP Reuters (2006). *The Sydney Morning Herald*, September 12.

Barnaby, F. (2002)'The New Terrorism: A 21st Century Biological, Chemical and Nuclear Threat.' Policy Paper: Oxford, Oxford Research Group.

Benjamin, D. et al . (2004). *The Transatlantic Dialogue on Terrorism*. Washington DC: Center for Strategic and International Studies.

Boulden, J. and Weiss, T. (2004).'The Security Council and Counter Terrorism.' In J. Boulden and T. Weiss (Eds.), *Terrorism and the UN: Before and After September 11th* (1-15). Bloomington, IN: Indiana University Press.

British Government (2000). *Terrorism Act 2000*. London: The Stationary Office.

Bush, G. W. (2006). *Le Monde Diplomatique*. September (p. 5).

Cole, D. (2006). *Le Monde Diplomatique*. September (p. 6).

Golub, P.S. (2006). 'The Will to Undemocratic Power.'*The Guardian Weekly*. London-Sydney, October 20-26.

Hart, W.B. and Hassencahl, F. (2002). 'Dehumanizing the Enemy in Editorial Cartoons.' In B.S. Greenberg (Ed.), *Communication and Terrorism: Public and Media Responses to 9/11* (140-156). Newark, NJ: Hampton Press.

Luck, E.C. (2004). 'The US, Counter Terrorism, and the Prospects for a Multilateral Alternative.' In J. Boulden and T. Weiss (Eds.), *Terrorism and the UN: Before and After September 11th* (80-91). Bloomington, IN: Indiana University Press.

Marshall, M. and Gurr, T.R. (2005). *Peace and Conflict Report*. Baltimore, MD: University of Maryland Press.

Nye, J. (2004). 'The Role of Soft Power in the War of Ideas.' *Futures Direction International*, July, (pp.16-27).

Pape, R.A. (2005). *Dying to Win: The Strategic Logic of Suicide Terrorism*. New York: Random House.

Powell, C. (2006). *Le Monde Diplomatique*. September (p. 6).

Rubenstein, R. (2001). Unpublished Talk at George Mason University, Fairfax, VA, September 11.

Wilcox, P. C. (2002). 'Defining Terrorism: Is One Man's Terrorist Really Another Man's Freedom Fighter.' Talk to Conflict Resolution and Prevention Forum. Washington, DC: Search for Common Ground, February 12.

United Nations Development Program. (2002). *Human Development Report*. New York: Oxford University Press.

Zulaika, J. and Douglass, W.A. (1996). *Terror and Taboo: The Follies, Fables and Faces of Terrorism*. London /New York: Routledge.

In: Nonviolence: An Alternative for Defeating...　　　　ISBN: 978-1-60021-812-5
Editors: S. Ram and R. Summy, pp. 257-277　　　　© 2008 Nova Science Publishers, Inc.

Chapter 15

DEFEATING TERRORISM NONVIOLENTLY: AN ENQUIRY INTO AN ALTERNATIVE STRATEGY[1]

Ralph Summy

One must ask constantly whether the problem being considered can be solved within the given set of assumptions used or whether what is required is a review of basic hypotheses. One must be prepared to start again on another basis...

[John Burton 1979, 26]

ABSTRACT

This chapter examines a few critical questions about how to respond effectively to the terrorism of irregular cell-based groups. Since a counter-strategy of state terrorism — one committed to 'shock and awe' and 'smokin them out' — has manifestly proved to be a failure, its protagonists woefully falling into a strategic trap set by Osama bin Laden, why did President Bush in his State of the Union Address on January 10th 2007 basically outline a continuation of that failed strategy? Why are his 'surge' and 'surge boost' policies of adding 21,500-30,000 combat troops in Iraq likely to produce the same outcome or at best a short-term solution? Despite the best intentions of his newly appointed commander of US ground forces in Iraq, Lieut. General David Petraeus, what are the chances of his success in securing the stability that will enable reconstruction to begin in the chaotically violent city of Baghdad and the outer provinces? Why is a staged withdrawal from Iraq the only viable strategy to pursue? In shifting to an overall strategy against non-state terrorism that might prove effective, what should be its salient features? Is a nonviolent strategy a viable option? To what extent would this require a new paradigm that builds on a base of principled nonviolence? What are the obstacles; what are the chances of nonviolence becoming a dominant mode of thinking and way of waging conflict? In considering these questions the intention is to redirect the thinking on dealing with non-state terrorism along more realistic and hence promising lines.

---

[1] This essay is primarily a distillation of inspirations and ideas culled from the writings of four outstanding peace researchers to whom I am highly indebted: John Burton, Tom H Hastings, Glenn Paige and Gene Sharp.

INTRODUCTION

The current strategy of countering the minatory actions of irregular cell-based terrorists with unilateral and collective state terrorism appears irrational when the overwhelming evidence indicates not only the strategy's immorality but its gross ineffectiveness. The strategy undermines the very values, including the rule of law, that democratic powers seek to preserve at home and cultivate abroad, and it aids the opponent's recruitment campaign among the alienated, dispossessed and drifters of the world. It also helps to create a militant leadership among the Islamic young of the middle and upper classes, and to garner financial support from these classes and from sympathetic Muslim governments.

That this violent counter-strategy has repeatedly failed when used by the Israelis against the Palestinians, the Russians against the Chechens, the U.S. and its 'Coalition of the Willing' against the Iraqis, Mujaheddin, etc does not seem to have registered on the thinking of many policymakers. They hold tenaciously to the view that elites — when challenged at the level of retaining or advancing their power position — have no option but to threaten or overwhelm their opponent with superior firepower. As laid down five hundred years ago in the advice of Machiavelli (1469-1527) to Cesare Borgia in *The Prince*, the first efforts of a ruler should be to dominate by the guile and craftiness of a 'fox', but should that method fail, the ruler should not hesitate to strike with the fury and viciousness of a 'lion.' [1908, ch. 6, 17]. An influential figure in the development of modern political realism, Machiaveli contended that 'He who establishes a tyranny and does not kill Brutus, and he who establishes a democratic regime and does not kill the sons of Brutus, will not last long' [1910, bk. III, 3]. This hardline pragmatism — when coupled with the retributive justice of an 'eye for an eye' instead of the restorative justice of asking questions about what causes human beings to resort to the vile actions of indiscriminate killing in the first place — prefigures a lose/lose outcome for all parties in the long run.

Every empire created at the point of a gun eventually declines and loses its dominance. The U.S. is not likely to be an exception. Although its dominance is based more on cultural and economic influence and the credibility of its military power than on the direct administration of colonies, it will have only one legacy to ponder. When its time comes to collapse, what sort of future will it have provided for those it managed and manipulated? The verdict for all empires is usually negative, but some leave less disaster in their wake. Britain certainly generated less disaster than Rome or Belgium or France. But what will be inherited from the U.S.? Despite its best intentions, will it transmit to the nationals of its empire a viable cultural, democratic and economic future? The prospects in the early 21st century are looking quite bleak.

To avert this possibility of a negative outcome where all the parties become victims, an alternative worth considering would be to shift the paradigm away from imperial militarism (the Violence model of counter-terrorism set out in the book's Introduction) to the upholding of human rights and the promotion of nonviolence (the Legal and Nonviolent models). While a nonviolent strategy upon examination might initially seem as catastrophic as the one previously in place and the slightly altered one announced in President George W. Bush's State of the Union Address in January 2007, it certainly merits examination. Yet nothing along these lines has been entertained — as far as I can determine — among the West's politicians or in major non-government think-tanks such as the Australian Institute of

Strategic Studies, the Brookings Institution or the International Institute for Strategic Studies. When it comes time for the governing elites and their supporters to consider applying the ultimate sanction, one voice generally prevails — the roar of the lion. The only major difference, for example, between the two main parties in Australia is whether the same existing counter-insurgency strategy should be applied in distant lands or confined primarily to the Southeast Asia/South Pacific area. And in the case of formulating an immediate strategy for Iraq, the Government automatically endorses the Bush 'surge' and 'surge boost' policies, while the Opposition proposes a long drawn-out staged withdrawal. While the latter proposal contains the merit of corresponding to the more pragmatic thinking of the James Baker-Lee Hamilton Iraq Study Group, neither political party has stressed the basic need to go to the roots of the terrorist problem.

HALF WAY IS NO WAY

Introducing a nonviolent strategy for the West into the imbroglio of Middle East politics means that one starts with the situation as it currently exists. What sort of strategy in early 2007 is feasible for Iraq, Afghanistan, Iran, and the Palestinian-Israeli conflict? Since developing a specific nonviolent strategy for all these 'trouble spots,' as well as others that are likely to erupt, would comprise the material for an entire book, my observations will be primarily confined to the salient issue of Iraq. The general nonviolent strategy on terrorism that follows will then provide pointers suggesting ways of countering the unchecked brutality associated with the many other areas.

President Bush's new 'surge' counter-insurgency strategy for Iraq does show a slight shift in thinking and even contains some important elements of nonviolence. The appointment of Lieut. General David Petraeus as the new overall commander of ground forces reflects a rejection of former Secretary of Defense Donald Rumsfeld's strategy of sending hi-tech armed strike-troops into an area to put down uprisings and then retreating to the sanctuary of well-protected garrisons. Petraeus, together with Marine Colonel Jim Mattis wrote a counter-insurgency manual in June 2006 that challenged this existing strategy. They proclaimed nine paradoxes of counter-insurgency, including assertions like 'the more force used, the less effective it is,' and 'the more you protect your force, the less secure you are' [Petraeus and Mattis 2006]. The manual stressed a focus on community policing, communication with the populace and strengthening the society's infrastructures.

Petraeus had previously been given an opportunity to put his ideas into practice back in April 2003. Given the command of 20,000 troops and ordered to secure the city of Mosul, he quickly established a presence in the streets with his soldiers. They patrolled their assigned areas like policemen on a beat, and reported to patrol bases analogous to police precincts. The soldiers were given instructions to treat the Iraqis with respect, to restrain from using force unless first attacked and then to ensure that no bystanders were hurt. As Joe Klein reports, 'Knocking down doors was replaced by knocking on doors' [2007, 11]. Whenever force had to be used, a task force followed up by going into the affected neighborhood to clean up and take down information on damage claims. Petraeus conducted elections for a city council. He saw to the dispersal of funds to reopen schools and factories, to repair streets, and to create recreation programs. Although this classic form of counter-insurgency proved successful as a first step in Mosul, it was scorned by the Pentagon and top brass in Iraq who saw nation building as a job for social workers, not soldiers. Petraeus and his troops were replaced by another unit of only 5,000 troops who resorted to the established practices of the U.S. military — patrolling the streets in high cost, thick armoured, hi-tech vehicles, and turning the maintenance of civic order over to the Iraqis. In short time the city descended into chaos [Klein 2007, 11].

The question now remains: will the addition of 21,500-30,000 troops — along with an extra supplement of $245 billion to cover war costs in Iraq and Afghanistan, together with the appointment of Petraeus who appreciates the classic nuances of counter-insurgency strategy — be enough to quell the anarchic violence in Iraq? By the very standards that Petraeus advanced in his writings and implemented in practice, the chances for success of the President's new 'surge' would appear minimal in the long term. The reasons can be set out as follows:

- As occupiers the troops have not been trained to cooperate with the citizenry and build civil structures. Their whole orientation has been directed to the killing of people and the destruction of their resources.
- Part of the problem lies within the military leadership itself which is inclined to view peacekeeping and peacebuilding as respectively the roles of police officers and social workers. For instance, until recently the subject of counter-insurgency only appeared as an elective in senior year at the nation's foremost military academy, West Point.
- According to Petraeus' own manual an effective, enduring counter-insurgency strategy requires a ratio of 20 soldiers per 1,000 residents. This means that a city the size of Baghdad would require 120,000 troops. However, the additional 20,000 troops that the President is providing for the city would only bring the total to about 35,000.
- With opposition mounting among the American people and their Congressional representatives, morale can be expected to deteriorate among the troops, especially when their tours of duty are extended and National Guard units are called on to return to action sooner than expected.
- Doubts are raised whether a counter insurgency strategy can be applied in Iraq where the fighting has taken the form of a civil war. The government of Prime Minister Nouri al-Maliki cannot be seen as an independent authority combating impartially the full range of insurgent forces when its survival depends on the support of the Shia militias.
- If it were possible to successfully implement a counter-insurgency strategy in Iraq along the lines of the Petraeus model, the time-line — as Mosul demonstrated and is estimated by experts — would take up to ten years to complete, a period well beyond the patience of Congress and the American public and probably the military's endurance.

In short, the half measures proposed by Bush appear to be a recipe for digging a deeper hole and opening up greater opportunities for terrorist exploitation. Explained historian Arthur Schlesinger Jr, in one of his last writings in the *New York Times* in December 2005:

Once American troops are out of Iraq, people around the world will rejoice that we have recovered our senses. What's more, the killing of Americans and the global loss of American credibility will diminish….

In a memorandum to President Kennedy, roughly three months after his inauguration (in 1961) I wrote with respect to Vietnam: 'There is no clearer example of a country that cannot be saved unless it saves itself.'

Today, Iraq is an even clearer example [Cited in *The Australian* 2007].

Two years later, Senator Carl Levin, Chairman of the Armed Services Committee, put it more bluntly: the 'surge', he said, is more like 'a plunge into the sectarian cauldron, a plunge into the unknown' [Quoted in Hulse and Zeleny 2007]. Iraq — which under the tyrant Saddam Hussein had effectively resisted the penetration of the ultra fundamentalist Wahhabis — is now not only destabilized but prone to becoming a terrorist base for operations throughout the Middle East. As Senate Majority Leader Harry Reid pointed out, the Bush policy in Iraq has been and continues to be the 'biggest American foreign policy mistake in the nation's history' [2007].

In the fight against the perpetrators of 9/11, the realistic choice back in the days of pre-invasion Iraq lay between the twin evils of a tyrant's order or insurrectional lawless pluralism. Regrettably the lesser evil of a stable tyranny was cast aside by Washington's neoconservatives in favor of 'plung(ing) into the sectarian cauldron.' Almost four years later, as noted by Richard Falk,

The White House continues to be steered by neoconservative hard liners when it comes to foreign policy. Well ahead of the speech (State of the Union) it was widely publicized that these new tactics of escalated deployment in Baghdad had been mainly crafted by Frederick Kagan of the American Enterprise Institute, a hawkish signatory of the pre-9/11 neoconservative blueprint for American foreign policy published under the auspices of the Project for a New American Century [207, 1].

While 'staying the course' with the same old formula of unleashing massive firepower — despite Petraeus' appointment — may reaffirm the President's reputation of gritty determination, it represents to the majority of Americans and most of the world a misguided attempt to rescue an unsalvageable situation at too late an hour. It is seen as strengthening the base of Islamic terrorism with potentially dire global implications. Although the nonviolent advocate would concur with such an assessment, he or she would argue that terrorism will never be defeated by imposing democracy through the backdoor of military conquest. From the outset the strategy of a global war against terrorism, particularly as it was applied in Iraq, was going nowhere. It was a 'no way' street to disaster.

ASSUMPTIONS BEHIND A NONVIOLENT STRATEGY

Terrorism lodged by a covert irregular group against a nation-state outside its borders constitutes a vastly different form of warfare than that conducted by nation-states against each other. That being an accepted and indisputable fact, one would think it follows that the response to meet this new kind of threat might also have to be different. At the very least it should provoke an enquiry that the response utilize a different form of warfare (as, for example, Petraeus and Mattis prescribed in their Manual). Proponents of a nonviolent strategy would take the analysis a step further and argue that the concept of warfare is itself inappropriate in countering terrorism. Instead, one is dealing with criminals — something more than a group of guerrillas or warriors whose fanaticism and ruthlessness happens to show no bounds. When the Bush administration and its allies declared a 'war on terror/terrorism', they committed a major blunder. A nonviolent strategist would reframe the problem, starting from the assumption that one is engaged in a police action. Why is this distinction important?

First, to declare war on terror dignifies the terrorists, elevating them to a position that equates them with a state. Only states and groups with credible aspirations to become states or to replace existing governments can legally be participants in a war. An individual or group without credible pretensions to statehood that engages in violence is committing an act of criminality.[2] September 11th, the Kuta and Australian embassy bombings, the train bombing in Madrid, the London tube and bus bombings, the Beslan atrocity, etc were vile criminal acts perpetrated outside the bounds of universally acceptable human behavior. To glorify these infamous deeds of al-Qa'ida and Jemaah Islamiah (JL), along with their amorphous network of co-Islamic criminals, with the designation of war actions is tantamount to bestowing the credibility of state legitimacy on pernicious thuggery.

Second, apart from giving militant *jihadists* an elevated status, one is engaged in a struggle that defies the way wars are traditionally fought. In terrorism there is no clear target that can be identified, nor a fixed location that can be captured and secured. The terrorist is a shadowy figure, constantly on the move and vanishing into the populace. Instead of something concrete to attack, one is facing criminal malevolence that passes itself off as high-minded religious or nationalist doctrine. One is fighting an insidious idea.

Third, whenever one declares a war on terror/ism — or on poverty or on drugs — one is mouthing an oxymoron with disastrous consequences. A commitment is made to engage in a war without end. However, wars are conceived as having exact and tangible resolutions. Senator Kerry during his campaign for the presidency was perceptive to say 'we have to return…to where terrorists are not the focus of our lives, but they're a nuisance' [Quoted in Eccleston 2004, 8]. While proclaiming a 'war against terror/ism' may generate patriotic passion and *hubris* among the citizenry in the short term, at some point in a prolonged campaign morale is bound to deteriorate and shatter the united support, both domestic and international, required to track down and bring the criminals to trial.

Finally, to declare a 'war on terror/ism' suggests a purely military operation. On the other hand, pursuing gangs of criminals implies a police action calling for a multi-dimensional and multi-lateral approach. President George W. Bush has termed his war strategy 'taking the battle to the enemy' [2002]. This is exactly the same strategy that failed when applied to the 'war on drugs' (ironically declared by President George Bush, Snr). Its strategic architects directed their fire at the cartels and 'drug lords' that smuggle narcotics, at the peasants who produce the coca, and at the 'pushers' who conduct the street sales. They corresponded to the armies to be defeated on the battlefield. Meanwhile, relatively little was done to provide the

---

[2] When a sovereign state is challenged for sovereign control within its own borders, it usually demeans its opponent with epithets such as 'rebel,' 'outlaw,' 'communist' or 'terrorist.' In some instances the charge of 'terrorist' is clearly justified if the opponent is engaged in what unequivocally constitutes an act of terrorism. A case in point is the Beslan atrocity committed by Chechen nationalists. Interestingly, some of their fellow independence fighters denounced this slaughter of children and other innocents as 'inexcusable terrorism'.

millions of addicts with education, treatment and rehabilitation programs. The complex conditions on the consumer side were neglected in the same way the conditions that turn young people into consumers of Islamic-based terrorism have been neglected. To cut off the demand for narcotics would destroy the trade. Similarly, to cut off the demand for an ideology that provides a catharsis for an anger formed out of desperation would eventually leave a terrorist leadership bereft of followers and the prospect of successors.

OUTLINING A NONVIOLENT STRATEGY FOR MIDDLE SIZE MEMBERS OF THE 'COALITION OF THE WILLING'

Proposing a nonviolent strategy and implementing it cannot be seen as discrete processes. The knowledge gained from practical experience will constantly require the revising and updating of the original plan. Despite this *caveat*, one has to begin somewhere with a preliminary proposal, recognizing the fact that it needs far more detailed analysis as well as the confirmation that comes from testing it under actual field conditions.

Six elements have been singled out as primary building blocks in configuring a viable nonviolent strategy for a country the size of Australia. These interdependent elements do not comprise an exhaustive list but set out a general template.

6) Unilateral Withdrawal from the 'Coalition of the Willing'

The first step is an obvious but very necessary one. It is also negative: it calls for reversing the existing counter-productive policy of participating in a 'war on terror' in Iraq. To prolong a war by helping to worsen conditions is neither in the long term interests of the Iraqis nor the people on the other side whose leaders have misled them into a war. Assisting the American elite to gain control of the Iraqi oil fields and to exercise political dominion over the Middle East will not advance the cause of defeating terrorism. Indeed, it does much to effect the process of backfire in Iraq, where temporary military success has rebounded into political defeat, as Brian Martin attests in his recently released book, *Justice Ignited* [ch 9, 2006]. The 'liberators'of Iraq are seen to be responsible for creating an intolerable degree of violence since the President's 'Mission Accomplished' boast. The Iraqis' humiliation at being so easily defeated, compounded by the continued presence of the occupiers and the atrocities of their undisciplined troops, has led to the mobilizing of more Islamic terrorists in Iraq and throughout the world. Moreover, it makes any of the participant nations an obvious target in the sights of the expanding terrorist network.

2) Preserving Traditional Values

Joining the 'Coalition of the Willing' in the 'war on terror' in order to protect one's way of life can lead to the self-inflicted loss of cherished values without the enemy firing a single shot. Values of respect for human rights and civil liberties are always tested in times of trial. A nation that abandons the high moral ground not only plays into the hands of the criminals by gaining them supporters, but undermines the strength of its own foundations, commencing a process of social dissolution at home. Senthil Ram refers to this overall exercise, initiated by the insurgent but requiring the self-destruction of the counter-insurgent, as 'terror jiu-jitsu' [see Ch 6].

When Vice President Dick Cheney announced to fellow Americans after 9/11, 'We have to work...the dark side of the street,' he opened up a can of worms that has plagued the conduct of the 'war.' Much of Cheneys 'work' has been exposed to the detriment of American credibility. The practice of 'extraordinary renditions' — in which terrorist suspects are snatched from one country and then taken to another like Egypt or Syria for questioning with methods that are claimed by subsequently released detainees to have included degraded forms of torture — became a very common but secret operation. Although the President, in this context, disclaimed the use of torture, he declined to define what he meant when admitting to 'tough interrogation' techniques.

The passage of the Patriot's Act has come under fire by civil libertarians who have challenged some of its provisions successfully in the courts. Other cases have been lost. The overall effect of this piece of legislation is to drastically curb the speech and movement of people coming under the jurisdiction of U.S. law. Sometimes the White House has directly defied domestic law specifically designed to rein in presidential abuse of civil rights. For instance, the President ordered the National Security Agency to eavesdrop on U.S. citizens without first securing the approval of a special court set up after the Watergate affair to ensure there was some institutional check on presidential powers to secretly monitor citizens.

To Cheney the President's actions were part of what became known as the 'one-percent doctrine.' He summed up its meaning as follows:

> Even if there's just a one per cent chance of the unimaginable coming due, act as if it is a certainty. It's not about our analysis. It's about our response. Justified or not, fact-based or not, our response is what matters. [Quoted in Suskind 2006, 5].

When faced with a crisis there is no time to waste with analysis or policy discussions. Fast action is required: suspects need to be rounded up, held without warrants and not mollycoddled with liberal niceties. In the climate of fear nurtured and sustained long after the immediate anxiety that followed al-Qa'ida's attacks on the Twin Towers and the Pentagon, the secret arrests and under-cover operations of the CIA, FBI and Homeland Security have continued unabated. An ambience has thrived that has led to the maltreatment of prisoners such as those at Abu Grab. A pervasive fear has enabled detainees to be incarcerated at Guantanamo Bay for indefinite periods without trial, laying of charges or facing their accuser. In other words, they have been denied *habeas corpus*, the cornerstone of a free society. Not surprisingly, the way has been has been paved for some American soldiers to engage in the frenzied killing of unarmed civilians.

Because the Australian Government has not raised resolute objections to these violations of human rights and dignity, a more sinister connotation can be given to the term 'Coalition of the Willing'. Failure of the Government to press for the release of its national, David Hicks, for trial in Australia — instead subjecting him to a U.S. military trial in which basic judicial rights are denied — reflected poorly on the nation's vaunted sense of fairness. The issue was not one of Hick's guilt or innocence, but whether after five years in detention, he was at least entitled to a trial in accordance with well-established procedures of Western jurisprudence.

Another paradigm case of how the overzealous reactions of Australian Federal Police and Government ministers can undermine basic principles of legal protection and guaranteed rights occurred over the holding without charges in July 2007 of hospital registrar, Dr Mohamed Haneef. He was detained for giving his SIM card with a small amount of unexpired credit on it to his second cousin, Sabeel Ahmed, when leaving Britain. The Sim card was allegedly passed on to Sabeel's brother, Kafeel Ahmed, who, according to the police, had the Card in his possession (later proved false) when attempting a suicide bomb attack on Glasgow airport. When the Government came to charging Haneef under one of its anti-terrorist acts, it was on the basis that giving the unexpired SIM card to Sabeel, who is now charged in Britain with withholding information on terrorism, constituted, on the part of Haneef, 'reckless' support for a terrorist group. If convicted, the charge carries a maximum penalty of 15 years in prison. Bail, however, was granted to Haneef as the Magistrate found the case presented by the prosecution was 'exceptionally weak.' The Attorney-General Philip Ruddock then proceeded to criticize the decision, noting it was 'the intention of Parliament that there would be a presumption against bail in serious offences involving terrorism' [Quoted in Stewart 2007]. The Immigration Minister Kevin Andrews agreed but went one step further, as he overturned the magistrate's granting of bail. He cancelled Haneef's visa and placed him in immigration detention where he was to be held until his case could be heard before a court. The minister said he had taken this action because Haneef failed to pass the good 'character test' specified in the Migration Act. He claimed there was more evidence against Haneef than was revealed in the affidavit opposing bail, but its substance was withheld since it was too critical to the ongoing investigation for public scrutiny. At the proper time it would be publicly released. In the meantime, a spate of inconsistencies in the testimony of the prosecution at the bail hearing came to light, casting grave doubts on the competency of the police and the credibility of the Government. Leading members of the legal profession expressed their misgivings at the way the arrest and interrogation were conducted, and the case was presented to the Magistrate. Questions were raised by the media and public about the reasons for the Government's overreactions when federal elections were fast approaching. Was the Government attempting to foment fear as an electoral ploy to stem the tide of its ebbing popularity? Whatever the answers, the Government's overreaction has strategically played into the hands of the terrorists without them apparently having to lift a finger.

Hallowed traditions of legalized rights were unreservedly abandoned when the U.S. Congress passed in September 2006 the Military Commissions Act (MCA). This Act gives the President — any U.S. President — the authority to set up a separate judicial system for the trying of alien unlawful enemy combatants. Who qualifies as an 'alien unlawful enemy combatant' can be determined by the President or his designee without recourse to due process of law. The MCA allows the government to use "coerced" interrogation to obtain evidence. Indeed, President Bush now claims the unlimited right to define "torture" and the phrase, "materially support(ing) hostilities". He also asserts the authority to declare any American citizen an 'enemy combatant'. Those swooped up in the net have no right to challenge the legitimacy of their confinement or treatment. Their rights have been abrogated by a provision in the (MCA) that disallows appeals to the Geneva Conventions, despite the fact that the U.S. signed the treaty and agreed to abide by its terms [See Wolf 2007, 15-17].

Enacting laws that defy liberal democratic norms and resorting to extra-judicial procedures that include torture, have been a hallmark of the 'war on terror.' Instead of defeating terrorism, they are more likely to boomerang and undermine the perpetrators. They taint both the reputation of the individual perpetrator and detrimentally shape the character of the offending nation. A nonviolent strategy would not only reject abominations like the 'one-percent doctrine,' the 'extraordinary renditions,' and the MCA, but would make a concerted effort to ensure that suspected criminals received the full benefits of a fair judicial hearing and were treated with civility and respect while awaiting trial or serving a sentence — no matter how heinous their crime.

For the nonviolent strategist the means should converge as much as possible with the ends, since they represent ends in the making. This dictum is not confined to a minority of nonviolent practitioners like Gandhi but forms a centerpiece of Western thought. For instance, identifying liberty with ends and means has long been inscribed in the American political ethic, yet all too frequently is forgotten and overridden in practice. Justice Louis Brandeis reminded his fellow Americans in his famous Supreme Court opinion rendered in the case of *Whitney v. California* [1927] that

> Those who won our independence believed that the final end of the State was to make men free to develop their faculties, and that in its government the deliberative forces should prevail over the arbitrary. They valued liberty both as an end and as a means.

The allies of America would do well to draw on this other stronger America.

3) Enforcement of the Law

Francis Boyle, a professor of international law at the University of Illinois, observes, 'Normally acts of terrorism are dealt with as a matter of international and domestic law enforcement...not an act of war' [2002, 20]. Is it possible, however, to enforce the law nonviolently, to not ultimately have to rely on the sanction of violence? The answer is mixed. Force may have to be used as sometimes happens when domestic police arrest felons. Yet police are trained not to endanger the lives of other people when making an arrest. Any violent action must be defensive in nature, taken only when physically attacked or clearly threatened with an attack. Thus only when the suspect violently resists can there be a physical transgression of the nonviolent ethic. If police use excessive force against a suspect or harm a bystander, they may find themselves facing prosecution. Contrast this procedure with the way the 'Coalition of the Willing' has pursued criminals like Osama bin Laden, Mullah Omar and the late Abu Musab al-Zarqawi by firing penile-shaped missiles at soft targets and in the process killing tens of thousands of children, women, and other innocent people [Hil 2004].

To its credit the Australian Government has followed the legal path in assisting Indonesia with the arrest of suspects in the Bali bombing of October 12, 2002. A cooperative relationship has unfolded between Indonesian authorities and the Australian Federal Police which has supplied expertise in the joint forensic work. The capture and trial of principal culprits has taken between one and four years without the need to launch armed attacks on civilians and terrorize villages. As Tom Hastings notes, 'It seems that violence has its limits and good police work with the intent of bringing the criminal to the bar to answer for his (sic) misdeeds is still the more functional approach' [2004, 62].

Operating alone, without the active cooperation of the international community, turns international law into a quiescent and sterile relic. In a nonviolent strategy, genuine coalition-building must receive top priority. Moreover, it is reasonable to assume that if a terrorist network operates at a global level, the legal counter approach should likewise emanate from a united global partnership. The antithesis, a pre-emptive military strike or 'anticipatory defense' in the language of Condoleeza Rice, will eventually return to haunt the perpetrators. It stands in clear defiance of the cooperative model of an international police force (preferably under the aegis of the UN) implementing international law and collecting evidence based on shared intelligence.

The findings that lead to arrests should be disclosed to the entire world, not withheld secretly by one nation as in the case of the Guantanamo Bay detainees. The next step is to indict any suspects before an international tribunal set up to try such cases; and it is before this tribunal that appeals for extradition can be lodged, compelling countries that are harboring suspects to turn them over to the special tribunal for a fair trial. Failure of a country to comply for whatever reason would set in train an international police action not only to apprehend the criminals but to bring to justice anyone acting in the role of an accessory, including governmental leaders.

Admittedly, achieving the unity for such a strategy is not easy. There are many people and nations that either openly or silently applaud what is happening to the U.S. and its compliant allies. Unfortunately, the 'Coalition of the Willing' have aggravated their own predicament. However, if they, together with the UN and groups such as the G7, were to implement the other constructive strands of the nonviolent strategy, the prospects of forging united police actions against suspected criminal terrorists would be greatly enhanced.

In addition to securing the unified support of the international community, the creation of an effective nonviolent police force requires a special kind of training for its members. Since their assignment is to enforce the law and protect the lawful and not to conquer and subdue, they should not be drawn from regular military personnel whose training is predicated on how to overpower an enemy. They should, instead, constitute a permanent corps, preferably attached to the UN, and possess the capabilities of armed peacekeepers if need be [See McElwee, ch 12]. If this all sounds like 'pie in the sky', the question arises: Does humankind have any other choice but to begin the process of chipping away at national sovereignty — an institution that points to more and greater disasters in the future. Middle powers like Australia and Sweden, two nations prominent at the birth of the UN, could provide a lead in moving towards a permanent police force at the UN's disposal.

4) Negotiating with Terrorists

Time and time again politicians have uttered the mantra that 'you can't negotiate with terrorists'. As an article of faith it justifies the adversarial approach of the militarist to annihilate the enemy. Nonviolent votaries take a different stance. They argue that a central plank in the strategy of countering irregular terrorism must be a willingness to negotiate. Without entering into talks, the hatred will remain and the fighting in all probability will continue and even intensify. An agreement to meet with terrorists does not mean capitulating on central values. The words of the late President John F. Kennedy are worth recalling in this respect. He impugned his fellow Americans to, 'Let us never negotiate out of fear, but let us never fear to negotiate.' [1961].

Being prepared to negotiate is premised on the view that everyone, irrespective of the deeds s/he has committed, is a member of the human family, and as such is worthy of respect. Who can say with certainty that if subjected to similar experiences they would not have acted in the same way? Conflict resolution calls for an understanding of the opponent, not their dismissal as some sub-human species. Although radical Islamic *jihadists* may be badly misguided in their actions, they see themselves as motivated in the name of Allah to preserve their culture and to rescue the unfortunate from poverty and oppression. In their eyes they are liberation fighters embarking on a righteous cause. The question needs to be asked: Where does one draw the line between a suicide bomber who blows up the embassy of an occupying power and a high flying aircraft that bombs a building reported by intelligence to contain terrorists but is subsequently revealed to have housed innocent civilian families? The so-called 'Other' can have altruistic motives, and the 'We' can have blood on their hands. Acknowledging one's violence is a good beginning. Labelling people or nations 'evil' is not the path to opening up negotiations.

In the end, despite previous disclaimers, governments often do negotiate with terrorists. Prominent past examples include Britain whose governments have met with Sein Fein, Israel where Shimon Peres followed up the Oslo Accords with Yasser Arafat, the Organization of American States bringing the Guatemalan guerrillas into discussions that produced the 1996 peace process, and the U.S. negotiating with its 'evil' enemy, North Korea. The Bush Administration was prepared to offer North Korea guarantees against any attack and normalization of relations, if it abandoned its nuclear program. No such offer at this writing (November 2007) has been extended to another nuclear threat and member of the 'evil axis,' Iran.

The willingness of President Ronald Reagan to negotiate with Iran in the early 1980s over the release of American hostages set in train a highly complicated deal. While U.S. officials Robert McFarlane and Oliver North were offering arms in exchange for the hostages in order to assist Iran in its war with Iraq, another official, Donald Rumsfeld, negotiated the sale of arms to Iraq's Saddam Hussein for money which was taken by North and William Casey, Director of the CIA, to the Nicaraguan *contras* who were waging a terrorist campaign against the socialist Sandinistas. Thus the no-negotiations Reagan regime was not averse to making deals with terrorists that included the supplying of weapons and money in direct violation of U.S. and international law [See Woodward 1987, 227 et seq; Chomsky 1992, 257-62].

An example of two well-known terrorist groups coming to the negotiating table occurred in South Africa. Both the apartheid government and the African National Congress engaged in some of the worst acts of brutality imaginable, and yet when the historical opportunity for negotiations came, they seized it. The initial talks did not deal with the deep-rooted issues but discussed areas around the periphery that might lessen tensions and create the atmosphere for making future talks fruitful — a system referred to as 'light prevention' [Mial, Ramsbotham and Woodhouse 1999, 98]. It worked; a bloodbath was prevented; and successful nation-wide elections followed. The process of healing was then advanced with the creation of the Truth and Reconciliation Commission headed by Bishop Desmond Tutu. It sought to bring together the gross violators of human rights and their victims in a spirit of confession and forgiveness.

Its underlying ethos was enshrined in the principle of *ubantu*, a word in the Nguni group of languages which literally means the 'essence of being human'. The Commission enjoyed considerable success, in large part because it embraced its cultural heritage of *ubantu*, recognizing that my humanity is caught up in your humanity. I am because you are. 'A person is a person through other people.' In *ubantu* one does not give up on a perpetrator but sees him/her with a capacity to change for the better. The healing bridge is finally crossed when both sides confirm in heart and mind their desire to restore the relationship [Tutu 1999, 34-36 *passim* and Munithi 2000].

Today, all the countries fighting in Iraq are committed to a no-negotiation policy with hostage takers. Yet when confronted with the situation of one of their nationals facing execution, they tend not to hesitate to engage in behind-the-scenes bargaining with intermediaries. Thus, the Italian government paid an undisclosed amount of money to release two women hostages. The British government sought negotiations to prevent the beheading of engineer Ken Bigley. The Filipino government negotiated the withdrawal of its troops in order to save the life of one of its nationals. And following the train bombing in Madrid a change of government in Spain brought about the withdrawal of Spanish troops in Iraq.

The disasters that can result from a refusal to negotiate were spelled out horrifically when the Russian government chose to mount a military assault to save the Beslan schoolchildren and their teachers. A fictional version of a hostage-taking situation forms the baseline story of a novel, *Bel Canto* by Ann Patchett [2001]. She depicts the human side of the terrorists and the close relationships they formed with their hostages. The two groups came to experience the love of *agape*[3] but in the end their ethos of understanding and forgiveness was brutally crushed by the state's exercise of its retributive powers — a telling indictment of what can be lost by repudiating the Other's humanity.

5) Applying Nonviolent Sanctions

Long before considering the use of violent sanctions there is a vast array of nonviolent coercive techniques to explore. Nonviolently imposed restrictions can take the form of social, religious, diplomatic or economic sanctions [Sharp1973, 183-213, 219-284, 340-347]. If intelligently applied, they can be most effective in countering terrorists or bringing them to the negotiating table. How the dynamics of these techniques operate and can be utilized, as well as how to engage in nonviolent strategic planning, tends not to be fully appreciated by anti-terrorist forces [See Sharp 1973, 449-810; 2003, *passim*; 2005, 359-524; and Ackerman. And Kruegler 1994, 1-53].

While cutting off the financial funding of terrorist groups like al-Qa'ida is highly desirable, it presents many difficulties. A former special adviser to the U.S. Secretary of the Treasurer explains that al-Qa'ida raises funds in four different ways: through legal commercial channels, through criminal operations (e.g. drug trade or black market gun running), through donations from wealthy supporters, and through smaller donations often secured via Muslim charities whose major contributions go to legitimate causes [Wechsler 2001, 131-153]. The way the money is moved parallels, for the most part, the methods used

---

[3] *Agape* is a form of love described by Martin Luther King, Jr. as 'understanding and creative, redemptive goodwill for all men' [1961, 5].

by legitimate operators, so that tracking transfers poses a major problem. Nonetheless, while pursuing the transactions may not be completely satisfactory, if economic sanctions are applied robustly they can hamper the activities of the terrorist networks, especially when used in conjunction with other forms of nonviolent action.

Economic sanctions can more effectively be applied against nation-states that harbor and financially aid terrorists than they can be used directly against terrorists. However, nation-states are more apt to respond positively to economic incentives than to punitive measures. Whether it is sticks or carrots, the two most telling features of a successful nonviolent policy will come down to the moral power that is wielded and the extent to which comprehensive international endorsement, beyond mere rhetoric, has been secured.

If a country provides military and economic assistance to authoritarian regimes that violate basic human rights, its moral authority is apt to be dismissed by potential allies as hypocrisy. It also feeds the propaganda machine of the terrorists, revention the effect of any sanctions since the resolve to resist has been reinforced. In the last half century Michael Parenti discloses that the U.S. government gave over 250 billion dollars in military aid (not economic) to prop up the military forces of more than eighty nations, many of them undemocratic [2002, 74]. Its military sales continue to lead the world, with Russia coming in a distant second. In 2003, the US signed deals representing 53.6 percent of all global arms sales to developing nations [Shanker 2004, 2]. Many of the weapons were purchased to maintain the security of despotic leaders rather than the security of their citizenry. This investment in despotism has generated a negative world view of the U.S. as a sponsor of state terrorism, a nation concerned only with its own strategic and material interests and lacking concern for the poor and oppressed of the world. Its highly uncritical allies, the other members of the 'Coalition of the Willing' are beginning to attract the same international opprobrium.

'Economic sanctions work best when backed by many countries' [Clemens 1998, 155]. The Burmese government has not felt the full brunt of world sanctions, mainly because China and Southeast Asian countries have shown a reluctance to interfere. The UN has relied frequently on sanctions to compel nations to desist from terrorist acts and human rights abuses, to meet minimal environment standards, and to halt drug trafficking, but its successes have been mixed [See Cortright, Lopez and Gerber 2002]. The limited sanctions imposed on the Taliban prior to September 11 did not cover the shipment of arms to Afghanistan, albeit the stated purpose was to induce the Taliban to disarm the terrorists and hand over Osama bin Laden to appropriate authorities [Cortright and Lopez 2000, 127]. Even if there had been an arms embargo, it probably would have failed since the neighboring Muslim countries were less than enthusiastic about securing the borders, and the restrictions were only imposed on aviation flights and overseas Taliban funds.

By contrast, the global community had far greater success with the economic and sporting bans placed on the terrorist regime of South Africa in the 1970s and 1980s. They were nearly comprehensive in coverage and participation (despite resistance that came from the Thatcher government in Britain). Two other factors contributed to their success. First, the impetus came from a well organized grassroots movement that used the techniques of nonviolence to pressure their governments to take firm action. Australia's nonviolent protesters played a prominent role in the external nonviolence movement against apartheid, demanding bans on sporting contacts that began with the cricket and rugby union teams in the early 70s [See Harris 1972]. A second factor ensuring success can be attributed to the fact that the ANC and other anti-apartheid forces within South Africa called for the sanctions. While they were conducting their own nonviolent campaign against the apartheid regime, they were joined by an outside movement of solidarity to create 'probably the largest grassroots eruption of diverse nonviolent strategies in a single struggle in human history' [Walter Wink cited in Zunes 1999, 203-204].

6) Going to the Root Causes

An Australian nonviolent strategy against terrorism entails going to the core of the problem. Instead of a coercive strategy centered solely on prevention, John Burton points to the need for what he calls 'proventive' solutions [1990, 13-24 *et seq*; 1996, 11 and 38; and 1997, *passim*]. Prevention seeks to contain or suppress a conflict — that is, to enforce a settlement; whereas revention is

> Concerned with the analysis and solving of the problems, whether human, institutional, or both, that give rise to conflicts, and the discovery of the options that meet the needs of those involved.... Provention implies the promotion of an environment conducive to harmonious relationships.... (It) thus enters the fields of political philosophy and policy making [1990, 1-2].

Provention starts from the assumption that everyone has basic human needs that may have to be considered in the process of reaching an enduring conflict resolution. What needs theory does, explains Burton, is to distinguish 'between *negotiable interests* and *non-negotiable needs* (his italics), between disputes and conflicts' [1997, 35]. The former can be handled by legal and bargaining processes. The latter can be steamrolled by political power and suppressed in the short term, but rankling, unfulfilled needs will prolong a conflict. Non-negotiable needs, insists Burton, require processes that 'lead to altered perceptions by the parties concerned, and in some cases agreed structural change' [1997, 35].

The conflict with the terrorists is about needs deprivation. A reflective response to the September 11th tragedy would have been to ask the question why some people would be so desperate as to commit such a dastardly act. None of the governments of the Coalition of the Willing, to my knowledge, has seriously pursued an analysis of the event from a perspective of thwarted basic needs.

Two ontological needs that transcend all cultural and historical barriers — and are relevant to an understanding of terrorist criminality — are 1) identity, self respect and self worth, and 2) survival and security. Terrorist organizations draw recruits into their network primarily from the *déclassé* of the Arab and Third World as well as the disaffected of the upper and middle classes throughout the Muslim world. It is people like the Palestinian refugees — crowded into the most densely populated area of the world and living in appalling sub-human conditions whose biological needs of food, shelter and living space are denied and their self respect weakened and debased — who respond to an ideology that explains their miserable predicament, offering hope of a way out, if not for themselves in this earthly life, for their family and the future of the community. On the other hand, the economically secure, who are attracted to the ideology of *jihad* against Western cultural and structural dominance, are driven primarily (one can surmise) by the need to fulfil a sense of identity (which they perceive as under threat) and gain a feeling of pride in their self worth.

While the more zealous, as reflected in the top leadership, may never gain a sense of identity fulfillment, despite greater Western efforts to respect Islamic culture and apply a more even-handed approach to the Israeli/Palestinian conflict,[4] inroads can be made to satisfy the needs of the Third World's dispossessed. These potential recruits for terrorism — the roughly two to three billion victims of globalization living on $US2 a day or less, and the 1.2 billion earning $1 a day or less [Henerson 2001; Eccleston 2004, 10] — share the same economic fate as the Palestinians. The world's dispossessed constitute not only a seemingly endless supply of suicide bombers, but a sizeable body of sympathizers and sideline spectators ready to offer moral and logistical support. If the UN member-states or the G7 members came together to end world poverty, the dispossessed could become a positive force in the struggle against terrorism. Metaphorically, the head or terrorist leadership would be severed from its body, the world's poor.

James Wolfensohn, former president of the World Bank, sees poverty, military spending, trade barriers and peace as all interwoven, yet the 'way the world is dealing with problems of poverty and peace seem to be disconnected' [Quoted in Eccleston 2004, 10]. He notes that military spending worldwide is around the $US1000 billion mark, and subsidies and tariffs to bolster the agricultural products in the First World countries come to about $US300 billion. Against these figures the rich countries offer no more than $US50-60 billion in aid to developing countries while blocking most of their agricultural exports — virtually the only way these countries can become solvent and pull themselves out of poverty.

Wolfensohn begins by reflecting on the consequences that flow from the extreme poverty existing among two-thirds of the world's population. His deduction:

> If you can't give them hope, which comes from getting a job or doing something productive, giving them their self-respect, these people become the basis on which terrorists or renegades or advocacy groups can flourish... you could spend $US2 trillion on military expenditure, but if you do nothing about poverty and development you're not going to have stability. So my message is a simple one: You cannot take your eye off the ball of poverty [Quoted in Eccleston 2004, 10].

There are many steps that can be taken to eliminate world poverty. As a middle power enjoying good relations with the U.S., the Australian government, for example, could use its influence in world forums to advance the eight goals set forth in the Millennial Declaration (MDG) of the UN. The eight goals are 1) eradicate poverty and hunger, 2) achieve universal primary education, 3) promote gender equality and empower women, 4) reduce child mortality, 5) improve maternal health, 6) combat HIV/AIDS, malaria and other diseases, 7) ensure environmental sustainability, and 8) develop a global partnership for development. Both nations signed this important document in 2001, and are obligated to make reports on the measures they are taking to reach the goals by 2015. Their records thus far have fallen woefully short of the designated targets. Indeed, as long as nations (and it is mostly the developed nations) continue to forego global economic and environmental sustainability, preferring to fatten military budgets, the targets of MDG will never be realized.

---

[4] Moreover, the West would never want to endorse the extreme patriarchal values and obsessive intolerance to differing opinions that fundamentalists like the Taliban seek to implement.

Initiatives to realize basic human needs will probably have to emanate from the grassroots and from the more perceptive and caring sectors of the elite community. Governments and transnational corporations tend to be slow to act. They act more as reflectors than as initiators of policy change, especially when their actions might adversely affect the military/security/industrial complex. Therefore, concerned people of the developed world, marching arm in arm with the most aggrieved victims of violence, will need to mobilize a massive global nonviolent movement to pressure governments and corporations to reassess their violence-creating policies.

Conclusion

While this chapter has outlined a general strategy for nonviolently defeating non-state and state terrorism, it has particularly been directed at the role that can be played by affluent, middle level, Western powers. Despite the different circumstance that set these states apart, their differences are far outweighed by factors they share in the anti-terrorist struggle. To draw on Australian experiences has therefore seemed appropriate and justified.

Overall, six strands of a nonviolent strategy have been outlined: (1) withdrawal from the war-oriented 'Coalition of the Willing;' (2) upholding of humane values at home and abroad; (3) engagement in a law-enforcing exercise against criminals; (4) willingness to negotiate with terrorists; (5) application of nonviolent sanctions; and (6) tackling the global problem of basic needs deprivation. Others to leaven the loaf (fully dealt with in earlier chapters) would include an educational policy that emphasized critical thinking, cultivated nonviolent values and taught the techniques and dynamics of nonviolent conflict resolution. In addition, the role of the popular media in shaping public policy would be challenged to be more critical of orthodox thinking and more receptive to the model of nonviolence. A functional democracy (and not one in name only) depends on the public's media literacy to ensure that information is exchanged freely and openly. As The Carnegie Commission on Preventing Deadly Conflict observed,

> A strong emphasis must be placed on freedom of the press — or the media in the broadest sense — with fair access for all parties, particularly for minority groups, and full freedom of political and cultural expression. This freedom also includes the opportunity to investigate governmental activities and to criticize all parties, even though the harshness of such criticism is often unpleasant and sometimes quite unfair [1997, 153].

Although in a country like Australia the media (and other cultural mechanisms) fall far short of this ideal, enlightened minorities can significantly mitigate the situation. They can resort to letters to editors, articles, photographs and staged events to broaden and deepen the information that filters through to the public. And beyond the oligarchy of media giants a viable network of alternative news sources can be developed to communicate greater diversity of views.

A free and fearless society is one of many components that make up a peace-oriented society. And, as the Carnegie Commission concludes, 'where peace and cooperation prevail, so do security and prosperity' [165]. Thus, there is a practical as well as a moral value to integrating all the elements of nonviolence that have been discussed in this book into a single project against terrorism and its fear.

A nonviolent strategy against terrorism is a holistic strategy (also referred to as principled nonviolence[5]) that no longer thinks and reacts in tribal idioms. The 'other' has disappeared. Its negative energy of fear and hate has been transformed into a positive image of the 'self as other' and the 'other as self'. Once that happens asylum seekers are no longer criminals requiring a policy of 'border protection.' The word 'sorry' can be uttered from a prime minister's lips for the terrible transgressions committed by his forefathers against the indigenous people. In Australia this small gesture would become the first step in a reconciliation process that honors a people and their culture that has survived for at least 40,000 years. When present generations can identify with future generations, economic growth does not come at the expense of the environment. In a society where *agape* prevails, foreign policymakers show respect for the principle of international cooperation, abandon pre-emptive war and unilateral adventurism, refrain from attacks on the UN and its agencies, and demonstrate leadership rather than 'followship' in the wake of the American man-of-war.

For all this to happen — for a nonviolent strategy to fall into place — a prodigious united effort will be required on the part of many global citizens. The task is formidable but not impossible. Necessity is its strength. The key is how well they are able to communicate and implement the strategy. In this endeavor, every individual can play a part. While few (if any) may be as brilliant and tireless as a Noam Chomsky, as attention-getting as a Michael Moore, or as noble and courageous as an Aung San Suu Kyi, the nonviolent paradigm and the strategies and policies that flow from it will not happen unless enough people make a contribution, large or small, and assume the responsibility that goes into creating a critical mass for real change.

The questions to be faced: Will humans answer to life triumphing over death? Will they address the root causes of terror rather than limit their response to suppressing the symptoms? Will they treat non-state terrorism as a criminal act and not a declaration of war? Will they take the initiative to halt the arms race and arms sales? Will they recognize terrorists as human beings and consider assessing their needs? Are they prepared to shed the tribalism that passes for national security? And finally, is the source of violence a lack of will and imagination, rather than the inevitability of human nature, as averred by Hobbes and Freud? To answer 'yes' to all these questions — and to build upon them other questions — shapes the nonviolent strategy. Unfettered materialism, power unchecked, ignorance about nonviolence, and false belief in the congenital violence of human beings are therefore some of the major challenges to overcome.

As human beings we need to keep reminding ourselves that questions must always be asked. The power of words must not be lost. In the Greek myth of Philomele — which appeared in Sophocles' partly lost play of *Tereus* and has been reworked into the modern opera *The Love of the Nightingale* — the dramatist unfolded a tale of terrible brutality, rape and mutilation. The characters, whether in the name of state grandeur or personal power and revenge, were locked into a vicious, ascending and inescapable cycle of violence. To transcend the cycle's trap through the power of words that question the futility of violence, to be replaced by *agape*, the principal characters had to metamorphose into birds: a nightingale,

---

[5] There is extensive literature on the subject of principled nonviolence. An excellent detailed account appears in the encyclopedia entry of R. Woito [1997, 357-363].

swallow and hoopoe. While we may not be able to break the cycle of violence by metamorphosing into birds, we can question it and find the language of legal justice and nonviolence (espoused in this book) that will speak to our own transformation into a much better world.

AUTHOR

Ralph Summy is an Adjunct Professor attached to the Australian Centre for Peace and Conflict Studies, The University of Queensland. He also is the founder and a current co-editor of *Social Alternatives*. He has written books and many articles on peace-related topics. Over the past ten years he has served as a Convenor or Co-Convenor of the Nonviolence Commission of the International Peace Research Association. Officially, he has been retired for the past six years from The University of Queensland and the University of Hawaii where respectively he had been the founder and coordinator of its peace and conflict major/double major, and the Director of the Spark M. Matsunaga Institute for Peace.

REFERENCES

Ackerman, P. and Kruegler, C. (1994). *Strategic Nonviolent Conflict: The Dynamics of People Power in the Twentieth Century.* Westport, CT/London: Praeger.

Boyle, F. A. (2002). *The Criminality of Nuclear Deterrence: Could the US War on Terrorism Go Nuclear?* Atlanta, GA: Clarity.

Brandeis, L. D. (1927). Whitney v. California, 274 U. S. 357, 375.

Burton, J. (1973). *Deviance Terrorism and War: The Process of Solving Unsolved Social and Political Problems.* Canberra: Australian National University Press.

Burton, J. (1990). *Conflict: Resolution and Provention.* London: Macmillan Press.

Burton, J. W. (1996). *Conflict Resolution: Its Language and Processes.* Lanham, MD/London: Scarecrow Press.

Burton, J. W. (1997). *Violence Explained: The Sources of Conflict, Violence and Crime and Their Provention* (Manchester/New York: Manchester University Press.

Bush, G. W. (2002). *Address at West Point Graduation Ceremony.* (June).

Carnegie Commission on Preventing Deadly Conflict (co-chairs David A. Hamburg and Cyrus R. Vance). (1997). *Preventing Deadly Conflict.* Washington, DC: Carnegie Corporation of New York.

Chomsky, N. (1992). *Deterring Democracy.* London: Vintage Books.

Clemens Jr., W. C. (1998). *Dynamics of International Relations: Conflict and Mutual Gain in an Era of Global Interdependence.* Lanham, MD: Rowman and Littlefield.

Cortright, D. and Lopez, G. (2000). *The Sanctions Decade: Assessing UN Strategies in the 1990s.* Boulder, CO: Lynne Rienner Publishers.

Cortright, D., Lopez, G. A., with Gerber, L. (2002). *Sanctions and the Search for Security: Challenges to Un Action.* Boulder, CO: Lynne Rienner Publishers.

Eccleston, R. (2004). 'No Peace Without Hope'. *The Australian* (4 February).

Eccleston, R. (2004) 'Oil Price Leap Fuels Fire under President'. *The Australian* (13 October).

Falk, R. (2007). 'President Bush's Iraq Policy Renewed.' http://www.wagingpeace.org/ articles'2007/01/11_falk_Iraq.htm , 1-3.

Harris, S. (1972). *Political Football: The Springbok Tour of Australia, 1971.* Melbourne: Gold Star Publications.

Hastings, T. H. (2004). *Nonviolent Response to Terrorism.* Jefferson, NC/London: McFarland and Co.

Henderson, H. (2001) 'Mr Bush's Win-Win Option.' *Los Angeles Times Op-Ed* on the Internet (14 September).

Hil, R. (2004). 'Civilian Casualties and the Forgotten Cost of the Iraq War.' Seminar paper. Australian Centre for Peace and Conflict Studies, University of Queensland, 8 October.

Huse, C. and Zeleny, J. (2007). 'Senate Rejects Renewed Effort to Debate Iraq.' *New York Times*, http://www.nytimes.com, 18 February.

Kennedy, J. F. (1961). Inaugural Address. 20 January.

King Jr., M. L. (1961). 'Love, Law and Civil Disobedience.' *New South,* December 3-11.

Machiavelli, N. (1908, 1515). *The Prince* (trans. W. K. Marriott). London: Morgan Inc.

Machiavelli, N. (1910). *Discourse Upon the First Ten Books of Livy* (trans. L. J. Walker). London: Morgan, Inc.

Martin, B. (2006). *Justice Ignited: The Dynamics of Backfire.* Lanham, MD: Rowman and Littlefield.

Mial, H., Ramsbotham, O. and Woodhouse, T. (1999). *Contemporary Conflict Resolution: The Prevention, Management and Transformation of Deadly Conflicts.* Oxford: Polity Press.

Murithi, T. (2000). 'Practical Peacemaking Wisdom from Africa: Reflections on Ubantu.' Paper presented at the annual conference of the British International Studies Association, Forum on Africa and International Relations, University of Bradford, 18-20 December.

Parenti, M (2002). *The Terrorism Trap: September 11 and Beyond.* San Francisco: City Light Books.

Patchett, A. (2001). *Bel Canto.* New York: Perennial.

Petraeus, D. and J Mattis, J. (2006). 'Counterinsurgency (Final Draft – Not for Implementation).' Headquarters, Department of the Army, United States of America, available online on September 21st, http://www.fas.org/irp/doddir/army/fm3-24fd.pdf#search=%22Counterinsurgency%20Petraeus%20final%20draft%22

Reid, H. (2007). Interview on CNN, 16 February.

Schlesinger Jr, A. (2007). *The Australian* (quoting *New York Times* (December 2005). (2 March), p. 17.

Sharp, G. (1973). *The Politics of Nonviolent Action.* Boston, MA: Porter Sargent Publisher.

Sharp, G. (2003). *There Are Alternatives.* Boston, MA: The Albert Einstein Institution.

Sharp, G. (2005). Waging Nonviolent Struggle: 20th Century Practice and 21st Century *Potential.* Boston, MA: Extending Horizons Books.

Shanker, T. (2004). 'US and Russia Still Dominate Arms Market, but World Total Falls.' *New York Times.* (http://www.nytimes.com/2004/08/30/international/europe/ 30weapons.html) The figures were originally taken from US Congressional Research Service's study, 'Conventional Arms Transfers to Developing Nations.'

Stewart, C. (2007). 'Trial by Leak in the Age of Terror.' *The Weekend Australian*, (21-22 July), p. 23.

Suskind, R. (2006). *The One Percent Doctrine: Deep Inside America's Pursuit of Its Enemies Since 9/11*. New York: Simon and Schuster.

Tutu, D. (1999). *No Future Without Forgiveness*. Sydney/London: Rider.

Wechsler, W. F. (2001). 'Strangling the Hydra: Targeting al-Qa'ida's Finances'. In J. F. Hoge Jr, and G. Rose (Eds.), *How Did This Happen? Terrorism and the New War*, edited by James F. Hoge Jnr and Gideon Rose (pp. 131-153). New York: Public Affairs.

Wolf, N. (2007). *The End of America: Letter of Warning to a Young Patriot*. Melbourne: Scribe.

Woodward, B. (1987). *Veil: The Secret Wars of the CIA 1981-1987*. New York: Simon and Schuster.

Zunes, S. (1999). 'The Role of Nonviolence in the Downfall of Apartheid'. In S. Zunes, L. R. Kurtz and S. B. Asher (Eds), *Nonviolent Social Movements: A Geographical Perspective* (203-230). Oxford: Blackwell Publishing.

INDEX

D

H

J

K

L

S